ASEAN and Human Trafficking

International Studies in Human Rights

VOLUME 109

The titles published in this series are listed at *brill.com/ishr*

ASEAN and Human Trafficking

Case Studies of Cambodia, Thailand and Vietnam

By

Naparat Kranrattanasuit

BRILL
NIJHOFF

LEIDEN | BOSTON

Library of Congress Cataloging-in-Publication Data

Kranrattanasuit, Naparat, author.
ASEAN and human trafficking : case studies of Cambodia, Thailand and Vietnam / By Naparat Kranrattanasuit.
p. cm. -- (International studies in human rights ; volume 109)
Includes bibliographical references and index.
ISBN 978-90-04-26517-2 (hardback : alk. paper) -- ISBN 978-90-04-26518-9 (e-book)
1. Human trafficking--South East Asia. 2. ASEAN. 3. Human trafficking--Cambodia. 4. Human trafficking--Thailand. 5. Human trafficking--Vietnam. I. Title.

KNC982.H86K73 2014
345.259'025--dc23

2014016829

This publication has been typeset in the multilingual "Brill" typeface. With over 5,100 characters covering Latin, IPA, Greek, and Cyrillic, this typeface is especially suitable for use in the humanities.
For more information, please see www.brill.com/brill-typeface.

ISSN 0924-4751
ISBN 978-90-04-26517-2 (hardback)
ISBN 978-90-04-26518-9 (e-book)

This book is printed on acid-free paper.

The Author dedicates this book to all *victims of human trafficking*

Contents

Preface

His Majesty King Bhumibol Adulyadej of Thailand, who has devoted his life for better living condition for *all* Thai people, has inspired and empowered the author to complete this book. In return for his grace, the author wishes to play a small role in reinforcing his wishes by sharing the anti-human trafficking research, which addresses the loopholes of national and ASEAN regional laws and practices. and the needs of ASEAN legal reform against human trafficking, in order to educate all ASEAN residents, including Thai civilians.

Acknowledgments

The substantive advice, frequent revision, encouragement, and benevolence of Professor Janie Chuang have strengthened my knowledge on the issue of human trafficking. Her dedication and guidance has truly helped in the completion of my book. Therefore, I would like to express my highest gratitude to her. I am also indebted to Professors Paul Williams and Ingrid Nifosi-Sutton for their valuable commentary, encouragement, generosity, and precious time. Their intellectual perspectives have helped me to fulfill this academic work. I have benefitted from various knowledgeable practitioners and scholars who have provided me with their varied counter-human trafficking perspectives and suggestions. I would also like to give credit for the completion of this book to Mr Matthew Friedman (former regional project manager of the United Nations Inter-Agency Project on Human Trafficking or UNIAP) and former and current staff member of UNIAP (Dr Lisa Rende Taylor, Mr Paul Buckley, Pattarin Wimolpitayarat, Mr Saw Morris, Ms. Pornnipa Buddee, Anyamanee Tabtimsri, and Ms. Chantana Supprasit), Dr Sriprapha Petcharamesree (Professor at Mahidol University), Mr Chainon (Thai legal counselor at Kret-Tra-Karn shelter), and Yuyun Wahyuningrum.

With my highest respect, I would like to thank all human trafficking victims for sharing their tragic experiences that have helped me to better comprehend the cycle of human trafficking. My sincere gratitude goes to Professor Mary Clark for her comments, generous editing, care, and encouragement. Also, I would like to give special thanks to Professor Donna Bain Butler, Erica Simpson, and Courtney Dredden for their outlining and writing courses. It is a good opportunity for me to thank American University Washington College of Law SJD program, Professors Lia Epperson, Amy Tenley, Hillary Lappin, and Diana Sawyer for their greatest contribution and support. Also, I wish to thank all Pence Law Library staff (including Professor Adeen Postar, Amy Taylor, Renee Cuthbert, Ripple Weistling, Susan J. Lewis, Cathy Carpousis, and Allen Hengst). Particularly, I would like to express my high appreciation to Bill Ryan for his greatest contribution on the citation and formatting of varied sources. Similarly, I would like to thank all staff of the Office of Technology (including Arjay Wright, John Bolt, and Mark Burrowes) for their technical advice and kindness.

I would like to extend my special thanks to all of my Thai and foreign supporters for their generosity, encouragement, and care. It is worth listing their names: Aunt Oranart and the Montian family, Srinin, Professor Harriet Bloom-Wilson, JoAnne, Joyce, LaDonna, Kanokthip, Jeff and Pam Thompson,

Charinda, Suzanne FitzGerald, Darla, Kim, Butler, and Monica. Also, I greatly value the friendship and encouragement of Dr Radwa Elsaman, Tong, Seo Young, Xiaolu, Dana Wolf, and Basma. Particularly, I profoundly appreciate Sophia for her caring box, respect, and care. This list would not be complete without mentioning the greatest contribution and commitment to infinite revision of Khelani Clay. I would like to express my deepest appreciation to her as my best editor and friend for her generosity, accountability, tolerance, and friendship.

I would like to express my appreciation to all WCL security officers (including Felicia Brooks) for their 24/7 security service. Even though snow storms attacked Washington, DC in December 2012, I could continue my study in the library because Doreen Hodges offered me the heater, which is warmer than other normal one.

I would never have accomplished any educational level without the greatest sacrifice, encouragement, and support of my oldest sister, Mrs Siriluck Khunphanichkij. Her enormous financial contribution has allowed me to pursue the SJD program and complete this book. Also, the advocacy, love, and care of other siblings (Ms. Saowaluck, Ms. Hussadee, Ms. Suphaluck, Ms. Aungkhana, and Mr Pasut Kranrattanasuit) have driven me to overcome all challenges. Last but not least, I wish to mention my beloved parents and oldest brother; I wish they could have acknowledged my highest educational achievement as they wished. Thank you all again for your kindness I will never forget any of you for the rest of my life.

List of Abbreviations

ABBREVIATION	ORGANIZATION OR ENTITY
ACMW	ASEAN Committee on the Implementation of the ASEAN Declaration on the Protection and Promotion of the Rights of Migrant Workers
ACTV	ASEAN Commission on the Promotion and Protection of the Rights of Trafficking Victims
ACWC	ASEAN Commission on the Promotion and Protection of the Rights of Women and Children
ADTV	ASEAN Declaration on the Promotion and Protection of the Rights of Trafficking Victims
AEC	ASEAN Economic Community
AICHR	ASEAN Intergovernmental Commission on Human Rights
AMMTC	ASEAN Ministerial Meeting on Transnational Crimes
APSC	ASEAN Political-Security Community
ARF	ASEAN Regional Forum
ARTIP	Asia Regional Trafficking in Persons Project
ASCC	ASEAN Socio-Cultural Community
ASEAN	Association of Southeast Asia Nation
CEDAW	Convention on the Elimination of All Forms of Discrimination Against Women
CoE	Council of Europe
COMMIT	Coordinated Mekong Ministerial Initiative Against Trafficking in Persons
CRC	Convention on the Rights of the Child
FDI	Foreign Direct Investments
MLAT	Treaty on Mutual Legal Assistance in Criminal Matters among Like-Minded ASEAN Member Countries
MOU	Memorandum of Understanding
SEANWFZ	Treaty on the Southeast Asia Nuclear Weapon-Free Zone
SIREN	Strategic Information Response Network
SOMTC	Senior Officials Meeting on Transnational Crime
TAC	Treaty of Amity and Cooperation
TIP Report	Trafficking In Persons Report
TOR	Terms of Reference

U.N. Palermo Protocol	Protocol to Prevent, Suppress and Punish Trafficking in Persons, especially Women and Children, supplementing the United Nations Convention against Transnational Organized Crime 2000
UNIAP	United Nations Inter-Agency Project on Human Trafficking
ZOPFAN	Zone of Peace, Freedom and Neutrality

CHAPTER 1

Introduction

1.1 The Statement of Problem and the Objectives of the Research

Trafficking in persons is a serious crime that affects the human rights, dignity, and integrity of all its victims including women, men, and children[1] in the Association of Southeast Asia Nation (ASEAN) region.[2] ASEAN has made efforts in the fight against human trafficking[3] through the establishment of its regional counter-human trafficking laws,[4] structure,[5] and human rights

---

1 Anne T. Gallagher, *Human Rights and the New u.n. Protocols on Trafficking and Migrant Smuggling – a Preliminary Analysis*. 23 Hum.Rts Q. 975, 986–987 (2001) (addressing that "Trafficking in Persons" contains three elements: "1. An action, consisting of: Recruitment, transportation, transfer, harboring or receipt of persons; 2. By means of: Threat or use of force or other forms of coercion, abduction, fraud, deception, abuse of power or position of vulnerability, giving or receiving payments or benefits to achieve consent of a person having control over another; 3. For the purpose of: Exploitation (including, at a minimum, the exploitation of the prostitution of others, or other forms of sexual exploitation, forced labor or services, slavery or practices similar to slavery, servitude, or the removal of organs)"); Wolfgang Benedek et al., The Role of Regional Human Rights Mechanisms, European Parliament, EXPO/B/DROI/2009/25, 20 (Nov. 2010), *available at* http://www.europarl.europa.eu/committees/en/droi/studiesdownload.html?languageDocument=EN&file=33385; The World Bank, *Human Trafficking: A Brief Overview* 1 (Social Development Notes: Conflict, Crime and Violence, No. 122, Dec. 2009), http:///siteresources.worldbank.org/EXTSOCIALDEVELOPMENT/Resources/244362-1239390842422/6012763-1239905793229/Human_Trafficking.pdf.

2 Annuska Derks, Combating Trafficking in South-East Asia: Review of Policy and Programme Response 16 (2000) (discussing the plenary expansion of ASEAN member countries refers to Brunei, Cambodia, Indonesia, Lao, Malaysia, Myanmar, Philippines, Singapore, Thailand, and Vietnam); U.S. Dep't of State, Trafficking in Persons Report 2010 8 (2010), *available at* http://www.state.gov/documents/organization/142979.pdf [hereinafter TIP Report 2010] (estimating that 3 per 1000 inhabitants have been trafficked in Asia and the Pacific region, compared with 1.8 per 1000 inhabitants of the world).

3 Derks, *supra* note 2, at 16 (commenting ASEAN has initiated its commitments against human trafficking since the late 1990s).

4 Ahmad Shah Pakeer Mohamad et al., *The Phenomenon of Human Trafficking Activities in Southeast Asia*, 1 Int'l J. Human. & Soc. Sci. 13, 168, 172 (2011).

5 ASEAN, Roadmap for an ASEAN Community 2009–2015 [hereinafter ASEAN Roadmap] (2009), *available at* http://www.asean.org/images/2012/publications/RoadmapASEANCommunity.pdf; Yuyun Wahyuningrum, *Understanding asean: Its Systems and Structure*

 | DOI 10.1163/9789004265189_002

bodies[6] in order to instruct the best norms and practices for its member countries. Despite these efforts, ASEAN has been unable to get this problem under control.

The International Labour Organization (ILO) recently declared that there are more than 11.7 million forced labor victims in the Asia-Pacific region[7] encompassing the biggest concentration of forced labour victims in the world.[8] These efforts have focused mostly on helping women and children, but approximately forty-five percent of victims around the world are men and boys.[9] The United Nations General Assembly resolution (A/RES/64/178)[10] has addressed the global economic recession, which has impacted not only trafficking in women and children, but also men.[11] Even though one third of Southeast Asian women and children are vulnerable to human trafficking,[12] the Strategic Information Response Network (SIREN) demonstrates that there is a growing number of men being trafficked in construction, agriculture, and fishing industries.[13]

(Dec. 2009), *available at* http://www.scribd.com/doc/81600447/ASEAN-Structures-Mechanisms-Yuyun-10-03-04-Copy.

6 *See* ASEAN Intergovernmental Commission on Human Rights (AICHR), Terms of Reference § § 4, 4.8 (Oct. 2009), *available at* http://www.asean.org/images/2012/publications/Terms%20of%20Reference%20of%20ASEAN%20Intergovernmental%20Commission%20on%20Human%20Rights.pdf [hereinafter AICHR Terms of Reference]; ASEAN Commission on the Promotion and Protection of the Rights of Women and Children (ACWC), Terms of Reference (Feb. 2010), *available at* http://www.asean.org/images/2012/publications/TOR%20of%20ACWC%201.pdf [hereinafter ACWC Terms of Reference] (describing the establishment of the ASEAN Intergovernmental Commission on Human Rights (AICHR) and the ASEAN Commission on the Promotion and Protection of the Rights of Women and Children (ACWC) to deal with human trafficking).

7 *Summary of the ILO 2012 Global Estimate of Forced Labour: Executive Summary*, International Labour Organization, *available at* http://www.ilo.org/wcmsp5/groups/public/---ed_norm/---declaration/documents/publication/wcms_181953.pdf [hereinafter *2012 ILO Global Estimate*] (explaining that there are fifty six percents of the global number compared to globally 20. 9 million victims of forced labour).

8 Press Release, International Labour Organization, 21 Million People are Now Victim of Forced Labour ILO Says (June 1, 2012) [hereinafter ILO Press Release], available at http://www.ilo.org/washington/WCMS_181961/lang--en/index.htm.

9 *2012 ILO Global Estimate, supra* note 7.

10 G.A. Res. 64/178, *supra* note 7, at 3.

11 Id.

12 Nicola Piper, *A Problem by a Different Name? A Review of Research on Trafficking in South-East Asia and Oceania* 43 Int'l Migration, no. 1–2, 2005 at 203, 203 (2005) (explaining that "The largest number of children and women are said to be *within* or *from* Asia").

13 TIP Report 2010, *supra* note 2, at 8.

Further, even though some ASEAN member countries have enacted human trafficking laws and mechanisms, for the last ten years, the US Department of State *Trafficking In Persons Report* (TIP Report)[14] has placed most ASEAN member countries on a Tier 2 Watch List because of the high number of victims and the lack of increasing efforts or advanced commitments.[15] Thus, it implies that these ASEAN member countries have not provided sufficient domestic human rights laws and mechanisms against trafficking in persons because they lack common and efficient anti-human trafficking standards in the ASEAN region.

It is imperative that ASEAN strengthen its regional methods and strategies by designing a new regional anti-human trafficking law or ASEAN Declaration on the Promotion and Protection of the Rights of Trafficking Victims (ADTV) stipulating sufficient measures of prevention, protection, and prosecution, and creating a monitoring human rights body or ASEAN Commission on the Promotion and Protection of Trafficking Victims (ACTV) specializing in preventing human trafficking, protecting all groups of trafficking victims, and

---

14 U.S. Dep't of State, Trafficking in Persons Report 2006 29 (2006), *available at* http://www.state.gov/documents/organization/66086.pdf [hereinafter TIP Report 2006]; U.S. Dep't of State, Trafficking in Persons Report 2007 11–12, 14–15 (2007), *available at* http://www.state.gov/documents/organization/82902.pdf [hereinafter TIP Report 2007]; U.S. Dep't of State, Trafficking in Persons Report 2008 12–13 and 15 (2008), *available at* http://www.state.gov/documents/organization/105501.pdf [hereinafter TIP Report 2008]; U.S. Dep't of State, Trafficking in Persons Report 2009 11–14 (2009), *available at* http://www.state.gov/documents/organization/123357.pdf [hereinafter TIP Report 2009]; TIP Report 2010, *supra* note 2; U.S. Dep't of State, *Tier Placements*, Trafficking in Persons Report 2011 (2011), *available at* http://www.state.gov/j/tip/rls/tiprpt/2011/164228.htm [hereinafter TIP Tier Placements 2011] ; U.S. Dep't of State, Trafficking in Persons Report 2012 60 (2012), *available at* http://www.state.gov/documents/organization/192594.pdf [hereinafter TIP Report 2012] (explaining that Tier 1 means fully compliant country with the TVPA's minimum standards – No ASEAN member countries ever earn tier 1. Tier 2 refer that the government's performance did not meet the TVPA's minimum criteria; however, the government made vital progress in the compliance with the TVPA's minimum criteria. Tier 2 Watch List implies that the governments' anti-human trafficking response did not meet the TVPA's minimum standards. Tier 3 means that the government does not reach the TVPA's minimum standard, and the government does not demonstrate the future commitments to battle against human trafficking).

15 *See,* e.g. U.S. Dep't of State, Trafficking in Persons Report 2011 100, 104, 110, 192, 224, 244, 296, 320, 353, and 384 (2011) , *available at* http://www.state.gov/documents/organization/142979.pdf [hereinafter TIP Report 2011]; *see also,* e.g. TIP Report 2012, *supra* note 13, at 60 (giving examples of Tier 2 Watch List which include Brunei from 2010 to 2011, Cambodia in 2007 and 2009; Malaysia and Thailand from 2010 to 2012, Vietnam between 2010 and 2011; Myanmar in 2012; and Philippines in 2009).

prosecuting perpetrators of human trafficking in order to guide its member countries in to the right direction against trafficking in persons.

1.2 The Reasons of Examining Cambodia, Thailand, and Vietnam as Case Studies

This research examines the domestic laws and mechanisms of Cambodia, Thailand, and Vietnam because these member countries have made additional commitments to strengthen their laws through the COMMIT Process[16] where the United Nations Inter-Agency Project on Human Trafficking (UNIAP) serves as the Secretariat.[17] COMMIT has underscored the necessity of providing protection for all women, children, and men victims of all kinds of human trafficking.[18] The process has adopted labour policies and monitoring system of employment recruitment agencies to combat the crime.[19] Also, this process exemplifies "a mutually shared framework for cooperation"[20] as Dr Susu

16 *See* Gerald Smith, The Criminal Justice Response to Human Trafficking: Recent Developments in the Greater Mekong Sub-Region 13 (2010), *available at* http://www.no-trafficking.org/reports_docs/siren/GMS-08_eng.pdf (explaining that the COMMIT MoU on TIP paves a way with guidance of national and sub-regional coordination).

17 Special Rapporteur on Trafficking in Persons, *Summary of Regional and Sub-Regional Structures and Initiatives to Counter Trafficking in Persons* 11 (Dec., 2010), *available at* http://www.ohchr.org/EN/Issues/Trafficking/Pages/DakarConsultationoct2010.aspx (scroll down to "Summary of Regional Structures and Initiatives") (Based on submissions received from regional mechanisms in response to questionnaire of the U.N. Special Rapporteur on Trafficking in Persons, Especially Women and Children, the Special Rapporteur's 2010 Report to the Human Rights Council and more recent submissions).

18 United Nations Inter-Agency Project on Human Trafficking (UNIAP), The COMMIT Sub-Regional Plan of Action (COMMIT SPA): Achievements in Combating Human Trafficking in the Greater Mekong Sub-Region, 2005–2007 (Dec. 2007), *available at* http://www.no-trafficking.org/reports_docs/commit/commit_spa1_achievements.pdf [hereinafter COMMIT SPA]; Susan Kneebone and Julie Debeljak, Transnational Crime and Human Rights: Responses to Human Trafficking in the Greater Mekong Subregion 203 (2012).

19 COMMIT SPA, *supra* note 18, at 29, 38, and 40; Kneebone & Debeljek, *supra* note 18, at 203.

20 Kneebone & Debeljek, *supra* note 18, at 210; Rebecca J. Miller, What is the Added Value of Coordination?: An Institutional Analysis of the United Nations' Response to National and Regional Coordination of Human Trafficking in the Greater Mekong Subregion 200 (2008) (Ph.D. Thesis, University of Auckland), *available at* https://researchspace.auckland.ac.nz/handle/2292/3396 (describing "some donors indicate another motive for the attraction to the UNIAP – its cooperative approach.").

Thatun considers this process as a master plan for collaborative exercise.[21] Therefore, all COMMIT member countries have equal chances to share their comments and concerns.

Further, these three countries can represent other ASEAN member countries' strengths and weaknesses of the fight against human trafficking. The example of their strengths includes the enactment of their anti-human trafficking laws to implement the Protocol to Prevent, Suppress and Punish Trafficking in Persons, especially Women and Children (the U.N. Palermo Protocol), which is the first international legal instrument that defines "trafficking in persons." The second strength is that their governments' actions have demonstrated several efforts in criminal justice responses to human trafficking.

In contrast, these countries have been remiss in implementing the U.N. Palermo Protocol, which ASEAN has urged its member countries to comply with in order to fight human trafficking. Despite enactment of domestic anti-human trafficking laws, several reports have revealed the lack of essential provisions as set forth in the U.N. Palermo Protocol. For instance, even though all ASEAN member countries have adopted the 1999 Bangkok Declaration on Irregular Migration[22] emphasizing the need of redressing irregular migrant workers dilemma, their government officials have deported trafficking victims without identifying them as victims because they are irregular migrant workers with no legal documents.

1.3 The Significant Substance and Structure of this Book

Since ASEAN has a vision of community integration for 2015, this research highlights its achievements and challenges of its anti-human trafficking laws

21 Kneebone & Debeljek, *supra* note 18, at 211 (mentioning Susu Thatun, Challenges and Breakthrough in Regional Cooperation: the Case of the COMMIT Process (Paper delivered to Workshop on National and Regional Responses to Trafficking: Lessons for a Global Response, Metropolis Conference, Melbourne Australia, 9 Oct. 2007).

22 The Bangkok Declaration on Irregular Migration, *International Symposium on Migration: Towards Regional Cooperation on Irregular/Undocumented Migration* (Apr. 21–23, 1999) *available at* http://www.iom.int/jahia/webdav/site/myjahiasite/shared/shared/mainsite/policy_and_research/rcp/APC/BANGKOK_DECLARATION.pdf; Ma. Lorena Macabuag, *asean Committee on Migrants Workers, in* 49 FOCUS Asia-Pacific, Sept. 2007, at 8, *available at* http://www.hurights.or.jp/asia-pacific/049/focus49.pdf (describing that 1999 Bangkok Declaration on Irregular Migration affirms to enumerate sources and positive and negative (namely human trafficking) impacts that affect migration (including irregular migration) in origin, transit, and destination countries).

and mechanisms in order to raise awareness of strengthening insufficient methods and strategies against human trafficking. With its deficiencies, this research proposes the establishment of specific counter-human trafficking measures like ASEAN Declaration on the Promotion and Protection of Trafficking Victims (ADTV) and the formation of ASEAN Commission on the Promotion and Protection of Trafficking Victims (ACTV) comprised of experts, who specialize in suppressing human trafficking, protecting victims, and prosecuting offenders.

Chapter Two elaborates on ASEAN's historical background and discusses ASEAN's focus on political-security and economic integration. It will also evaluate ASEAN's influence in internal and external communities to look at whether their influence can mobilize countries to engage in anti-human trafficking efforts. Lastly, this chapter discusses the main principles of the ASEAN influence, or ASEAN Way on the region's approach to human rights, including counter-human trafficking. It will be concluded that ASEAN should not completely follow its rules because they can decelerate anti-human trafficking development in the ASEAN region.

Chapter Three discusses three issues, in order to assert the need of establishing a new anti-human trafficking law and body in ASEAN, they include: counter-human trafficking law, structure, and power of human rights bodies. ASEAN's existing legal instruments and guidelines will be examined to determine whether they contain sufficient measures that promote and protect the rights of all trafficking victims. This chapter will next explore whether ASEAN's anti-human trafficking structure can tackle the trafficking of all trafficking victims. And lastly point out the strengths and weaknesses of the ASEAN human rights bodies that deal with anti-human trafficking in order to respond whether ASEAN has adequately given these bodies' basic authorities to equally promote and protect all trafficking victims.

Chapter Four focuses on four areas. First, it examines the causes of the increase in human trafficking in these three countries. Second, it examines these countries' implementation and non-implementation of their commitment under the U.N. Palermo Protocol because six ASEAN member countries have ratified to this treaty. Third, it analyzes their governments' criminal justice responses to human trafficking. This chapter aims to demonstrate why the governments of Cambodia, Thailand, and Vietnam need a regional anti-human trafficking mechanism like the ACTV to assist them in addressing the root causes of trafficking in persons.

Chapter Five proposes the creation of the ASEAN Declaration on the Promotion and Protection on the Rights of Trafficking Victims (ADTV) because ASEAN lacks a regional legal instrument and mechanism that can address and tackle trafficking of all victims, including men. This chapter aims to draw attention to vital matters of the ADTIP and to special characteristics of the ACTV with monitoring power. This section also considers the feasibility of ASEAN's acceptance of the ACTV. Chapter Six provides a conclusion and recommendations for the establishment of ADTV and the formation of ACTV (Figure 1).

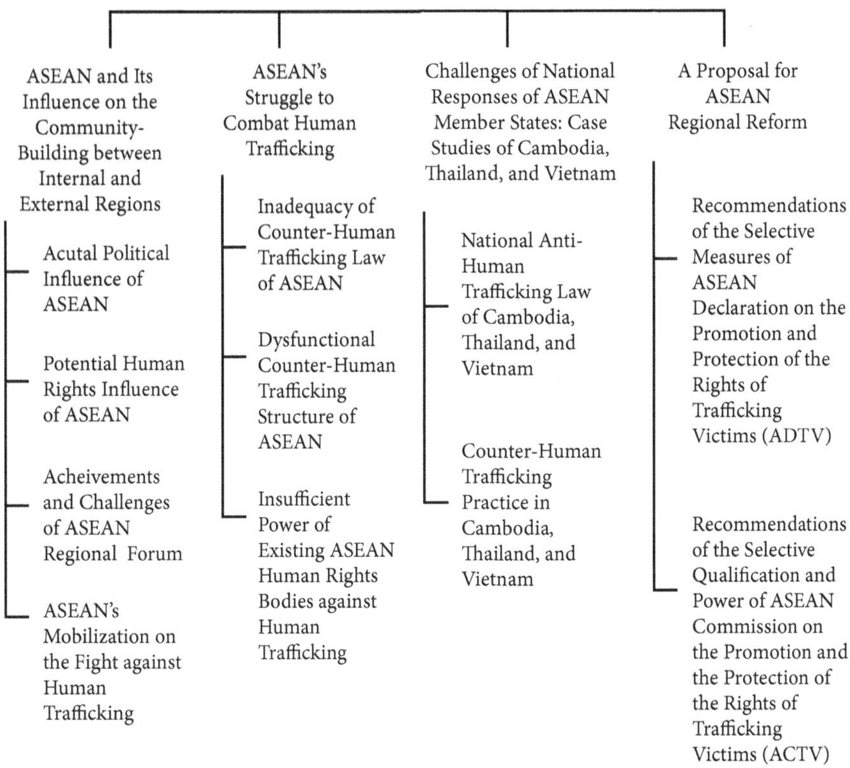

FIGURE 1 *Structure of the book.*

CHAPTER 2

Overview of ASEAN and Its Influence on Community-Building between Internal and External Regions

ASEAN is a regional organization comprised mostly of vulnerable member countries; therefore many concerns have been raised about the region's political, economic and social development as well as their approach to security management.[1] Critics feel that this combination has prevented ASEAN from becoming a strong organization capable of tackling its regional dilemmas,[2] including the scourge of human trafficking. This chapter argues that despite its stature, ASEAN has the potential to serve its member countries and non-member countries as a center of identifying various concerns and exchanging their best methods and strategies to redress such transnational crimes based on its existing influences towards these communities.

In order to fully understand the issue of human trafficking in the region, it is important to look at its origin and current vision for development. The first section of this chapter traces the internal and external political security challenges that ASEAN member countries have faced in establishing ASEAN. ASEAN's role in dispute settlement to sustain peace and stability during numerous political conflicts in the region illustrates their influence both within the region and the international community. For instance, ASEAN played a diplomatic role in Vietnamese ending the territorial attack of the Vietnamese government following its invasion of Cambodia.[3]

ASEAN also played a neutral role in South China Sea conflict[4] demonstrating its efforts in preventing intensive political conflict. In addition to political

---

1 Christopher B. Roberts, *State Weakness and Political Values: Ramifications for the ASEAN Community, in* ASEAN and the Institutionalization of East Asia 12 (Ralf Emmers, ed., 2012).

2 Id.

3 Amitav Acharya, *Ideas, Identity and Institution-Building: From the 'ASEAN Way' to the 'Asia-Pacific Way?'* 10 Pac. Rev. 3, 319, 319–346 (1997); Kyu Deug Hwang, The Mechanisms of Politico-Security Regionalism in Southeast Asia and Southern Africa: A Comparative Case Research of ASEAN and SADC 120 (Sep. 27, 2006) (unpublished Ph.D. dissertation, University of Pretoria), *available at* http://upetd.up.ac.za/thesis/available/etd-09272006-154344/.

4 Jianming Shen, *China's Sovereignty over the South China Sea Islands: A Historical Perspective,* Chinese J. Int'l L. 94, 97 (2002); Kingsford, Michael, Can the ASEAN Regional Forum have a Role in Maintaining Regional Security? 6 (Shedden Papers 2012), *available at* http://www.defence.gov.au/adc/docs/Publications2012/SheddenPapers12_120306_ARF_Kingsford.pdf.

 | DOI 10.1163/9789004265189_003

influence, ASEAN has attempted to play a role in promoting human rights through "the three-pillar community."[5] ASEAN has also planned to advocate its member countries to promote and protect the rights of people through political-security, economic, and socio-cultural communities. While the notion of the "ASEAN Way"[6] has been an influence on these communities, this section points out its core principles in order to perceive the main concept and method of dealing with security concerns of ASEAN.

Section two of this chapter discusses the debates on the human rights approach of ASEAN to confirm that ASEAN has planned to provide fundamental rights for its people. ASEAN has attempted to maintain peace and unity through the establishment of the ASEAN Charter[7] (its first legally-binding instrument of human rights) and ASEAN Intergovernmental Commission on

5 Declaration of ASEAN Concord II (Bali Concord II), Oct. 7, 2003, *available at* http://www.asean.org/news/item/declaration-of-asean-concord-ii-bali-concord-ii-2 [hereinafter Bali Concord II]; I.B.R. Supancana, *Special Note: The Roadmap toward the Creation of ASEAN Security Community in 2015: Legal Perspectives*, 1 J.E. Asia & Int'l 323, 328 (2008).

6 Treaty of Amity and Cooperation (TAC) in Southeast Asia, Feb. 24, 1976, 1025 U.N.T.S. 316, *available at* http://www.asean.org/asean/asean-summit/item/treaty-of-amity-and-cooperation-in-southeast-asia-indonesia-24-february-1976 [hereinafter TAC]; Amitav Acharya, *Regional Military-Security Cooperation in the Third World: A Conceptual Analysis of the Relevance and Limitations of ASEAN (Association of Southeast Asian Nations)* 29 J. of Peace Research 7 (1992); Lee Leviter, *The ASEAN Charter: ASEAN Failure or Member Failure?* 43 Int'l L. and Pol. 159, 161, 168 (2010).

7 Ong Keng Young, *At Close Quarters with the Drafting of ASEAN Charter*, *in* The Making of ASEAN Charter, 107–108 (Tommy Koh, Rorario G Manalo & Walter Woon eds., 2009); Working Group for an ASEAN Human Rights Mechanism, *Terms of Reference of the ACWC completed at the 15th ASEAN Summit*, Hum. Rts. Herald, Jan. 2010, at 6–7, *available at* http://www.aseanhrmech.org/downloads/Human_Rights_Herald_Jan2010_Issue.pdf.; *See*, e.g. Joint Statement of the Fifth ASEAN Plus Three Ministerial Meeting on Transnational Crime (5th AMMTC + 3) Consultation §6, Oct. 12, 2011, http://www.asean.org/news/asean-statement-communiques/item/joint-statement-of-the-fifth-asean-plus-three-ministerial-meeting-on-transnational-crime-5th-ammtc3-consultation-2 [hereinafter ASEAN + 3 5th Joint Statement]; Wilfrido V. Villacorta, *Strengthening the Foundation for An ASEAN Community*, *in* ASEAN Matters!: Reflecting on the Association of Southeast Asian Nations 306–307 (Lee Yoong Yoong, ed., 2011); The Cebu Declaration on the Blueprint of ASEAN Charter, Jan. 13, 2007, *available at* http://www.asean.org/asean/asean-summit/item/cebu-declaration-on-the-blueprint-of-the-asean-charter-cebu-philippines-13-january-2007 [hereinafter Cebu Declaration]; Chairman's Statement of the 13th ASEAN Summit, *One ASEAN at the Heart of Dynamic Asia*, Nov. 20, 2007, http://www.asean.org/asean/asean-summit/item/chairman-s-statement-of-the-13th-asean-summit-one-asean-at-the-heart-of-dynamic-asia-singapore-20-november- [hereinafter Chairman's Statement of the 13th ASEAN Summit]; *About ASEAN: Overview*, Association of Southeast Asian Nations, http://www.asean.org/asean/about-asean (last visited Dec. 12, 2012).

Human Rights (AICHR).[8] However, both the ASEAN Charter and AICHR represent ASEAN's human rights development under the auspices of the ASEAN Way. Even though the seemingly meek approach of ASEAN Way helped to alleviate the political conflict of Vietnamese invasion of Cambodia, in the case of human rights violations, including human trafficking, the application of the principles of ASEAN Way, specifically non-interference, because it can decelerate development of human rights development in the ASEAN region. Further, even if ASEAN has not efficiently accomplished dispute settlement during traditional security concerns (such as in the dispute over the South China Sea), they have been successful in persuading dialogue partners to collaborate during non-traditional threats, such as natural disasters, counterterrorism, and epidemic diseases. ASEAN has also made efforts to fight human trafficking in addition to other non-traditional crimes.

2.1 Establishment of ASEAN

In order to entirely understand how ASEAN deals with threats such as human trafficking, it is necessary to look at the core missions and strategies for maintaining relationships with member countries and other stakeholders in their efforts to deal with various regional and international insecurities. For over forty-five years, ASEAN has been one of the most sustainable regional organizations even though its members are overwhelmingly underdeveloped and developing countries.[9] These countries have also experienced periods of internal political tension and external invasion by threats such as communism.[10] Even though numerous territorial disputes and external threats have taken place in Asian countries, these insecurity issues have not hindered ASEAN's establishment. ASEAN has aimed to concentrate not solely on political, socio-cultural, or economic approaches, but wants to address these issues as a

8 Charter of the Association of Southeast Nations [ASEAN Charter], art. 14(1), Nov. 20, 2007, *available at* http://www.asean.org/archive/publications/ASEAN-Charter.pdf; Working Group for an ASEAN Human Rights Mechanism, *supra* note 77; Misun Woo, *Voicing Women's Concerns to ASEAN*, 22 Asia Pac. F. Women L. & Dev., no. 1, 2009 at 8, *available at* http://apwld.org/pdf/ForumNews/APWLD-Forum-News-june-09-22-1.pdf; *Frequently Asked Questions on the ASEAN Charter*, MARUAH: Singapore Working Group for an ASEAN Human Rights Mechanism, http://maruah.org/asean-charter/ (last visited Mar. 5, 2013).

9 Roberts, *supra* note 1, at 12–16.

10 Tim Huxley, *International Relations, in* An Introduction to Southeast Asian Studies 228–229 (M. Halib and Tim Huxley, eds., 1996); Amitav Acharya, The Quest for Identity: International Relations of Southeast Asia 78 (2000); Acharya, *supra* note 6, at 7, 13.

whole in an effort to strengthen their organization. Multiple approaches demonstrate how ASEAN has designed their policies to promote human rights based upon the core principles of ASEAN Way and applied them in order to mitigate political conflicts, namely the aforementioned Vietnamese invasion of Cambodia and dispute over the South China Sea.

2.2 The Origin and Evolution of ASEAN

Before the formation of ASEAN, most Asian countries had experienced colonialism, territorial conflicts, and communist invasions by neighboring countries.[11] Colonial expansion impacted their perception of international and regional collaboration[12] because these countries lack fundamental political, cultural, social, and economic standards.[13] Even though most of the countries gained independence after the Second World War, they remained unstable and void of any real regional identity.[14] In the post-colonial era, Southeast Asian countries experienced the threats of communism and insurgency,[15] which weakened their stability.[16] These internal and external threats pressured Asian countries to create a strong institution to help them mitigate this tension.

---

11 Shaun Narine, Explaining ASEAN: A Regionalism in Southeast Asia 9–10 (2002); *see also* Hwang, *supra* note 3, at 69.

12 Id.

13 Hwang, *supra* note 3, at 68–69.

14 Id. at 69.

15 Id. at 16, 70; Bernard Gordon, *Problems of Regional Cooperation in Southeast Asia*, 16 World Pol. 222, 222–235 (1964) (summarizing from these sources that the communist insurrection in Southeast Asia prevailed in Cambodia, Vietnam, Lao PDR, Malaysia, Myanmar, and Thailand and that these political conflicts damaged intra-regional relations amongst these countries).

16 Acharya , *supra* note 10, at 43–74; Buzan, Barry, People, States and Fear: An Agenda for International Security Studies in the Post-Cold War Era 96–107 (1991); Buzan, Barry, *Is International Security Possible*?, *in* New Thinking about Strategy and International Security 45–46 (Bjorn Hettne, Andras Inotai & Osvaldo Sunkel eds., 1991); Hwang, *supra* note 3, at 66 (finding that weak or strong states refer to the degree of "socio-political cohesion within a state", "while weak or strong powers refer to the traditional distinction among states in respect of their military and economic capability in relation to each other", and "[a]ccording to Buzan's definitions of 'weakness' and 'strength' as a state characteristics, all ASEAN member countries excluding Singapore could be categorized as 'weak states'").

There were various attempts by Asian countries to establish cooperative organizations,[17] namely the establishment of the Southeast Asian Treaty Organization (SEATO),[18] the Asia-Pacific Council (ASPAC),[19] Southeast Asia (ASA),[20] and Malaya, Philippines, and Indonesia (MAPHILINDO).[21] The fragmentation of their individual countries had caused them severe uncertainty without mediating organization. Many of these organizations ultimately failed because of the inconsistent political opinions of the member countries.

Malaysia, Philippines, and Thailand founded Southeast Asia (ASA) in 1961 to reinforce regional cooperation, economic benefits included the sharing of import and export data, accommodation of customs services and the feasibility of expanding the number of the ASA member countries. The establishment of the ASA was a scheme, where Southeast Asian countries could share internal concerns such as political, social, and economic issues.[22] The ASA member countries desired to "work closely together" for their own mutual benefit. Even though Malaysia, the Philippines, and Thailand successfully created the ASA, the 1962 territorial dispute between Malaysia and the Philippines over Sabah (or North Borneo) caused the collapse of the ASA.

In 1964, the Philippines and Thailand participated with the U.S. and other countries, including Britain, France, Australia, New Zealand, and Pakistan to establish the Southeast Asian Treaty Organization (SEATO) to strengthen political-security affairs in the region.[23] In 1966, other Southeast Asian countries banded together to form the Asia-Pacific Council (ASPAC) with the goal of

---

17 Frank Frost, *Introduction: ASEAN Since 1967-Origins, Evolution and Recent Developments, in* ASEAN into the 1990s 2–4 (Alison Broinowski ed., 1990) (summarizing that the instances of different organizations include the Southeast Asian Treaty Organization (SEATO), Southeast Asian countries instituted the Asia Pacific Council (ASPAC), Southeast Asia (ASA), and the Greater Malayan Confederation (MAPHILINDO)).

18 Id.; Hwang, *supra* note 33, at 70.

19 Frost, *supra* note 17, at 2–4; Hwang, *supra* note 3, at 70–71.

20 Acharya, *supra* note 10, at 78; Yuen Foong Khong, *ASEAN and the Southeast Asian Security Complex, in* Regional Orders: Building Security in a New World 329 (David A. Lake & Patrick Morgan eds., 1997); Hwang, *supra* note 3, at 71; Acharya, *supra* note 6, at 13.

21 John Brown Gordon, Dimension of Conflict 22–25(1966); *see also* Hwang, *supra* note 3, at 72; Muthiah Alagappa, *The Dynamics of International Security in Southeast Asia: Change and Continuity*, 45 Austl. J. of Int'l Aff. 1, 18 (1991) (noting that Malaysia, a mark of "neocolonialism," implied a threat to the Indonesia's territorial security because Indonesia desired to be a leader of the "emerging force" of other developing countries).

22 Acharya, *supra* note 10, at 78; Khong, *supra* note 20, at 329 (David A. Lake & Patrick Morgan eds., 1997); Hwang, *supra* note 33, at 71; Acharya, *supra* note 6, at 13.

23 Frost, *supra* note 17, at 2–4.

abolishing communism in neighboring countries, namely Vietnam.[24] Most countries in the region refrained from joining SEATO and ASPAC because of their narrow focus on eliminating communism.[25]

The MAPHILINDO alliance also proved to have its own problems, including Indonesia's opposition to Malaysian imperialism. Malaysia had essentially been made obsolete by the aforementioned territorial dispute between the Philippines and Malaysia in Sabah. Worse was the Indonesian policy known "Konfrantasi" or "Confrontation against the Federation of Malaysia" which eventually destabilized the MAPHILINDO.[26]

Despite Asian countries' efforts in founding a regional institution, most Southeast Asian countries did not believe that the establishment of ASEAN would make a difference at the outset. However, the Southeast Asian countries acknowledged that the threat from communism and external powerful countries was enormously intimidating and that their "interdependence" could assist in protecting their sovereignty.[27] ASEAN eventually promulgated concrete institutional structures and goals in order to build their internal security management schemes.[28]

Even though their geographical size, ethnic groupings, socio-cultural identities, and colonial and post-colonial experiences differ,[29] the five ASEAN founding members, Malaysia, Indonesia, Philippines, Thailand, and Singapore shifted their political tension in the region into harmonious relationships among their neighboring countries and established ASEAN,[30] and envisioned that this regional organization would help its member countries deal with both internal and external threats, including communism.[31] Even with a wide range of dissimilarities in economics, politics, cultures, and languages, they agreed to accept their differences and sustain peace through the establishment of this regional organization.[32] Thus, ASEAN was established in Bangkok, Thailand on August 8, 1967.[33]

---

24 Id.

25 Id.

26 Brown, *supra* note 21, at 22–25; Hwang, *supra* note 3, at 72.

27 Hwang, *supra* note 3, at 68–72.

28 Id. at 72.

29 Tommy Koh, *Foreword, in* ASEAN Matters!: Reflecting on the Association of Southeast Asian Nations ix (Lee Yoong Yoong, ed., 2011); *see also* id. at 66.

30 Hwang, *supra* note 3, at 68–72.

31 Acharya, *supra* note 10, at 87.

32 Koh, *supra* note 29, at ix; Sivkant Tiwari, *ASEAN's Perception Problem, in* ASEAN Matters!: Reflecting on the Association of Southeast Asian Nations 30 (Lee Yoong Yoong, ed., 2011).

33 Koh, *supra* note 29, at ix.

Over time, ASEAN grew to include another five countries, Brunei, Cambodia, Laos, Myanmar, and Vietnam. These ten member countries to a certain degree are politically divergent, with communist regimes in Vietnam and Laos, "soft authoritarian regimes and limited democracy" in Myanmar, Malaysia, Singapore and Brunei, and "constitutionalism and transitional justice" in Cambodia, the Philippines, Thailand, and Indonesia.[34] In fact, Thailand is the only member country that has not been colonized.[35]

While ASEAN has focused on constructing peace and sustainable conformity through ASEAN, international communities have questioned whether ASEAN has the potential to maintain peace and unity while using their influence to promote and protect human rights. The next part will point out the actual political and potential human rights influences of ASEAN.

2.3 Actual Political Influence of ASEAN

To better understand its influence on political conflict dispute management it is necessary to examine ASEAN's political role in both the regional and international communities.[36] ASEAN was able to stop the Vietnamese invasion of Cambodia through its diplomatic efforts and served a neutral role in alleviating the intensive territorial dispute and other dialogue partners in case of South China Sea conflict.

2.3.1 *Vietnamese Invasion of Cambodia*

The traditional practice of consensus decision-making concentrates on avoiding the political confrontation of ASEAN member countries.[37] However, it is asserted here that its role in mediating the Vietnamese invasion of Cambodian between 1978 and 1990 exemplifies their cohesion in reconciling political conflict.[38] It is clear that there was a balance of ASEAN's outstanding hegemony and "mediating role."[39]

---

34 Rule of Law for Human Rights in the ASEAN Region: A Base-line Study 8 (2011), *available at* hrrca.org/system/files/Rule_of_Law_for_Human_Rights_in_the_ASEAN_Region.pdf [hereinafter Base-Line Study].

35 Tiwari, *supra* note 32, at 29–30.

36 *See* Huxley, *supra* note 10; *see also* Acharya, *supra* note 10, at 78; Acharya, *supra* note 66, at 13.

37 Acharya, *supra* note 3, at 3, 319–346; *see also* Hwang, *supra* note 3, at 120.

38 Hwang, *supra* note 3, at 88.

39 Amitav Acharya, *Arguing about ASEAN: What Do We Disagree About?*, 22 Cambridge Rev. of Int'l Aff. 493, 497 (2009).

Even though ASEAN supports consensus decision-making through consultation and the principle of the non-interference in the internal affairs of other countries, ASEAN has joined in other countries' internal affairs when they impact neighboring countries.[40] For instance, ASEAN interfered in the Vietnamese invasion of Cambodia in December 1978 in an effort to reduce the role of external powers in Southeast Asia,[41] and thwart the establishment of a "Vietnamese-installed regime," which could threaten the peace and stability of ASEAN.[42]

These actions in the dispute between Vietnam and Cambodia exhibited ASEAN's influence in calling for collaboration between its internal and external communities.[43] This involvement has also illustrated ASEAN's accomplishment at applying the consensus decision-making and consultation principle for this sort of dispute settlement.[44] The leaders of ASEAN member countries have used diplomatic methods to negotiate with other supporters, particularly the United Nations, the United States, and China.[45]

Though Vietnam was not a member country during this conflict, ASEAN claimed that its invasion of Cambodia's sovereignty breached the non-interference and non-armed force principles set forth in Treaty of Amity and Cooperation (TAC) in Southeast Asia.[46] The TAC calls for cooperation in establishing "peace, harmony and stability in the region."[47] But the Vietnamese government failed to acknowledge the treaty and invaded Cambodia.[48]

The active diplomatic role and regional coherence demonstrated by ASEAN persuaded the United Nations General Assembly to take action against the

---

40 Rodolfo C. Severino, *ASEAN: What It Cannot Do, What It can and Should Do*, *in* ASEAN Matters!: Reflecting on the Association of Southeast Asian Nations 5 (Lee Yoong Yoong ed., 2011).

41 Hwang, *supra* note 33, at 82 (explaining that both Vietnam and Cambodia did not join ASEAN during this conflict, these countries joined respectively in 1995 and 1999).

42 Amitav Archarya & Alastair Iain Johnston, *Comparing Regional Institutions: An Introduction*, *in* Crafting Cooperation: Regional International Institutions in Comparative Perspective 42 (Amitav Archarya & Alastair Iain Johnston eds., 2007).

43 Kavi Chongkittavorn, *Covering ASEAN for Three Decades*, *in* ASEAN Matters!: Reflecting on the Association of Southeast Asian Nations 40 (Lee Yoong Yoong, ed., 2011).

44 *See* Mely Caballero-Anthony, Regional Security in Southeast Asia: Beyond ASEAN Way 106–107 (2005); *see also* Archarya & Johnston, *supra* note 42, at 44.

45 Chongkittavorn, *supra* note 43, at 40; Jens-Uwe Wunderlich, Regionalism, Globalisation and International Order: Europe and Southeast Asia 149 (2007).

46 Id. at 149.

47 TAC, *supra* note 6.

48 Wunderlich, *supra* note 45, at 149.

Vietnamese invasion of Cambodia and the Vietnamese-backed government policy in Phnom Pen in November 1979.[49] The United Nations General Assembly commanded the Vietnamese government to instantly remove its military from Kampuchea.[50] The United Nations General Assembly had required all countries to evade all forms of violent "acts and threats" and interference in the internal affairs of other countries.[51] More importantly, the result of the resolution was the Paris Peace Agreement of 1991 that terminated the Vietnamese and Cambodian disputes.[52] Martin Löffelholz and Danilo A. Arao correctly posit praise for ASEAN and its active mobilization, which has presented "the arrival of a mature organi[z]ation with a growing impact on the regional security order."[53]

This successful movement during the Vietnamese invasion of Cambodia represents their influence in the region. ASEAN has applied its consensus decision-making principle and harmonious concept to settle this conflict. Also, their role in mediation throughout the international community has built up its regional identity as an active institution.[54]

2.3.2 *South China Sea Dispute*

In addition to their diplomatic role, ASEAN also displayed their efforts at political conflict management during the conflict of the South China Sea between China and some member countries.[55] Efforts have been made to minimize tension between concerned parties.[56] More specifically the confirmation of China on the South China Sea in 2010 concerned all claimant countries as well as the United States.[57] This conflict created difficulty retaining ASEAN's solidity because

49 G.A. Res. 34/22, U.N. Doc. A/RES/34/22 (Nov. 14, 1979), pp. 16–17, *available at* http://www.un.org/documents/ga/res/34/a34res22.pdf.

50 Id.; Wunderlich, *supra* note 45, at 149.

51 Id.

52 *See* Caballero-Anthony, *supra* note 44, at 106–107; *see also* Archarya & Johnston, *supra* note 422, at 44.

53 Martin Löffelholz & Danilo A. Arao, The ASEAN Guide: A Journalist's Handbook to Regional Integration in Southeast Asia 48 (2010).

54 Wunderlich, *supra* note 45, at 149–150.

55 Shen, *supra* note 4, at 94, 97; Kingsford, *supra* note 4, at 6 (listing the parties of the South China Sea dispute as China, Brunei, Malaysia, Vietnam, the Philippines, and Taiwan).

56 ASEAN, ASEAN Regional Forum: Annual Security Outlook-2011, 12 ARF ASO 34 (2011), *available at* http://aseanregionalforum.asean.org/files/ARF-Publication/ARF-Annual-Security-Outlook/ARF%20Annual%20Security%20Outlook%202011.pdf [hereinafter Annual Security Outlook-2011].

57 *See* Gilbert Rozman, *East Asian Regionalism*, *in* Routledge Handbook of Asian Regionalism 26 (Mark Beeson & Richard Stubbs eds., 2012).

of the confrontation between China and the United States over this territory.[58] To reassure intra-relations amongst the ASEAN Regional Forum (ARF) parties, ASEAN called on China and its member countries to adopt the Declaration on the Conduct of Parties in the South China Sea in 2002.[59] This Declaration shows the feasibility of creating a dispute settlement mechanism to resolve this conflict based on common trust and collaboration through practical methods.[60] The Declaration also required China and ASEAN member countries to affirm their commitment to decrease the possibility of the use of force.[61] This commitment included application of peaceful methods in managing the territorial disputes, implementation of the rule of self-control in taking actions in the region, and enhancement of sharing perspectives between their governments.[62]

It is clear that the Declaration on the Conduct of Parties in the South China Sea contains both advantages and disadvantages.[63] On the positive side, it symbolizes the acknowledgement of all ASEAN member countries and claimant countries on the issues of "economic development, and food security."[64]

---

58 *See* id.; *see also American Shadow Over South China Sea,* Global Times (26 July, 2010), http://www.globaltimes.cn/opinion/editorial/2010-07/555723.html (stating that "[r]egional stability will be difficult to maintain if the countries concerned allow themselves to be controlled by the strategic guidance of the US...China offered a solution of "shelving disagreement and joint development" to help foster trust and move the issue forward. China's objective is clear: to build strategic trust with neighboring countries *under China's tolerance and patience*...Southeast Asian Countries need to understand any attempt to maximize gains by playing a balancing game between China and the US is risky...China will never waive its right to protect its core interests with military means.")

59 Zeng Lingliang, *ASEAN-China Relations: An International Law Perspective, in* China-ASEAN Relations: Economic and Legal Dimensions 39 (John Wong, Zou Keyuan & Zeng Huaqun eds., 2006) (describing that ASEAN member countries and China signed the Declaration on the Conduct of Parties in the South China Sea at the Eighth ASEAN Summit on 4 November 2002); *see also* Kingsford, *supra* note 4, at 7.

60 Lingliang, *supra* note 59, at 39.

61 Id.

62 Id.

63 Ian Storey, *The Institutionalization of ASEAN-China Relations: Managing the South China Sea Dispute, in* ASEAN and the Institutionalization of East Asia 144 (Ralf Emmers, ed., 2012); Ralf Emmers & See Seng Tan, *The ASEAN Regional Forum and Preventive Diplomacy: A Review Essay,* in ASEAN and the Institutionalization of East Asia 100 (Ralf Emmers, ed., 2012); Lee Jones, *ASEAN's Unchanged Melody? The Theory and Practice of "Non-Interference" in Southeast Asia,* 23 The Pac. Rev. 479 (2010); *See* Declaration on the Conduct of Parties in the South China Sea, Phnom Peh, Nov. 4, 2002, *available at* http://www.asean.org/news/item/declaration-on-the-conduct-of-parties-in-the-south-china-sea-2.

64 Storey, *supra* note 63, at 144.

Further, all signatories have agreed to maintain peace and stability.[65] In contrast, the declaration also contains several weaknesses, including the fact that because of China's policy of constraining Taiwan's territory, the agreement does not recognize one of the claimant countries.[66] In addition, this declaration is ambiguous and fails to specify territorial protection and provide sanctions against non-compliant countries.[67] The declaration is also extremely ambitious, particularly under paragraph five, which demands all claimants to cease any additional action that may elevate tensions on unavailable atolls.[68]

According to the Declaration on the Conduct of Parties in the South China Sea, China and ASEAN claimants need to confer their individual military forces in order to forge reliance and diffuse pressures.[69] They should also participate in "annual defense and security forums."[70] In an effort to promote cooperative confidence-building measures,[71] these countries should engage in several methods to mitigate tensions. One such method might be requiring claimant countries to provide "advanced notification of military exercises and naval patrols" in the territorial conflict when no country shares such activities that cause disputes.[72] Going forward, China and ASEAN claimant countries should continue to research the most appropriate methods to improve their conflicts even though the failure of negotiating table between the United States and China.[73]

Even though ASEAN has yet to initiate a multilateral code of conduct with China,[74] they have attempted to undertake confidence building measures to compromise with China in the South China Sea conflict.[75] The Parties approved their mutual collaboration on "marine environmental protection and scientific

65 Id.

66 Id.

67 Id.; *see also* Ian Storey, *Implementing cbms in the 2002 DOC: A Roadmap to Managing the South China Sea Dispute*, Program for East SEA (South China Sea) Studies (Aug. 2, 2011, 8:20 AM), http://nghiencuubiendong.vn/en/conferences-and-seminars-/second-international-workshop/ 602-602-.

68 Id.

69 Id.

70 Storey, *supra* note 63, at 144; Storey, *supra* note 67.

71 Id.

72 Id.

73 Id.

74 Leng Thearith, ASEAN Security and Its Relevency 80 (Cambodian Institute for Cooperation and Peace E-Book, No. 1, June 2009), *available at* http://www.cicp.org.kh/download/CICP%20E-Book/cicp%20e-book%20no%201.pdf.

75 Id.

research, safety of navigation, search and rescue operation and combating transnational crime."[76] ASEAN has been hesitant to engage in conflict resolution out of concern that any rigid political action may drive China to cease or suspend its partnership in the ASEAN Regional Forum (ARF).[77]

The Declaration on the Conduct of Parties in the South China Sea instructs the concerned Parties to make a mutual political pledge and diminish any amplification of conflict.[78] Subsequently, the government of China has released a report of relations between China and ASEAN. In that report, they confirm that whether or not the global community revolutionizes, China will continue maintain a partnership with ASEAN.[79] China has also declared that they will persistently enhance ASEAN's leadership in all dialogue forums.[80] So far the establishment of ASEAN, its vision of community integration and the core principles of the ASEAN Way have been studied, the next section covers ASEAN's approach to human rights in an effort to show that ASEAN has the potential to protect human rights in its region.

Apart from its political influence, ASEAN has also played a role in promoting and protecting the rights of people through their three-pillar community integration, which is divided by political-security, economic and socio-cultural affairs. This three-pillar approach addresses the promotion of human rights in order to ensure that its people are entitled to obtain fundamental rights and to be protected from human rights violations, including human trafficking. This discussion is integral to understanding ASEAN's vision of community development and its role in developing its institutional capacities and promoting and protecting the rights of people.

2.4 Potential Human Rights Influence of ASEAN

The strife that individual ASEAN member countries experienced made them realize that they could achieve a peaceful atmosphere only through cohesion as a regional group.[81] Since 1967, ASEAN has attempted to regulate its regional

76 Lingliang, *supra* note 59, at 39.

77 Thearith, *supra* note 74, at 80.

78 *See* Declaration on the Conduct of Parties in the South China Sea, *supra* note 63.

79 *See China-ASEAN Cooperation: 1991–2011*, China Daily (Nov. 16, 2011, 08:03 AM), http://www.chinadaily.com.cn/cndy/2011-11/16/content_14101968.htm.

80 See id.

81 Hwang, *supra* note 3, at 68–72.

agreements to guarantee stability among its member countries.[82] Even though numerous threats[83] have impacted political, economic, and social conditions of ASEAN, this research acknowledges that ASEAN has not only desired to sustain solidarity among its member countries, but it has also planned to concentrate on promoting and protecting the rights of people through political-security, economic, and socio-cultural community integration. The three-pillar approach discussed above has traditionally been applied in compliance with the key principles of ASEAN Way, particularly non-interference and consensus decision-making. Section Two includes a vital discussion of whether these principles can help ASEAN promote and protect its people's rights.

2.4.1 *Three-Pillar Community Integration*

Despite numerous security agreements,[84] ASEAN has been ambitious in accomplishing integration of political-security, economic, and socio-cultural communities by 2015.[85] At the 9th ASEAN Summit in 2003, all ten ASEAN

---

82 Löffelholz & Arao, *supra* note 53, at 48; Rudolfo C. Severino, Toward in ASEAN Security Community 5 (2004); I.B.R. Supancana, *supra* note 5, at 327.

83 *See* Huxley, *supra* note 10, at 228–229; *see also* Acharya, *supra* note 10, at 78; Acharya, *supra* note 6, at 13.

84 ASEAN Declaration (Bangkok Declaration), Thailand, Aug. 8, 1967, 6 I.L.M. 1223, *available at* http://www.asean.org/component/zoo/item/the-asean-declaration-bangkok-declaration [hereinafter ASEAN Declaration]; Zone of Peace, Freedom and Neutrality Declaration, Kuala Lumpur, Nov. 27, 1971, http://cil.nus.edu.sg/rp/pdf/1971%20Zone%20of%20Peace%20Freedom%20and%20Neutrality%20Declaration-pdf.pdf; TAC, *supra* note 66; ASEAN Declaration on the South China Sea, Manila, July 22, 1992, http://cil.nus.edu.sg/rp/pdf/1992%20ASEAN%20Declaration%20on%20the%20South%20China%20Sea-pdf.pdf; Treaty on the Southeast Asia Nuclear Weapon-Free Zone, Dec. 15, 1995, *available at* http://www.asean.org/asean/asean-summit/item/treaty-on-the-southeast-asia-nuclear-weapon-free-zone; ASEAN Vision 2020, Dec. 15, 1997, *available at* http://www.aseanhrmech.org/downloads/Asean-Vision-2020.pdf; Löffelholz & Arao, *supra* note 533, at 48; Severino, *supra* note 82, at 5; Supancana, *supra* note 5, at 327–328 (2008) (summarizing that at the outset of ASEAN establishment (between 1967 and 1983), ASEAN intended to strengthen political security; but it also succeeded in enhancing economic and socio-cultural cooperation and integration. Numerous agreements have demonstrated these various approaches. These agreements include the ASEAN Declaration (Bangkok Declaration), the Zone of Peace, Freedom and Neutrality (ZOPFAN), and the Treaty of Amity and Cooperation (TAC). During the Enlargement of Membership (between 1984 and 1999), ASEAN has created several agreements to ensure security in its region. For instance, ASEAN established the ASEAN Declaration on the South China Sea, Treaty on the Southeast Asia Nuclear Weapon-Free Zone, ASEAN Vision 2020).

85 *See* Bali Concord II, *supra* note 5; Supancana, *supra* note 5, at 328.

member countries agreed to create a three-pillar community to strengthen prosperity and peace.[86] This three-pillar community includes the ASEAN Political-Security Community (APSC), ASEAN Economic Community (AEC), and ASEAN Socio-Cultural Community (ASCC).[87] ASEAN member countries have committed to establish these communities by 2015.[88] ASEAN is not just an economic organization. Their precepts have elaborated detailed actions of the development of these communities.[89] It is imperative that ASEAN member countries provide serious commitment and collaboration in implementing all action activities to establish these efficient three communities[90] in order to provide basic rights for its people.

a ASEAN Political-Security Community (APSC):

In 2005, ASEAN member countries produced a statement entitled "One Vision, One Identity, One Community"[91] addressing the plan of action towards the establishment of ASEAN Security Community (ASC).[92] This statement called for cohesion among ASEAN member countries to maintain peace and security in the region with the potential to reinforce ASEAN in the fight against transnational crimes, including human trafficking.[93] Subsequently, ASEAN developed the ASC to the ASEAN Political-Security Community (APSC).[94] The APSC aims

---

86 *See* Bali Concord II, *supra* note 55.

87 *See* id.; Supancana, *supra* note 5, at 328.

88 Cebu Declaration, *supra* note 7 (affirming the strong commitment to establish the three pillar community by 2015).

89 *See* ASEAN, Roadmap for an ASEAN Community 2009–2015 [hereinafter ASEAN Roadmap] 5–94 (2009), *available at* http://www.asean.org/images/2012/publications/RoadmapASEANCommunity.pdf; Yuyun Wahyuningrum, *Understanding ASEAN: Its Systems and Structure* (Dec. 2009), *available at* http://www.scribd.com/doc/81600447/ASEAN-Structures-Mechanisms-Yuyun-10-03-04-Copy.

90 Nicholas T. Dammen, *Relevance of ASEAN in Forging Regional Peace, Security, and Prosperity, in* ASEAN Matters!: Reflecting on the Association of Southeast Asian Nations 66 (Lee Yoong Yoong ed., 2011).

91 Chairman's Statement of the 11th ASEAN Summit, *One Vision, One Identity, and One Community Statement*, Dec. 12, 2005, http://www.asean.org/asean/asean-summit/item/chairman-s-statement-of-the-11th-asean-summit-one-vision-one-identity-one-community.

92 *See* id.; *see also* ASEAN Roadmap, *supra* note 89, at 5–19.

93 Mely Caballero-Anthony, *UN Peace Operations and Asian Security, in* UN Peace Operations and Asian Security 7 (Mely Caballero-Anthony & Amitav Acharya eds., 2005).

94 Mely Caballero-Anthony, *Non-Traditional Security Challenges, Regional Governance, and the ASEAN Political Security Community* (*APSC*), in ASEAN and the Institutionalization of East Asia 33 (Ralf Emmers, ed., 2012).

to boost regional cooperation and guarantee that people in ASEAN member countries live in peace and in the atmosphere of justice, democracy, and coherence in the region.[95]

The APSC involves three core attributes. First is "a rules-based community of shared values and norms"[96] that aim to achieve a rules-based community of shared values and norms, ASEAN underlines political collaboration in advancing democracy to reinforce good governance and the rule of law, and to promote and protect human rights and fundamental freedoms.[97]

Second is "a cohesive, peaceful and resilient region with shared responsibility for comprehensive security."[98] ASEAN envisions that a cohesive, peaceful and resilient region with shared responsibility for comprehensive security (including traditional and non-traditional security matters) is possible through economic, socio-cultural, and environmental development.[99] In addition, ASEAN focuses on conflict avoidance to decrease intensification of disputes among its member countries.[100]

Third is "a dynamic and outward-looking region in an increasingly integrated and interdependent world."[101] ASEAN aims to intensify external relationships with other non-ASEAN member countries by providing various regional and international dialogue forums to strengthen ASEAN's mutual benefits.[102] ASEAN's dialogue forums with external member countries could assist ASEAN construct three efficient communities.[103]

b ASEAN Economic Community (AEC):

The ASEAN Economic Blueprint shows its serious commitment to strengthen collaboration to regional economic unity, by aiming to create a single market and production base in the ASEAN region, a fair competitive economic region, and an external economic approach.[104] In essence, the single market and production base in the ASEAN region requires a free flow of goods, services, investment, capital, and skilled labor.[105] Therefore, the creation of the

95 *See* ASEAN Roadmap, *supra* note 89, at 5.
96 *See* id. at 6–11.
97 *See* id. at 6.
98 *See* id. at 11–17.
99 *See* id. at 11.
100 *See* ASEAN Roadmap, *supra* note 89, at 11.
101 *See* id. at 17–18.
102 *See* ASEAN Roadmap, *supra* note 89, at 17.
103 See id.
104 *See* Löffelholz & Arao, *supra* note 53, at 50; *see also* id. at 21–38.
105 *See* ASEAN Roadmap, *supra* note 89, at 22.

AEC can ensure establishment of regional economic and trade strategies and principles that can magnetize a large-scale of investment groups.[106] These investors can promote business growth for all ASEAN underdeveloped countries.[107] In order to accomplish its single market plan, ASEAN requires the AEC to accommodate the labor movement by issuing work permit visas for ASEAN professionals and skilled labors working in member countries' trade and investment companies.[108] This working permit method will promote free movement of migration that can accelerate economic growth in its region.

c ASEAN Socio-Cultural Community (ASCC):

ASEAN addressed the need for building the ASEAN Socio-Cultural Community (ASCC) at the 13th ASEAN Summit held in Singapore on November 20, 2007.[109] The ASCC blueprint features six major dimensions with detailed action programs: (1) human development, (2) social welfare and protection, (3) social justice and rights, (4) ensuring environmental sustainability, (5) building ASEAN identity, and (6) narrowing the development gap.[110] In order words, ASEAN designed the ASCC to strengthen the life conditions, promote an ASEAN identity, and provide equal public welfare and rights for people in ASEAN region.[111] The strategies for the establishment of ASCC consist of strengthening human resources for employment; reducing poverty, social and economic inequality; and improving life condition of people, including vulnerable groups such as those in the countryside.[112]

---

106 David Jay Green, *The Role of ASEAN Economic Community as a Commitment to Policy Certainty*, 25 ASEAN Econ. Bull. 209, 227 (2008); ASEAN Secretariat, ASEAN Socio-Cultural Community Blueprint 1 (2009), *available at* http://www.asean.org/images/archive/5187-19.pdf [hereinafter Socio-Cultural Community Blueprint].

107 Green, *supra* note 106, at 227.

108 *See* ASEAN Roadmap, *supra* note 89, at 29.

109 Socio-Cultural Community Blueprint, *supra* note 106, at 1; ASEAN Roadmap, *supra* note 89, at 68, 73.

110 ASEAN Roadmap, *supra* note 89, at 68.

111 Socio-Cultural Community Blueprint, *supra* note 106, at 1.

112 Socio-Cultural Community Blueprint, *supra* note 106, at 1; ASEAN Roadmap, *supra* note 89, at 68, 73; Rhanch Macalalad et al., A Guidebook on Spaces for Children's Participation in ASEAN 16 (2011), *available at* http://forum-asia.org/2010/Spaces%20for%20Childrens%20Participation%20%28May%2012%29%20FINAL.pdf (This research summarizes from these sources that ASEAN has done bounds to take into account the protection of women, children, and other vulnerable groups through measures such as providing for their social security and protection in the ASCC. Compared to APSC and AEC, the ASCC emphasizes the creation of strategies and measures to enforce children's rights. For instance, ASEAN has implemented the CRC by creating action plans for "child survival, development and

After tracing the historical background and vision of ASEAN, it is noteworthy to address that even though ASEAN has confronted political conflicts in the past, they have not involved military force.[113] ASEAN believes that it can build regional institutions by strengthening political security, without the use of the military.[114] ASEAN member countries prefer to maintain security of their own government rather than use regional military force.[115]

There have been affirmative statements which illustrate the non-implementation of military force by ASEAN member countries.[116] For instance, Indonesia and the Philippines asserted that ASEAN will not use "a security pact" to support great powerful countries or its member countries.[117] Philippine Foreign Minister Narciso Ramos also persisted that an individual country has its rights of internal "security" management.[118] ASEAN member countries believe that regional security can be maintained through economic, political, and socio-cultural approaches, *not* military force.[119] According to the former Prime Minister of Malaysia, Hussein Onn, ASEAN member countries feel that the use of force can cause political disputes among them and threaten their harmony.[120] Additionally, the former Thai Foreign Minister has insisted that ASEAN has never acknowledged military collaboration because it implies that use of military force has been superseded.[121] ASEAN has supported its member countries in managing border insurgencies (such as the dispute between Malaysia and Indonesia) as regional security collaboration through the bilateral agreement.[122] ASEAN has preferred reinforcing regional security cooperation through non-military methods, namely diplomatic channels or the negotiating process because military force has proved improper and redundant for ASEAN.[123]

---

protection." ASEAN also involves "persons with disabilities" in the decision-making process of creating policies and methods of their rights because their physical or psychological incompetence can render them to become vulnerable people to human trafficking).

113 Acharya, *supra* note 6, at 10, 12; Hwang, *supra* note 3, at 75.

114 Hwang, *supra* note 33, at 75; Acharya, *supra* note 10, at 96.

115 Anja Jetschke, *ASEAN*, *in* Routledge Handbook of Asian Regionalism 334 (Mark Beeson & Richard Stubbs eds., 2012); Acharya, *supra* note 10, at 96.

116 Jetschke, *supra* note 115, at 334; Amitav Acharya, Constructing a Security Community in Southeast Asia: ASEAN and the Problem of Regional Order 90 (2d ed. 2009).

117 Jetschke, *supra* note 115, at 334.

118 *See* id.; *see also* Acharya, *supra* note 116, at 89.

119 Löffelholz & Arao, *supra* note 53, at 41.

120 Acharya, *supra* note 10, at 91.

121 Id. at 95.

122 Id. at 95.

123 Id. at 96.

2.4.2 *ASEAN Way*

ASEAN has required its communities to respect the concept of the "ASEAN Way" in order to maintain peace and security. It is necessary to explore the main principles making up this notion of the "ASEAN Way" in order to understand ASEAN's approach to political conflict management.[124] The ASEAN Way sets forth five principles of security management through the ASEAN Bangkok Declaration 1967 and the Treaty of Amity and Cooperation (TAC) in Southeast Asia 1976, including: "(1) 'Mutual respect for the independence, sovereignty, territorial integrity of all nations'; (2) 'The right of every state to lead its national existence free from external interference, subversion and coercion'; (3) 'Non-interference in the internal affairs of one another'; (4) 'Settlement of differences and disputes by peaceful means'; and (5) 'Renunciation of the threat of use of force.'"[125] These principles illustrate that ASEAN member countries have made a pledge to respect the individual country's sovereignty and jurisdiction in order to avoid political intervention within its member countries. They have also agreed on consensus decision-making in all concerns in order to promote equal voting system that each member country has one vote.

In their view, this concept has the potential to establish trust, understanding and peaceful relations amongst the ASEAN member nations.[126] It focuses on mediation rather than forceful conduct and dispensable order.[127] Those focusing on the region have found that the ASEAN Way is a diplomatic measure, which can be used to promote stability and regional organization through the use of conflict management and dispute settlement mechanisms.[128] ASEAN applies ASEAN Way as its main instrument of world peace through cultural correlations.[129]

2.5. Debates on Human Rights Approach of ASEAN

Even though ASEAN's vision of three-pillar community integration has addressed human rights, critics have questioned the feasibility of its achievement in providing fundamental rights for its populations. This section will

124 Löffelholz & Arao, *supra* note 53, at 38.

125 TAC, *supra* note 66; *see also* Acharya, *supra* note 66, at 7; Leviter, *supra* note 6, at 161, 168.

126 Beverly Loke, *The 'ASEAN Way': Towards Regional Order and Security Cooperation*? 30 Melbourne J. of Politics, 2005, at 8–38.

127 Id.

128 Id.; Löffelholz & Arao, *supra* note 53, at 38.

129 Id.; *see also* Michael Haas, The Asian Way to Peace: A Story of Regional Cooperation 2 (1989).

discuss ASEAN's current human rights instruments, the ASEAN Charter and AICHR TOR, which require application of the ASEAN Way. Even though this ASEAN Way was successful in settling the Vietnamese invasion of Cambodia, this approach will not be as successful in the case of human rights infringements such as human trafficking as this type of action is inadequate for providing protection for trafficking victims' rights. And while ASEAN has yet to show any progress in settling the dispute over the South China Sea, they have exhibited positive responses to non-traditional security concerns, namely natural disasters, counterterrorism, and epidemic diseases. Except for other non-traditional crimes, ASEAN has also focused on ending human trafficking through collaboration with the regional and international communities.

2.5.1 *Discussion of the "ASEAN Way"*

Human rights is a new focus in the region and ASEAN has responded by establishing their first legally-binding instrument, the ASEAN Charter,[130] and creating

---

130 Young, *supra* note 7, at 107–108; Hum. Rts. Herald, *supra* note 7, at 6–7; ASEAN + 3 5th Joint Statement, *supra* note 7 at §6; *see also* Villacorta, *supra* note 7, at 306–307; Cebu Declaration, *supra* note 7 Chairman's Statement of the 13th ASEAN Summit, *supra* note 7; *Frequently Asked Questions on the ASEAN Charter*, *supra* note 8; *About ASEAN*, *supra* note 7 (summarizing that even though ASEAN was originally considered an informal group without any constitutional or legal character, its member countries acknowledged the necessity of the development of a regional legal framework to build up its regional identity and address human rights in its region. Pursuant to the formation of ten plenary member countries in 1999, ASEAN convened meetings to develop the ASEAN Charter as its first legally binding international instrument and frequently held various forums to discuss the adoption of AICHR. The member countries made serious efforts and commitments to strengthen their regional regime by creating the ASEAN Charter despite the long process of its development. For the first time, in June 2004, the Foreign Affairs Ministers concurred to establish this Charter which builds an institutional framework for the region. ASEAN member countries recognized the action plan for the advancement of the ASEAN Charter as one of main objectives of the Vientiane Action Programme (VAP). ASEAN leaders adopted the Declaration on the Establishment of ASEAN Charter in December 2005. This Declaration designated the Eminent Persons Group (EPG) to suggest specific rules and legal procedures to be indoctrinated in the ASEAN Charter. The Eminent Persons Group provided its recommendations, and attached them to the Cebu Declaration on the Blueprint of ASEAN Charter signed by ASEAN leaders at the 12th ASEAN Summit in 2007. The Cebu Declaration also called on ASEAN member countries to create of the High Level Task Force (HLTF) which was charged with drafting the ASEAN Charter. The draft was endorsed by leaders in 2007. The ten ASEAN member countries ratified the ASEAN Charter, and it was entered into force on December 15, 2008. As a result, the ASEAN Charter has become the ASEAN Constitution and a binding agreement among the ten ASEAN Member States).

a regional human rights body (AICHR)[131] in an effort to prove that ASEAN intends to provide fundamental rights to people in its region. ASEAN has demonstrated its power of mobilization to drive its member countries to acknowledge and promote human rights through its Charter and human rights mechanisms. However, there is much more room for improvement in ASEAN's approaches to ensure their citizens enjoy their primary rights. In accordance with other critics, it is clear that ASEAN needs to refrain from adhering to the restrictive principles of the ASEAN Way to fully battle human rights violations.

ASEAN has made a concerted effort to drive member countries to promote human rights by creating the ASEAN Charter and AICHR, but still there have been several debates over these instruments.[132] There is no doubt that the

---

131 ASEAN Charter, *supra* note 8, at art. 14(1); Hum. Rts. Herald, *supra* note 7, at 6–7; Woo, *supra* note 8; *Frequently Asked Questions on the ASEAN Charter, supra* note 8 (concluding that regardless of the long process of establishing the ASEAN Charter, ASEAN formed AICHR to promote human rights. In 1993, the Foreign Ministers conceded that ASEAN should take into account the creation of an effective human rights body. Also in the same year, the Human Rights Committee of LAWASIA designated the Working Group for an ASEAN Human Rights Mechanism to accelerate ASEAN to develop the human rights body. In 1998, ASEAN Foreign Ministers approved the Working Group's involvement in the formation of a human rights mechanism. The Working Group completed a "Draft Agreement for the Establishment of ASEAN Human Rights Commission" and proposed it to ASEAN Senior Officials in 2000. Between 2001 and 2009, the Working Group arranged workshops on the ASEAN human rights body where ASEAN member countries and other organizations participated in dialogue about human rights. Notwithstanding its sluggish progress in creating a human rights body, between 2004 and 2010, ASEAN undertook the Vientiane Action Program (VAP) that prescribes plans of action on human rights. ASEAN called for the Working Group's support on the VAP. The Working Group responded to the request by organizing numerous workshops, namely in 2001 and 2006 in Jakarta; in 2002 and 2007 in Manila; in 2003 and 2009 in Bangkok; in 2006 in Kula Lumpur; and in 2008 in Singapore. Between 2005 and 2007 ASEAN concentrated on the establishment of the ASEAN Charter stipulating the creation of an ASEAN human rights body. Human rights and relevant concepts are specified in Article 14(1) requiring establishment of a regional human rights mechanism to implement the objectives and principles of the ASEAN Charter pertaining to the promotion and protection of human rights and fundamental freedoms.[131] Further, Article 14(2) mandates ASEAN Foreign Ministers Meeting (comprising of ASEAN Senior Officials) to determine the creation of ASEAN human rights body. ASEAN Foreign Ministers took action by delegating a High Level Panel (HLP) to draft the Terms of Reference for ASEAN Human Rights Body (AICHR TOR) in 2008. All ten ASEAN member countries ratified the TOR AICHR in the same year. ASEAN Foreign Ministers approved the TOR of ASEAN Intergovernmental Commission on Human Rights (AICHR) in 2009).

132 Chongkittavorn, *supra* note 43, at 41; Tan Sri Ahmad Fuzi bin Abdul Razak, *Facing Unfair Criticisms, in* The Making of ASEAN Charter 18 (Tommy Koh, Rorario G Manalo, & Walter Woon eds., 2009).

ASEAN Charter symbolizes progressive development[133] and promotes moving towards a new approach that advances the promotion and protection of human rights.[134] In addition, the AICHR has the potential to lead ASEAN to be an effective regional organization by allowing mechanisms for ASEAN member countries to share their human rights concerns.[135]

Nonetheless, these instruments contain shortcomings that must be improved. For instance, the Charter addresses the coalition's movement towards a "people-centered" standard, which reinforces the involvement of its populations and civil society organizations in regional forums to build a regional community.[136] However, people should have the right to receive information and participate in the regional community-building process by sharing their views with member countries.[137]

Even though the Indonesian President of Indonesia Susilo Bambang Yuhoyoo has intoned that ASEAN values various perspectives,[138] in practice,

---

133 Razak, *supra* note 132, at 18.

134 *South East Asia Regional Office (2008–2009): Human Rights Context*, OHCHR, http://www.ohchr.org/EN/Countries/AsiaRegion/Pages/SouthEastAsiaSummary0809.aspx (last visited Mar. 1, 2013) [hereinafter *Human Rights Context*].

135 Le Thu Huong, *Many Faces and One Identity? ASEAN in the Case of Human Rights Regime*, Asia-Pacific J. Soc. Sci., Special Issue No. 1, 56, 64 (2010), *available at* http://www.academia.edu/2092999/Many_Faces_and_One_Identity_ASEAN_in_the_Case_of_Human_Rights_Regime; *un High Commissioner for Human Rights Boosts Human Rights Development in ASEAN*, ASEAN Secretariat News, Nov. 29, 2011, *available at* http://www.asean.org/news/asean-secretariat-news/item/un-high-commissioner-for-human-rights-boosts-human-rights-development-in-asean (reprinting the remarks of the The Secretary-General of ASEAN, Dr. Surin Pitsuwan, that the AICHR opens opportunity for ASEAN and all levels of organizations to discuss human rights issues. The United Nations High Commissioner for Human Rights (OHCHR), Ms. Navanethem Pillay commended ASEAN's establishment of the AICHR represented ASEAN's commitment to provide the primary rights for people that can hasten its community-building).

136 *See* ASEAN Charter, *supra* note 8; Melissa Curley, *Human Security's Future in Regional Cooperation and Governance?*, 66 Ausl. J. of Int'l Aff. 527 (2011).

137 Chheang Vannarith, *Asia Pacific Security Issues: Challenges and Adaptive Mechanism* 3 (Cambodian Institute for Cooperation and Peace, CICP Policy Brief No. 3, July 2010), *available at* http://www.cicp.org.kh/download/CICP%20Policy%20brief/CICP%20Policy%20brief%20No%203.pdf.

138 Susilo Bambang Yuhoyoo, On Building ASEAN Community: The Democratic Aspect, Lecture on the occasion of the Thirty-Eighth Anniversary of the Association of Southeast Asian Nations, ASEAN Secretariat News (Aug. 8, 2005) http://www.asean.org/resources/2012-02-10-08-47-56/leaders-view/item/on-building-the-asean-community-the-democratic-aspect; Rizal Sukma, ASEAN *Charter: Neither Bold Nor Visionary*, *in* The Road to Ratification and Implementation of ASEAN Charter 48 (Pavin Chachavalpongpun d., 2009).

the actual method of this involvement is not outlined in the Charter.[139] The Charter focuses solely on the participation of government representatives. ASEAN should bridge this gap by designing a means of exchanging information between member countries' governments and their citizens and civil society organizations.[140] This has the potential strengthen the interaction between these entities.[141] This can also help ASEAN accelerate its community-building.

The second debate is over the ASEAN Charter and the Terms of Reference of the AICHR, which have adhered to the principles of ASEAN Way,[142] particularly its approaches of consensus decision-making and non-interference, which weaken promotion and protection of human rights. The ASEAN Way has the potential to establish trust, understanding and peaceful relations in the ASEAN region.[143] Its focus is on mediation rather than forceful conduct and dispensable order.[144] Those focusing on the region have found that the ASEAN Way is a diplomatic measure, which can be used to promote stability and regional organization through the use of conflict management and dispute settlement mechanisms.[145] ASEAN applies the ASEAN Way as its main instrument of world peace through cultural correlations.[146]

One of the major criticisms of the ASEAN Way has been that it is an informal decision-making process.[147] Scholars criticize that the consensus principle aims to prevent "losing face" with its member countries.[148] Such consensus decision-making is an unreliable principle that ASEAN leaders apply it to

139 Curley, *supra* note 136; Sukma, *supra* note 138, at 47–48.

140 Sukma, *supra* note 138, at 48.

141 Id.

142 *See* TAC, *supra* note 6; *see also* Acharya, *supra* note 6, at 7; Leviter, *supra* note 6, at 161, 168; ASEAN Intergovernmental Commission on Human Rights (AICHR), Terms of Reference § 3 (Oct. 2009), *available at* http://www.asean.org/images/2012/publications/Terms%20of%20Reference%20of%20ASEAN%20Intergovernmental%20Commission%20on%20Human%20Rights.pdf [hereinafter AICHR Terms of Reference] (including the principles of "(1) 'Mutual respect for the independence, sovereignty, territorial integrity of all nations'; (2) 'The right of every state to lead its national existence free from external interference, subversion and coercion'; (3) 'Non-interference in the internal affairs of one another'; (4) 'Settlement of differences and disputes by peaceful means'; and (5) 'Renunciation of the threat of use of force.'")

143 Loke, *supra* note 126, at 8–38.

144 Id.

145 Id.

146 Id.; Haas, *supra* note 129, at 2.

147 Acharya, *supra* note 39, at 494.

148 Mark Beeson, Institutions of the Asia-Pacific: ASEAN, APEC, and Beyond 21 (2009).

maintain their power.[149] When compared to other regional organizations such as those in Europe and North America, it also exhibits informal organization.[150] Such informality practiced in East Asia has been criticized by some as "undeveloped."[151] In this regard, Acharya and Johnston have argued that this informality has had an effect on consensus decision-making within ASEAN and has defined the regional standards of some of the parties.[152] Because some parties exhibit more formal schemes, including majority voting, positive collaboration has not always been generated amongst the parties.[153]

Although consensus decision-making through consultation decelerates ASEAN's operations, the process can in fact eliminate the superiority of more powerful countries.[154] Because of the availability of a mutual foreign policy, consensus decision-making is advantageous because it can "balance" benefits for both powerless and powerful ASEAN member countries.[155] This decision process prevents powerful ASEAN member countries from manipulating powerless countries[156] and emphasizes developing partnerships without them losing sovereignty,[157] which makes them feel "comfortable."[158] These member countries believe that this concept can maintain their stability as a regional institution.[159]

Non-interference regarding state sovereignty has also raised concerns to the international community because while ASEAN wants to take a hands-off approach and apply the principle of non-interference, human rights abuses are taking place.[160] According to scholar I.B.R. Supancana, it is obvious that

---

149 Id.

150 *See* Fredrik Söderbaum, *Theories of Regionalism*, *in* Routledge Handbook of Asian Regionalism 20 (Mark Beeson & Richard Stubbs eds., 2012).

151 *See* id.; *see also* Young Jong Choi & James A. Caporaso, *Comparative Regional Integration*, *in* Handbook of International Relations 485 (W. Carlsnaes, T. Risse & B. Simmons, eds., 2002).

152 *See*: Regional International Institutions, *in* Comparative Perspective 268–269 (Amitav Acharya & Alastair Iain Johnston eds., 2007), *see also* Söderbaum, *supra* note 150, at 20.

153 Id.

154 Loke, *supra* note 126, at 8–38.

155 Löffelholz & Arao, *supra* note 53, at 9.

156 Id. at 7, 9.

157 Id. at 38; Jűrgen Haacke, ASEAN's Diplomatic Culture: Origins, Development, and Prospects 3–4 (2003).

158 Löffelholz & Arao, *supra* note 53, at 38–39.

159 Id.; Alice D. Ba, *ASEAN Centrality Imperiled? ASEAN Institutionalism and the Challenges of Major Power Institutionalization*, *in* ASEAN and the Institutionalization of East Asia (Ralf Emmers ed., 2012); Severino, *supra* note 40, at 4–5.

160 Supancana, *supra* note 5, at 332; Shaun Narine, *Asia, ASEAN and the Question of Sovereignty: the Persistence of Non-Intervention in the Asia-Pacific*, *in* Routledge Handbook of Asian Regionalism 163 (Mark Beeson & Richard Stubbs, eds., 2012).

ASEAN has interpreted the non-interference principle as non-intervention through the use of military force and movement in politics, economics, and culture,[161] and has applied them with "respect of sovereignty, territory integrity, political independence and self-determination."[162] The historical experiences of the ASEAN member countries illustrate the reasons that they have emphasized maintenance of their "sovereignty" above all else.[163] All of the member countries, except Thailand, have cherished their "sovereignty" after suffering colonization by European countries, the United, and Japan.[164] These countries have asserted that human rights fall under the realm of the internal affairs of an individual country; therefore, as a "prerogative of state sovereignty" each country should be accountable for their own citizens' rights.[165] Consequently, these countries rarely intervene when other countries are involved in human rights abuses.[166]

Nevertheless, it has been observed that in responding to economic, environmental, and human security threats the ASEAN Way has originated "delayed, inadequate and ineffective" processes.[167] Specifically, this non-interference principle has deteriorated ASEAN credibility in protesting the Myanmar State Peace and Development Council's (SPDC) policies against ethnic minorities while other Western countries condemn and sanction Myanmar.[168]

Even though ASEAN has applied a principle of "constructive engagement"[169] that construes peaceful negotiation and consent, this approach has not been effective in Myanmar.[170] The ASEAN Way has been applied not for diplomatic

---

161 Supancana, *supra* note 5, at 332 (2008); Acharya, *supra* note 116, at 58; Wunderlich, *supra* note 45, at 153.

162 Supancana, *supra* note 5, at 332.

163 Narine, *supra* note 160, at 157.

164 Id.

165 Sou Chiam, *Asia's Experience in the Quest for a Regional Human Rights Mechanism*, 40 Victoria U. Wellington L. Rev. 127, 129, 146 (2009).

166 Id. at 127, 129, 147.

167 Alastair Iain Johnston, *Socialization in International Institutions: ASEAN Way and International Relations Theory*, *in* International Relations Theory and the Asia-Pacific 124 (G. John Ikenberry & Michael Mastanduno eds., 2003); Kasira Cheeppensook, ASEAN Way on Human Security 20 (Paper from the International Development Studies Conference of Mainstreaming Human Security: The Asian Contribution, held on Oct. 4–5, 2007), *available at* http://humansecurityconf.polsci.chula.ac.th/Documents/Presentations/Kasira.pdf ; Loke, *supra* note 126, at 8–38.

168 Loke, *supra* note 126, at 8–38.

169 Id.; *see also* Leszek Buszynski, *Thailand and Myanmar: The Perils of "Constructive Engagement*, 11 Pac. Rev. 290–305 (1998); Acharya, *supra* note 116, at 89–90.

170 Loke, *supra* note 126, at 8–38.

reasons, but as it seems to avoid a rapid response there.[171] ASEAN may have to determine if the non-interference principle has caused ASEAN to be unsuccessful in its mission of mediation with Myanmar.[172] It is clear that ASEAN's failure to mediate with Myanmar is an example of the drawbacks of the ASEAN Way.[173]

While the ASEAN Way has been useful and indispensable in addressing past conflicts, the application of these principles of non-interference and consensus decision-making have proven to be inconsistent and impractical tools for promoting and protecting human rights in the current landscape.[174] This approach has both strengths and weaknesses. For instance, it has been instrumental in eradicating inequity in authority,[175] and its norms have helped maintain peace and stability in the region. However, even former UN Secretary General, Kofi Annan, has insisted that state sovereignty should not prevail in the case of human rights violations such as human trafficking.[176] In this era of globalization, the principle of state sovereignty is not always practical because countries are now so interconnected and the world has become much smaller through technology such as online connection channels, which have all but eliminated frontier of state sovereignty.[177]

2.5.2 *Achievements and Challenges of ASEAN Regional Forum*

ASEAN has convened the ARF, where its dialogue partners can share their concerns and best actions against both traditional and non-traditional crimes, including human security concerns. This seems to be a step towards some hope for a process, which would promote and protect human rights. ASEAN's role in the forum is crucial in persuading its member countries to respond these threats, especially as they apply to non-traditional crimes.

Even though ASEAN has not been successful in fully convincing both member countries and non-member countries to moderate political conflicts of Vietnamese invasion of Cambodia and South China Sea, it has been able to engage other non-member countries to participate in the ARF. The ARF is a

171 Id.

172 Id.; Jusuf Wanandi, *ASEAN's Problem with Myanmar*, The Jakarta Post (July 13, 2005, 7:13 AM), http://www.thejakartapost.com/news/2005/07/13/ASEAN039s-problem-myanmar.html.

173 Loke, *supra* note 126, at 8–38.

174 Löffelholz & Arao, *supra* note 53, at 7; *see also* Rodolfo C. Severino, *Will There Be a New ASEAN in the 21st Century?*, 2 Asia Eur. J. 184 (2004).

175 Chiam, *supra* note 165, at 127, 129, 146.

176 Id. at 127, 129, 147.

177 Id.

multilateral security forum on traditional and non-traditional security. Here dialogue partners have an opportunity to share their concerns and best actions against both traditional and non-traditional crimes, including human security concerns. ASEAN has played a role in persuading its member countries to respond these threats, especially non-traditional crimes.

Although they have not served as a leader in these efforts, they have reinforced collaboration between member countries and other entities to address concerns and share their best practices on both traditional and non-traditional security measures.

Although many scholars criticize ASEAN's unaccountable and non-legally binding dialogues,[178] ASEAN's informal and formal discourses have enhanced a number of its partnerships.[179] Since the inception of the ARF in 1994 it has reinforced open and productive "dialogue and consultation on political and security issues" and to make progress in "confidence-building and preventive diplomacy" in the Asia-Pacific region[180] with the emphasis of upholding peace, security, and collaboration in ASEAN region.[181] The international community can applaud ASEAN for creating the ARF, which was "the first multilateral security forum."[182]

The ARF's biggest achievement has been its status as the "only regional security framework in the world," which has been successful in recruiting powerful countries, such as the United States, Russia, China, Japan, India, and European Union (Britain, France, and Germany).[183] Participation by these countries is an indication of ASEAN's influence in internal and external communities as a center

---

178 *See* Michael Leifer, ASEAN Regional Forum: Extending ASEAN's Model of Regional Security 53 (Adelphi Research, No. 302, 1996); *see also* Beeson, *supra* note 148, at 73; Otto von Feigenblatt, *ASEAN and Human Security: Challenges and Opportunities* 9 (Ritsumeikan Center for Asia Pacific Studies Working Paper No. 09-5, July 2009), *available at* http://papers.ssrn.com/sol3/papers.cfm?abstract_id=1442476&download=yes.

179 Archarya & Johnston, *supra* note 42, at 27; Alice Ba, *ASEAN Regional Forum: Maintaining the Regional Idea in Southeast Asia*, 52 Int'l J. 635, 644–645 (1997); Leifer, *supra* note 178, at 55; Mely Cabellero-Anthony, *Regionalization of Peace in Asia: Experiences and prospects of ASEAN, arf and un Partnership* 9 (The Institute of Defence and Strategic Studies, Working Research No. 42, Jan. 2003), *available at* http://www.rsis.edu.sg/publications/WorkingPapers/WP42.PDF.

180 *See* ASEAN, The First ASEAN Regional Forum, Bangkok, Thailand, July 25, 1994, Art. 4, Para. 3, *available at* http://aseanregionalforum.asean.org/files/ARF-Publication/ARF-Document-Series-1994-2006/01_Bangkok2006.pdf.

181 *See* id.; *see also* Vannarith, *supra* note 137, at 3.

182 *See* Acharya, *supra* note 10, at 146.

183 *See* id.; *see also, About the ASEAN Regional Forum*, ASEAN Regional Forum (ARF), http://aseanregionalforum.asean.org/about.html (listing the 28 member states of the ARF: Australia, Bangladesh, Brunei Darussalam, Cambodia, Canada, China, European Union,

of discussion.[184] This participation also reflects the fact that the ARF could provide them common interest even though this forum was created by small powerful countries.[185] ASEAN also has the competence to strengthen regional collaboration within its member countries and engage other non-member countries[186] to boost development and community-building.

Despite its lagging progress in the realm of political conflict management, the ARF has served as a central venue for its member countries and other dialogue partners to point out their concerns and share their best strategies to tackle non-traditional threats.[187] The ARF has set out three main platforms for security development: confidence-building measures (CBMs);[188] preventive diplomacy (PD);[189] and non-traditional security collaboration.[190]

The ARF has been most successful in the realm of non-traditional security collaboration. The dialogue partners have struggled with "confidence-building measures" and have been unable to make agreements for each forum. During the first meeting of the confidence-building agenda, there was a considerable amount of dissent amongst ARF's member countries.[191] Active countries, such as

---

India, Indonesia, Japan, Democratic Peoples' Republic of Korea, Republic of Korea, Laos, Malaysia, Myanmar, Mongolia, New Zealand, Pakistan, Papua New Guinea, Philippines, Russian Federation, Singapore, Sri Lanka, Thailand, Timor Leste, United States, Vietnam).

184 Amitav Acharya, *ASEAN at 40: Mid-Life Rejuvenation?* Foreign Aff. (Aug. 15, 2007), http://www.foreignaffairs.com/print/64249?page=show; *see also* Aileen S.P. Baviera, *Introduction, in* Regional Security in East Asia: Challenges to Cooperation and Community Building 1–12 (Aileen S.P. Baviera ed., 2008).

185 Acharya, *supra* note 10, at 147; Narine, *supra* note 160, at 157.

186 Sompong Sucharitkul, *ASEAN Society: A Dynamic Experiment for South-East Asian Regional Co-Operation,* 1 Asian Y.B. Int'l 113 (1991).

187 Nicholas Rees, *EU and ASEAN: Issues of Regional Security*, 47 Int'l Politics 402, 412 (2010).

188 Feigenblatt, *supra* note 178, at 9–10 (finding that confidence-building aims to forge trust between member countries and to eliminate insecurity by exchanging data. Its measures include "participation in small arms registration, announcements of military exercises, position papers regarding security, and arms control." The ARF has applied confidence-building measures and has approached to the second stage).

189 *See* Takeshi Yuzawa, *The ASEAN Regional Forum: Challenges and Prospects, in* Routledge Handbook of Asian Regionalism 341 (Mark Beeson & Richard Stubbs eds., 2012); *see also* Takeshi Yuzawa, *The Evolution of Preventive Diplomacy in the ASEAN Regional Forum: Problems and Prospects*, 46 Asian Survey 790, 790–791 (2006) (explaining that preventive diplomacy (PD) means a higher stage of security collaboration in the ARF agenda items).

190 Feigenblatt, *supra* not 178, at 9–10; Yuzawa, *The ASEAN Regional Forum, supra* note 189, at 340; *see also* Takeshi Yuzawa, Japan's Security Policy and the ASEAN Regional Forum: The Search for Multilateral Security in the Asia-Pacific 65 (2007).

191 Yuzawa, *The ASEAN Regional Forum, supra* note 189, at 340; Yuzawa, *supra* note 190, at 65.

the United States, Japan, Australia, and Canada, advocated for solid confidence-building measures to strengthen military force.[192] Hesitant countries (such as China), who are distrustful of military transparency, wanted to promote the confidence-building approach through the use of informal discourse and agreements.[193] In the late 1990s the dialogue partners agreed to emphasize non-traditional security more than traditional security affairs, which may include participation of defense authorities.[194] This involvement could strengthen law enforcement cooperation by sharing opinions and relevant data.[195]

Preventative diplomacy (PD) includes systematic and noncompulsory dialogues and demands on the ARF member countries to advocate "mediation, conciliation, enquiry, and negotiation."[196] Despite this, the dialogue partners have expressed divergent views about preventive diplomacy because of the ARF's lack of ability to develop "confidence and trust" among its partners.[197] Active countries favor implementation of preventive diplomacy measures in practice, specifically as effective enforcement mechanisms that can interpret the application of laws and administration.[198] In addition, these countries anticipate that the ARF can tackle all matters, including "traditional and non-traditional sources of conflict such as territorial disputes, political and legal disputes, terrorism, and human rights issues"[199]

Hesitant countries oppose preventive diplomacy measures that allow other partners to intervene in the domestic affairs of partners, especially in terms of religious and territorial conflicts.[200] For instance, Chinese Ambassador and Secretary-General of the Council for Security Cooperation in the Asia-Pacific (CSCAP) China assert "sovereignty" and non-interference principles.[201] The ARF envisions moving toward "elaboration and approaches to conflict;" they have been unable to reach this stage because it requires serious commitment from member countries.[202] In practice, consensus

192 Id.
193 Id.
194 Yuzawa, *The ASEAN Regional Forum, supra* note 189, at 341.
195 Id.
196 Feigenblatt, *supra* note 178, at 10.
197 Yuzawa, *The ASEAN Regional Forum, supra* note 189, at 341; *see also* Yuzawa, *The Evolution of Preventive Diplomacy, supra* note 189, at 790–791.
198 Id.
199 Yuzawa, *The ASEAN Regional Forum, supra* note 189, at 342.
200 Id. at 341; *see also* Yuzawa, *The Evolution of Preventive Diplomacy, supra* note 189, at 790–791.
201 Emmers & Tan, *supra* note 63, at 94.
202 Feigenblatt, *supra* note 178, at 10.

decision-making has kept ASEAN from making progress although the ARF reveres the consensus rule.[203]

Still, the ARF does have some potential, which can be seen through its support, trust, belief and loyalty of their dialogue partners and ASEAN's central role. The United States, China, and Japan have all found ASEAN to be a cooperative manager.[204] These powerful dialogue partners value the ARF as a productive multilateral platform that can create progressive collaboration on a variety of common security concerns.[205] Canada applauded the role of the ARF in alleviating and managing political conflicts based on preventive diplomacy, which has cut down on the costs of peace maintenance.[206] Canada has also recognized the significance of ASEAN's leadership in the ARF by strengthening effective plans of action and enhancing collaboration among participants.[207]

Even though the ARF originated from a seemingly powerless organization like ASEAN, this forum has opened a platform for all countries of all development and economic levels in order to spell out their political security views, thus creating global harmony. The ARF has provided a venue for its dialogue partners to propose coherent and sustainable strategies to deal with their concerns, or to exchange information and technical assistance, and to raise public awareness on mutual interests.

On the other hand, the resolutions of the meetings and the lessons from these partners' experiences have contributed to ARF in the form of institutional confidence-building and preventive diplomacy. In other words, the ARF has become both giver and taker. The United States has supported ASEAN's cooperative actions against transnational crimes through training programs for judges and prosecutors of Indonesia, the Philippines, Thailand, and Laos.[208] However, the ARF should regularly translate its partners' comments into concrete work plans of action so that the ARF can reach all stages of its development.

Although the ARF has not illustrated progress in preventive diplomacy,[209] it is clear that it is the only Asian-Pacific regional security forum, where its dialogue partners can discuss both traditional and non-traditional security

203 Id.

204 Ralf Emmers & See Seng Tan, *Conclusion: Trends and Driving Forces in East Asian Regionalism, in* ASEAN and the Institutionalization of East Asia 196 (Ralf Emmers ed., 2012).

205 Annual Security Outlook-2011, *supra* note 56, at 170.

206 *See* id. at 34 (providing the opinions of North and South Korea at ASEAN).

207 *See* id.

208 *See* id.

209 Yuzawa, *The ASEAN Regional Forum, supra* note 189, at 348.

collaboration.[210] The ARF persuades dialogue partners to raise concerns, exchange best practices, and share technical assistance, including natural disasters and transnational crimes.[211] ASEAN has played a central role in the ARF and has well served its own as well as external communities by calling for international collaboration between member countries and non-member countries.

However, there has been contentious debate over the fact that ASEAN has concentrated only on traditional security cooperation. Former internal and external threats in the region have made ASEAN take into consideration a broader understanding of the term "human security" instead of narrow perspective of protecting its populations. In the past, there had been contentious debate amongst scholars regarding the definition of "security" in the region.

Debates over the definition of "human security" encompassed two groups: broader and narrower advocates.[212] The UNDP's 1994 *Human Development Report* and a report called *"Human Security Now"* promulgated by the Commission on Human Security (CHS) proposed a broader definition.[213] According to the UNDP, "human security" involves human life and dignity or military and non-military threats.[214] The CHS report specified three freedoms of "human security":[215] "freedom from fear," "freedom from want," and "freedom

---

210 Id. at 343.

211 Annual Security Outlook-2011, *supra* note 56, at 5–171 (containing the comments of the ARF's participants in this outlook).

212 Okiko Fukushima, *East Versus West? Debate and Convergence on Human Security, in* Human Security in East Asia: Challenges for Collaborative Action 48–49 (Sorpong Peou ed., 2009).

213 Id. at 48 (explaining that "The CHS was established by Japan and chaired jointly by Sadako Ogata (former UN High Commissioner for Refugees and current President of the Japan International Cooperation Agency JICA) and Amatya Sen (former Master of Trinity College Cambridge and current Lamont Professor at Harvard University).").

214 United Nations Development Programme, Human Development Report: New Dimensions of Human Security 22–23 (1994), *available at* http://hdr.undp.org/en/reports/global/hdr1994/chapters/; *see also* Sorpong Peou, *Critical Challenges for Globalism in Human Security Studies, in* Human Security in East Asia: Challenges for Collaborative Action 14–15 (Sorpong Peou ed., 2009); Jörn Dosch, *The Concept and Management of Non-Traditional Security in the Southeast Asia*, 24 Security & Peace, no. 4, 2006, at 179, 180.

215 Fukushima, *supra* note 212, at 48; *see also* U.N. Commission on Human Security (UNCHS), Human Security Now 4 (2003), *available at* http://reliefweb.int/sites/reliefweb.int/files/resources/91BAEEDBA50C6907C1256D19006A9353-chs-security-may03.pdf (explaining

to live in dignity."[216] According to those who construe this concept more narrowly, this definition may also include the concept of "freedom from violence," which is closely related to the concept of "freedom from fear".[217] These advocates criticize the broader definition for being too vague.[218] It is clear though that both the broad and narrow definitions recognize "the protection of individuals," but they define different scopes of insecurity that a person is entitled to be protected.[219]

Over time, advocates of the both the broad and narrow approaches have agreed to acknowledge the same definition of human security.[220] Proponents of the broader definition have included the concept of freedom from fear, while narrower proponents have tried to advocate for the terminology "freedom from want".[221] Some critics have narrowly construed "security" in its traditional sense[222]

the term that "Human security means protecting fundamental freedoms – freedoms that are the essence of life. It means protecting people from critical (severe) and pervasive (widespread) threats and situations. It means using processes that build on people's strengths and aspirations. It means creating political, social environmental, economic, military and cultural systems that together give people the building blocks of survival, livelihood and dignity").

216 Fukushima, *supra* note 212, at 48; *see also* Human Security Centre, Human Security Report 2005: War and Peace in the 21st Century 127–152 (2005); Aninda Rahmasari, Human Security, Emancipation, and the Challenges towards the Establishment of ASEAN Security Community 2015 3 (Paper presented at the 4th International Conference on Human Rights & Human Development, Critical Connections: Human Rights, Human Development and Human Security, Chulalongkorn University, Aug. 18–19, 2011) (proposing the comprehension of human security that "…Freedom from want and freedom from fear should be achieved through a civil-government collaboration, resulted from a balanced state-society relationship…")

217 Fukushima, *supra* note 212, at 48.

218 Id. at 49 (quoting critic Andrew Mack).

219 Id. at 48–49 (quoting Simon Fraser who has studied the differences between the narrow and broad definitions of "human security").

220 Id. at 49.

221 Id. at 49; 2005 World Summit Outcome, G.A. Res. 60/1, U.N. Doc. A/RES/60/1 (Oct. 24, 2005), *available at* http://unpan1.un.org/intradoc/groups/public/documents/un/unpan021752.pdf (mentioning that the UN Outcome Document of the World Summit in September 2005 stipulates their endorsement as follows: "We stress the right of people to live in freedom and dignity, free from poverty and despair. We recognize that all individuals, in particular vulnerable people, are entitled to freedom from fear and freedom from want, with an equal opportunity to enjoy all their rights and fully develop their human potential.")

222 Thearith, *supra* note 74, at 16.

or only as only a military issue[223] so that it is the government that is responsible for the protection of its sovereignty. Others contend that this definition also includes non-military[224] or non-traditional issues such as climate change, infectious diseases, natural disasters, refugees, irregular migration, drugs and human trafficking, and so forth that have been growing in Southeast Asia.[225]

After the economic crisis starting in 1997 and the subsequent 9/11 tragedy, ASEAN has moved from a "state-centric" security approach to a human-centric security approach, which was introduced by the engagement of NGOs.[226] ASEAN now emphasizes citizens' security as trumping the protection of sovereignty; they along with the surrounding Asian countries acknowledge that they have an obligation to protect their citizens from these dangers.[227]

---

223 *See* William T. Tow & Russell Trood, *Linkage between Traditional Security and Human Security, in* Asia's Emerging Regional Order: Reconciling Traditional and Human Security 13 (William T. Tow, Ramesh Thakur, & In-Taek Hyun eds., 2000); *See also* id.

224 Alan Collins, *Non-Traditional Security, in* Routledge Handbook of Asian Regionalism 313–314, 319 (Mark Beeson & Richard Stubbs eds., 2012) (considering non-traditional security as a "threat to security that does not include the use of military force for coercive, or lethal, purposes." The objects of security are protecting country, society, and individuals from threats. "Threats" can be military ("loss of territory"), economic (loss of natural resource), political ("loss of sovereignty"), environmental (meaning what) or societal (such as "climate change or infectious disease" and "migration") sectors. Therefore, according to the Consortium of Non-Traditional Security Studies in Asia non-traditional security includes "climate change, resource scarcity, contagious diseases, natural disasters, irregular migration, famine, people smuggling, drug-trafficking and transnational crime…" However, Alan Collins notes that non-traditional security includes many categories of transnational crimes, except terrorism and piracy because these two criminal activities need military force in order to eradicate these threats. For instance, to ward against piracy, naval vessels guard the Straits of Malacca and the sea of the Somali coastline).

225 *See* Mely Callabero-Anthony & Ralf Emmers, *Understanding the Dynamics of Securitizing Non-Traditional Security, in* Non-Traditional Security in Asia: Dilemma in Securitization 1 (Mely Callabero-Anthony, Ralf Emmers, & Amitav Acharya eds., 2006); *see also* Thearith, *supra* note 74, at 17; Caballero-Anthony, *supra* note 94, at 27 (noting that "This definition of the term non-traditional security is used by the Consortium of Non-Traditional Security Studies in Asia, otherwise known as NTS-Asia. For more details, see the NTS-Asia website, www.rsis-ntsasia.org."); Dosch, *supra* note 214, at 179, 180.

226 Cheeppensook, *supra* note 167, at 5–6, 8–10, 20.

227 *See* Amitav Acharya, *Human Security: East Versus West*, 3 Int'l J. 442, 459 (2001); Dosch, *supra* note 214, at 179, 180; *see also* Fukushima, *supra* note 212, at 54; Phan Duy Hao, *The International and ASEAN Legal Framework Against Non-Traditional Security Issues* 4 (The China-ASEAN Project Occasional Paper Series, 2006), *available at* http://www.rsis-ntsasia.org/resources/publications/research-papers/Phan%20Duy%20Hao.pdf (Phan Duy Hao marks three differences between traditional and non-traditional threats. First, traditional

Even though ASEAN as a whole has acknowledged the concept of security as encompassing more than just military threats, the individual member-countries have given varying attention to the issue.[228] Singapore for example has displayed a more rigid approach because of its particular security needs because of its geographic position between Indonesia and Malaysia, who experience a considerable amount of political tension.[229] Despite its geography, Singapore has been able to strengthen its economic and political relationships with others by entering into numerous bilateral free trade agreements.[230]

---

security issues refer to "military threats" to a country while non-traditional security issues include "economic, environmental and human dimensions of security." For this reason, only "state actors" can manage traditional security threats as "other non-state actors" such as international organizations, non-governmental organizations, and civilians can advocate for "addressing or aggravating" non-traditional security matters. Similarly, even though non-traditional security refers to non-military force, the military still plays a vital role in "humanitarian and disaster relief (HADR) operation." Second, danger from traditional security threats can take place in the domestic territory of a country, but the consequences of non-traditional security damage can originate in both national and transnational territories. Third, the key object of traditional security issues is a country; however, the objects of non-traditional security include all people, namely victims of terrorist attacks, tsunamis, or other disasters); *see also* Collins, *supra* note 224, at 316 (finding that following the earthquake for instance, the United States military provided relief supplies and facilitated air and sea support to provide humanitarian aid during the Haitian relief operation in 2010); Peou, *supra* note 214, at 14–15; Lloyd Axworthy, The New Diplomacy: The UN, The International Criminal Court and the Human Security Agenda, Paper Presented at Conference on UN Reform, Kennedy School, Harvard University (April 25, 1998), *available at* http://www.international.gc.ca/mines/process-ottawa-processus/1998-04-25.aspx?lang=eng&view=d (articulating that "security goals should be primarily formulated and achieved in terms of human, rather than state, needs." All victims from any kinds of threat have the right to be protected by the government); Peou, *supra* note 214, at 15; *see also* S. Neil MacFarlane and Yuen Foong Khong, The UN and Human Security: A Critical History, Ch. 6 (2006) (commenting that the definition of vulnerable civilians should also include men and older people).

228 Dewi Fortuna Anwar, *Human Security: An Intractable Problem in Asia, in* Asian Security Order 536–537 (Multhiah Algappa ed., 2003); Rahmasari, *supra* note 216, at 2; Yukiko Nishikawa, Human Security in Southeast Asia 37–47 (2010) (describing that the ASEAN member countries have approached to human security and have implemented the concept human security in different arenas through their national rule, economic advancement, political solidarity).

229 Dosch, *supra* note 214, at 181–182.

230 Id. at 179, 182 (indicating Singapore's bilateral free trade agreements' partners that include "Australia, the European Free Trade Association, India, Japan, Jordan, New Zealand, South Korea, and the United States."); Ramkishen S. Rajang et al., Singapore and Free Trade Agreements: Economic Relations with Japan and the United States 76 (2001).

Singapore also showed acknowledgement of non-traditional or non-military security threats by contributing to the tsunami relief efforts in Indonesia.[231]

In contrast, Vietnam has been limited in assisting with non-traditional security threats seemingly because of its underdeveloped economic growth since the 1979 invasion of Cambodia.[232] Because of these varying degrees of adoption of nontraditional security approaches, it is imperative that ASEAN reinforces its member countries to allocate sufficient domestic budgets for responses non-traditional threats to ensure that their people can obtain adequate public protection and assistance.

ASEAN has to figure out how to move from a "security regime" to a "security community" approach that ASEAN has planned to approach both in the future.[233] The former demonstrates that member countries cooperate based on mutual behavioral principles that can build up a certain confidence in their partnership.[234] While member countries comply with common standards in a short period of time, they can anticipate long-term benefits.[235] However, this approach can urge the reliance of member countries because they are afraid of a member country's infringement of their rules. In this case, these member countries have to remove such potential concern.[236]

In contrast, member countries approaching the "security community" tend to share identification, including reputation and benefits.[237] Mutual identification of member countries takes place through their long-term relationships through numerous discourses[238] that allow its member countries to exchange their concerns and to generate mutual best actions against threats.[239]

ASEAN can move from a security regime to a security community by engaging government agencies and public involvement.[240] The creation of a Political-Security Community exercised by ASEAN Inter-Governmental Commission on

231 Dosch, *supra* note 214, at 179, 182.

232 *See* id.; *see also* Non-Traditional Security Issues in Southeast Asia 3 (Andrew T.H. Tan & J.D. Kenneth Boutin eds., 2001).

233 Löffelholz & Arao, *supra* note 53, at 46; *see also*, Alan Collins, *Forming a Security Community: Lessons from ASEAN*, 7 Int'l Rel. Asia-Pac. 203–225 (2007).

234 Löffelholz & Arao, *supra* note 53, at 46; *see also*, Collins, *supra* note 233, at 206.

235 Löffelholz & Arao, *supra* note 53, at 46.

236 Id.

237 Id.; *see also*, Collins, *supra* note 233, at 206.

238 Löffelholz & Arao, *supra* note 53, at 46; *see also*, Collins, *supra* note 233, at 208.

239 Id.

240 Löffelholz & Arao, *supra* note 53, at 46 (2010) (mentioning Alan Collins's proposal that a "security community is more than an organi[z]ation structure." According to him, "[i]t is something that has to be believed in, imbibed and nurtured by the people of a country."

Human Rights exemplifies ASEAN's security communities if the citizens in its region pay more attention to "security" by engaging in all processes of regional security through communication with relevant government authorities.[241] In addition, populations should have voices to inform and recognize non-traditional security scourges.[242]

The international community clearly regards human trafficking as an issue of human security.[243] Human security encompasses social and political threats, namely human rights violations, epidemic diseases, environmental pollution or climate change, and other threats to populations' well-being.[244] Further, the International Commission on Intervention and State Sovereignty (ICSS) enumerates that human security means "the security of people" including their physical, social and economic security; their right to be respected and to be protected as human beings published in the report, *the Responsibility to Protect*.[245] Consequently, human trafficking as a human security threat has affected all scales of the community, namely trafficked individuals and their families, society, politics, and economics.[246]

Similar to the international community, ASEAN understands "security" in political, military, economic, and social terms.[247] In addition, ASEAN has defined human security as its responsibility to tackle the insecurity of *all* people.[248] This includes taking into account the fact that human security refers to "people-oriented" values[249] including numerous human security issues such as natural disasters, economic downfalls, epidemic diseases, transnational crime, as well as trafficking in persons.[250]

ASEAN has pledged to provide the social justice and rights of women, children, migrant workers, the elderly and people with disabilities through regional

---

The shift from a security regime to a security community can happen "when the form of interaction among the members expands beyond intergovernmental contacts").

241 Id.

242 Id.

243 *See* Louise Shelley, *Human Security and Human Trafficking*, *in* Human Trafficking and Human Security 10 (Anna Jonsson ed., 2009).

244 *See* id.

245 *See* International Commission on Intervention and State Sovereignty (ICISS), The Responsibility to Protect 15 (2002); *see also* Nishikawa, *supra* note 228, at 20.

246 *See* Shelley, *supra* note 243, at 10–11; *See also* id. at 17.

247 Shaun Narine, *ASEAN and the Management of Regional Security*, 71 Pac. Aff. 195 (1998).

248 *See* Nishikawa, *supra* note 228, at 37; *see also* Amitav Acharya, Promoting Human Security: Ethical, Normative and Educational Frameworks in South-East Asia 21 (2007).

249 *See* Nishikawa, *supra* note 228, at 34.

250 *See* id. at 37; *see also* Acharya, *supra* note 248, at 21.

laws and policies according to the ASEAN socio-cultural community blueprint.[251] They have also created the ASEAN Commission on the Promotion and Protection of the Rights of Women and Children (ACWC) to monitor the implementation of the rights of women and children, including anti-trafficking protection of women and children.[252] Further, the ASEAN Commission on the Rights of Migrant Workers (ACMW) was established to examine the promotion of the migrant workers' rights, including counter-trafficking of migrant workers.[253]

The central role of ASEAN in the ARF has served its own as well as external communities by calling for international collaboration between member countries and non-member countries to tackle both traditional and non-traditional threats. ASEAN's competence in identifying non-traditional insecurity has been illustrated in many occasions, including natural disasters, counterterrorism, and epidemic diseases.[254]

a Natural Disaster Response

After the December 2004 tsunami in the Indian Ocean, ARF vigorously responded to various natural disasters through official guidance to advance cooperation amongst dialogue partners.[255] The guidance addresses "risk identification and monitoring, disaster prevention and preparedness, emergency response and disaster relief, and capacity-building" according to the statement adopted at the 13th and 14th ARF Ministerial Meeting in July 2006.[256] Also, ARF Ministers concurred to advocate collaboration in natural disaster relief assistance, namely "emergency relief, rehabilitation, and reconstruction."[257]

251 *See* Socio-Cultural Community Blueprint, *supra* note 106, at 12.

252 *See* ASEAN Commission on the Promotion and Protection of the Rights of Women and Children (ACWC), Terms of Reference (Feb. 2010), *available at* http://www.asean.org/images/2012/publications/TOR%20of%20ACWC%201.pdf [hereinafter ACWC Terms of Reference].

253 *See* ASEAN Declaration on the Protection and Promotion of the Rights of Migrant Workers, Cebu, Jan. 13, 2007, *available at* http://www.asean.org/communities/asean-political-security-community/item/asean-declaration-on-the-protection-and-promotion-of-the-rights-of-migrant-workers-3 [hereinafter ASEAN Migrant Workers' Declaration].

254 Rees, *supra* note 187, at 402, 412.

255 Yuzawa, *The ASEAN Regional Forum, supra* note 189, at 343.

256 Id. at 343–344.

257 Chairman's Statement of the Twelfth Meeting of the ASEAN Regional Forum (ARF), July 29 2005, http://www.asean.org/communities/asean-political-security-community/item/chairman-s-statement-of-the-twelfth-meeting-of-the-asean-regional-forum-arf-vientiane-29-july-2005-2; Mely Caballero-Anthony, *Nontraditional Security and*

Likewise, these Ministers agreed to create an advanced warning of natural disasters to alleviate severe damage.[258]

In particular, the ARF created "Strategic Guidance for Humanitarian Assistance and Disaster Relief" to aid victims of Cyclone Nargis in 2008.[259] This guidance focuses on the military involvement and practice in natural relief activities that lead to "voluntary demonstration of response" or "field exercise" in central Luzon in 2009.[260] Several ARF partners applied this demonstration of response to rescue victims of typhoon.[261]

The rapid responses of ARF and non-traditional security cooperation have increased. The "Vision Statement" paves a way for effective action in responding to widespread barriers taking place in the region, namely "terrorism and transnational crime," "disaster relief," "maritime security," and "non-proliferation and disarmament."[262] For instance, In March 2011, ASEAN organized the ARF Disaster Relief Exercise (ARF DiREx)[263] that encompasses three main focuses: Table-Top Exercises, Field Training Exercises, and Humanitarian Civic Action.[264] The objective of the exercises was to evaluate the participating countries' abilities and management of natural disaster relief efforts.[265] The evidence showed the ARF DiREx's success in recruiting over four thousand participants from twenty-five countries, including the ASEAN member countries and the United Nations.[266] The Relief provided by ARF can prevent the possibility of these natural disaster victims' migration that causes the risk of

---

Multilateralism in Asia: Reshaping the Contours of Regional Security Architecture, in Asia's New Multilateralism: Cooperation, Competition, and the Search for Community 314 (Michael J. Green & Bates Gill eds., 2009).

258 Id.

259 Yuzawa, *The ASEAN Regional Forum, supra* note 189, at 343–344.

260 Id. at 344.

261 Id.; *see also* Jurgen Haacke, *The ASEAN Regional Forum: From Dialogue to Practical Security Cooperation?*, 22 Cambridge Rev. of Int'l Studies 427, 439–442 (2009); Noel M. Morada, *The ASEAN Regional Forum: Origins and Evolution, in* Cooperation Security in the Asia-Pacific: The ASEAN Regional Forum 24–25 (Jurgen Haacke ed., 2010).

262 Yuzawa, *The ASEAN Regional Forum, supra* note 189, at 344; *see also* ASEAN Regional Forum Vision Statement, July 23, 2009, http://aseanregionalforum.asean.org/files/library/ARF%20Chairman%27s%20Statements%20and%20Reports/The%20Sixteenth%20ASEAN%20Regional%20Forum,%202008-2009/ARF_Vision_Statement.pdf.

263 Annual Security Outlook-2011, *supra* note 56, at 24.

264 Id.

265 Id.

266 Id. at 80.

their vulnerability to human trafficking because of their losses of shelter, job opportunity, and food.

This ARF DiREx presents the ARF participants' mutual concerns, namely the massive earthquake and tsunami, which happened in Japan right after the ARF conducted this exercise. The ARF has become the main center for its partners to spell out their experiences and to suggest the best techniques and training programs among them as Japan determined that the ARF is the best place to organize the regular ARF DiREx.[267]

b Counterterrorism[268]

After the September 11, 2001 terrorist attacks, ASEAN served as a diplomatic actor for the United States by encouraging ARF partners to undertake measures against the financial support for terrorist under the ARF Statement on Measures against Terrorist Financing agreed by ARF participants in 2002.[269] The measures against terrorist financing include freezing the assets of terrorists and their accomplices and providing technical assistance to other countries in strengthening laws and policies to battle financial contribution for terrorism and money laundering.[270] ARF participants also agreed to implement the international collaboration on exchanging data related to terrorist financing.[271]

The ARF Statement on Measures against Terrorist Financing reflected the influence that ASEAN had on the determination of itself and external communities. ASEAN enhanced the ARF Workshop on Financial Measures against Terrorism.[272] The result of this workshop suggested that ARF's participants take actions against the financing of terrorism.[273]

In addition, ASEAN has promoted collaboration among ARF partners on border security under the ARF Statement on Cooperative Counter-Terrorist

---

267 Id.

268 *See* ASEAN, ASEAN Documents on Combating Transnational Crime and Terrorism: A Compilation of ASEAN Declarations, Joint Declarations, and Statements on Combating Transnational Crime and Terrorism (2012), *available at* http://www.asean.org/resources/publications/asean-publications/item/asean-documents-on-combating-transnational-crime-and-terrorism?category_id=382.

269 *See* ASEAN, The Ninth ASEAN Regional Forum 234 (Bandar Seri Begawan, Brunei Darussalam, July 31, 2002), *available at* http://aseanregionalforum.asean.org/files/ARF-Publication/ARF-Document-Series-1994-2006/09_Brunei2006.pdf [hereinafter Ninth ASEAN Regional Forum].

270 *See* id. at 234–235.

271 *See* id. at 235.

272 *See* id. at 234.

273 *See* id. at 234.

Action on Border Security adopted in 2003.[274] The cooperation on border security can prevent terrorism and other transnational crimes, namely illicit trafficking in arms, drugs humans and other goods smuggling.[275] This Statement aims to discourage the demands of all types of transnational crimes by focusing on the mutual border security.

c Epidemic Diseases

In spite of its public relations and advocacy attributes, ASEAN regional collaboration and commitment can catalyze the national response to regional problems. ASEAN has helped its partners realize that their national problems are similar to others by grouping government and community representatives to share experiences on how to handle severe issues. For instance, two global pandemic diseases, Severe Acute Respiratory Syndrome (SARS) and H1N1 or Avian Influenza (Bird Flu), have impacted people around the world including in ASEAN member countries, Australia, Europe, North and South America since 2003.

The ARF served its participants by organizing a workshop to acknowledge the role of military and civil cooperation in the prevention and control of communicable diseases, namely Severe Acute Respiratory Syndrome (SARS) and Avian Influenza.[276] The representatives of the ARF, United Nations Office for the Coordination of Humanitarian Affairs Regional Office for Asia and Pacific (UN OCHA ROAP) attended this workshop.[277]

The ARF agenda was comprised of diverse presentations with effective strategic actions to respond widespread diseases such as developing the public awareness-raising system and advancing capacity to prevent and responses to these epidemic diseases, namely collecting vaccine supplies.[278] The ARF

274 *See* ASEAN, The Tenth ASEAN Regional Forum 273–276 (Phnom Penh, Cambodia, June 18, 2003), *available at* http://aseanregionalforum.asean.org/files/ARF-Publication/ARF-Document-Series-1994-2006/10_Cambodia2006.pdf [hereinafter Tenth ASEAN Regional Forum].

275 *See* id. at 275.

276 *See* ASEAN, ASEAN Regional Forum: Documents Series 2006–2009, 105–110 (2010), *available at* http://www.google.com/url?sa=t&rct=j&q=&esrc=s&source=web&cd=1&ved=0CDAQFjAA&url=http%3A%2F%2Fwww.asean.org%2Fresources%2Farchives%3Ftask%3Dcallelement%26format%3Draw%26item_id%3D5239%26element%3Da0c6d315-bb76-42c6-9ecf-c287d406937b%26method%3Ddownload&ei=NWe_UNScDaqQ0QHR24CgBQ&usg=AFQjCNELpftOR9t-G7LplLBG1zMGPfy6yw&sig2=TBgL-hHksuO-ux70b-OT_Q [hereinafter Documents Series 2006–2009].

277 *See* id. at 105.

278 *See* id. at 106–107.

workshop also provided lessons and responses to the outbreak of Avian Influenza and SARS from Thailand and China.[279] The attendees could learn lessons from these countries on the effective methods of preventing these infectious diseases, such as strategies of Emergency Infectious Disease Prevention and Control presented by China.[280] Finally, the workshop emphasized the vital role of civil-military collaboration in preventing and controlling these diseases, particularly strengthening the ability of quick evacuation.[281]

In addition, ASEAN created the Highly Pathogenic Avian Influenza (HPAI) task force in December 2004 and adopted the action plan to prevent and control bird flu in 2010.[282] While only five member countries present seem to be the most competent, the others need to advance their rapid responses.[283] ASEAN should also ease the application of non-interference and consensus decision making in light of the report on widespread contagious diseases in its member countries to in order prevent the growing number of infection.[284] It is, however, indisputable that ASEAN deserves to take credit for sharing data and creating the plans of action leading to "credible and effective policies."[285]

2.6 ASEAN's Mobilization on Human Trafficking

Apart from other non-traditional crime, ASEAN has raised its concerns about counter-human trafficking efforts. ASEAN has driven member countries and the international community to recognize the problem of human trafficking. Although there is great potential to end human trafficking in the ASEAN region, such crime has been handled through its regional anti-human trafficking strategies and various multilateral agreements.

It is clear from research that ASEAN has persuaded both its member countries and dialogue stakeholders to acknowledge and tackle human trafficking. For instance, the investigative cooperation among ASEAN member countries has exhibited ASEAN's influence in the battle against human trafficking.

279 *See* id. at 107.

280 *See* id. at 107–108.

281 *See* id. at 108.

282 Collins, *supra* note 224, at 322.

283 Id.

284 Id. at 322–323.

285 Id. at 322; *see also* Mely Caballero-Anthony, *Non-Traditional Security and Infectious Diseases in ASEAN: Going Beyond the Rhetoric of Securitization to Deeper Institutionalization*, 2 Pac. Rev. 507, 517 (2008).

The UN Special Rapporteur Joy Ngozi Ezeilo commends that ASEAN created the Heads of Specialist Trafficking Units (HSU)[286] Process, which can help its member countries advance investigative competence and collaboration between the police departments of each country.[287] This process has mobilized the authority of ASEAN member countries specialist trafficking units to cooperate in the exchange of information and operation in an investigation.[288] This collaboration has strengthened these countries' identification, salvation and repatriation of trafficking victim, as well as the capture of suspects.[289]

Considering the collaboration between ASEAN and other dialogue partners on the battle human trafficking, ASEAN documents have displayed its anti-human trafficking initiatives with the involvement of other non-ASEAN member countries through various forums, including other dialogue partners (USA, Australia, and India) and ASEAN Plus Three.[290] The recent agreement of ASEAN Plus Three (China, Japan, and South Korea) refers to *Joint Statement of the Fifth ASAN Plus Three Ministerial Meeting on Transnational Crime*.[291] This statement highlights the collaboration between ASEAN and its three other dialogue partners regarding the investigation of cybercrimes, which also have the potential to promote transnational crimes such as human trafficking.[292]

Likewise, the ASEAN-U.S. Joint Cooperation Committee (JCC) Meeting on June 20, 2012 affirmed their mutual collaboration and action plans on various concerns, including counter-human trafficking and other non-traditional

286 Fiona David et al., Progress Report on Criminal Justice Responses to Trafficking in Persons in ASEAN Region 135 (2011), *available at* http://www.artipproject.org/progress-report/Progress%20Report_Criminal%20Justice%20Responses%20to%20TIP%20in%20the%20ASEAN%20Region_2011.pdf.

287 Special Rapporteur on Trafficking in Persons, Especially Women and Children, *Report on Agenda Item 3: Promotion and Protection of all Human Rights, Civil, Political, Economic, Social and Cultural Rights, including the Right to Development*, U.N. Human Rights Council, U.N. Doc. A/HRC/14/32 (May 4, 2010) (by Joy Ngozi Ezeilo), *available at* http://daccess-dds-ny.un.org/doc/UNDOC/GEN/G10/132/11/PDF/G1013211.pdf?OpenElement [hereinafter U.N. Doc. A/HRC/14/32].

288 David et al., *supra* note 286, at 135–136.

289 Id. at 135.

290 The 5th SOMTC, 3rd SOMTC + 3 (CHINA, JAPAN, ROK), 3rd SOMTC + CHINA, 2nd SOMTC + JAPAN, 2nd SMTC + USA, 2nd SOMTC + AUSTRALIA and 1st SOMTC + INDIA, Siem Reap, Cambodia, June *13–17, 2005*, NCB-Interpol Indonesia (July 19, 2010, 12:09 PM) [hereinafter SOMTC Reports].

291 *See* ASEAN + 3 5th Joint Statement, *supra* note 77.

292 Id.

threats like disaster management.[293] Both parties are ambitious to intensify their plans of action and "raise the profile of ASEAN in the U.S." in order to achieve this aspiration, it is necessary for ASEAN to make solid commitments and efforts.[294]

Another instance of a multilateral agreement regarding the approach to anti-human trafficking includes Co-chairs' Statement of the Bali Regional Ministerial Conference on People Smuggling, Trafficking in Persons and Related Transnational Crime.[295] This forum shows that ASEAN has tried to intensify collaboration to prevent human trafficking, protect all groups of trafficking victims, and prosecute perpetrators by strengthening law enforcement mechanisms, domestic policies and measures, and multilateral cooperation in mutual criminal investigation.[296] Indonesia and Australia, this forum's

---

293 ASEAN News Desk, *Highlights of the 4th ASEAN-U.Sn jcc*, Zambotimes, June 22, 2012, http://www.zambotimes.com/archives/48745-Highlights-of-the-4th-ASEAN-U.S.-JCC.html; U.S. Dep't of State Office to Monitor and Combat Trafficking in Persons, Addressing Modern Slavery in the ASEAN Region (Nov. 20, 2012), *available at* http://www.state.gov/documents/organization/201097.pdf (certifying the United States' commitment to collaborate with ASEAN against human trafficking by strengthening counter-human trafficking norms, especially protection of trafficking victims and prosecution of trafficking perpetrators).

294 Id.

295 Co-Chairs Statement, Delivered at the Bali Ministerial Conference on People Smuggling, Trafficking in Persons and Related Transnational Crime (the Bali Process) (Feb. 26–28, 2002), *available at* http://www.baliprocess.net/files/ConferenceDocumentation/BRMC1.pdf ("The Bali Process encourages and facilitates regional cooperation in addressing the transnational crimes of people smuggling and trafficking in persons, including through effective information and intelligence sharing; law enforcement cooperation; cooperation on border and visa systems to detect and prevent irregular movements; increased public awareness to discourage these activities and warn those susceptible; enactment of national legislation to criminalize people smuggling and trafficking in persons; provision of appropriate protection and assistance to the victims of trafficking, particularly women and children; addressing the root causes of irregular migration; and assisting countries to adopt best practices in asylum management, in accordance with the principles of the Refugee Convention"). Co-chairs' Statement of the Fourth Bali Regional Ministerial Conference on People Smuggling, Trafficking in Persons and Related Transnational Crime, Bali, Indonesia, Mar. 29–30, 2011, http://www.asean.org/communities/asean-political-security-community/item/co-chairs-statement-of-the-fourth-bali-regional-ministerial-conference-on-people-smuggling-trafficking-in-persons-and-related-transnational-crime-bali-indonesia-29-30-march-2011 [hereinafter Co-chairs' Statement of the Fourth Bali Regional Ministerial Conference].

296 *See, e.g.*, Co-chairs' Statement of the Fourth Bali Regional Ministerial Conference, *supra* note 295.

foreign ministers have presented their ambition to uphold the management of undocumented migration through essential policies that uphold accurate data collection of irregular migration to constitute a rationale for their assistances and services.[297]

ASEAN has made progress in recognizing egregious human trafficking problems as community threat by participating with various discussions to better understanding the nature of human trafficking root cause and to uphold appropriate anti-human trafficking laws and policies. However, there is more opportunity for ASEAN to undertake measures from all dialogues into serious action because of the nascent acknowledgement of its member countries on human trafficking in its region needed a rapid management.

Conclusion

This review of the historical background and innovation of ASEAN shows that despite the fact that ASEAN is made up of small, seemingly powerless countries they have proven themselves nothing, but durable, reliable, and neutral for their internal and external communities. Whether internal and external conflicts have taken place, ASEAN has strived to preserve peace and stability in its region through its regional cooperation. However, ASEAN acknowledges that the external contribution and collaboration have assisted ASEAN accelerate the community building through numerous dialogues.

ASEAN community integration reflects the solid methods and strategies necessary to maintain peace, harmony, and prosperity in ASEAN region through its member countries' cooperation. Nonetheless, the evidence shows that there is much space for ASEAN to integrate all three economic, political, and socio-cultural communities that promote and protect human rights.

ASEAN has empowered itself through coherent cooperation among its member countries and strong commitments in peace and solidarity even though the intra-inter political tensions have raised concerns its confidence-building. However, ASEAN has overcome those pressures by highlighting peaceful dispute settlement instead of the use of force. As stipulated in all ASEAN's legal frameworks, ASEAN member countries have reaffirmed the maintenance of peace and stability in all of these agreements.

Despite ASEAN's ineffective conflict management, ASEAN has made efforts to neutralize all concerned parties to meet their mutual interests through a multilateral forum like ARF. The ARF's dialogue partners have praised ASEAN's

297 *See*, e.g., Id. (laying out the future activities on topic number 25).

central role. However, without the contribution of non-ASEAN member countries, ASEAN may take longer to develop its community. There is no doubt that ASEAN has valued the non-ASEAN member countries' dialogues as they have also played a vital role as providing practical actions, training programs, and other assistances.

The research acknowledges the challenges and prospects of ASEAN. For instance, ASEAN Way (principles of non-interference, consensus decision-making and consultation) has stamped ASEAN's dispute avoidance to reduce tensions among its member countries and non-ASEAN member countries. These principles may be functional for some cases, but ASEAN should take into account the flexible application of these principles in the case of transnational crimes, particularly anti-human trafficking, to accelerate the strengthening of the criminal justice responses of all ASEAN member countries.

As a result, ASEAN's central role of a multilateral dialogue forum, especially the ARF with the external community, has illustrated a certain level of its accomplishment in external relations. ASEAN's leading role of strengthening coherent cooperation among its member countries has demonstrated that ASEAN's influence can drive its community to handle different dilemmas, both traditional and non-traditional crimes, including human trafficking. The next question to be addressed in Chapter Three is what kind of challenges ASEAN has faced to tackle human trafficking in order to confirm this research's argument that ASEAN needs to establish a common standard against human trafficking such as ASEAN Declaration on the Promotion and Protection of the Rights of Trafficking Victims and form a monitoring human rights like ASEAN Commission on the Promotion and Protection of the Rights of Trafficking Victims in order to ensure that all human trafficking victims in its region will have the rights to receive assistance and protection from their governments.

CHAPTER 3

ASEAN's Struggle to Combat Human Trafficking

Human trafficking has tremendously affected the ASEAN region and has been on the ASEAN transnational crime agenda since the 1990s.[1] In an effort to tackle this scourge, ASEAN has created counter-human trafficking strategies, addressed it in various agreements as a transnational crime,[2] designed structures to counter-human trafficking,[3] and assigned two human rights bodies: ASEAN Inter-Governmental Commission on Human Rights (AICHR) and ASEAN Commission on the Promotion and Protection of the Rights of Women and Children (ACWC) to deal with this phenomena.[4]

Although ASEAN has established various legal instruments and guidelines, they contain ineffective mechanisms to deal with human trafficking. These instruments are unequal in their approaches at gender sensitivity, contain ambiguous and insufficient anti-human trafficking content, lack trafficking victims protection, and exhibit no common anti-human trafficking norms. In addition, even though ASEAN has created a three-pillar community to promote and protect the rights of people (including protection from human trafficking), it is ill-suited to this purpose because it separates the issue from labor migration, which is closely intertwined with the issue of human trafficking. Lastly, although ASEAN created AICHR and ACWC to protect the rights of all

---

1 *See* Annuska Derks, Combating Trafficking in South-East Asia: Review of Policy and Programme Response 16 and 20 (2000).

2 *See* Ahmad Shah Pakeer et al., *The Phenomenon of Human Trafficking Activities in Southeast Asia,* 1 Int'l J. Human. & Soc. Sci. 13, 168, 172 (2011).

3 ASEAN, Roadmap for an ASEAN Community 2009–2015 [hereinafter ASEAN Roadmap] (2009), *available at* http://www.asean.org/images/2012/publications/Roadmap ASEANCommunity.pdf; Yuyun Wahyuningrum, *Understanding ASEAN: Its Systems and Structure* (Dec. 2009), *available at* http://www.scribd.com/doc/81600447/ASEAN-Structures-Mechanisms-Yuyun-10-03-04-Copy.

4 *See* ASEAN Intergovernmental Commission on Human Rights (AICHR), Terms of Reference § § 4, 4.8 (Oct. 2009), *available at* http://www.asean.org/images/2012/publications/Terms%20of%20Reference%20of%20ASEAN%20Intergovernmental%20Commission%20on%20Human%20Rights.pdf [hereinafter AICHR Terms of Reference]; ASEAN Commission on the Promotion and Protection of the Rights of Women and Children (ACWC), Terms of Reference (Feb. 2010), *available at* http://www.asean.org/images/2012/publications/TOR%20of%20ACWC%201.pdf [hereinafter ACWC Terms of Reference].

 | DOI 10.1163/9789004265189_004

and prevent exploitation, ASEAN has failed to authorize them with the fundamental functions needed to do so, in particular a monitoring system.

Chapter 5 will further discuss the recommendation that ASEAN draft the ASEAN Declaration on the Promotion and Protection of the Rights of Trafficking Victims (ADTV), a new regional anti-human trafficking law which will stipulate sufficient measures of prevention, protection, and prosecution. These measures will be effectuated through the ASEAN Commission on the Promotion and Protection of Trafficking Victims (ACTV) a monitoring human rights body which will specialize in preventing human trafficking, protecting all groups of trafficking victims, and prosecuting perpetrators of human trafficking. This chapter, Chapter 3, is divided into three sections, which will cover the inadequacy of the current counter-human trafficking law, its dysfunctional counter-human trafficking structure, and insufficient powers for existing human rights bodies dealing with human trafficking in an effort to show the need for the creation of the ADTV and ACTV.

3.1 Inadequacy of Counter-Human Trafficking Law of ASEAN

Most significantly, ASEAN lacks common norms to address the crisis of human trafficking in its region. Despite this lack of cohesiveness, ASEAN has made an effort to curb human trafficking by creating various agreements. These agreements and legal instruments have numerous shortcomings that confirm the need to draft an instrument such as the ADTV. These laws have been criticized based on their lack of force through the use of "hard" law. It will be posited that ASEAN's traditional use of "soft" law mechanisms may very well be effective in tackling the problem of human trafficking in the region if coupled with a monitoring body that can help ASEAN strengthen its human trafficking laws and their implementation. A discussion of the advantages and disadvantages of using hard and soft law is necessary to better understand ASEAN's preferences in creating their laws and guidelines.

3.1.1 *Lack of Common Counter-Human Trafficking Norms*

Since not all of the ASEAN member countries have ratified the U.N. Palermo Protocol, the region lacks common standards for addressing human trafficking.[5] The majority of the member countries, except Brunei, Singapore, and

5 FIONA DAVID ET AL., PROGRESS REPORT ON CRIMINAL JUSTICE RESPONSES TO TRAFFICKING IN PERSONS IN ASEAN REGION 10 (2011), *available at* http://www.artipproject.org/progress-report/Progress%20Report_Criminal%20Justice%20Responses%

Thailand, have ratified the U.N. Palermo Protocol.[6] The three that have refrained from ratifying the U.N. Palermo Protocol are not bound by its definition of "trafficking in persons." In fact, Singapore has no anti-human trafficking law[7] and has not enacted any of the related domestic laws proscribed by this Protocol.[8]

Even though there is very little commonality in their counter-human trafficking standards,[9] ASEAN has addressed human trafficking as a transnational crime in various agreements.[10] While several scholars assert that hard-law instruments are the only possible outcome of a lawful process, ASEAN has created various soft laws against human trafficking[11] because they believe that soft law can provide concise details to explain hard law agreements. According to positivist theorists, hard law consists of three elements that should be considered by lawmakers during drafting process: the apparent obligation of parties and legal definitions, its legally-binding characteristics, and an enforcement mechanism.[12] Only hard law mechanisms symbolize

20to%20TIP%20in%20the%20ASEAN%20Region_2011.pdf; United Nations Convention against Transnational Organized Crime and the Protocol Thereto, Nov. 15, 2000, 2225 U.N.T.S. 209, G.A. Res. 55/25, Annex I, U.N. Doc. A/RES/55/25, Ch. 18: Penal Matters, *available at* http://www.unodc.org/documents/treaties/UNTOC/Publications/TOC%20Convention/TOCebook-e.pdf [hereinafter UNTOC]; Protocol to Prevent, Suppress and Punish Trafficking in Persons, especially Women and Children, supplementing the United Nations Convention against Transnational Organized Crime, Nov. 15, 2000, 2237 U.N.T.S. 319, Annex II (entered into force Dec. 25, 2003), *available at* http://www.unodc.org/documents/treaties/UNTOC/Publications/TOC%20Convention/TOCebook-e.pdf [hereinafter the U.N. Palermo Protocol].

6 David et al., *supra* note 5, at 10; UNTOC, *supra* note 5, at Chapter 18: Penal Matters; U.N. Palermo Protocol, *supra* note 5.

7 David et al., *supra* note 5, at 12.

8 Id.

9 Id. at 10; UNTOC, *supra* note 5, at Chapter 18: Penal Matters; U.N. Palermo Protocol, *supra* note 5.

10 *See* Mohamad et al., *supra* note 2, at 168, 172.

11 Sunsanee Sutthisunsanee, Response of ASEAN to Human Rights Violations in Southeast Asia: Case Studies of Cambodia and East Timor 25 (2006) (unpublished thesis, Mahidol University) (on file with Mahidol University).

12 Jeffrey L. Dunoff, Steven R. Ratner & David Wippman, International Law: Norms, Actors, Process: A Problem-Oriented Approach 94 (3d ed. 2010); Alison Duxbury, *ASEAN Features: Moving Towards or Turning Away from Institutions? The Future of International Organizations in Asia and the Pacific*, 11 SYBIL 177, 179 (2007), *available at* http://law.nus.edu.sg/sybil/downloads/articles/SYBIL-2007/SYBIL-2007-177.pdf (presenting the "the concept of legalization" and strong characteristics that

the form, subject matter, details of the law, and actors' will[13] that soft law fails to provide.

In turn, soft law is considered seemingly ambiguous. Scholar Anthony D'Amato has condemned the nature of soft-law as "a head without a body" because of its lack of detailed directives.[14] Even if the parties create a legally-binding tool, it could contain content of a soft nature. The 1995 Council of Europe Framework Convention on the Protection of National Minorities is an example of "*soft negotium*" meaning that the parties aimed not to stipulate a serious commitment based on Jean d'Aspremont,[15] which allows them to proclaim their non-legally binding intent.[16] This treaty allows its parties to impose the description of "minorities" under their domestic laws.[17] It confirms positivists' opinion that a legal act does not require the parties to specify their

---

should be taken into account during the law-making process. This concept of legalization is comprised of "precision" (clear definition), "obligation" (legally-binding instrument), and "delegation" (the third party's responsibility of application, implementation, and interpretation of the law)).

13 DUNOFF, RATNER & WIPPMAN, *supra* note 12, at 94.

14 Anthony D'Amato, *Softness in International Law: A Self-Serving Quest for New Legal Materials: A Reply to Jean d'Aspremont* (Faculty Working Paper 89, 2010), *available at* http://scholarlycommons.law.northwestern.edu/facultyworkingpapers/89/.

15 Jean d'Aspremont, *Softness in International Law: A Self-Serving Quest for New Legal Materials*, 19 EUR. J. OF INT'L L. 1075, 1078–1080, 1082–1087 (2008), *available at* http://www.ejil.org/pdfs/19/5/1700.pdf (intimating that the parties may establish a legally or non-legally binding instrument with soft substance. Jean d'Aspremont comments that if the parties express their intent to create a law, this intent can indicate softness through a "legal act" presenting the outcome of the parties' direct intent. Soft law includes "*soft instrumentum*" and "*soft negotium*." *Soft instrumentum* represents that the parties of agreement aim to create non-legally binding instrument or no intention to be officially bound by the agreement. While only the legal acts from *soft instrumentum* constitute legal effects that clarify substances of the agreement. Jan Klabber argues that legal acts from *soft instrumentum* can undermine the legalization of a law. Based on the positivist scholars' binary theory, a soft law instrument implies "a redundant concept" that contradicts with the binary concept of either "[hard] law or no law." Therefore, those positivists reject the presence of *soft instrumentum*.); Hartmut Hillgenberg, *A Fresh Look at Soft Law*, 10 EUR. J. INT'L L. 499, 505–506 (1999), *available at* http://ejil.oxfordjournals.org/content/10/3/499.full.pdf (noting that Hartmut Hillgenberg applies the parties' intention to demonstrate their commitment. "Subjectivity" illustrates that the parties create a law with the intent of their commitment according to the agreement. In contrast, "objectivity" suggests that the agreement derives from customary law or common practice, not from the parties' will of commitment).

16 d'Aspremont, *supra* note 15, at 1075, 1084.

17 Id. at 1075, 1085.

precise commitment.[18] Also, if the law solely provides persuasive content, then it amounts to a soft law instrument.[19] For instance, even though Article 1 of the Treaty of Amity, Economic Relations and Consular Rights 1955 between Iran and the United States concentrates on peace and friendship to strengthen "the commercial, financial and consular relations,"[20] but the parties of this treaty do not stipulate their responsibility.[21]

It is also possible that a non-legally binding outcome of a meeting can turn into a legally-binding commitment.[22] For instance, the Pacific Islands Forum resorted to a non-legally-binding instrument to address transnational crime because of its parties' non-compliance with the agreement.[23] Non-compliance has the potential to destabilize the accountability and effectiveness of a parties' governance.[24] For instance, it is possible that governments could decrease the impact of pivotal substances by creating ambiguous provisions.[25] Governments also could restrict the power of the enforcement powers responsible for application, implementation, and interpretation of the law in order to exert their judgment or determination.[26] This sort of constraint gives governments a chance to comply with the law under their own norms.[27]

Despite their level of force, laws must be legally binding.[28] Soft law takes into account moral and political matters, which cannot be undertaken in hard law agreements.[29] On the other hand, political agreements can be developed into binding legal agreements by the use of hard law, which has the potential

---

18 Id. at 1075, 1078–1080, 1084–1085.

19 Id. at 1075, 1086.

20 Id.

21 Id.

22 DUNOFF, RATNER & WIPPMAN, *supra* note 122, at 99.

23 Neil Boister, *New Directions for Regional Cooperation in the Suppression of Transnational Crime in the Southeast Pacific*, 9 J. S. PAC. L. 2 (2005), *available at* http://www3.paclii.org/journals/fJSPL/vol09no2/1.shtml.

24 Id.

25 Kenneth W. Abbott & Duncan Snidal, *Pathways to International Cooperation*, *in* THE IMPACT OF INTERNATIONAL LAW ON INTERNATIONAL COOPERATION: THEORETICAL PERSPECTIVES 54 (Eyal Benvenisti & Moshe Hirsch eds., 2004).

26 Id.

27 Id. (explaining that dimension of legalization refers to "a summary dimension where increases reflect overall movement towards a hard legal arrangement (i.e., an increase in obligation, precision, delegation, or some combination thereof), without differntiating the specific forms of softer legalization.")

28 DUNOFF, RATNER & WIPPMAN, *supra* note 12, at 95.

29 Matthias Goldmann, *We Need to Cut Off the Head of the King: Past, Present, and Future Approaches to International Soft Law*, 25 LEIDEN J. INT'L L. 335, 335–368 (2012).

to strengthen regimes by stipulating the enforcement necessary to implement the resulting legally-binding instrument.[30] Even though soft law can facilitate parties reaching flexible agreements, it fails to help parties generate a common standard of law.[31] Therefore, it stands that if parties were to consider transnational crime as a global threat, the parties should reinforce the application of a legally-binding instrument rather than an unofficial soft law instrument in order to suppress such crime.[32]

However, research shows that non-legally binding soft laws have the potential to provide a specific description. For instance, despite their informality, the World Guidelines on the Treatment of Foreign Direct Investment specifically delineate states' obligations, which may include compensation.[33] These guidelines define the persuasive term "appropriate" with "prompt, adequate, and effective" compensation.[34] Both developed and developing countries sustain this concept in bilateral and multilateral treaties, including Guidelines on the Treatment of Foreign Direct Investment that address "compensation for a specific investment taken by the State, which will be deemed 'appropriate' if it is adequate, effective and prompt."[35]

In addition, the non-enforceable nature of soft law persuades the parties to move towards serious obligations through no- or low-risk of loss according to the "loss avoidance theory."[36]

Many scholars believe that a soft law instrument is a persuasive tool to encourage parties to comply with agreements.[37] Parties adopt soft law

---

30 Id.

31 Tan Hsien-Li, *The ASEAN Human Rights Body: Incorporating Forgotten Promises for Policy Coherence and Efficacy*, 12 SINGAPORE Y.B. INT'L L. & CONTRIBUTORS 239, 252 (2008), *available at* http://law.nus.edu.sg/sybil/downloads/articles/SYBIL-2008/SYBIL-2008-239.pdf.

32 Boister, *supra* note 23.

33 DUNOFF, RATNER & WIPPMAN, *supra* note 12, at 99.

34 Id. at 100.

35 Id. at 100, 102 (providing the examples that "..0.3. Compensation will be deemed 'adequate' if it is based on the fair market value of the taken asset as such value is determined immediately before the time at which the taking occurred or the decision to take the asset became publicly known...7. Compensation will be deemed 'effective' if it is paid in the currency brought in by the investor where it remains convertible, in another currency designate as freely usable by the International Monetary Fund, or in any other currency accepted by the investor.").

36 Andrew T. Guzman & Timothy L. Meyer, *International Soft Law*, 2 J. LEGAL ANALYSIS 171 (2010), *available at* http://works.bepress.com/cgi/viewcontent.cgi?article=1040&context=andrew_guzman.

37 D'Amato, *supra* note 14, at 897; DUNOFF, RATNER & WIPPMAN, *supra* note 12, at 93; David Patterson et al., *Use of Soft Law to Address HIV/AIDS in Southeast Asia*, 12

instruments to regulate their practice regarding various issues such as economic and environment cooperation,[38] transnational crime,[39] and health concerns.[40]

An example is the Helsinki Final Act of 1975, which pertains to the security, economic collaboration, and human rights.[41] Even though the rules of these matters demonstrate a non-legally binding agreement, the parties express their intent to entirely undertake and implement this law.[42] It is notable that active parties can motivate non-compliant parties to undertake measures set forth under their agreements.[43] Even though parties to soft law instruments concentrate on shared concern and benefit,[44] in the case of ASEAN, it is clear that those member countries have neglected to comply with these non-legally binding agreements.

ASEAN asserts that hard law instruments are overly inflexible and are not malleable enough to deal with changing circumstances,[45] so soft law can provide an atmosphere to achieve the mutual benefits of ASEAN member countries.[46] ASEAN Member States prefer the use of peer pressure rather than the promulgation of legally-binding instruments.[47] As a result, ASEAN has used soft law mechanisms more frequently than hard law mechanisms in the setting of the regional normative content against human trafficking.[48] Soft law

---

HIV/AIDS POLICY & L. REV., no. 2/3, 2007, at 18, *available at* http://www.aidslaw.ca/publications/interfaces/downloadFile.php?ref=1277 (acknowledging the successful application of a non-legally-binding law which deals with HIV/AIDs contagion of migrant workers. The Cambodian government has adapted common direction and practical control of HIV between countries to its internal policy. A regional non-binding legal instrument constitutes a rapid process for parties to undertake relevant regional measures into domestic law compared to a hard law instrument).

38 Hillgenberg, *supra* note 15, at 499, 503.

39 Boister, *supra* note 23.

40 Patterson et al., *supra* note 37, at 18–19.

41 DUNOFF, RATNER & WIPPMAN, *supra* note 12, at 93 (describing that the Helsinki Fnal Act of 1975 was the outcome of the Conference on Security and Cooperation in Europe, a permanent international organization (OSCE)).

42 Id.

43 Id.

44 *See* Hillgenberg, *supra* note 15, at 499, 506–507.

45 *See* DUNOFF, RATNER & WIPPMAN, *supra* note 12, at 93.

46 *See* Daniel B. Braaten, *Human Rights and Soft Law: Alternative Paths for New Challenges*, *in* NEGOTIATING SOVEREIGNTY AND HUMAN RIGHTS: ACTORS AND ISSUES IN CONTEMPORARY HUMAN RIGHTS POLITICS 105 (Noha Shawki & Michaelene Cox eds., 2009).

47 Sutthisunsanee, *supra* note 11, at 25.

48 *See* Eugene K.B. Tan, *ASEAN Charter as "Legs To Go Places": Ideational Norms and Pragmatic Legalism in Community Building in Southeast Asia*, 12 SINGAPORE

contains international legal standards that are essentially guidelines for countries to include in their own domestic anti-human trafficking laws.

Therefore, some domestic anti-human trafficking legal frameworks basically stipulate provisions of protection and assistance for trafficking victims according to these Principles and Guidelines. Examples include the 2002 United Nations Recommended Principles and Guidelines on Human Rights and Human Trafficking, and the 2010 United Nations Recommended Principles and Guidelines on Human Rights and Human Trafficking, the Guidelines on the Protection of the Rights of Child Victims of Trafficking of the United Nations Children's Fund (UNICEF), and the Guidelines of the United Nations High Commissioner for Refugees.[49]

In particularly, ASEAN has used soft law to tackle the crime of human trafficking. Some of these approaches include the 2004 ASEAN Declaration against Trafficking in Persons, Particularly Women and Children and the Memorandum of Understanding on Cooperation against Trafficking in Persons in the Greater Mekong Sub-Region adopted in 2004 by the six member countries of the region. ASEAN also created the 2007 ASEAN Practitioner Guidelines on Effective Criminal Justice Responses to Trafficking in Persons and the 2007 Global Initiative to Fight Trafficking (GIFT) Recommendations on an Effective Criminal Justice Response to Trafficking in Persons. Cambodia and Thailand signed the Memorandum of Understanding on Bilateral Cooperation for Eliminating Trafficking in Children and Women and Assisting Victims of Trafficking.[50]

Y.B. INT'L L. & CONTRIBUTORS 171, 187 (2008), *available at* http://law.nus.edu.sg/sybil/downloads/articles/SYBIL-2008/SYBIL-2008-171.pdf; *see also* ASSOCIATION OF SOUTHEAST ASIAN NATIONS, ASEAN HANDBOOK ON INTERNATIONAL LEGAL COOPERATION IN TRAFFICKING IN PERSONS CASES 16 (2010), *available at* http://www.aseansec.org/publications/ASEAN%20Handbook%20on%20International%20Legal%20Cooperation%20in%20TIP%20Cases.pdf [hereinafter ASEAN HANDBOOK ON INTERNATIONAL LEGAL COOPERATION].

49 United Nations Office of the High Commissioner for Human Rights, *Recommended Principles and Guidelines on Human Rights and Human Trafficking: Commentary*, U.N. Doc. HR/PUB/10/2, U.N. Sales No. E.10.XIV.1, 24–26 (2010), *available at* http://www.ohchr.org/Documents/Publications/Commentary_Human_Trafficking_en.pdf. [hereinafter OHCHR COMMENTARY] (comparing to other international legal instruments, various vital international legal instruments in the area of human trafficking include non-legally binding or non-enforceable tools as soft law); TAN HSIEN-LI, THE ASEAN INTERGOVERNMENTAL COMMISSION ON HUMAN RIGHTS: INSTITUTIONALISING HUMAN RIGHTS IN SOUTHEAST ASIA 157 (2011) (Recent implementation of soft laws includes AICHR TOR, the ASEAN Political-Security and Socio-Cultural Community Blueprints that have no sanction of non-implementation of its law).

50 ASEAN HANDBOOK ON INTERNATIONAL LEGAL COOPERATION, *supra* note 48, at 16.

In order to motivate parties to implement the law, a hard law instrument may require member countries to pay compensation for their violations,[51] yet ASEAN member countries have yet to approve such coercive pressures.[52] According to critics, parties may resort to non-legally binding laws to instruct their application of the agreement when it is not possible to create a legally-binding law[53] because there is no feasibility of compliance.[54] However, it may very well be that the reason that ASEAN prefers soft law over hard law instruments is because the violation of its member countries' pledges cannot constitute any offense or sanction for their non-compliance with the agreement.[55] ASEAN could thereby avoid the risk of sanctions, which can have the potential to cause internal conflict among its member countries based on ASEAN vision of the maintenance of peace and stability in its region.[56] ASEAN has utilized soft law as a persuasive tool that provides a peaceful atmosphere for its member countries to collaborate and create regional counter-human trafficking structures in order to achieve the joint benefits of its member countries[57] without legal concern.

Further, the implementation of soft law allows for application of diplomatic channels for "interpretation, administration, and enforcement."[58] Specifically, ASEAN has created soft law that can detail the explanation of other legally-binding international and regional anti-human trafficking hard laws.[59] For instance, the ASEAN Handbook on International Legal Cooperation in Trafficking in Persons Cases[60] has been applied as a "non-binding promotional standard" that clarifies the interpretation and application provisions stipulated in the Treaty on Mutual Legal Assistance in Criminal Matters among Like-Minded ASEAN Member Countries (MLAT) as a "binding specific regulations" to advance criminal justice responses to human trafficking.[61]

---

51 D'Amato, *supra* note 14, at 897.

52 Tan, *supra* note 48, at 187–188.

53 D'Amato, *supra* note 14, at 897.

54 DUNOFF, RATNER & WIPPMAN, *supra* note 12, at 96–97.

55 Hillgenberg, *supra* note 15, at 499, 511.

56 ASEAN Declaration (Bangkok Declaration), Thailand, Aug. 8, 1967, *available at* http://www.asean.org/component/zoo/item/the-asean-declaration-bangkok-declaration [hereinafter ASEAN Declaration]; Julio Santiago Amador III, *ASEAN in the Asia Pacific: Central or Peripheral?* 2 ASIAN POLITICS & POLICY 601, 603 (2010).

57 *See* Braaten, *supra* note 46, at 105; Tan, *supra* note 48, at 187–188.

58 *See* Braaten, *supra* note 46, at 104.

59 *See* Tan, *supra* note 48, at 188.

60 *See* ASEAN HANDBOOK ON INTERNATIONAL LEGAL COOPERATION, *supra* note 48.

61 *See* Braaten, *supra* note 46, at 104; *see also* Treaty on Mutual Legal Assistance in Criminal Matters among Like-Minded ASEAN Member Countries, Nov. 29, 2004, *available*

3.1.2 *Deficiency of Current Counter-Human Trafficking Law*

This section examines the region's existing legal instruments to determine whether it is actually necessary for ASEAN to create an anti-human trafficking law such as ADTV. ASEAN has asserted that it has created several significant legal instruments and guidelines to combat human trafficking.[62] However, these legal instruments and guidelines contain shortcomings, namely non-specific anti-human trafficking provisions, unequal gender sensitivity, ambiguous and inadequate anti-human trafficking content, and no common anti-human trafficking norms. Even though these laws illustrate deficiency, this research insists that ASEAN should draft ADTV, which will require it to form a regional human rights monitoring body specializing in preventing human trafficking, protecting all groups of trafficking victims, and prosecuting traffickers.

a Unequal Gender Sensitivity

The 2004 ASEAN Declaration against Trafficking in Persons, particularly Women and Children (2004 ASEAN Declaration against Trafficking) exemplifies ASEAN's focus on preventing and protecting its populations from human trafficking.[63] To monitor the implementation of the ASEAN Declaration against Trafficking, the Senior Officials Meeting on Transnational Crime (SOMTC)[64]

---

at http://www.agc.gov.my/images/pdf/int/emam/mlatdoc/mutuallegalassisttreaty.pdf [hereinafter Treaty on Mutual Legal Assistance].

62 DAVID ET AL., *supra* note 5, at 1 (listing ASEAN's main legal instruments, namely the 1997 ASEAN Declaration on Transnational Crime, the 2004 ASEAN Declaration against Trafficking in Persons, particularly Women and Children, Treaty on Mutual Legal Assistance in Criminal Matters among Like-Minded ASEAN Member Countries 2004, 2007 ASEAN Declaration on the Protection and Promotion of the Rights of Migrant Workers, etc).

63 ASEAN Declaration against Trafficking in Persons, Particularly Women and Children, Vientiane, Nov. 29, 2004, *available at* http://www.asean.org/communities/asean-political-security-community/item/asean-declaration-against-trafficking-in-persons-particularly-women-and-children-2 [hereinafter ADTC]; Olivia Khoo, *Regional Approaches to Trafficking in Women in South-East Asia: the Role of National Human Rights Institutions and the New ASEAN Human Rights Body*, 15 AUSTL. J. OF HUM. RTS., no. 2, 2010, at 59, 69, *available at* http://www.austlii.edu.au/au/journals/AJHR/2010/3.pdf; Cheah Wuiling, *Assessing Criminal Justice and Human Rights Models in the Fight Sex Trafficking: A case Research of ASEAN Region*, 3 ESSEX HUM. RTS. REV 46, 57 (2006).

64 Ralf Emmers, Beth Greener-Barcham & Nicholas Thomas, *Institutional Arrangements to Counter Human Trafficking in the Asia Pacific*, 28 CONTEMP. S.E. ASIA 490, 495–496 (2006); Wuiling, *supra* note 63, at 56; ASEAN Declaration on Transnational Crime, Paragraph 8, Manila, Dec. 20, 1997, *available at* http://cil.nus.edu.sg/rp/pdf/1997%20

designated the Working Group on Trafficking in Persons in 2007.[65] The Working Group operates as a facilitator for ASEAN member parties to fight human trafficking and advance regional and international collaboration.[66]

However, it is clear from the focus of this declaration that ASEAN concentrates on trafficking involving women and children much more than that involving men.[67] Actually, because of the aforementioned conditions driving trafficking in the region, men are just as vulnerable as women and children to become victims. Still, the region's efforts to combat this problem have focused on raising awareness of trafficking in women and children.[68] It is imperative

---

ASEAN%20Declaration%20on%20Transnational%20Crime-pdf.pdf; ASEAN Plan of Action to Combat Transnational Crime, June 23, 1999, *available at* http://www.asean.org/communities/asean-political-security-community/item/asean-plan-of-action-to-combat-transnational-crime [hereinafter APACTC] (providing that while the 1997 ASEAN Declaration on Transnational Crime lacks specific methods to fight human trafficking, ASEAN has developed the "ASEAN Plan of Action to Combat Transnational Crime" to mobilize ASEAN member countries to strengthen the strategies against transnational crime through national, bilateral, and regional agreements. This is the only such plan that they have to improve regional criminal justice responses to transnational crime. Nonetheless, this plan of action broadly stipulates its goals and objectives in combating all categories of transnational crimes aside from human trafficking. This plan of action is limited – it emphasizes the development of mutual legal assistance, but fails to address measures of providing victim protection such as non-prosecution of trafficking victims, appropriate housing, and right to remedy that can help accelerate victims' recovery. Further, ASEAN created one comprehensive program to implement the ASEAN Plan of Action to Combat Transnational Crime and designated the Senior Officials Meeting on Transnational Crime (SOMTC) to respond to the ASEAN Ministerial Meeting on Transnational Crimes (AMMTC) approved measures on counter-transnational crime).

65 *See* Special Rapporteur on Trafficking in Persons, *Summary of Regional and Sub-Regional Structures and Initiatives to Counter Trafficking in Persons* 9 (Dec., 2010), *available at* http://www.ohchr.org/EN/Issues/Trafficking/Pages/DakarConsultationoct2010.aspx [hereinafter OHCHR] (positing that based on submissions received from regional mechanisms in response to questionnaire of the U.N. Special Rapporteur on Trafficking in Persons, Especially Women and Children, the Special Rapporteur's 2010 Report to the Human Rights Council and more recent submissions).

66 *See* OHCHR, *supra* note 65, at 11.

67 ADTC, *supra* note 63 (indicating that "Expressing the urgent need for a comprehensive regional approach to prevent and to combat trafficking in persons, particularly women and children" "acknowledging that social, economic and other factors that cause people to migrate also make them vulnerable to trafficking in persons").

68 ADTC, *supra* note 63, at para. 6 (enumerating that "Hereby Declare, ..., to undertake concerted efforts to effectively address an emerging regional problem, namely the trafficking in persons, particularly women and children").

that the focus is expanded, and steps are taken to ensure that public and private sectors recognize that trafficked men are equally as vulnerable to human trafficking.

A review of official documents from the East Asian and Pacific region finds that these countries very narrowly construe women and children as a critical vulnerable group that may be subject to human trafficking and have barely investigated trafficking in men and boys.[69] For instance, according to the UNODC *2009 Global Report on Trafficking in Persons*, many countries in East Asia and the Pacific region have narrowly construed the term "trafficking in persons" as only sexual exploitation of women and children.[70] This takes away from the broader issue, which also includes labor exploitation, forced and otherwise. In addition, a report by the UNIAP Strategic Information Response Network (SIREN) finds that the number of male Cambodian victims is actually higher than that of their female counterparts.[71] Similarly, non-governmental organizations in Vietnam have put more emphasis on assisting trafficked women and girls over male trafficking victims.[72] The Singaporean law applies only to women and girls[73] and is silent on which indicators present the involvement of trafficking of women and girls.[74] Also, Singapore's domestic law neglects to provide security and protection of adult male victims if they need safe temporary shelter.[75] Similarly, the laws of Myanmar and Vietnam emphasize the protection of women and children, and exclude men.[76]

The International Labour Organization suggests that women are more likely than men to depend upon agents, who may become human trafficking

---

69 SUSAN KNEEBONE AND JULIE DEBELJAK, TRANSNATIONAL CRIME AND HUMAN RIGHTS: RESPONSES TO HUMAN TRAFFICKING IN THE GREATER MEKONG SUBREGION 16 (2012).

70 Id. at 15–17; United Nations Office on Drugs and Crime (UNODC), Global Report on Trafficking in Persons 11 (2009), *available at* http://www.unodc.org/documents/human-trafficking/Global_Report_on_TIP.pdf.

71 KNEEBONE & DEBELJEK, *supra* note 69, at 137; United Nations Inter-Agency Project on Human Trafficking, Human Trafficking Sentinel Surveillance: Poipet, Cambodia 2009 –2010, 50 (2010), *available at* http://www.no-trafficking.org/reports_docs/2009-2010_UNIAP_sentinel_surveillance_Poipet.pdf [hereinafter UNIAP Human Trafficking Sentinel Surveillence].

72 KNEEBONE & DEBELJEK, *supra* note 69, at 149.

73 DAVID ET AL., *supra* note 5, at 12.

74 Id. (referring to the WOMEN'S CHARTER OF SINGAPORE, Ch. 353, Sec. 141).

75 Id. at 118–119.

76 Id. at 119.

perpetrators.[77] It also reveals that migration initiatives tend to help female migrant workers seeking domestic work, more than they do male migrant workers.[78] While ASEAN should be commended for prioritizing the protection of women and children, it seems that they should also be concerned with the growing number of trafficked men in the construction, agriculture, and fishing industries.[79] The U.N. Special Rapporteur Joy Ngozi Ezeilo posits that most regional organizations have fallen short in identifying men and boys as trafficking victims because they have concentrated on only the promotion and protection of women and girls.[80] It is obvious that there is no sufficient protection and aid for male victims in the ASEAN region. If human trafficking in the region is to be countered, it will be necessary for ASEAN to persuade its member countries to collaborate on providing protection for trafficking victims because their cooperation can also help end the impunity of traffickers. It is also vital that ASEAN draws attention to male trafficking victims because they are just as vulnerable as other victims and deserve to be protected by the governments and civil society organizations of the ASEAN member countries.

---

77 International Labour Office (ILO), A Global Alliance against Forced Labour: Global Report Under The Follow-Up to the Ilo Declaration on Fundamental Principles and Rights at Work 58 (Mar. 1, 2005), *available at* http://www.ilo.org/wcmsp5/groups/public/—ed_norm/—declaration/documents/publication/wcms_081882.pdf.

78 Id.; G. Moreno-Fontes Chammartin, *The Feminization of International Migration* (Labour Education Paper, No. 29, Apr. 2002), *available at* http://www.ilo.org/wcmsp5/groups/public/—ed_dialogue/—actrav/documents/publication/wcms_111462.pdf.

79 U.S. Dep't of State, Trafficking in Persons Report 2010 8 (2010), *available at* http://www.state.gov/documents/organization/142979.pdf [hereinafter TIP Report 2010]; *see also Initiatives: Support to Underserved Victims,* United Nations Inter-Agency Project on Human Trafficking (UNIAP), http://www.no-trafficking.org/init_underserved.html (last visited Mar 1, 2013); Interview with Mr Matthew Friedman, Regional Project Manager, The United Nations Inter-Agency Project on Human Trafficking (Jan. 6, 2011) (viewing that men in the Greater Mekong Sub-region have been sufficiently promote and protect their rights).

80 Special Rapporteur on Trafficking in Persons, Especially Women and Children, *Report on Agenda Item 3: Promotion and Protection of all Human Rights, Civil, Political, Economic, Social and Cultural Rights, including the Right to Development,* U.N. Human Rights Council, U.N. Doc. A/HRC/14/32 (May 4, 2010) (by Joy Ngozi Ezeilo), *available at* http://daccess-dds-ny.un.org/doc/UNDOC/GEN/G10/132/11/PDF/G1013211.pdf?OpenElement [hereinafter U.N. Doc. A/HRC/14/32] at 18, para. 98.

b Ambiguous and Insufficient Content

Several of the legal instruments studied contain vague and inadequate anti-human trafficking mechanisms. The first is the 2004 ASEAN Declaration against Trafficking, which is effective in persuading ASEAN member countries to respect the rights and dignity of trafficking victims.[81] Despite this, it still illustrates loose and deficient provisions for assistance for trafficking victims[82] such as calling for regional cooperation to undertake measures against human trafficking and urging member countries to implement such measures through their internal laws.[83] In addition, although it also provides for essential assistance measures such as medical care and repatriation,[84] its language is vague and only encourages ASEAN member countries to provide trafficking victims "with such *essential* medical and other forms of assistance deemed *appropriate*."[85] There is no clear definition of the terms "essential" and "appropriate" as the World Guidelines on the Treatment of Foreign Direct Investment[86] defines the persuasive term "appropriate" with "prompt, adequate, and effective."[87] Accordingly, it is imperative that ASEAN provides indicators that determine the minimum standard of "essential" medical treatment and "appropriate" assistance. Such guidance can help ASEAN member countries understand how to care for trafficking victims and can educate victims to acknowledge their pivotal health rights.[88]

Second, the Treaty on Mutual Legal Assistance in Criminal Matters among Like-Minded ASEAN Member Countries 2004 (ASEAN MLAT)[89] calls for mutual legal assistance in "criminal matter[s]"[90] (including human trafficking).[91] This treaty shows that ASEAN does not sanction traffickers' impunity.[92] In fact,

---

81 ADTC, *supra* note 63, at para. 6.

82 Id. at para. 5.

83 Id. at para. 6; KNEEBONE & DEBELJEK, *supra* note 69, at 191.

84 ADTC, *supra* note 63, at para. 5.

85 Id.; Wuiling, *supra* note 63, at 57.

86 DUNOFF, RATNER & WIPPMAN, *supra* note 12, at 99.

87 Id. at 100.

88 *See*, e.g., INTERNATIONAL ORGANIZATION FOR MIGRATION, CARING FOR TRAFFICKED PERSONS: GUIDANCE FOR HEALTH PROVIDERS (Cathy Zimmerman ed., 2009), *available at* http://publications.iom.int/bookstore/free/CT_Handbook.pdf.

89 Treaty on Mutual Legal Assistance in Criminal Matters, *supra* note 61.

90 Treaty on Mutual Legal Assistance in Criminal Matters, *supra* note 6161, at Art. 1 (1); ASEAN HANDBOOK ON INTERNATIONAL LEGAL COOPERATION, *supra* note 48, at 36.

91 Treaty on Mutual Legal Assistance in Criminal Matters, *supra* note 61.

92 ASEAN, CRIMINAL JUSTICE RESPONSES TO TRAFFICKING IN PERSONS: ASEAN PRACTITIONER GUIDELINES, Pt. II (D)(1) (2007), *available at* http://www.artipproject.org/

it implies assistance in sharing evidence and legal documents for criminal investigations and proceedings, including against traffickers and purveyors.[93] Also, this instrument requires its member countries to present the person for legal proceedings to assist in recovering compensation for victims, including forfeiture actions.[94]

However, ASEAN MLAT is silent on the obligation to assist in arresting or detaining a person for extradition, and transferring that person for prosecution.[95] If the purpose of the ASEAN MLAT is to fully advocate for non-impunity of human trafficking offenders, it should include guidelines, which govern both assistance in arrest or detention as well as extradition and transfer of alleged human traffickers.[96]

While the ASEAN MLAT requires the requested country to instantly respond the requesting country's needs,[97] it also shows restrictions on the requested country's support by giving the requested country too much power over whether it should respond to the request.[98] For instance, under this instrument, a requested country can decline assisting in investigation, prosecution, and punishment if "there are substantial grounds" that can constitute "prejudice" to a person's race, nationality, religion, gender, ethnic group, or political views that differ from people of the requested country.[99] The purpose of this restriction is to curtail unfair investigation and prosecution. But the instrument itself fails to provide any idea of what constitutes "substantial" reasons for the country to arbitrarily or irrationally reject the request for assistance. Accordingly, ASEAN MLAT should be more precise so that all member countries have a common understanding of this treaty. Such precision can reduce confusion in interpretation and curtail conflicts among ASEAN member countries.

---

artip-tip-cjs/tip-cjr/recent_developments/ASEAN-PG_Web_English_Final.pdf [hereinafter ASEAN PRACTITIONER GUIDELINES]; ASEAN HANDBOOK ON INTERNATIONAL LEGAL COOPERATION, *supra* note 48, at 36.

93 Treaty on Mutual Legal Assistance in Criminal Matters, *supra* note 61.

94 Id. at Art. 14, 18, and 22.

95 Id. at Art. 2.

96 ASEAN PRACTITIONER GUIDELINES, *supra* note 92, at Pt. One (A)(4).

97 Treaty on Mutual Legal Assistance in Criminal Matters, *supra* note 61, at Art. 5, 6, and 7.

98 Id. at Art. 3.

99 Id. at Art. 3 (1)(c) (stipulating that "The Requested Party shall refuse assistance if, in its opinion -(c) there are substantial grounds for believing that the request was made for the purpose of investigating, prosecuting, punishing or otherwise causing prejudice to a person on account of the person's race, religion, sex, ethnic origin, nationality or political opinions")

The ASEAN Practitioner Guidelines on Effective Criminal Justice Responses to Trafficking 2007 (ASEAN Practitioner Guidelines)[100] is directed at law enforcement officials, special investigators, prosecutors, and judges, and lay out comprehensive criminal justice responses.[101] In addition, these guidelines reflect their mission to assist member countries in providing justice for victims and curtailing traffickers' impunity.[102]

The ASEAN Practitioner Guidelines recommend that the member countries advance their anti-human trafficking or relevant laws.[103] However, these ASEAN Practitioner Guidelines are silent on defining the terms of "trafficking victim" and do not have provisions giving trafficking victims immunity.[104] These guidelines articulate the significance of effective cooperation between government authorities in investigating, prosecuting, and adjudicating human trafficking cases;[105] but they fail to emphasize cooperation between front line law enforcement officers[106] and specialist investigators.[107]

ASEAN needs to encourage collaboration between front line law enforcement authorities and special investigators because it is imperative in the first 24 hours of the revelation of a human trafficking case that national front line law enforcement authorities find trafficking victims and investigate key elements of trafficking.[108] If front line law enforcement authorities are unable to identify victims, the ASEAN regional instruments should encourage them to consult with special investigators. This can decrease arbitrary deportation of trafficking victims without properly identifying whether or not they are trafficking victims. These shortcomings are indicative of the weak performance of front line law enforcement officials in most of the ASEAN member countries.[109]

---

100 ASEAN PRACTITIONER GUIDELINES, *supra* note 92.

101 Id.

102 Id.

103 Id. at pt. 1(A).

104 Id.

105 Id. at pt. 1(B)(6)-(7), (C)(1), (F)(1)(5).

106 GERALD SMITH, THE CRIMINAL JUSTICE RESPONSE TO HUMAN TRAFFICKING: RECENT DEVELOPMENTS IN THE GREATER MEKONG SUB-REGION 7 (2010), *available at* http://www.no-trafficking.org/reports_docs/siren/GMS-08_eng.pdf (illustrating that the front line law enforcement officers refer to "general duties police, border guards, and immigration and customs officials").

107 ASEAN PRACTITIONER GUIDELINES, *supra* note 92.

108 DAVID ET AL., *supra* note 5, at 55.

109 Id. at 65–66.

ASEAN should require member countries to provide appropriate housing, education and care, consider the characteristics of victims, namely their age, gender and special needs, particularly those of child victims.[110] In addition, throughout all stages of the investigation and trial, trafficking victims should be allowed to choose their residences, operated by either public or private organizations, in places that they prefer.[111] Allowing trafficking victims to choose their own shelters might contribute to their physical and psychological well-being thus making them more effective witnesses.

c Lack of Trafficking Victims Protection

Human trafficking has significantly impacted migrant workers, particularly those that are undocumented.[112] In response, ASEAN created the 2007 ASEAN Declaration on Migrant Workers to promote and protect these migrants.[113] It prescribes the commitments of countries of origin and destination to promote and protect the rights of migrant workers.[114] Nevertheless, ASEAN has neglected to call for protection of migrant workers in the countries of origin and destination.[115] Particularly, because of their undocumented status, ASEAN

110 U.N. Palermo Protocol, *supra* note 5, at Art. 6(4).

111 Naparat Kranrattanasuit, Memorandum of Anti-Human Trafficking Law of Vietnam (2011) (unpublished paper submitted to UNIAP) (on file with author) (presenting questions by Dr Lisa Rende Taylor, Counter Trafficking Technical Specialist at the United Nations Inter-Agency Project on Human Trafficking (UNIAP)).

112 Shiwei Ye, *Migrant Workers in Southeast Asia Need Stronger Protection*, ASIA CATALYST (May 19, 2010, 12:38 PM), http://asiacatalyst.org/blog/2010/05/migrant-workers-in-southeast-asia-need-stronger-protection.html.

113 ASEAN Declaration on the Protection and Promotion of the Rights of Migrant Workers, Cebu, Jan. 13, 2007, *available at* http://www.asean.org/communities/asean-political-security-community/item/asean-declaration-on-the-protection-and-promotion-of-the-rights-of-migrant-workers-3 [hereinafter ASEAN Migrant Workers' Declaration]; DAVID ET AL., *supra* note 5, at 1.

114 ASEAN Migrant Workers' Declaration, *supra* note 113.

115 International Labour Organization (ILO), *Ensuring the Right to Social Security for ASEAN Migrant Workers Through Social Security Agreements* 2 (ILO Research Series: Social Security Extension Initiatives in Asia), *available at* http://www.ilo.org/public/english/region/asro/bangkok/events/sis/download/paper20.pdf (last visited Dec. 12, 2012); Susan Kneebone, *ASEAN: Setting the Agenda for the Rights of Migrant Workers?*, *in* HUMAN RIGHTS IN THE ASIA-PACIFIC REGION: TOWARDS INSTITUTION BUILDING 161(Hitoshi Nasu & Ben Saul eds., 2011) (placing a quote that "strengthen and raise the visibility of labour attachés and consular staff in collecting and providing information, and responding to rights violations against women and men migrant workers. This should

does not consider the protection of irregular migrant workers[116] despite both documented and undocumented migrant workers having been "vulnerable to poor working and living conditions."[117] As a result most migrant workers have encountered difficulty in obtaining social security benefits.[118]

In addition, Susan Kneebone gives several observations of the 2007 ASEAN Declaration on the Rights of Migrant Workers.[119] For instance, this agreement is silent on defining "migrant worker" as Article 2 underscores that migrant workers, who "subsequently become undocumented," will obtain aid for "humanitarian reasons rather than as an entitlement."[120] Article 4 clarifies that the declaration does not apply to undocumented migrant workers.[121] Although the declaration provides obligations for sending and receiving countries, it is silent on their mutual responsibilities that can decelerate development on this matter.[122]

Provisions for immunity for trafficking victims have been another challenge.[123] Only five member countries allow for victims' protection from prosecution.[124] The Indonesian anti-human trafficking law provides precise provisions for trafficking victims' immunity ensuring that the law does not criminalize or punish trafficking victims for criminal conduct committed at the behest of traffickers.[125]

---

be achieved through close engagement with the migrant community and employers, and in cooperation with authorities of the host countries").

116 *See* ILO, *supra* note 115, at 2; *see also* ASEAN Migrant Workers' Declaration, *supra* note 113, General Principles 4 (stating that "[n]othing in the present Declaration shall be interpreted as implying the regularisation of the situation of migrant workers who are undocumented.")

117 South East Asia Regional Cooperation in Human Development (SEARCH), *Promoting a Process of Change: The Task Force on ASEAN Migrant Workers, available at* http://www.docstoc.com/docs/74046970/Task-Force-on-ASEAN-Migrant-Workers-Civil-Society—Trade-Union-Consultation-Process-Towards-an-ASEAN-FRAMEWORK-INSTRUMENT-FOR-THE-PROTECTION-AND-PROMOTION-OF-THE-RIGHTS-OF-T (last visited Mar. 2, 2013).

118 *See* ILO, *supra* note 115, at 2.

119 Kneebone, *supra* note 115, at 160–161.

120 Id. at 160.

121 Id. at 160–161.

122 Id. at 161.

123 DAVID ET AL., *supra* note 5, at 26.

124 Id. at 23 (naming Indonesia, Malaysia, Myanmar, Philippines, and Thailand).

125 DAVID ET AL., *supra* note 5, at 24 (mentioning unofficial translation, Law of the Republic of Indonesia Number 21 of Year 2007 on Eradication of the Criminal Act of Human Trafficking, Article 18).

Moreover, only four ASEAN member countries have developed national legal protections for trafficking victims, specifically immediate protection and support.[126] Immediate protection and support includes the provision of appropriate temporary shelter,[127] physical and psychological treatment,[128] vocational education,[129] and other essential services as provided by the U.N. Palermo Protocol.

Through legal instruments and guidelines (such as the 1997 ASEAN Transnational Crime, ASEAN MLAT, and ASEAN Practitioner Guidelines), ASEAN has emphasized mutual legal assistance and cooperation among member countries. In their view, the member countries cannot fight human trafficking as individuals, but rather should do so as an institution. However, the ASEAN legal instruments and guidelines fail to provide detailed methods and strategies for criminal justice responses to end human trafficking. Also, ASEAN needs to address the significance of non-prosecution of trafficking victims under its laws thus increasing collaboration in investigation and prosecution.

Although the ASEAN Practitioner Guidelines suggest that member countries facilitate trafficking victims as witnesses, they are devoid of detailed provisions for the protection and shelter of trafficking victims.[130] The guidelines stipulate that ASEAN member countries should promptly provide trafficked victims with protection, but they fail to describe the scope of that protection. As a result, the member countries lack the necessary protection and support for all trafficked victims, witnesses, and their families.[131]

The Malaysian anti-human trafficking law does not stipulate guidelines for the protection of victim-witnesses.[132] It is imperative that legal instruments address the nature of trafficking victims' protection, specifically, privacy and

---

126 Id. 21–23.

127 ANTI-TRAFFICKING IN PERSONS ACT B.E 2551 §37 (2008) (Thai), *available at* http://www.no-trafficking.org/content/Laws_Agreement/laws_agreement_pdf/trafficking_in_persons_act_b.e%202551%20%28eng.%29.pdf; DAVID ET AL., *supra* note 5, at 22.

128 Law on Child Protection, Care and Education, No. 25/2004/QH11, Art. 32 (June 15, 2004), *available at* https://docs.google.com/viewer?a=v&q=cache:RCoGyArRVUcJ:www.hsph.harvard.edu/population/trafficking/vietnam.child.04.doc+&hl=en&gl=us&pid=bl&srcid=ADGEESh8XXn7M0OWkRJNIo1J_VwYnM4-OXpQlclT5I10pCrKogaSINgmXh6n6DmcCRMLio6AOsPXBJkYGRUjG7-SBdQqfj0DN-XtQ770fpYW5C08MkZ1i7Ukg8sXo62ozpZyP5iK1avm&sig=AHIEtbSbVcVVfFRPTgJqFDcXzLODJfh_Gw (last visited Jan. 12, 2013); *see also* DAVID ET AL., *supra* note 5, at 22.

129 DAVID ET AL., *supra* note 5, at 22 (referring to the Anti-Trafficking in Persons Law (Law No. 5/2005) (Myanmar)).

130 ASEAN PRACTITIONER GUIDELINES, *supra* note 92, at pt. 1(C).

131 DAVID ET AL., *supra* note 5, at 118–119.

132 Id. at 119.

identity of trafficking victims,[133] physical, psychological and social recovery of victims, which includes appropriate housing,[134] counseling and legal rights,[135] medical treatment,[136] employment, education, and training opportunities.[137] Additionally, the ASEAN Practitioner Guidelines lack provisions on shelter conditions, which can lead member countries to place trafficking victims in inconvenient and improper environments at times, for instance settings that mix children with unrelated adults in the same living quarters.

Because of the ineffective anti-human trafficking strategies of ASEAN, it is proposed that ASEAN create the ADTV to create common anti-human trafficking norms applicable for its member countries. There have, however, been numerous debates regarding the concept of "hard" and "soft law," it is imperative to assess what type of anti-human trafficking law ASEAN should undertake in order to address this problem. When talking about human trafficking laws in the region, it is necessary to evaluate whether existing laws or the ADTV would be more functional to combat human trafficking. Many have contended that only hard law can be used as a legitimate and effective instrument, but it is argued here that a soft-law scheme coupled with a regional monitoring mechanism can help ASEAN strengthen its anti-human trafficking strategies and policies.

The question addressed here is whether this new pact against human trafficking should be created as a soft or hard law. The evidence reveals that since 2007, ASEAN leaders have agreed to delegate Ministers in charge of Transnational Crimes or ASEAN Ministerial Meeting on Transnational Crimes (AMMTC) to task Senior Officials Meeting on Transnational Crime (SOMTC) to further research the possibility of creating an "ASEAN Convention on Trafficking in Persons."[138] It is worth noting that the AMMTC has yet to make a resolution. However, it is argued that ASEAN can resort to a soft-law instrument that addresses anti-human trafficking much like ADTV on one condition of establishing a specific monitoring body like ACTV.

Considering ASEAN's resort to soft law, historically, it is believed that as a non-legally binding tool, ADTV can urge and guide its member countries to

---

133 U.N. Palermo Protocol, *supra* note 5, at Art. 6(1).

134 Id. at Art. 6(3)(a).

135 Id. at Art. 6(3)(b).

136 Id. at Art. 6(3)(c).

137 Id. at Art. 6(3)(d).

138 Joint Communiqué of the Sixth ASEAN Ministerial Meeting on Transnational Crime (AMMTC), Nov. 6, 2007, http://www.asean.org/news/item/joint-communique-of-the-6th-ammtc-bandar-seri-begawan-6-november-2007 [hereinafter Sixth Joint Communiqué]; ASEAN Leaders' Joint Statement in Enhancing Cooperation against Trafficking in Persons in Southeast Asia, May 8, 2011, http://www.asean.org/archive/Joint_Statement_TIP.pdf.

mitigate human trafficking through its specific anti-human trafficking information that provides a specific explanation and scope of both soft- and hard-law.[139] For instance, ADTV stipulates a common standard of the explicit measures of preventing human trafficking, protecting trafficking victims, and prosecuting trafficking offenders in order to clarify existing hard-law agreements[140] such as the Treaty on Mutual Legal Assistance in Criminal Matters among Like-Minded ASEAN Member Countries (MLAT). Also, because ASEAN lacks a specialized anti-human trafficking monitoring body, ASEAN needs to create ACTV specializing in preventing all forms of human trafficking, protecting all trafficking victims, and prosecuting perpetrators to provide sufficient and rapid responses against human trafficking for its member countries in order to ensure that all groups of trafficking victims can enjoy their rights through ASEAN member countries' implementation of the law. Such a scheme would allow ASEAN to construct mutual basic norms against human trafficking in the region. The discussion now turns to the legal structure of counter-human trafficking of ASEAN in order to address whether ASEAN counter-human trafficking is functional to lead its community into the right direction of suppressing human trafficking in its region.

3.2 Dysfunctional Counter-Human Trafficking Structure of ASEAN

Apart from the establishment of various laws, ASEAN has designed a three-pillar community to battle human trafficking. However, its structure may not accelerate the promotion and protection of the rights of trafficking victims because it divides the issues of human trafficking and labor migration, which are in fact inter-related issues. It is critical that ASEAN reinforces the collaboration between its human rights bodies by providing regular meetings in its anti-human trafficking mechanisms. This will create an effective measure of prevention, protection, and prosecution that can be instrumental in decelerating the scourge of human trafficking.

3.2.1 *Background of Counter-Human Trafficking Structure*

According to "ASEAN Integration 2015,"[141] ASEAN classified transnational crime as part of the political security community and labor migration affairs in the

139 Anne Gallagher, The International Law of Human Trafficking 142 (2010).

140 Id. at 142–143.

141 ASEAN Roadmap, *supra* note 3; Wahyuningrum, *supra* note 3.

socio-cultural community.[142] Their vision has been to create a fully integrated "ASEAN community" by 2015.[143] The structural and functional formulation of the three ASEAN communities is the ASEAN Economic Community (AEC), ASEAN Political-Security Community (APSC), and ASEAN Socio-Cultural Community (ASCC) (*see* ASEAN Three-Pillar Community 2015).[144] These three entities are aiming for community integration and mutual collaboration in economics, politics, and socio-culture in 2015.[145]

ASEAN has categorized trafficking in persons as a political security community dealing with transnational crime.[146] They have assigned the ASEAN Intergovernmental Commission on Human Right (AICHR) to promote and protect the rights of people, including countering human trafficking.[147] In addition, ASEAN has created ASEAN Commission on the Promotion and Protection of the Rights of Women and Children (ACWC) to monitor the implementation of the rights of women and children (including anti-trafficking protection of women and children)[148] and ASEAN Committee on the Implementation of the ASEAN Declaration on the Protection and Promotion of the Rights of Migrant Workers (ACMW) to implement the Declaration, to reinforce the promotion of the migrant workers' rights, and to enhance the prevention of counter-trafficking of migrant workers.[149] It is vital

---

142 ASEAN ROADMAP, *supra* note 3, at 15, 79; Wahyuningrum, *supra* note 3.

143 Vientiane Action Programme 2004–2010, Nov. 29, 2004, *available at* http://cil.nus.edu.sg/rp/pdf/2004%20Vientiane%20Action%20Programme%202004-2010-pdf.pdf; ASEAN, ASEAN POLITICAL-SECURITY COMMUNITY BLUEPRINT (2009), *available at* http://www.asean.org/archive/5187-18.pdf; Tan Sri Ahmad Fuzi bin Abdul Razak, *Facing Unfair Criticisms*, *in* THE MAKING OF ASEAN CHARTER 26 (Tommy Koh, Rorario G Manalo, & Walter Woon eds., 2009); Christopher Roberts, *ASEAN Institutionalization: The Function of Political Values and State Capacity* 1 (The S. Rajaratnam School of International Studies, Working Research Series No. 217, 2010), *available at* http://www.rsis.edu.sg/publications/WorkingResearchs/WP217.pdf.

144 Vientiane Action Programme, *supra* note 143; ASEAN POLITICAL-SECURITY COMMUNITY BLUEPRINT, *supra* note 143; RAZAK, *supra* note 143, at 26; Roberts, *supra* note 143, at 1.

145 *See* Roberts, *supra* note 143, at 1–2.

146 *See* Un Sovannasam, *ASEAN Efforts in Dealing with Transnational Crime*, *in* ASEAN MATTERS!: REFLECTING ON THE ASSOCIATION OF SOUTHEAST ASIAN NATIONS 79 (Lee Yoong Yoong ed., 2011).

147 AICHR TERMS OF REFERENCE, *supra* note 4, at § 4, 4.8.

148 ACWC TERMS OF REFERENCE, *supra* note 4.

149 Statement on the Establishment of ASEAN Committee on the Implementation of ASEAN Declaration on the Protection and Promotion of the Rights of Migrant Workers, July 13, 2007, http://www.asean.org/communities/asean-political-security-community/

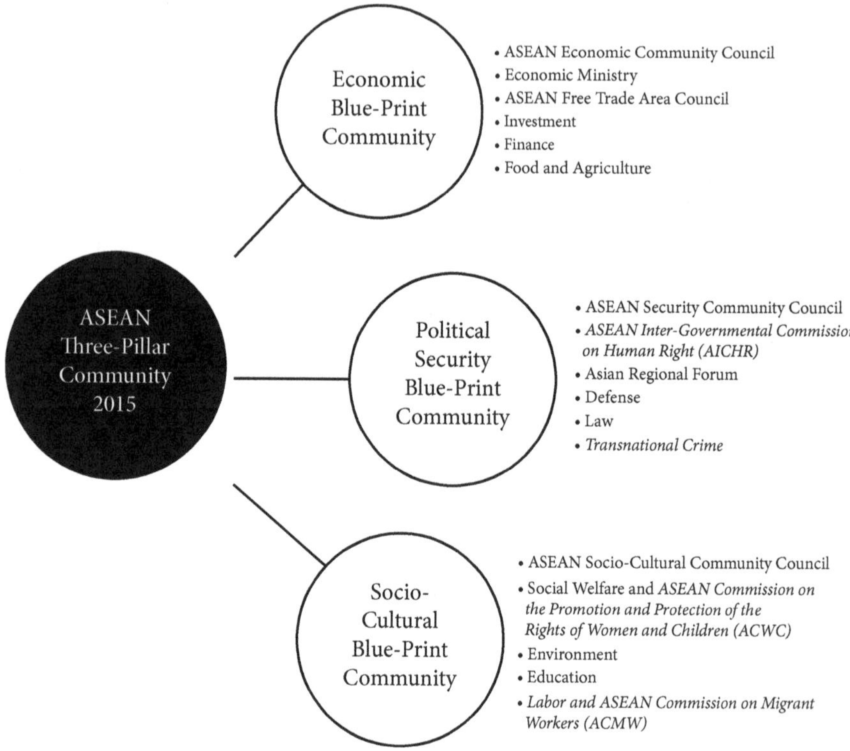

FIGURE 2 *ASEAN three-pillar community 2015*[150]

to address that ASEAN has placed both ACWC and ACMW under ASCC (Figure 2).[151]

3.2.2 *Critique of the Separation between Human Trafficking and Labour Migration*

ASEAN has broadened its human security approaches in the realm of both traditional (military) and non-traditional (non-military) matters (Chapter 2).

---

item/statement-of-the-establishment-of-the-asean-committee-on-the-implementation-of-the-asean-declaration-on-the-protection-and-promotion-of-the-rights-of-migrant-workers; ASEAN Migrant Workers' Declaration, *supra* note 113.

150 Wahyuningrum, *supra* note 3; ASEAN IN THE GLOBAL COMMUNITY: ANNUAL REPORT 2010–2011 (2011), *available at* http://www.asean.org/images/2012/publications/Annual%20Report%202010_2011.pdf; EVOLVING TOWARDS ASEAN 2015: ASEAN ANNUAL REPORT 2011–2012 (2012), *available at* http://www.aseansec.org/documents/annual%20report%202011-2012.pdf.

151 ASEAN, ASEAN ROADMAP, *supra* note 3, at 15, 79.

Therefore, it is imperative to further analyze whether the functional structure of the political security and socio-cultural communities to determine whether ASEAN's anti-human trafficking structural vision has the potential to effectively address and tackle human trafficking. It is clear that ASEAN recognizes the relationship between trafficking in persons and labour migration; however, the division between these two issues has reduced the strength of ASEAN counter-human trafficking efforts because in essence, the process of migration has the potential to lead to all categories of trafficking in persons.

Even with the creation of a three-pillar community, the ASEAN anti-human trafficking structure may not be effective at combating this threat because it separates the issue of human trafficking from labor migration. According to "ASEAN Integration 2015,"[152] ASEAN has classified transnational crime as part of the political security community, and labor migration affairs in the socio-cultural community.[153] It is their vision to create an "ASEAN community" by 2015.[154] The structural and functional formation includes the: ASEAN Economic Community, ASEAN Political-Security Community, and the Social and Cultural Community (*see* ASEAN Three-Pillar Community 2015).[155] These three entities will lead to community integration and mutual collaboration in economics, politics, and socio-culture.[156]

Trafficking in persons is categorized as a political security challenge that AICHR serves under this community[157] while labor migration is considered a social and cultural challenge that ACWC and ACMW work under this community.[158] This creates a problem because if ASEAN is seriously committed to

---

152 ASEAN ROADMAP, *supra* note 3; Wahyuningrum, *supra* note 3.

153 ASEAN ROADMAP, *supra* note 3, at 15, 79; Wahyuningrum, *supra* note 3.

154 Vientiane Action Programme, *supra* note 143; Charter of the Association of Southeast Nations [ASEAN Charter], art. 14(1), Nov. 20, 2007, *available at* http://www.asean.org/archive/publications/ASEAN-Charter.pdf; ASEAN POLITICAL-SECURITY COMMUNITY BLUEPRINT, *supra* note 143; RAZAK, *supra* note 143, at 26; Roberts, *supra* note 143, at 1.

155 Vientiane Action Programme, *supra* note 143; ASEAN Charter, *supra* note 154; ASEAN POLITICAL-SECURITY COMMUNITY BLUEPRINT, *supra* note 143; RAZAK, *supra* note 143, at 26; Roberts, *supra* note 143, at 1.

156 *See* Roberts, *supra* note 143, at 1–2.

157 *See* Sovannasam, *supra* note 146, at 79; Wahyuningrum, *supra* note 3 (noting that to deter human trafficking growth, ASEAN created two mechanisms, the AMMTC and SOMTC, to strengthen ASEAN collaboration in the battle over transnational crimes, including human trafficking. ASEAN places the SOMTC and the AMMTC under ASEAN Sectoral Ministerial Bodies).

158 ASEAN ROADMAP, *supra* note 3, at 15, 79.

combating human trafficking, this issue must be considered in tandem with labor migration. In order to address this crisis, specialists from both fields are required.[159]

The scourge of human trafficking surely affects migrant workers. Even though they contain very different natures, human trafficking and migration issues are in fact very much connected to one another.[160] Migration[161] itself involves movement of a person from one place to another either through regular or irregular methods.[162] Whether they cross legally or illegally migrant workers,[163] who cross borders, are engaged in the act of migration.[164] On the

---

159 Marwaan Macan-Markar, *Human Trafficking Exposes ASEAN's Underbelly*, INTER PRESS SERVICE (June 17, 2011), http://wwipsnews.net/print.asp?idnews=51857.

160 MIKE KAYE, THE MIGRATION-TRAFFICKING NEXUS: COMBATING TRAFFICKING THROUGH THE PROTECTION OF MIGRANTS' HUMAN RIGHTS 3 (Nov. 2003), *available at* http://www.antislavery.org/includes/documents/cm_docs/2009/t/the_migration_trafficking_nexus_2003.pdf; ROUNDTABLE ON USING CEDAW TO PROTECT THE RIGHTS OF WOMEN MIGRATION WORKERS AND TRAFFICKED WOMEN IN SOUTH AND SOUTHEAST ASIA, REPORT, MAY 6–9, 2009, KUALA LUMPUR, MALAYSIA 24 (2009), *available at* http://www.iwraw-ap.org/publications/doc/Roundtable_on_Migration_and_Trafficking_report.pdf [CEDAW ROUNDTABLE]; *Beyond Borders: Exploring Links between Trafficking and Migration* 5 (GAATW Working Paper Series, 2010), *available at* http://www.gaatw.org/publications/WP_on_Globalisation.pdf; Kneebone, *supra* note 115, at 147; KNEEBONE & DEBELJEK, *supra* note 69, at 28; Patrick Taran, *Human Rights of Migrants: Challenges of the New Decade*, 38 INT'L MIGRATION 6, 7, 8 (2000).

161 Kneebone, *supra* note 115, at 146 (referring to the attributes of "migration" as "'repeat,' 'circular' or 'temporary', and including 'regular' (legal) and 'irregular' (illegal) migration"); *Beyond Borders*, *supra* note 160, at 5 (highlighting that "migrant" means "an overarching term that covers many special categories of migrants, including refugees, smuggled, trafficked and undocumented persons").

162 KAYE, *supra* note 160, at 3.

163 Elaine Pearson, *Destination Factors in the Trafficking of Children and Young Women in the Mekong Sub-Region*, *in* THE MEKONG CHALLENGE- HUMAN TRAFFICKING: REDEFINING DEMAND 7 (2005), *available at* http://www.ilo.org/wcmsp5/groups/public/–asia/–ro-bangkok/documents/publication/wcms_bk_pb_29_en.pdf (describing Article 2(1) of the U.N. Convention on the Protection of the Rights of All Migrant Workers and Members of Their Families (1990) that "a migrant worker is any person who is to be engaged, is engaged or has been engaged in a remunerated activity in a State of which he or she is not a national.").

164 KAYE, *supra* note 160, at 3; Id. at 7–8 (explaining Article 5 of the U.N. Convention on the Protection of the Rights of All Migrant Workers and Members of Their Families (1990) that irregular migrant workers "(a) Are considered as documented or in a regular situation if they are authorized to enter, to stay and to engage in a remunerated activity in the State of employment pursuant to the law of that State and to international agreements to

other hand, human trafficking involves the movement of a person using means of force, coercion, threat, or deception, and generally applies in situations, where it is done for the purposes of exploitation.[165] The migration process itself is an open avenue for traffickers to target regular and irregular migrant workers.[166] In essence, human trafficking impacts an individual's security while migration smuggling affects state sovereignty and security.[167] Human trafficking relates to and is effectuated by various elements of migration.[168]

In the ASEAN region, human trafficking and migration are generally dealt with as separate issues, yet there are other international and regional laws illustrating the relationship between migration and human trafficking.[169]

---

which that State is a party; (b) Are considered as non-documented or in an irregular situation if they do not comply with the conditions provided for in subparagraph (a) of the present article." Therefore, an "irregular migrant" means an "undocumented migrant." However, human trafficking can be either regular or irregular migrants).

165 Id.

166 Id.; KNEEBONE & DEBELJEK, *supra* note 69, at 55; Special Rapporteur on Violence Against Women its Causes and Consequences, *Integration of the Human Rights of Women and the Gender Perspective: Violence against Women*, U.N. Eco. & Soc. Council, U.N. Doc. E/CN.4/2001/73/Add.2 (Feb. 6, 2001) (by Radhika Coomaraswamy, para. 15 (Feb. 6, 2001), *available at available at* http://daccess-dds-ny.un.org/doc/UNDOC/GEN/G01/108/65/PDF/G0110865.pdf?OpenElement (referring "traffickers fish in the stream of migration.").

167 *See* Natalia Ollus, *Protocol against the Smuggling of Migrants by Land Air and Sea supplementing the United Nations Convention against Transboundary Organized Crime: A Tool for Criminal Justice Personnel*, 1 INT'L LEGAL STUD. PROGRAM L. J., 1, 1, 33 (2000), *available at* http://www.wcl.american.edu/journal/ilsp/v1/1/ilsplj_v1_1.pdf?rd=1; *see also* Maggy Lee, *Introduction: Understanding Human Trafficking, in* HUMAN TRAFFICKING 10–11 (Maggy Lee ed., 2007).

168 Richard Danziger, Janathan Martens & Mariela Guajardo, *Human Trafficking and Migration Management, in* STRATEGIES AGAINST HUMAN TRAFFICKING: THE ROLE OF THE SECURITY SECTOR 261 (Cornelius Friesendorf ed., 2009), *available at* http://www.acrath.org.au/multimedia/downld/var/Strategies_Against_Human_Trafficiking-The_Role_of_the_Security_Sector_Vienna&Geneva_Sep2009.pdf.

169 Id. at 267–268 (illustrating international laws that show the relationship between migration and human trafficking the International legal tools consist of 1948 Universal Declaration of Human Rights and the 1966 International Covenant on Civil and Political Rights (ICCPR), 1951 Geneva Convention Relating to the Status of Refugees, 2000 Protocol to Prevent, Suppress and Punish Trafficking in Persons, especially Women and Children (U.N. Trafficking Protocol), 1990 International Convention on the Protection of the Rights of all Migrant Workers and Members of their Families (ICRMW), International Labour Organization (ILO) Conventions. Regional laws comprise of 2005 Council of Europe Convention on Action against Trafficking in Human Beings and 2004 Arab

There are several regional agreements pertaining to migrant workers, which illuminate the link between human trafficking and migration.[170] For instance, the ASEAN Declaration on the Promotion and Protection of the Rights of Women and Children[171] exemplifies ASEAN's apprehension of human

Charter on Human Rights explaining that "The Universal Declaration of Human Rights states that every person has the right to freedom of movement within the borders of each state, that everyone has the right to leave any country, including his own and that everyone has the right to seek asylum." Moreover, articles 3, 4 and 5 of the Declaration make reference to the right to life, liberty and security of person; the right to be free from slavery or servitude; and the right to not be subjected to torture or cruel, inhuman or degrading treatment. Although the Declaration was not originally binding, its content has become customary international law and can therefore be considered binding on states. The ICCPR mentions that individuals lawfully residing in a state have the right to liberty of movement. The ICCPR also makes reference to an individual's right to leave any country, including his own and that no one should be arbitrarily deprived of the right to enter his own country (Article 12). Not only is the ICCPR binding on states that ratify it but, if a state also ratifies the first Optional Protocol to the ICCPR, individuals may also take complaints to the Human Rights Committee after all national remedies have been exhausted).

170 Ma. Lorena Macabuag, *ASEAN Committee on Migrants Workers, in* 49 FOCUS ASIA-PACIFIC, Sept. 2007, at 8, *available at* http://www.hurights.or.jp/asia-pacific/049/focus49.pdf; ASEAN Migrant Workers' Declaration, *supra* note 113; The Bangkok Declaration on Irregular Migration, *International Symposium on Migration: Towards Regional Cooperation on Irregular/Undocumented Migration* (Apr. 21–23, 1999) *available at* http://www.iom.int/jahia/webdav/site/myjahiasite/shared/shared/mainsite/policy_and_research/rcp/APC/BANGKOK_DECLARATION.pdf; Declaration of ASEAN Concord II (Bali Concord II), Oct. 7, 2003, *available at* http://www.asean.org/news/item/declaration-of-asean-concord-ii-bali-concord-ii-2 [hereinafter Bali Concord II] (First, the 1997 ASEAN Vision 2020 concentrates on collaboration among its member countries in managing regional predicaments, namely trafficking in women and children. Second, Hanoi Plan of Action 1998 requires ASEAN member countries to create action plans focusing on regional cooperative advancement in the fight against trafficking in women and children. Third, the 1999 Bangkok Declaration on Irregular Migration enumerates sources and positive and negative (namely human trafficking) impacts that affect migration (including irregular migration) in origin, transit, and destination countries. Fourth, the 2004 ASEAN Declaration against Trafficking in Persons Particularly Women and Children creates a "regional focal network" to intercept and tackle human trafficking in ASEAN. Fifth, the 2003 Bali Concord II promotes the use of regional entities and human rights bodies to reinforce national and regional competences to redress transnational crime, namely human trafficking. Sixth, the ASEAN Declaration on the Protection and Promotion of the Rights of Migrant Workers provides the needs to undertake substantial measures to obstruct human trafficking by criminalizing all people engaged in this business).

171 ADTC, *supra* note 63.

trafficking and recognition of the intersection of migration and human trafficking.[172] Also, the ASEAN Plan of Action for Cooperation on Immigration Matters aims to advance migration collaboration that reinforces data sharing about irregular migration, human trafficking, and other transnational crimes.[173] It also urges multilateral cooperation between ASEAN member countries and their stakeholders.[174]

Similarly, the Financing Agreement under the Migration and Border Management Program between ASEAN and the EU is aimed at advancing improvement of trans-border management in an effort to accommodate the legal movement of people and merchandise, and to fight against transnational crimes, including trafficking in persons and unlawful migration.[175] Many civilian counter-human trafficking and migrants' rights organizations have asserted that migration and trafficking are linked.[176] As a result, governments and human rights advocates have attempted to quell the issue by inhibiting trafficking.[177]

The connection of trafficking in persons and labour migration demonstrates that ASEAN should promote its human rights bodies, AICHR, ACWC, and ACMW to share their information of trafficking circumstances of all groups of trafficking victims in order to strengthen its regional norms. Therefore, the next part will illustrate the significance of enhancing the cooperation among ASEAN human rights bodies through their regular meeting.

3.2.3 *Need for Collaboration among Human Rights Bodies*

Even though ASEAN has divided these human rights mechanisms into different communities, ASEAN should urge collaboration among AICHR, ACWC, and ACMW through a specific meeting on counter-human trafficking in order to ensure the promotion and protection of the rights of all trafficking victims. This analysis will make it clear that although ASEAN divides political security

---

172 Id.; Khoo, *supra* note 63, at 69.

173 ASEAN Plan of Action for Cooperation on Immigration Matters, *available at* http://www.asean.org/communities/asean-political-security-community/item/asean-plan-of-action-for-cooperation-on-immigration-matters (last visited Dec. 12, 2012).

174 Id.

175 NNT, *Cabinet Approves Addendum to ASEAN-EU Financing Agreement*, PATTAYA MAIL (May 16, 2012), http://www.pattayamail.com/business/cabinet-approves-addendum-to-asean-eu-financing-agreement-12718.

176 GAATW & La Strada International, NGO Priority for EU Anti-Trafficking Day 2009: Focus on Human Rights 22 (Paper presented at the EU Ministerial Conference: Towards Global EU Action against Trafficking in Human Beings, Oct. 18, 2009).

177 Id.

dealing with counter-human trafficking from socio-cultural community managing the labor migration and the rights of women and children, ASEAN should require these two communities to collaborate in abating human trafficking. Regular meetings between these entities would be beneficial because their collaboration can help them create better norm because of their better understanding of the problem.

Based on a review of its official documents, it seems that ASEAN will pursue this suggestion in practice, particularly the cooperation in promoting and protecting human rights.[178] For instance, the Term of Reference of the ASEAN Intergovernmental Commission on Human Rights (AICHR TOR) stipulates that AICHR has to exchange information with other ASEAN mechanisms in order to promote human rights.[179] Specifically, AICHR can interact with all three-pillar communities, including the Political-Security, Socio-Cultural Community, and the Economic Community[180] while ACWC can only exercise within the socio-cultural community by submitting a report to the ASEAN Ministers Meeting on Social Welfare and Development (AMMSWD) and to the ASEAN Committee on Women (ACW) and other sectoral bodies.[181] ASEAN has demanded that ACWC shares information and collaborates among its offices, but it has stipulated that ACWC carries on "independently and separately" from other human rights bodies.[182]

During its 17th meeting on December 2, 2011, the AICHR had a meeting with ACWC to share their statuses, mandates, and work plans.[183] It is clear that

---

178 Irene Pietropaoli, *Challenges for ASEAN Human Rights Mechanisms: the Case of Lao pdr from a Gender Perspective*, *in* HUMAN RIGHTS IN THE ASIA-PACIFIC REGION: TOWARDS INSTITUTION BUILDING 168 (Hitoshi Nasu & Ben Saul eds., 2011).

179 *See* AICHR Terms of Reference, *supra* note 4, at § § 4, 4.8.

180 *See* id. at § 4.7; Alistair D.B. Cook & Priyanka Bhalla, *Regional Champions – Examining the Comparative Advantages of aichr and acwc*, CENTRE FOR NON-TRADITIONAL SECURITY STUDIES INSIGHT 1 (2010), *available at* http://www.rsis.edu.sg/nts/HTML-Newsletter/Insight/NTS-Insight-jun-1001.html (explaining that the terms of reference theoretically directs AICHR to interact with other human rights bodies by providing "technical advice on human rights" and the rights of women and children).

181 Cook & Bhalla, *supra* note 180, at 1.

182 *ASEAN to Proceed with Commission on the Promotion and Protection of the Rights of Women and Children*, WORKING GROUP FOR AN ASEAN HUMAN RIGHTS MECHANISM, http://www.aseanhrmech.org/news/asean-to-proceed-with-commission.html (last visited Dec. 12, 2012); Khoo, *supra* note 63, at 70.

183 Press Release, Assoc. of Southeast Asian Nations (ASEAN), Press Release of the Seventh Meeting of the ASEAN Intergovernmental Commission in Human Rights (AICHR) (Dec. 2, 2011), *available at* http://www.asean.org/news/asean-secretariat-news/item/press-release-of-the-seventh-meeting-of-the-asean-intergovernmental-commission-in-human-rights-aichr.

despite their division, the two human rights bodies are capable of convening a meeting. The purpose for this meeting was to address human trafficking, a transnational crime affecting men, women, and children, who coincidentally may also be migrants. Current anti-human trafficking legislation and policies have also had the effect of affecting the freedom of movement of migrant workers. However, to date, there has been no evidence of cooperation to combat human trafficking among AICHR, ACWC, and ACMW.[184]

ASEAN must authorize all three human rights bodies (AICHR, ACWC, and ACMW) to convene a regular anti-human trafficking forum so that they can share and learn different aspects of the problems relevant to human trafficking. Such a forum has the potential to strengthen ASEAN member countries' counter-human trafficking laws and practices even though they have been assigned to different communities. This proposal was supported by the report of the IWRAW, the GAATW, and CARAM Asia and shows that policymakers consider human trafficking and migration in the same agenda[185] because anti-human trafficking policies can impact migrant workers, who are subject to human trafficking.[186] Such a joint discourse can broaden their views on particularly preventing human trafficking and protecting trafficking victims.

Migrants should be afforded fundamental rights and legal protections with support of anti-human trafficking policies.[187] However, preventive measures against human trafficking can have the extraneous effect of limiting migration in an effort to deter trafficking of migrant workers.[188] For instance, the ASEAN Declaration on the Promotion and Protection of the Rights of Women and Children has concentrated on the sharing of information regarding migration and border controls.[189] It mentions the idea of "management" of migration, which in practice has been found to constrain the fundamental rights of

---

184 Tess Bacalla, *ASEAN Urged to Set Up Mechanism for Migrant Rights*, VERA FILES (Sept. 10, 2012), http://oppenheimer.mcgill.ca/ASEAN-urged-to-set-up-mechanism (providing an interview of Philippine Representative to AICHR Rosario Manalo that "Since migrant workers' rights fall under the purview of human rights, coordination between the ACMW and AICHR on the issue of migrant workers is expected. Since migrant workers' rights fall under the purview of human rights, the expectation is that the ACMW and AICHR would be coordinating on the issue of migrant workers. There is no engagement between the two").

185 CEDAW ROUNDTABLE, *supra* note 160, at 24–25.

186 Id.

187 Id.

188 Id.

189 Khoo, *supra* note 63, at 69.

migrants'[190] because most preventive measures have equated "anti-migration" with "anti-trafficking." This connotation is made to discourage women's migration and thus seemingly hopefully diminish the occurrence of sex trafficking.[191]

Such measures have proven detrimental. Although aimed at preventing human trafficking, many sources have reported that restrictions on migration increase the risk of trafficking because migrant workers might seek out the services of smugglers in order to gain access to other countries.[192] For instance, in its efforts to decrease the number of Cambodian forced laborers in Malaysia, the Cambodian government has proscribed limitations on their "travel rights."[193] This law has done little to reduce human trafficking and exploitation and has really only affected Cambodian women legally seeking domestic work in Malaysia.[194]

Considering human trafficking and migrant worker protection in the same agenda can help AICHR, ACWC, and ACMW better understand the plight of migrants and uphold their protection. It is critical that these three human rights bodies promote standardization of "migration" procedures from and to their lands. Their governments should concentrate on compliance with international law, and more specifically protection of rights and freedom of movement.[195] Even though the government can regulate boundaries and scrutinize requirements for entering its country,[196] they need to guarantee the fundamental rights of all individuals residing on its land, particularly undocumented

---

190 Danziger, Martens & Guajardo, *supra* note 168, at 262.

191 Id. at 271–272; Mike Dottridge, *Introduction* to COLLATERAL DAMAGE 13–14 (Global Alliance against Trafficking in Women/Amarin 2007), *available at* http://www.gaatw.org/Collateral%20Damage_Final/singlefile_CollateralDamagefinal.pdf.

192 Danziger, Martens & Guajardo, *supra* note 168, at 275; *Beyond Borders*, *supra* note 160, at 11.

193 U.S. DEP'T OF STATE, TRAFFICKING IN PERSONS REPORT 2012 108 (2012), *available at* http://www.state.gov/documents/organization/192594.pdf [hereinafter TIP REPORT 2012].

194 GAATW & La Strada International, *supra* note 176 (describing that "At the core of anti-trafficking measures is the goal of stopping exploitation of migrant workers; however, current restrictive migration policies; for example, the limits to legal labour migration possibilities despite abundant demand for cheap labour and services in destination countries) and labour policies continue to discriminate against poor people creating opportunities for exploitation of migrants. Years of implementing a restrictive approach to migration and immigration policies by the EU have not resulted in a decreased migration, but rather have left migrants more vulnerable to irregular forms of migration, including smuggling and trafficking for labour and other forms of exploitation").

195 Danziger, Martens & Guajardo, *supra* note 168, at 262–263.

196 Id. at 266.

migrants.[197] Despite the sovereign authority to formulate immigration rules, residence permission and disapproval of migrants, individual countries must acknowledge that they have to ensure the migrants' enjoyment of movement.[198] However, many countries have neglected their responsibility to protect and respect human rights while dealing with migration issues.[199]

These three bodies should address the causes of human trafficking amongst migrants[200] including the problem of victim identification, lack of victims' collaboration in investigation, and insufficient supportive proof.[201] The current criminal justice response to fighting human trafficking has proven itself to be an inadequate strategy to approach this dilemma, which has caused the vulnerability of people, particularly migrants.[202]

Mutual collaboration of AICHR, ACWC, and ACMW can help ASEAN educate law enforcement authorities to recognize that migrants even if undocumented and considered "illegal" are in fact trafficking victims because they do not have legal status in their transit or destination countries. In some instances these people may already migrated with legal documents, but then loses them.[203] It is very important that ASEAN recognizes these instances and considers the fact that illegal immigration is closely related to transnational human trafficking crimes.[204] The negative outcomes of constraining migration have caused a growing number of potential trafficking victims[205] that reflects more irregular than regular migrants.[206]

---

197 Id. at 266–267.

198 Id. at 267.

199 Id.

200 CEDAW ROUNDTABLE, *supra* note 160, at 24–25.

201 Danziger, Martens & Guajardo, *supra* note 168, at 284.

202 Id.

203 *Beyond Borders*, *supra* note 160, at 5; INTERNATIONAL COUNCIL ON HUMAN RIGHTS POLICY, IRREGULAR MIGRATION, MIGRANT SMUGGLING AND HUMAN RIGHTS: TOWARDS COHERENCE 15 (2010), *available at* http://www.ichrp.org/files/reports/56/122_report_en.pdf.

204 *See* KNEEBONE & DEBELJEK, *supra* note 69, at 11, 54.

205 Shanthi Dairiam, *Failing Women: Why We Need a New Approach to Human Trafficking*, 6 GLOBAL ASIA 3 (Sept. 2011), http://www.globalasia.org/V6N3_Fall_2011/Shanthi_Dairiam.html; Marie Segrave, *Human Trafficking and Human Rights*, 14 AUSTL. J. OF HUM. RTS. 2, 71, 82 (2009); ANDREAS PETER, BORDER GAMES: POLICING THE US-MEXICO DIVIDE 7 (2000) (explaining that migration and border control rules have "actually structured, conditioned, and even enabled (often unintentionally) clandestine border crossings.")

206 Dairiam, *supra* note 205.

In addition to convening regular meetings to address the issue of human trafficking and cooperation among AICHR, ACWC, and ACMW, ASEAN should create a specialized anti-human trafficking body like the ASEAN Commission on the Promotion and Protection of the Rights of Trafficking Victims (ACTV) in order to assist AICHR, ACWC, and ACMW monitor and address up-to-date human trafficking situation in the ASEAN region that can broaden these three bodies' knowledge against human trafficking. The ACTV should be created under the auspices of the political-security community to assist AICHR, ACWC, and ACMW with addressing the root causes of human trafficking, redressing this dilemma in the right direction, and providing sufficient prevention and protection for all trafficking victims. This issue will be discussed further in Chapter 5.

In order to ensure collaboration between these human rights bodies, the ADTV should require regular meetings on anti-human trafficking through ADTV to give the ASEAN member countries opportunities to better understand the problem of human trafficking and share methods and strategies to combat human trafficking. This type of dialogue would allow individual countries to create sufficient measures of prevention, protection, and prosecution. Since ASEAN lacks a specialized anti-human trafficking body like ACTV, the next section will examine whether ASEAN's current legal instruments addressing human trafficking, AICHR and ACWC are sufficient to ensure the promotion and protecting of trafficking victims' rights. This examination is necessary to determine whether there is a need to create an anti-human trafficking body like ACTV.

3.3 Insufficient Powers of Existing ASEAN Human Rights Bodies against Human Trafficking

Human rights bodies have the potential to assist member countries in addressing human rights violations and concerns and mobilize countries to undertake measures to combat them while also tackling domestic breaches that result from the practices or negligence of the government.[207] Even though the ASEAN human rights bodies, AICHR and ACWC, which address human trafficking,[208]

207 Macabuag, *supra* note 170, at 1.

208 ACWC TERMS OF REFERENCE, *supra* note 4; James Kon, *ASEAN Body on Rights of Women, Children Established*, SULTANATE (Apr. 8, 2010), http://www.sultanate.com/news_server/2010/8_apr_4.html; *About Us*, WORKING GROUP FOR AN ASEAN HUMAN RIGHTS MECHANISM, http://www.aseanhrmech.org/aboutus.html (last visited Dec. 12,

have been created, this section will question whether ASEAN has authorized basic powers in order to ensure that they can help ASEAN member countries address counter-human trafficking circumstance and enhance the protection of people from human trafficking. Therefore, it is vital to examine whether they have the authority to monitor, assess, and compile information on the challenges and prospects of national and regional anti-human trafficking policies. In addition, it is important to ascertain whether they admit State or individual complaints. Even though ASEAN has established AICHR and ACWC, they cannot effectively promote anti-human trafficking and protect all trafficking victims because they lack the requisite monitoring and complaint powers.

3.3.1 *The Lack of Monitoring, Evaluation, and Data Collection on Achievements and Challenges of the National and Regional Policies*

ASEAN claims that the establishment of AICHR and ACWC can bridge the gap between national and international criteria levels and have the power to urge ASEAN member countries conform to international human rights principles.[209] The shortcomings of these bodies show that they may have increased human rights issues, including trafficking in persons.[210] This deficiency

---

2012) (addressing that the Terms of Reference of ASEAN Commission for the Promotion and Protection of the Rights of Women and Children (ACWC TOR) requires ACWC to serves as a "bridge for the well-being, development, empowerment and participation of both women and children in the community-building process." Also, ACWC TOR demands ACWC to encourage ASEAN member parties to implement regional and international instruments adhered by the member parties. These international instruments encompass the Protocol to Prevent, Suppress and Punish Trafficking in Persons, especially Women and Children (the U.N. Palermo Protocol); the Convention on the Elimination of All Forms of Discrimination Against Women (CEDAW), Dec. 18, 1979, http://www2.ohchr.org/english/law/cedaw.htm; and the Convention on the Rights of the Child (CRC). This ACWC's role will help ASEAN member countries understand and acknowledge fundamental anti-human trafficking cooperation at the same level).

209 *See* SRIPRAPHA PETCHARAMESREE ET AL., TOWARDS AN ASEAN COMMISSION ON THE PROMOTION AND PROTECTION OF THE RIGHTS OF WOMEN AND CHILDREN 112–113 (2008).

210 AICHR TERMS OF REFERENCE, *supra* note 4, at Art. 4(3)-(6); Yuval Ginbar, *Human Rights in ASEAN—Setting Sail or Treading Water?*, 10 HUM. RTS L. REV. 504, 515–516 (2010), *available at* http://hrlr.oxfordjournals.org/content/10/3/504.full.pdf+html; *Compromising – Even on Human Rights*, ASIAVIEWS (July 25, 2009, 6:12 AM), http://www.asiaviews.org/index.php?option=com_content&view=article&id=5302:colcomalias1266&catid=3:column-a-commentaries&Itemid=10; Yuyun Wahyuningrum, *Can aichr Promote and Protect Human Rights?*, 5 ASIAN HUM. RTS. DEFENDER, no. 2, 2009, at 4, 7;

includes the lack of monitoring, evaluating, and compiling information on its member countries' achievement and dilemma of their anti-human trafficking strategies.[211]

While AICHR has the power to receive member countries' data on domestic laws and policies that reinforce human rights, its term of reference has not required AICHR to examine and assess these laws and policies.[212] The ACWC encourages member countries to carry out regular evaluations of their domestic laws, measures, policies, and criminal justice responses to the violations of women and children's rights,[213] and recommend "appropriate" approaches to prevent and eradicate infringement against women and children's rights.[214]

ACWC began its research on preventing, protecting, and assisting victims of violence against women and children in the region by visiting the Vientiane Counseling and Protection Centre for Women and Children an organization providing aids and services for a variety of victims, including domestic violence and human trafficking.[215] The purpose of this visit was to learn and understand what individual ASEAN member countries have exercised to assure that their contributions will meet the needs of victims.[216]

ASEAN also mentions the report on "*Regional Dialogue on U.N. Engagement with ASEAN Human Rights System*" stipulating the ACWC five-year action plan.[217] This priority plan highlights the establishment of "indicators" for

---

Asia, INTERNATIONAL JUSTICE RESOURCE CENTER, http://ihrlaw.org/ihr-reading-room/regional/asia/ (last visited Mar. 5, 2013) (giving the view that the Terms of Reference of the AICHR "limit the Commission's role to promotion and protection, as a consultative body of ASEAN"); *ASEAN Body to Address Rights of Women and Children*, INQUIRER.NET (Apr. 7, 2010, 07:43 PM), http://newsinfo.inquirer.net/breakingnews/world/view/20100407-262920/ASEAN-body-to-address-rights-of-women-and-children.

211 *See* PETCHARAMESREE, *supra* note 209, at 112–113.

212 *See*, e.g. AICHR TERMS OF REFERENCE, *supra* note 4, at Art. 4.10.

213 *See*, e.g. ACWC TERMS OF REFERENCE, *supra* note 4, para 5.10.

214 *See*, e.g. id. at para. 5.12.

215 Press Release, Assoc. of Southeast Asian Nations (ASEAN), Third Press Release of the ASEAN Commission on the Promotion and Protection of the Rights of Women and Children (AWC) (Feb. 18, 2012), available at http://www.asean.org/news/asean-secretariat-news/item/third-press-release-of-the-asean-commission-on-the-promotion-and-protection-of-the-rights-of-women-and-children-acwc.

216 Id.

217 UNDP Asia Pacific Regional Centre & OHCHR Regional Office for Southeast Asia, *Report on Regional Dialogue on u.n. Engagement with ASEAN Human Rights System* 5 (Sept. 6, 2010), *available at* http://bangkok.ohchr.org/files/Regional_Dialogue_ASEAN_Report.pdf.

monitoring, evaluating, collecting data on achievements and challenges, and submitting recommendations.[218] It is expected that if ACWC develops "indicators" for data collection, ACWC will be able to help ASEAN member countries establish their national report based on the same indicators. However, to date, ACWC has not published any report on violence or human trafficking affairs.

ASEAN tends to rely upon other agencies, including the recently expired Asia Regional Trafficking in Persons Project (ARTIP),[219] for support on data collection on achievements and challenges of the national and regional policies.[220] The reports include *ASEAN Responses to Trafficking in Persons*, published in 2006[221] and the *Progress Report on Criminal Justice Responses to Trafficking in Persons in ASEAN region* published in 2011.[222] ASEAN cooperated with the International Organization for Migration in creating a report, *ASEAN and Trafficking in Persons: Using Data as a Tool to Combat Trafficking in Persons*.[223]

Although ASEAN member countries provided the information, they were prepared by other organizations and are produced sporadically.[224] It is imperative that ASEAN assigns regional human rights mechanisms to regularly compile information on the challenges and accomplishments of its member countries' national laws and policies in order to ensure the efficacy of these responses.

Despite the impotence of AICHR and ACWC's monitoring powers, ASEAN has potentially accepted such monitoring system.[225] For instance, the report

218 Id.

219 *See* ASIA REGIONAL TRAFFICKING IN PERSONS PROJECT (ARTIP), http://www.artipproject.org; *see also* KNEEBONE & DEBELJEK, *supra* note 69, at 200 (adding that "the ARTIP project was wound up in 2011 and will be replaced with a new project in 2012.")

220 *See ASEAN Makes Public Anti-Human Trafficking Report*, VIETNAMPLUS (Aug. 24, 2011, 11:15 AM), http://en.vietnamplus.vn/Utilities/PrintView.aspx?ID=20456.

221 *See* ASSOCIATION OF SOUTHEAST ASIAN NATIONS, ASEAN RESPONSES TO TRAFFICKING IN PERSONS: ENDING IMPUNITY FOR TRAFFICKERS AND SECURING JUSTICE FOR VICTIMS (2006), *available at* http://www.artipproject.org/artip-tip-cjs/resources/specialised_publications/ASEAN%20Responses%20to%20TIP_2006.pdf.

222 DAVID ET AL., *supra* note 5; *ASEAN Makes Public Anti-Human Trafficking Report*, *supra* note 220.

223 ASEAN AND TRAFFICKING IN PERSONS: USING DATA AS A TOOL TO COMBAT TRAFFICKING IN PERSONS, INTERNATIONAL ORGANIZATION FOR MIGRATION (Fiona David ed., 2008), *available at* http://www.iom.or.id/publications/pdf/16_MIL6010112_ASEAN_lo.pdf.

224 Id. (revealing that only Cambodia, Indonesia, Philippines, and Thailand cooperated in this report).

225 *Asia*, *supra* note 210.

Post-Nargis Needs Assessment and Monitoring: ASEAN's Pioneering Response shows that ASEAN has practically admitted a monitoring system.[226] This report examined ASEAN disaster relief strategies and methods, including lessons learned, such as needed strong collaboration of various groups,[227] and challenges such as information inaccuracy.[228] It provides vital recommendations to prevent further mistakes and the use of training programs to create more effective disaster management for all relevant public and private staff.[229] The report describes thorough operations and working processes, particularly a timeline of events for each group to exercise and complete their plans,[230] as well as to visualize the situations through maps and diagrams.[231]

In addition to this preliminary monitoring process, ASEAN should assign its Commission on the Promotion and Protection of the Rights of Trafficking Victims specializing in the fight against human trafficking to help AICHR and ACWC monitor, evaluate, and compile information on the accomplishments and challenges of ASEAN member countries' anti-human trafficking laws and practices. As a monitoring system,[232] it can mobilize a country to comply with

---

226 JOHANNA WEGERDT & SIU SUE MARK, POST-NARGIS NEEDS ASSESSMENT AND MONITORING: ASEAN'S PIONEERING RESPONSE 31–56, 63(2010), *available at* http://www.asean.org/images/2012/publications/Post-Nargis%20Needs%20Assessment%20and%20Monitoring%20ASEAN's%20Pioneering%20Response.pdf.

227 Id. at 31.

228 Id.

229 Id. at 31–56, 63.

230 Id. 21, 23, 29.

231 Id. 10–12, 27, 39, 41, 52, 54, 57.

232 Mike Dottridge, *Research Needs Concerning the Monitoring, Evaluation and Impact Assessment of Both Research about Human Trafficking and Projects and Programmes to Address Human Trafficking, in* HUMAN TRAFFICKING: NEW DIRECTIONS FOR RESEARCH 69–70 (2008), *available at* http://www.iom.ch/jahia/webdav/shared/shared/mainsite/microsites/IDM/workshops/ensuring_protection_070909/human_trafficking_new_directions_for_research.pdf (describing that the Organization for Economic Co-operation and Development (OECD) Development Assistance Committee (DAC) define the term "Monitoring" and "Evaluation" on a glossary. "Monitoring" means "An ongoing process to collect data systematically about the results of anti-trafficking initiatives either by a single agency or a group of agencies, in order to inform the agencies' management and other stakeholders about what is being achieved. Specific indicators can be used to assess the extent of progress and achievement of the objectives of an individual organization, a single project or a group of organizations that are working together or pursuing a common objective." "Evaluation" means "While monitoring should be

the law.[233] The level of compliance depends on "the frequency and extent to which State performance is monitored—as well as the strength and sanctioning capacity of the monitoring body."[234] Anne T. Gallagher has pointed out the various virtues of "effective monitoring."[235] First, it can provide a comprehensive explanation of international laws that can strengthen its implementation.[236] Second, an effective monitoring mechanism can indicate and redress the hurdles of implementation of the laws.[237] And third, monitoring can address the conflict between international and local norms.[238] In addition, the sixteen member countries of the Pacific Islands Forum (PIF)[239] confirm that a regional human rights commission could suggest and encourage its member countries to implement the member countries' adhered internal and regional norms[240] through the regional mechanism commission's monitoring system.[241]

Even though ASEAN has occasionally reinforced its human rights bodies with data collection procedures, member countries still must provide that information. It seems that ASEAN member countries conflate the idea of "state

continuous, "evaluations occur periodically. In the case of projects they generally occur near the end of an intervention, or half way through (in order to see if any changes of plan are needed). The aim of an evaluation is to determine the relevance and fulfillment of objectives, efficiency (in terms of use of resources), effectiveness impact and sustainability. An evaluation should provide information that is credible and useful, enabling lessons to be learned so that these can be taken into account when consideration is given to continuing or modifying an activity. In some instances evaluation involves the definition of appropriate standards, the examination of performance against those standards and an assessment of actual and expected results.").

233 GALLAGHER, *supra* note 139, at 465.

234 Id.

235 Id.

236 Id.

237 Id.

238 Id.

239 Kathryn Hay, *A Pacific Human Rights Mechanism: Specific Challenges and Requirements*, 40 VICTORIA U. WELLINGTON L. REV. 195, 195 n.1 (2010) (intimating that "[t]he Pacific Islands Forum [PIF] member states include Australia, Cook Islands, Federated States of Micronesia, Fiji Islands, Kiribata, Nauru, New Zealand, Niue, Palau, Papua New Guinea, Republic of Marshall Islands, Samoa, Solomon Islands, Tonga, Tuvalu and Vanuatu").

240 Id. at 213.

241 Id.; DAVE PEEBLES, PACIFIC REGIONAL ORDER 2 (2005).

reporting"[242] with "confrontation" or "adjudication."[243] This is not the case, it simply means that a country will submit a report of its implementation of law to a human rights monitoring body[244] in order to strengthen the domestic legal framework and practice.[245] In return, the state reporting procedure helps the treaty body recognize the impact of "compliance" and facilitate the states' best options.[246]

Although the reporting system can help ASEAN member countries strengthen their exercises,[247] ASEAN member countries might assert to respect the non-interference principle against the reporting function because they do not favor the controlling methods of their performances.[248] Indeed, compared to ASEAN's reporting experience, recent evidence reveals that all ten ASEAN member countries have provided individual reports to international human rights body, namely CEDAW[249] even though they may have deferred submission of their report. Individual reports have also been submitted to the Human Rights Resource Centre at the University of Indonesia, so that they may examine the domestic rule of law in the ASEAN region. It is clear that by providing information for these reports ASEAN member countries do not consider reporting mechanisms invasions of their sovereignty or violations of their adherence to the principle of non-interference.[250]

---

242 Fekadeselassie F. Kidanemariam, Enforcement of Human Rights under Regional Mechanisms: a Comparative Analysis 33 (Jan. 1, 2006) (unpublished LL.M. thesis, Univ. of Georgia School of Law), *available at* http://digitalcommons.law.uga.edu/cgi/viewcontent.cgi?article=1079&context=stu_llm; *see also* MARK FREEMAN AND GIBRAN VAN ERT, INTERNATIONAL HUMAN RIGHTS LAW 386 (2004) (State reporting means the dialogue between a state and its adhered agreement body on the state's implementation of the agreement).

243 Kidanemariam, *supra* note 242, at 34; *see also* RHONA K.M. SMITH, INTERNATIONAL HUMAN RIGHTS 146 (2003).

244 Kidanemariam, *supra* note 242, at 33; *see also* FREEMAN & VAN ERT, *supra* note 242, at 386.

245 Kidanemariam, *supra* note 242, at 34; *see also* EVELYN A. ANKUMAH, THE AFRICAN COMMISSION ON HUMAN AND PEOPLES' RIGHTS: PRACTICE AND PROCEDURES 80 (1996).

246 Kidanemariam, *supra* note 242; *see also* ANKUMAH, *supra* note 245, at 80.

247 Jina Kim, *Development of Regional Human Rights Regime: Prospects for and Implications to Asia*, *in* THE SYLFF 2007 REGIONAL FORUM SELECTED PAPERS ON HUMAN RIGHTS AND CREATIVE LEADERSHIP 64 (Foreword by Yozo Yokota, 2009).

248 Id.; Khoo, *supra* note 63, at 70.

249 Convention on the Elimination of All Forms of Discrimination against Women, Ch. 4, Dec. 18, 1979, 1249 U.N.T.S. 13, *available at* http://www2.ohchr.org/english/law/cedaw.htm [hereinafter CEDAW].

250 RULE OF LAW FOR HUMAN RIGHTS IN THE ASEAN REGION: A BASE-LINE STUDY 13 (2011), *available at* hrrca.org/system/files/Rule_of_Law_for_Human_Rights_in_the

A related discussion is how ASEAN should respond to the Universal Periodic Reviews (UPR) mechanism, which requires member countries to submit reports and engage in a forum with the Human Rights Council on their commitment to human rights promotion and protection under the system of UPR every five years.[251] Although no ASEAN human rights body appears to call for member countries to submit their anti-human trafficking laws and measures to ensure their compliance with the requisite legal instruments, there are several reasons that ASEAN will encourage member countries to implement the UPR mechanism. First, even though the UPR embraces an "inter-governmental process," the U.N. Secretary-General articulated that the UPR or "peer review" that can evade the "confrontation and politicization and selectivity."[252] It is noted that the "non-confrontational and non-politicized manner"[253] reflects ASEAN's preferences in order to alleviate the political conflict mentioned in its legal instruments, namely the Treaty of Amity and Cooperation (TAC) and the ASEAN Charter.

Second, despite its key objectives to advance human rights circumstances and aid member countries in complying with their duties and accountabilities,[254] the UPR does not emphasize evaluation of these member countries' operations. It is critical to observe that even though ASEAN member countries cooperate with ASEAN in providing reports of their domestic laws and policies; these countries prefer recommendation rather than

_ASEAN_Region.pdf [hereinafter BASE-LINE STUDY] (enumerating that "our country researchers have also undertaken a textured and detaild qualitative analysis of the data they have gathered as evinced in their annexed individual country reports").

251 Robin Ramcharan, *ASEAN's Human Rights Commission: Policy Considerations for Enhancing Its Capacity to Protect Human Rights*, 3 UCLA HUMAN RIGHTS REV. 199, 221 (2010); Ivan Shearer & Naomi Hart, *The Engagement of Asia-Pacific States with the U.N. Human Rights Committee: Reporting and Individual Petitions*, *in* HUMAN RIGHTS IN THE ASIA-PACIFIC REGION: TOWARDS INSTITUTION BUILDING 17 (Hitoshi Nasu & Ben Saul eds., 2011) (explaining that the UN. Human Rights Council created the Universal Periodic Review (UPR) that "[t]his procedure surveys the observance of human rights in all U.N. member states, irrespective of their party status to particular treaty instruments, but does not replace the reporting obligations under those instrument").

252 Shigeki Sakamoto, *Challenges to a Human Rights Mechanism in the Asia-Pacific Region: the Experience of the Universal Periodic Review of the U.N. Human Rights Council*, *in* HUMAN RIGHTS IN THE ASIA-PACIFIC REGION: TOWARDS INSTITUTION BUILDING 53 (Hitoshi Nasu & Ben Saul eds., 2011); U.N. General Assembly, *In Larger Freedom: Towards Development, Security and Human Rights for All Report of the Secretary-General*, U.N. Doc. A/59/2005/Add.1 (May 23, 2005), *available at* http://www2.ohchr.org/english/bodies/hrcouncil/docs/gaA.59.2005.Add.1_En.pdf.

253 Sakamoto, *supra* note 252, at 53.

254 Id. at 51.

assessment by scoring their operational responses. The aforementioned ASEAN publications show that each report has not evaluated governments' performances by a grading score such as that used by the Human Rights Resource Centre of University of Indonesia in its report *Rule of Law for Human Rights in the ASEAN Region: A Base-line Study*.[255]

3.3.2 *The Lack of State or Individual Complaints Admission*

Even though the admission of a human rights body's complaints can help promote and protect human rights, ASEAN claims that its human rights bodies do not need such authority. ASEAN should acknowledge that an effective human rights body should encompass crucial authorities and personalities, including admission of an individual and an inter-state complaint,[256] an independent attribute, a provider of transparent information on its decisions, concerns, and recommendations). In addition, a regional human rights mechanism should be able to accept individual and interstate complaints as well as collaborate with other international human rights mechanisms to advance the human rights structure.[257] Therefore, if an ASEAN human rights body can obtain individual petitions, it may help diminish the high risk of human rights infringement and a prejudiced human rights body that only pays attention to what its government demands.[258]

It is obvious that the creation of AICHR and ACWC reflects a "bold" human rights approach of ASEAN.[259] However, both AICHR and ACWC serve as

255 BASE-LINE STUDY, *supra* note 250, at 13 (explaining that "We have captured the results of our base-line study in an ASEAN Rule of la Grid,...To be clear, this grid is not designed to reduce data into a single summary score to 'rank' country performance. In fact, the grid is merely a tabular representation of our primary findings in relation to the central principles identified...and ASEAN countries' reception of core international human rights and humanitarian law instruments").

256 Kidanemariam, *supra* note 242, at 24 (describing "inter-state complaint" that a government issues its complaint to oppose another government's human rights violation and calls for such government's accountabilities. Presently, many international entities consider inter-state complaint as "one of the means of human rights enforcement."); FREEMAN & VAN ERT, *supra* note 242, at 397; SMITH, *supra* note 243, at 147.

257 *A Regional Human Rights Mechanism for The Pacific?: Lessons Learnt from Developments in other Regions*, 3 HUM. RTS. MONITOR Q., no. 3, 2010, at 32.

258 *See* WOLFGANG BENEDEK ET AL., THE ROLE OF REGIONAL HUMAN RIGHTS MECHANISMS, EUROPEAN PARLIAMENT, EXPO/B/DROI/2009/25, 20 (Nov. 2010), *available at* http://www.europarl.europa.eu/committees/en/droi/studiesdownload.html?languageDocument=EN&file=33385.

259 Pietropaoli, *supra* note 178, at 165; AICHR TERMS OF REFERENCE, *supra* note 4; ACWC TERMS OF REFERENCE, *supra* note 4.

consultative bodies,[260] and their advisory role and non-enforceable advice hamper their protective responsibility.[261] These two human rights bodies have approached promotion more than it has protection.[262] For instance, AICHR disregards assurance of implementing human rights protection[263] because ASEAN aimed to assign AICHR to play a political mediating role for its member countries, not an "independent watchdog."[264] The Foreign Ministers of ASEAN allege that ASEAN initially aimed to create AICHR to raise awareness of human rights within the ASEAN member countries.[265]

Similarly, ACWC is required to create awareness of the women and children's rights, but it is silent on protection.[266] It is imperative to acknowledge that ASEAN has anticipated the collaboration between AICHR and ACWC in advancing the protection of human rights.[267] Not only does the ACWC have to support

260 AICHR TERMS OF REFERENCE, *supra* note 4; ACWC TERMS OF REFERENCE, *supra* note 4.

261 PETCHARAMESREE, *supra* note 209, at xix.

262 *ASEAN Body to Address Rights of Women and Children*, *supra* note 210; BENEDEK ET AL., *supra* note 258, at 20.

263 Martin Löffelholz & Danilo A. Arao, THE ASEAN GUIDE: A JOURNALIST'S HANDBOOK TO REGIONAL INTEGRATION IN SOUTHEAST ASIA 36 (2010); Wahyuningrum, *supra* note 210, at 7–8.

264 Termsak Chalermpalanupap, *ASEAN Is Working to Promote and Protect Human Rights*, THE NATION [THAILAND] (Dec. 18, 2008), http://www.nationmultimedia.com/2008/12/18/opinion/opinion_30091288.php; Termsak Chalermpalanupap, *ASEAN Charter Is a New Commitment to Rights*, THE NATION [THAILAND] (Dec. 19, 2008), http://www.nationmultimedia.com/2008/12/19/opinion/opinion_30091372.php; Leila Salaverria, *Toothless Rights Body Would Hurt ASEAN Group*, PHILIPPINE DAILY INQUIRER (June 30, 2009, 2:58 AM), http://newsinfo.inquirer.net/inquirerheadlines/nation/view/20090630-213089/Toothless-rights-body-would-hurt-ASEAN-group; LÖFFELHOLZ & ARAO, *supra* note 263, at 36; *ASEAN: The ASEAN Foreign Ministers' Meeting with High Level Panel on an ASEAN Human Rights Body (HLP)*, THAI PRESS REPORTS (Mar. 2, 2009), *available at* http://www.accessmylibrary.com/coms2/summary_0286-36872935_ITM; Tan Hsien-Li, *Persistent Engagement and Insistent Persuasion: The Role of the Working Group for an ASEAN Human Rights Mechanism in Institutionalizing Human Rights in the Region*, *in* HUMAN RIGHTS IN THE ASIA-PACIFIC REGION: TOWARDS INSTITUTION BUILDING 132–133 (Hitoshi Nasu & Ben Saul eds., 2011); Termsak Chalermpalanupap, *10 Facts about ASEAN Human Rights Cooperation*, http://www.asean.org/images/archive/HLP-OtherDoc-1.pdf (last visited Dec. 12, 2012) (responding to criticism criticism of "the AICHR's lack of teeth" from other scholars by saying that "ASEAN would not have come this far it its Member States want[ed] to bite one another with sharp teeth just to get things done their own way").

265 LÖFFELHOLZ & ARAO, *supra* note 263, at 36; *ASEAN: The ASEAN Foreign Ministers' Meeting with High Level Panel on an ASEAN Human Rights Body (HLP)*, *supra* note 264.

266 ACWC TERMS OF REFERENCE, *supra* note 4, at Art. 2. (defining its "purposes").

267 Cook & Bhalla, *supra* note 180, at 1.

AICHR to accomplish their goals, ACWC also needs to aid ASEAN member countries in improving the promotion and protection of the rights of women and children.[268] However, these two bodies have no authority to receive any petition of human trafficking case.[269]

Supporters feel that it is premature for ASEAN to make a serious commitment to the protection approach, especially the admission of the State complaints. At the outset, ASEAN created AICHR and ACWC to prioritize the promotion of human rights rather than protection. Both AICHR and the ACWC have endorsed a principle of "non-confrontational" to promote and protect human rights.[270] Also, the ASEAN Security-General Surin Pitsuwan has articulated that ASEAN member countries should not be "too ambitious" about the functions of its human rights body because they lack investigative and prosecutorial powers.[271] Despite ASEAN's conflict avoidance concept, ASEAN does not have to require ACTV to accept an interstate complaint because its member countries can raise their concerns in other ASEAN regional forums, namely the ARF.[272]

In order to compile information on the human trafficking situation in the region, ASEAN should consider providing for an individual complaint procedures in the proposed ACTV as a regional enforcement mechanism.[273] These petitions can broaden ASEAN's views and help member countries strengthen their national anti-human trafficking laws on preventing human trafficking, protecting trafficking victims, and prosecuting trafficking offenders.[274] These effective measures can also help mitigate the growth of human trafficking. In addition, ASEAN should reinforce the ACTV to engage the public and private sectors, especially regular anti-human trafficking forums, in order to advance regional and national anti-human trafficking laws and policies. This method

---

268 Id.

269 AICHR TERMS OF Reference, *supra* note 4, at Art. 4(3)-(6); ACWC TERMS OF REFERENCE, *supra* note 4, at Art. 5 (1)-(3); Ginbar, *supra* note 210, at 515–516; *Compromising – Even on Human Rights*, *supra* note 210; Wahyuningrum, *supra* note 210, at 7.

270 *See* AICHR TERMS OF REFERENCE, *supra* note 4, at Art. 2.4 and Art. 3.6.

271 Khoo, *supra* note 63, at 72.

272 Ramcharan, *supra* note 251, at 222.

273 Id.; *Asia*, *supra* note 210; DINAH L. SHELTON, REGIONAL PROTECTION OF HUMAN RIGHTS 1067 (2008).

274 Press Release. United Nations Office of the High Commissioner for Human Rights, Address by the U.N. High Commissioner for Human Rights on the 7th Official Meeting of the ASEAN Intergovernmental Commission on Human Rights (Nov. 28, 2011), *available at* http://bangkok.ohchr.org/news/press/address-high-commissioner-asean-inter governmental-commission-human-rights.aspx.

has the potential to prevent internal conflict among the ASEAN member countries.[275]

Conclusion

There are three main concerns that ASEAN should take into account to strengthen counter-human trafficking in its region. First, most of the ASEAN legal instruments and guidelines prioritize the trafficking of women and children more than trafficking in men. Even though many men in ASEAN member countries have experienced forced labour exploitation, they have not been properly represented or given fundamental assistance and legal protection[276] by the public or private sectors.

Second, ASEAN's anti-human trafficking function and structure shows that ASEAN should consider convening a regular counter-human trafficking and migration forum among its human rights bodies in the same agenda because of the interrelation between these two issues. To accomplish this goal, ASEAN should promote collaboration among human rights bodies through the ADTV, which should require regular meetings on counter-human trafficking in ADTV. The meeting can provide more opportunities to share information and cooperation leading to better norms against human trafficking because they can better understand the root causes of problem.

Third, while AICHR and ACWC are anticipated to help ASEAN member countries to raise awareness of the prevalence of human trafficking, their competences are restricted to provide protection for all trafficking victims because there are no crucial functions like monitoring and individual complaint systems.

ASEAN should establish the ADTV, which will be the regional common standards against human trafficking. The corresponding ACTV should be

275 Soren C. Prebensen, *Inter-State Complaints under Treaty Provisions-The Experience under the European Convention on Human Rights*, *in* INTERNATIONAL HUMAN RIGHTS MONITORING MECHANISMS: ESSAYS IN HONOUR OF JAKOB TH. MÖLLER 459 (Gudmundur Alfredsson et al., 2d Revised ed., 2009) (offerring that there are different comments on the virtues and shortcomings of an inter-state complaint system. For instance, Peter van Dijk (former judge of the Court) and G.J.H. van Hoof have criticized that "such applications have hardly been effective." Judge Pettiti of the Court inserts that "by lowering the level of protection afforded by the Convention institutions, State applications have had the unfortunate effect of 'normalising' the matters complained of").

276 Victoria E. Kalu, *Issues in Human Trafficking and Migrant Smuggling in the Context of Illegal Migration*, 1 INT'L LEGAL STUD. PROGRAM J. 27 (2009).

established to strengthen criminal justice responses to human trafficking. The next chapter examines the national anti-human trafficking laws and mechanisms of Cambodia, Thailand, and Vietnam as representatives of other ASEAN member countries to evaluate whether these three countries have created effective anti-human trafficking laws and have made progressive efforts to redress human trafficking in order to conclude that these three countries need to embrace the ADTV and ACTV because of their insufficient responses to human trafficking.

CHAPTER 4

Challenges of National Responses of ASEAN Member States to Human Trafficking

Case Studies of Cambodia, Thailand and Vietnam

Since trafficking in persons is a growing phenomenon in Cambodia, Thailand, and Vietnam,[1] the governments of these countries have collaborated with international and intergovernmental organizations to create various plans of action to tackle trafficking-in-persons.[2] However, these three governments have been incompetent in addressing this issue and diminishing the growth of human trafficking in their countries. Therefore, this chapter aims to demonstrate the shortcomings of their laws and practices to show that the impetus is on ASEAN to create the ASEAN Declaration on the Promotion and Protection of Trafficking Victims (ADTV) and the ASEAN Commission on the Promotion and Protection of Trafficking victims (ACTV) to assist and direct them the best practices of counter-human trafficking.

It is very important especially for these three countries because the sources of human trafficking in these countries are truly interconnected. Further, these countries have shown their adherence to international mechanisms, particularly the Protocol to Prevent, Suppress and Punish Trafficking in Persons, especially Women and Children (UN Palermo Protocol), that ASEAN has encouraged its member countries to implement these international agreements in order to make the common human rights standards (including anti-human trafficking) in its region.

The second section of this research discusses the legal commitments and practices against human trafficking in Cambodia, Thailand, and Vietnam based on the UN Palermo Protocol because the anti-human trafficking laws and actions in Cambodia, Thailand, and Vietnam present general anti-human trafficking strengths and weaknesses of other ASEAN member countries. It also explores the counter-human trafficking challenges in Cambodia, Thailand, and Vietnam can explain which measures ASEAN should address and emphasize in ADTV, and which role ASEAN should assign ACTV to play in order to assist these three countries redress human trafficking that will be discussed in Chapter 5.

It is argued that even though Cambodia, Thailand, and Vietnam have pledged to reinforce the application of these international instruments, they

1 *See* Annuska Derks, Combating Trafficking in South-East Asia: Review of Policy and Programme Response 5 (2000).

2 Id.

 | DOI 10.1163/9789004265189_005

have failed to demonstrate a true commitment to such agreements for fighting human trafficking that can cause the risk of vulnerability of people to human trafficking in these three countries. As a result, it is imperative that ASEAN creates its common anti-human trafficking standards after the ADTV, which provides the specific methods and strategies that these three countries and other ASEAN member countries urgently need to tackle human trafficking. Also, ASEAN should form ACTV to serve these three countries and other ASEAN member countries as a regional monitoring human rights body specializing in counter-human trafficking in order to guide them sufficient responses to human trafficking.

4.1 Background of Cambodia, Thailand, and Vietnam

This section contains two parts: a discussion of the origin of the human trafficking phenomenon and memberships in international law mechanisms against human trafficking by Cambodia, Thailand, and Vietnam. While the root causes of human trafficking in Cambodia, Thailand, and Vietnam exhibit the link among these three countries, their memberships of international agreements illustrate their common norms against human trafficking.

4.1.1 *Origin of Human Trafficking Phenomenon in Cambodia, Thailand, and Vietnam*

In an effort to demonstrate the root causes of this unique and problematic phenomenon, this section evaluates the factors contributing to human trafficking in these three countries. Cambodia and Thailand have become a source, transit point, and destination for trafficked men, women, and children who have been subjected to all forms of human trafficking, specifically forced labour and sex trafficking.[3] Like Cambodia and Thailand, Vietnam has been a source and destination of trafficking in persons.[4] Both internal and cross-border trafficking has taken place in and from these three countries.[5] The source of the human trafficking phenomenon in these three countries does not initiate solely from lack of education of the victims, but also from the lack job opportunities, economic boom, and war in Vietnam.

3 U.S. DEP'T OF STATE, TRAFFICKING IN PERSONS REPORT 2011 109, 351 (2011), *available at* http://www.state.gov/documents/organization/142979.pdf [hereinafter TIP REPORT 2011] (Reports of Cambodia and Thailand).

4 TIP REPORT 2011, *supra* note 3, at 383.

5 United Nations Inter-Agency Project on Human Trafficking (UNIAP), Strategic Information Response Network (SIREN) Human Trafficking Datasheets: Mekong Region 2, 17, 30–31,

a Lack of Job Opportunity

Lack of job opportunity tends to become a main cause of human trafficking and has caused such migration from countries such as Cambodia and Vietnam to Thailand. As mentioned above, Cambodia, Thailand, and Vietnam are a major source of human trafficking gin the ASEAN region.[6] The lack of job opportunity does not support the reason for people's migration in all three countries; however, this factor is the main cause of Cambodian and Vietnamese workers' migration.[7]

People in Cambodia live below the poverty line on less than $1.00 (U.S.) per day.[8] Many Cambodians cannot afford to provide their children with sufficient nutrition thus leading to an exorbitant rate of infant mortality in Cambodia.[9] In addition to poverty, malnutrition, and low education, the country has also sustained long periods of drought and flooding, which have driven Cambodian men, women, and children to seek other employment opportunities in other countries,[10] particularly Thailand.[11]

While the majority of Cambodian migrants are trafficked to Thailand, Vietnamese migrants are likewise trafficked to Taiwan.[12] Based on the statistical

---

(Sept. 2010), *available at* http://www.no-trafficking.org/reports_docs/siren/uniap_2010ht_datasheets.pdf [hereinafter SIREN HUMAN TRAFFICKING DATASHEETS: MEKONG REGION].

6 TIP REPORT 2011, *supra* note 3, at 109, 351, 383 (Reports of Cambodia and Thailand).

7 SIREN HUMAN TRAFFICKING DATASHEETS: MEKONG REGION, *supra* note 5, at 2; INTERNATIONAL COUNCIL ON SOCIAL WELFARE (ICSW), TRAFFICKING AND RELATED LABOUR EXPLOITATION IN ASEAN REGION 34–35 (Nov. 2007), *available at* http://www.icsw.org/doc/Trafficking%20Labour%20Exploitation%20in%20ASEAN%2007.pdf.

8 *See* ICSW, *supra* note 7, at 33; *see also Cambodia—Background*, UNITED NATIONS CHILDREN'S FUND (UNICEF), http://www.unicef.org/infobycountry/cambodia_2190.html (last updated Feb. 26, 2003); United Nations Inter-Agency Project on Human Trafficking (UNIAP), United Nations Inter-Agency Project on Human Trafficking (UNIAP), Strategic Information Response Network (SIREN) Human Trafficking Data Sheet: Cambodia 1 (Mar. 2008), *available at* http://www.no-trafficking.org/reports_docs/cambodia/datasheet_cambodia_march08.pdf [hereinafter HUMAN TRAFFICKING DATASHEET: CAMBODIA].

9 ICSW, *supra* note 7, at 33.

10 *See* id. at 34–35; *see also* INTERNATIONAL LABOUR OFFICE, THE MEKONG CHALLENGE—DESTINATION THAILAND: A CROSS-BORDER LABOUR MIGRATION SURVEY IN BANTEAY MEANCHEY PROVINCE, CAMBODIA viii (Jan. 3, 2005), *available at* http://www.ilo.org/asia/whatwedo/publications/WCMS_BK_PB_69_EN/lang—en/index.htm (page from the pdf file); HUMAN TRAFFICKING DATASHEET: CAMBODIA, *supra* note 8, at 1, n.6; SIREN HUMAN TRAFFICKING DATASHEETS: MEKONG REGION, *supra* note 5, at 30 (revealing that Cambodian migrants also seek employment in Vietnam).

11 SIREN HUMAN TRAFFICKING DATASHEETS: MEKONG REGION, *supra* note 5, at 21.

12 TIP REPORT 2011, *supra* note 3, at 383; LOUISE SHELLEY, HUMAN TRAFFICKING: A GLOBAL PERSPECTIVE 164 (2010).

record, trafficking has affected Vietnamese men, women, and children.[13] In fact, Vietnamese women and children have become more vulnerable to human trafficking trap than Vietnamese men because of gender discrimination, and women's lack of social and financial power.[14] There is more demand for women and children for sexual exploitation and forced labour in factories or as housemaids in Vietnam.[15] Even worse is that there is a growing demand for children and virgins to work in prostitution.[16] There have been many Vietnamese cases reporting this trafficking that a Taiwanese couple and seventy-three accomplices were charged with luring Vietnamese women to Taiwan, Malaysia, and Singapore for forced labour or brokered marriages.[17] Men tend to be subjected to forced labour in other industries such as fishing, agriculture, and construction.[18]

In addition, internal migration of Vietnamese people has been affected by the lack of employment opportunities in rural areas.[19] The Vietnamese Ministry of Justice reports that between 2005 and 2007 there was immensity in the number of women and children trafficked throughout the cities of Vietnam, there were: 29 cases in Hanoi;[20] 62 cases in Lao Cai;[21] and 54 cases in Quang Ninh.[22] Because of the high migration of rural populations, approximately

---

13 SIREN HUMAN TRAFFICKING DATASHEET: CAMBODIA, *supra* note 8, at 21; DANG NGUYEN ANH, FORCED MIGRATION IN VIETNAM: HISTORICAL AND CONTEMPORARY PERSPECTIVES 10 (2004).

14 SIREN HUMAN TRAFFICKING DATASHEET: CAMBODIA, *supra* note 8, at 21; ANH, *supra* note 13, at 10.

15 SHELLEY, *supra* note 12, at 164.

16 HUMAN TRAFFICKING DATASHEET: CAMBODIA, *supra* note 8, at 21; DANG NGUYEN ANH, A REVIEW OF LITERATURE AND INFORMATION ON THE CURRENT SITUATION OF HUMAN TRAFFICKING IN VIETNAM 31(2006).

17 SHELLEY, *supra* note 12, at 164; *Trafficking of Men Appears in Border Provinces*, HUMAN TRAFFICKING BLOG (Oct. 1, 2007), http://humantrafficking21.blogspot.com/2007/10/trafficking-of-men-appears-in-border.html; *Human Trafficking & Modern-day Slavery in the Early Years of the 21st Century—2000 to 2010* [Vietnam], GVNET, http://gvnet.com/humantrafficking/Vietnam.htm (last visited Mar. 5, 2013).

18 SHELLEY, *supra* note 12, at 164.

19 HUMAN TRAFFICKING DATASHEET: CAMBODIA, *supra* note 8, at 21; Thi Hoai Thu Nguyen et al., *Assessment on Urban Migration Policy* 89 (Parliamentary Committee for Social Affairs Research Paper 2005).

20 MINISTRY OF JUSTICE OF VIETNAM, (DRAFT) REPORT: SURVEY FINDINGS ON THE ENFORCEMENT OF LAWS AND REGULATIONS ON INVESTIGATION, PROSECUTION, AND TRIAL OF CRIMINALS IN WOMEN AND CHILDREN TRAFFICKING 3 (Report Draft Project 4-CT 130/CP, June 2008).

21 Id. at 4.

22 Id.

forty-five percent of the Vietnamese population will reside in cities by 2020.[23] Therefore, it is possible that there will have more human trafficking victims in Vietnam if the Vietnamese government lacks effective prevention measures to suppress all forms of human trafficking.

b Economic Boom in Thailand

Despite the fact that Cambodia, Thailand, and Vietnam are all developing countries, the economic boom in Thailand has made it more of a destination country and has attracted more foreign migrants seeking employment.[24] The economic boom began in the 1990s and has caused massive upheaval in the migration of foreign workers.[25] At that time, Thailand needed more migrant laborers to work in the factories and agricultural sectors.[26] Thailand recruited workers without enacting a migration law and many migrant workers from neighboring countries, including Cambodia and Laos, crossed the border to Thailand to work in these fields.[27] In 1996, the Thai government passed a resolution allowing for temporary work permits for migrant workers, including Cambodians and Laotians. These resolutions paved the way for foreign migrants to be employed in Thailand.[28] In 2004, the number of foreign migrants increased to 1.28.[29]

Based on *Strategic Information Response Network* (SIREN) report, migrant workers with no legal documentation, no Thai language skills, or no knowledge of Thai law were allowed to be exploited by perpetrators.[30] The UN Special Rapporteur found both sexual and labor exploitation in Thailand.[31] With

---

23 HUMAN TRAFFICKING DATASHEET: CAMBODIA, *supra* note 8, at 21; Nguyen, *supra* note 19, at 89.

24 SUSAN KNEEBONE & JULIE DEBELJAK, *Combating Transnational Crime in the Greater Mekong Subregion: the Cases of Laos and Cambodia, in* TRAFFICKING AND HUMAN RIGHTS: EUROPEAN AND ASIA-PACIFIC PERSPECTIVES 1, 134 (Leslie Holmes ed., 2010).

25 Id.

26 Id.

27 Id.; Louise Shelley, *International Trafficking: An Important Component of Transnational Crime, in* HUMAN SECURITY, TRANSNATIONAL CRIME AND HUMAN TRAFFICKING: ASIAN AND WESTERN PERSPECTIVES 141 (Shiro Okubo & Louise Shelly eds., 2011).

28 KNEEBONE & DEBELJAK, *supra* note 24, at 1, 134 (Leslie Holmes ed., 2010).

29 Id.

30 HUMAN TRAFFICKING DATASHEET: CAMBODIA, *supra* note 8, at 18.

31 Press Release, Office of the High Commissioner for Human Rights, Thailand Must Do More to Combat Human Trafficking Effectively and Protect the Rights of Migrant Workers Who are Increasingly Vulnerable to Forced and Exploitative Labor, Says Special

regard to labor exploitation, trafficking victims work in various private sectors, namely seafood processing, fishing, garment, and domestic work.[32]

The economic expansion in Thailand has attracted many migrant workers from Myanmar, Cambodia, and Lao PDR to serve in dangerous, difficult, and dirty ("3-D") work.[33] Lao PDR, Myanmar, and Cambodia are victimized in domestic servitude in Thailand.[34] Approximately 200,000 Cambodian and Myanmese men and boys have been victims on fishing boats in Thailand.[35] Regardless workers from Cambodia, Myanmar, and Laos PDR, mostly ethnic minorities have been vulnerable to human trafficking because of their undocumented statuses.[36] Men, women and children have been immensely trafficked in Thailand as a result of these immigration policies.[37] In addition, Thailand has been attractive to Cambodian men working in the fisheries and construction because they have the potential to earn, respectively, seven and two times the wages they could earn in Cambodia (Figure 3).[38]

Rapporteur on Trafficking in Persons, Especially Women and Children, Joy Ngozi Ezeilo (Aug. 19, 2011), http://www.ohchr.org/en/NewsEvents/Pages/DisplayNews.aspx?NewsID=11319&LangID=E (suggesting that Thailand should do more to combat human trafficking effectively and protect the rights of migrant workers who are increasingly vulnerable to forced and exploitative labor).

32 SIREN HUMAN TRAFFICKING DATASHEETS: MEKONG REGION, *supra* note 5, at 24.

33 WORLD VISION, GMS HUMAN TRAFFICKING: A CHANGING LANDSCAPE: MEKONG REGION 2, *available at* http://wvasiapacific.org/downloads/factsheets/regionaltraff.pdf (last visited Mar. 5, 2013) (stating that 25,000 Vietnamese women were coerced to marry in Korea between 2002 and 2007, and 24,600 in Taiwan between 2003 and 2005); SUZANA CRASSARD, COUNTRY PROFILE: CAMBODIA, at 2, *available at* http://www.iom.int/jahia/webdav/shared/shared/mainsite/activities/countries/docs/country_profile_cambodia.pdf (last visited Dec. 12, 2012).

34 WORLD VISION, *supra* note 33, at 2.

35 WORLD VISION, *supra* note 33, at 2.

36 *uniap Thailand*, UNITED NATIONS INTER-AGENCY PROJECT ON HUMAN TRAFFICKING (UNIAP), http://www.no-trafficking.org/thailand_who.html (last visited Mar. 1, 2013).

37 Kanchana Tangchonlatip & Kerry Richter, *Gender and Migration*, *in* THAILAND MIGRATION REPORT 2011: MIGRATION FOR DEVELOPMENT IN THAILAND: OVERVIEW AND TOOLS FOR POLICYMAKERS 113 (Jerrold W. Huguet & Aphichat Chamratrithirong eds., 2011), *available at* http://www.un.or.th/documents/TMR-2011.pdf.

38 H.E. Dr Ing Kantha Phavi, *Managing Return Migration when Entry or Stay is not Authorized*, *available at* http://www.iom.int/jahia/webdav/shared/shared/mainsite/microsites/IDM/workshops/managing_return_migration_042108/presentations_speeches/idm_pres_apr22.pdf (last visited Dec. 12, 2012).

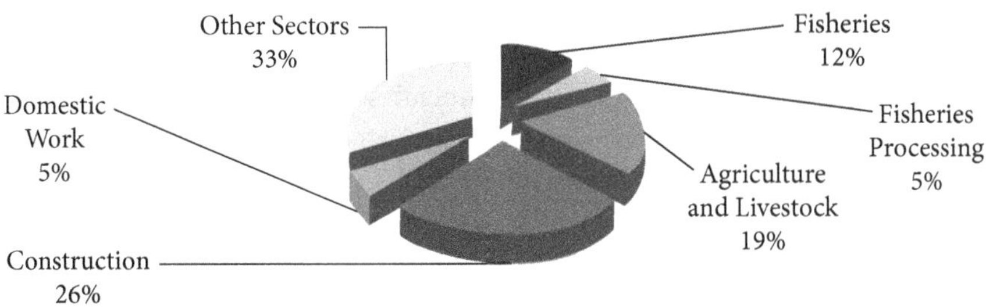

FIGURE 3 *Industries employing Cambodian migrants in the ASEAN region*

The United Nations Inter-Agency on Human Trafficking Project (UNIAP) reports that in 2009–2010, 124,902 Cambodian migrant workers received work permits from the Thai government.[39] These Cambodian migrant workers provided services in various business sectors: 14,988 in fisheries, 6020 in fisheries processing, 24,118 in agriculture and livestock, 32,483 in construction, 6591 in domestic work, and 40,702 in other sectors.[40] The research of the International Organization for Migration reported that almost 248,000 undocumented Cambodian migrant workers lived and worked in Thailand in 2008.[41] These undocumented migrant workers are vulnerable to human trafficking than documented workers.[42] Many undocumented migrant workers did not call for help from Thai authorities when they were trafficked[43] because they were afraid of being arrested or deported as a result of unlawful migration.[44]

A famous labor exploitation case called *Poipet* refers to the recession in Cambodia and neighboring countries, which forces many workers to migrate for employment purposes.[45] The International Labour Organization

39 UNIAP Human Trafficking Sentinel Surveillance, *supra* note 45, at 22.

40 Id.

41 Id.; *see also* BRUNO MALTONI, ANALYZING THE IMPACT OF REMITTANCES FROM CAMBODIAN MIGRANT WORKERS IN THAILAND ON LOCAL COMMUNITIES IN CAMBODIA (June 2010), *available at* http://www.iom.int/jahia/webdav/shared/shared/mainsite/published_docs/studies_and_reports/report_on_remittances.pdf.

42 SIREN HUMAN TRAFFICKING DATASHEETS: MEKONG REGION, *supra* note 5, at 25.

43 Id.

44 Id.

45 United Nations Inter-Agency Project on Human Trafficking, Human Trafficking Sentinel Surveillance: Poipet, Cambodia 2009–2010, 21 (2010), *available at* http://www.no-trafficking.org/reports_docs/2009-2010_UNIAP_sentinel_surveillance_Poipet.pdf [hereinafter UNIAP Human Trafficking Sentinel Surveillance].

(ILO)[46] and International Organization for Migration (IOM)[47] conducted research on the benefits of migrant labor.[48] It is clear from research that while the country of origin earns financial support of migrant workers as "remittances," the country of destination gains labor support of migrant workers because of insufficient laborers.[49] In effect, Cambodia earned income from Cambodian citizens, who were migrant workers in Thailand; while Thailand was able to recruit more migrant laborers to develop its economy. *Poipet* also includes non-human trafficking issues.[50] The non-human trafficking aspects of the case indicate no cheating or exploitation while the human trafficking aspects exemplify cheating, deception, and exploitation.[51]

c War in Vietnam

Historical evidence reveals that the war in Vietnam is another possible cause of the high density of trafficking in Vietnam and Thailand.[52] While in transit to Vietnam, both French and American military men traveled to Thailand for the purpose of patronizing prostitution,[53] thus causing the human trafficking of migrant workers. The support of the War by the Vietnamese and Thai governments only spurred the immense growth in trafficking.[54]

During the Vietnam War, demand for prostitutes and trafficked persons increased, causing an increase sexual exploitation in both Thailand and Vietnam.[55] The sex industry in Thailand also increased,[56] and migrating women and children were subjected to sexual exploitation because of the

---

46 Id. at 23; *see* AREE JAMPAKLAY & SIRINAN KITTISUKSATHIT, MIGRANT WORKER REMITTANCES: CAMBODIA, LAO PDR AND MYANMAR (2009), *available at* http://www.ilo.org/wcmsp5/groups/public/@asia/@ro-bangkok/documents/publication/wcms_111543.pdf, for more information.

47 UNIAP Human Trafficking Sentinel Surveillance, *supra* note 45, at 23; *see* MALTONI, *supra* note 41.

48 UNIAP Human Trafficking Sentinel Surveillance, *supra* note 45, at 23.

49 Id.; JAMPAKLAY & KITTISUKSATHIT, *supra* note 46; *see more information in* MALTONI, *supra* note 41.

50 UNIAP Human Trafficking Sentinel Surveillance, *supra* note 45, at 40, 44.

51 Id.

52 SHELLEY, *supra* note 12, at 160.

53 Id.

54 Diana Betz, Human Trafficking in Southeast Asia: Causes and Policy Implications 37–38 (June 2009) (unpublished M.A Thesis, Naval Postgraduate School), *available at* http://edocs.nps.edu/npspubs/scholarly/theses/2009/Jun/09Jun_Betz.pdf.

55 SHELLEY, *supra* note 12, at 160.

56 Betz, *supra* note 54, at 38.

growing number of demands for prostitutes.[57] The Thai government did not take serious action against the sex business.[58] Based on previous Thai law, prostitutes were required by the Thai government to register and pay taxes.[59] But since the 1980s, the Thai government no longer supports this sex industry.[60] Despite the cancellation of the tax law, critics have repeatedly commented that corruption of the Thai officers has caused human trafficking scourge by accepting money from trafficking perpetrators.[61] This criticism has generated suspicion[62] that past prostitution in Thailand compounded with the demand from the Vietnam War influenced the attitude of some Thai government authorities and has allowed for the toleration of trafficking in human-beings.

The cycle of human trafficking has continually haunted men, women, and children in Cambodia, Thailand, and Vietnam. This cycle was initiated by the lack of job opportunities for Cambodian migrants. Also, the economic boom expanded the need for foreign workers in Thailand. The war in Vietnam, as the possible starting point of the sex industry, turned migrating people into trafficking victims.

4.1.2 *Membership of Cambodia, Thailand, and Vietnam*

Apart from the interrelation of human trafficking sources, Cambodia, Thailand, and Vietnam has participated in the same international legal agreements and organizations enhancing counter-human trafficking that most ASEAN member countries have joined, except COMMIT Mekong.[63] For instance, Cambodia has

57 *See* RON O'GRADY, THE CHILD AND THE TOURIST 92–101 (1992); *see also* Betz, *supra* note 54, at 38.

58 Betz, *supra* note 54, at 37–38.

59 Id.

60 Id. at 38; U.S. DEP'T OF STATE, TRAFFICKING IN PERSONS REPORT 2008 243 (2008), *available at* http://www.state.gov/documents/organization/105501.pdf [hereinafter TIP REPORT 2008].

61 TIP REPORT 2011, *supra* note 3, at 353.

62 Betz, *supra* note 54, at 38; KAREN LEITER ET AL., NO STATUS: MIGRATION, TRAFFICKING, AND EXPLOITATION OF WOMEN IN THAILAND—HEALTH AND HIV/AIDS RISKS FOR BURMESE AND HILL TRIBE WOMEN AND GIRLS 27 (2004), *available at* https://s3.amazonaws.com/PHR_Reports/thailand-women-trafficking-2004.pdf; SHELLEY, *supra* note 12, at 162 (describing how the Vietnam War encouraged the growth of the human trafficking as a way for the people and the Thai government to earn extra income in Thailand and Vietnam).

63 *Where We Work*, UNITED NATIONS INTER-AGENCY PROJECT ON HUMAN TRAFFICKING (UNIAP), http://www.no-trafficking.org/where.html (last visited Mar. 1, 2013); SOUTH EAST ASIA NATIONAL HUMAN RIGHTS INSTITUTIONS FORUM (SEANF) PAPER ON MIGRANT WORKERS 14 (2010), *available at* http://www.aseannhriforum.org/attachments/059_SEANF_Paper_on_Migrant_Workers_-_Final.pdf [hereinafter SEANF

joined the Association of Southeast Asian Nations (ASEAN), the Coordinated Mekong Ministerial Initiative against Trafficking (COMMIT Mekong), the United Nations Convention against Transnational Organized Crime (UNTOC), and the UN Palermo Protocol and the government has enacted a national anti-human trafficking law to implement the UN Palermo Protocol (Table 1).[64]

Similar to Cambodia, Vietnam joined ASEAN, COMMIT Mekong, the UNTOC, and the UN Palermo Protocol.[65] The Vietnamese government has presently

TABLE 1 *Memberships in Cambodia, Thailand & Vietnam*

	Cambodia	Thailand	Vietnam
ASEAN	Yes	Yes	Yes
COMMIT Mekong	Yes	Yes	Yes
UNTOC	Yes	Signed	Yes
Palermo Protocol	Yes	Signed	Yes
CEDAW	Yes	Yes	Yes
CRC	Yes	Yes	Yes

PAPER ON MIGRANT WORKERS] (explaining that Cambodia, Lao PDR, Myanmar, Thailand, and Vietnam have joined the COMMIT Mekong that provides specific anti-human trafficking directions and action plans that apply to all trafficking victims).

64 *See ASEAN Member States*, ASSOCIATION OF SOUTHEAST ASEAN NATIONS (ASEAN), http://www.asean.org/asean/asean-member-states (last visited Dec. 12, 2012); *COMMIT: The Coordinated Mekong Ministerial Initiative Against Trafficking*, UNITED NATIONS INTER-AGENCY PROJECT ON HUMAN TRAFFICKING (UNIAP), http://www.no-trafficking.org/commit.html (last visited Mar. 1, 2013); United Nations Convention against Transnational Organized Crime and the Protocol Thereto, Nov. 15, 2000, 2225 U.N.T.S. 209, G.A. Res. 55/25, Annex I, U.N. Doc. A/RES/55/25, Ch. 18: Penal Matters, *available at* http://www.unodc.org/documents/treaties/UNTOC/Publications/TOC%20Convention/TOCebook-e.pdf [hereinafter UNTOC] at Chapter 18: Penal Matters; Protocol to Prevent, Suppress and Punish Trafficking in Persons, especially Women and Children, supplementing the United Nations Convention against Transnational Organized Crime, Nov. 15, 2000, 2237 U.N.T.S. 319, Annex II (entered into force Dec. 25, 2003), *available at* http://www.unodc.org/documents/treaties/UNTOC/Publications/TOC%20Convention/TOCebook-e.pdf [hereinafter the U.N. Palermo Protocol]; TIP REPORT 2011, *supra* note 3, at 110; U.S. DEP'T OF STATE, TRAFFICKING IN PERSONS REPORT 2012 106–108 (2012), *available at* http://www.state.gov/documents/organization/192594.pdf [hereinafter TIP REPORT 2012].

65 *ASEAN Member States*, *supra* note 64; *COMMIT*, *supra* note 64; UNCTOC, *supra* note 64, at Chapter 18: Penal Matters; U.N. Palermo Protocol, *supra* note 64.

applied its first national anti-human trafficking law in 2012.[66] Thailand has joined ASEAN and COMMIT Mekong, but its government has only signed the UNTOC and the UN Palermo Protocol.[67] While the Thai government has not ratified the UN Palermo Protocol, its government has enacted a national anti-human trafficking law.[68]

In addition, Cambodia, Thailand and Vietnam have ratified CEDAW and CRC[69] to provide the basic rights for women and children, including the prevention and protection from human exploitation. However, based on a review of these instruments, it is clear that Thailand has entered reservations to CEDAW and CRC that can constitute the risk of vulnerability of women and children to human trafficking because the governments have not provided the full rights of women and children.

As memberships of several international agreements as mentioned above, Cambodia, Thailand, and Vietnam should prevent human trafficking, protect trafficking victims, and prosecute trafficking perpetrators by enacting their domestic anti-human trafficking law and transforming their law into actions as stipulated in these international laws, specifically the UN Palermo Protocol that is the main anti-human trafficking instrument.

4.2 Arguments of Legal Commitments of Cambodia, Thailand, and Vietnam to Counter-Human Trafficking and National Anti-Human Trafficking Law of Cambodia, Thailand, and Vietnam

Since Cambodia, Thailand, and Vietnam have adhered to various international legal instruments, including the UN Palermo Protocol, in order to ensure the

---

66 *Counter-Trafficking Action in Vietnam*, UNITED NATIONS INTER-AGENCY PROJECT ON HUMAN TRAFFICKING (UNIAP), http://www.no-trafficking.org/vietnam_action.html (last visited Mar. 1, 2013).

67 *ASEAN Member States*, *supra* note 64; *COMMIT*, *supra* note 64; UNTOC, *supra* note 64, at Chapter 18: Penal Matters; U.N. Palermo Protocol, *supra* note 64, at 41, Annex II; TIP REPORT 2011, *supra* note 3, at 355.

68 *ASEAN Member States*, *supra* note 64; *COMMIT*, *supra* note 64; UNTOC, *supra* note 64; U.N. Palermo Protocol, *supra* note 64; TIP REPORT 2011, *supra* note 3, at 352; TIP REPORT 2012, *supra* note 64, at 338–342.

69 Convention on the Elimination of All Forms of Discrimination against Women, Ch. 4, Dec. 18, 1979, 1249 U.N.T.S. 13, *available at* http://www2.ohchr.org/english/law/cedaw.htm [hereinafter CEDAW]; Convention on the Rights of the Child, entered into force Sept. 2, 1990, 15 U.N.T.S. 3, http://www.ohchr.org/EN/ProfessionalInterest/Pages/CRC.aspx.

promotion and protection of the rights of trafficking victims, these three governments should attempt to tackle human trafficking according to these international norms even though the UN Palermo Protocol encompasses several deficiencies.

This section discusses the advantages and disadvantages of the UN Palermo Protocol in order to confirm that Cambodia, Thailand, and Vietnam should implement this agreement to fight human trafficking that ASEAN has urged its member countries to comply with. Also, this research examines the domestic anti-human trafficking law enacted in Cambodia, Thailand and Vietnam to see if they comport with the provisions of the UN Palermo Protocol. The reasons that these three countries cannot identify or tackle human trafficking through their national laws will be made clear by taking into account the key factors of their legislations, namely the definition of trafficking in persons, legal protection for trafficking victims, the right to a remedy for trafficking victims, and criminalization of traffickers. In order to ensure that these three countries can transform their domestic anti-human trafficking law into action, these laws must first be examined to determine if they contain adequate measures of preventing human trafficking, protecting trafficking victims, and prosecuting offenders.

4.2.1 *Discussion over the Protocol to Prevent, Suppress and Punish Trafficking in Persons, especially Women and Children*

Even though many critics have pointed out the ineffectiveness of the UN Palermo Protocol, it represents the minimum standards of indicators for primary anti-human trafficking efforts. The instance of its deficiency is that it requires the parties to protect "privacy and identity" of trafficking victims before, during, and after the proceedings;[70] however, this protection can be applied only "in appropriate cases and to the extent possible under its domestic law."[71] This reflects flexible phrase that cannot assure trafficking victims that they will fully be given protection of privacy and identity through confidential proceedings by the parties.

The UN Palermo Protocol persuades a member country to provide physical protection for trafficking victims while they stay in that country.[72] In the case

70 U.N. Palermo Protocol, *supra* note 64, at Art. 6.

71 U.N. Palermo Protocol, *supra* note 64, at Art. 6; Jan J.M. Van Dijk, *Empowering Victims of Organized Crime: on the Concurrence of the Palermo Convention with the un Declaration on Basic Principles of Justice for Victims*, 9 INT'L REV. OF VICTIMOLOGY 15, 19 (2002).

72 U.N. Palermo Protocol, *supra* note 64, at Art. 6; Van Dijk, *supra* note 71, at 15, 19.

of trafficking victims serving as witnesses in criminal legal proceedings, there is no requirement for the destination country to provide protection of trafficking victims and their family after repatriation.[73] Also, the UN Palermo Protocol disregards involvement of non-governmental organizations in providing assistance, particularly shelter, for trafficking victims.[74]

The UN Palermo Protocol has concentrated on effective prevention and collaboration in criminal justice responses,[75] but it has contained insufficient protection for victims.[76] For instance, the UN Palermo Protocol falls short on addressing the protection of trafficking victims and their family members while they reside in their countries of origin. Retaliation has been known to occur against trafficking victims and their families;[77] so many trafficking victims are hesitant to testify against perpetrators in court.[78] In addition, the UN Palermo Protocol is silent on compensation from government funds even though in practice, trafficking offenders have failed to compensate to victims,

---

73 U.N. Palermo Protocol, *supra* note 64, at Art. 6; Van Dijk, *supra* note 71, at 15, 19.

74 U.N. Palermo Protocol, *supra* note 64, at Art. 6; Van Dijk, *supra* note 71, at 15, 19.

75 *See* SUSAN KNEEBONE AND JULIE DEBELJAK, TRANSNATIONAL CRIME AND HUMAN RIGHTS: RESPONSES TO HUMAN TRAFFICKING IN THE GREATER MEKONG SUBREGION 179 (2012) (laying out provisions of prevention in the U.N. Palermo Protocol, *supra* note 64, Arts. 4, 10(2), 9 (1)-(5)).

76 *See* id. at 13.

77 U.N. Palermo Protocol, *supra* note 64, at Art. 6; Van Dijk, *supra* note 71, at 15, 20.

78 U.N. Palermo Protocol, *supra* note 64, at Art. 6; Van Dijk, *supra* note 71, at 15, 20, 26 (insisting that because trafficking victims are often required to testify against traffickers, origin and destination countries should collaborate to protect victims and their families before, during, and after criminal proceedings for both "humanitarian" purposes and counter-human trafficking efficiency); *Action against Trafficking in Human Beings for the Purpose of Sexual Exploitation: Recommendation No. R (2000) 11 of the Committee of Ministers and Explanatory Memorandum*, at 10, (May 19, 2000), *available at* http://www.coe.int/T/E/human_rights/trafficking/PDF_Rec%282000%2911_E.pdf (mentioning the Committee of Ministers of the Council of Europe has suggested that the parties (country of origin and destination) to the UN Palermo Protocol regulate methods and strategies containing sufficient prevention of the risk of trafficking victims' vulnerability to human trafficking and protection of trafficking victims and their families); ANGELIKA KARTUSCH, REFERENCE GUIDE FOR ANTI-TRAFFICKING LEGISLATIVE REVIEW WITH PARTICULAR EMPHASIS ON SOUTH EASTERN EUROPE 63–66 (Sept. 2001), *available at* http://www.osce.org/odihr/13986 (explaining that the United States and certain European countries, namely Germany, Belgium, The Netherlands, and Italy, have stimulated trafficking victims' legal proceeding collaboration by offering them residence during the trial proceedings in order to protect trafficking victims and/or their family members from reprisals and intimidation by traffickers).

especially in the case of great penalties.[79] As a result, many trafficking victims have struggled to get compensation from offenders because of the failure of enforcement.[80]

As the first international treaty to recognize the definition of "trafficking in persons," the UN Palermo Protocol contains "persuasive" contents.[81] The vital legal protection and assistance for trafficking victims set forth in the UN Palermo Protocol only urges its member parties to make efforts.[82] The member parties should create measures to serve trafficking victims,[83] including physical and psychological treatment.[84] Also, the UN Palermo Protocol indicates that its member parties should design measures to prevent human trafficking, namely awareness-raising.[85] Legal protections for trafficking victims should include temporary or permanent immigration relief, appropriate housing, information and legal counseling, medical assistance, employment, education and training opportunities, compensation, and voluntary repatriation.[86]

The UN Palermo Protocol provides specific guidelines for cooperation in the fight against human trafficking.[87] The UN Palermo Protocol articulates standardized measures of the development of state-to-state law enforcement authorities' communication and collaboration.[88] Also, the protocol promotes mutual legal assistance, assistance in extradition proceedings, and creation of mutual investigation teams at the bilateral and multilateral level.[89] More significantly, the UN Palermo Protocol enumerates measures

---

79 Van Dijk, *supra* note 71, at 15, 22; Jo Goodey, *Compensating Victims of Violent Crime in the European Union: The Case for State Restitution, in* REPARATION AND VICTIM-FOCUSSED SOCIAL WORK 16–33 (Brian Williams, ed., 2002).

80 Van Dijk, *supra* note 71, at 15, 22.

81 Janie Chuang, *Beyond a Snapshot: Preventing Human Trafficking in the Global Economy*, 13 IND. J. GLOBAL LEGAL STUD. 137, 148 (2006) (mentioning U.N. Palermo Protocol, *supra* note 64, art. 6–8).

82 U.N. Palermo Protocol, *supra* note 64, at Art. 6–8.

83 Chuang, *supra* note 81, at 137, 148.

84 Id.

85 Chuang, Id. at 81, 148–149 (discussing U.N. Palermo Protocol, *supra* note 64, art. 9).

86 U.N. Palermo Protocol, *supra* note 64, at art. 6–8.

87 Chuang, *supra* note 81, at 137, 148 (discussing Articles 16, 18, 19, 27, 28 of the United Nations Convention against Transnational Organized Crime, *supra* note 64).

88 U.N. Palermo Protocol, *supra* note 64, at Art. 10 & 11.

89 U.N. Palermo Protocol, *supra* note 64, at Art. 8 & 9; Chuang, *supra* note 81, at 137, 148 (discussing Articles 16, 18, 19, 27, 28 of the United Nations Convention against Transnational Organized Crime, *supra* note 64).

on the prevention of trafficking in persons and the protection of trafficking victims.[90]

Although the UN Palermo Protocol emphasizes enforcement against human traffickers, it provides insufficient protection and assistance for trafficking victims.[91] Because the protocol stipulates restricted protection measures, trafficking victims may be afraid to serve as witnesses in human trafficking cases.[92] Without the cooperation of trafficking victims in investigations and prosecutions, the parties cannot accomplish the UN Palermo Protocol's goal of arresting and convicting perpetrators.[93]

It is critical to note that many countries that have adhered to the protocol have modified their laws to comply with it[94] while many ASEAN member countries have ratified this protocol.[95] The protocol has driven sixty-three percent of 155 ratified countries to adopt anti-human trafficking laws. Also, over half of the UN Palermo Protocol member countries have initiated plans of action against human trafficking.[96]

Even if the UN Palermo Protocol's several provisions do not require its parties' strict obligations,[97] the protocol has mobilized its parties, non-parties, and other anti-human trafficking agencies to take action and express their low tolerance policy of human trafficking by enacting or modifying domestic laws.[98] For instance, the United States created the Trafficking Victims Protection Act (TVPA) to convict traffickers and to protect trafficking victims.[99] The United Arab Emirates (UAE) has created a legal framework to deter all types of human

---

90 U.N. Palermo Protocol, *supra* note 64, at Art. 9–13; Chuang, *supra* note 81, at 137, 148 (2006) (mentioning the U.N. Palermo Protocol, Art. 6–8).

91 Carol S. Brusca, *Palermo Protocol: The First Ten Years after Adoption*, 2 GLOBAL SECURITY STUD., no. 3, 2011, at 8, 15, *available at* http://globalsecuritystudies.com/Brusca%20Palermo%20Final%20One.pdf; Ryszard Piotrowicz, *The unhcr's Guidelines on Human Trafficking*, 20 INT'L J. REFUGEE L. 242, 244–245 (2008).

92 Brusca, *supra* note 91, at 15.

93 Id.

94 Matthew Berger, *Rights: Govts Pledge to Renew Fight against Human Trafficking*, INTER PRESS SERVICE (May 14, 2009), http://www.ipsnews.net/2009/05/rights-few-govts-serious-about-human-trafficking-un-finds/.

95 U.N. Palermo Protocol, *supra* note 64, at Ch. 18: Penal Matters.

96 JAY S. ALBANESE, TRANSNATIONAL CRIME AND THE 21ST CENTURY: CRIMINAL ENTERPRISE, CORRUPTION, AND OPPORTUNITY 62 (2011).

97 Chuang, *supra* note 81, at 137, 148 (discussing to U.N. Palermo Protocol, *supra* note 64, Art. 6–8).

98 Brusca, *supra* note 91, at 16.

99 Id.

trafficking.[100] The Coalition to Fight against Exploitation, a non-governmental organization in Thailand, has campaigned for the punishment of human trafficking perpetrators and demands (namely customers of human trafficking).[101] Europe seems to have the largest number of investigations and criminal proceedings for human trafficking that involves sexual exploitation.[102]

It is clear that even though this Protocol has demonstrated several deficiencies in its anti-human trafficking mechanisms, there is much more space for the world community, especially ASEAN member countries such as Cambodia, Thailand, and Vietnam to strengthen their domestic laws on preventing human trafficking, protecting trafficking victims, and prosecuting perpetrators to meet the standards of the UN Palermo Protocol.[103] The UN Palermo Protocol directs all member countries, including Cambodia, Thailand, and Vietnam to establish basic anti-human trafficking procedures.[104] As a result, it is necessary that all of the countries studied here, Cambodia, Thailand, and Vietnam ensure that trafficking victims can enjoy their human rights by providing primary protection for victims according to pivotal provisions of the UN Palermo Protocol.

4.2.2 *National Anti-Human Trafficking Law of Cambodia, Thailand, and Vietnam*

All should transform their counter-human trafficking laws, measures, and strategies into actions to ensure the rights of trafficking victims and implement international legal norms,[105] particularly through instruments adhered to by governments. This section will examine whether Cambodia, Thailand, and Vietnam have made a serious commitment to battle human trafficking in compliance with the UN Palermo Protocol, their core instrument against trafficking in persons. It is clear that the anti-human trafficking law of Cambodia

100 Id.; Jessica Caplin, *Mirage in the Desert Oasis: Forced Labor in Dubai and the United Arab Emirates*, HARVARD INT'L REV., Mar. 21, 2009, http://hir.harvard.edu/rethinking-finance/mirage-in-the-desert-oasis.

101 Brusca, *supra* note 91, at 16.

102 *See* id.; *see also* Nathalie Vandystadt, *Justice and Home Affairs Commission to Revise EU Action Against Human Trafficking*, EUROPOLITICS (Oct. 17, 2008), *available at* http://www.europolitics.info/commission-to-revise-eu-action-against-human-trafficking-artr151215-10.html (mentioning that there were 128 cases in Austria, 353 cases in Germany, 214 cases in Italy, 65 cases in Portugal, and 65 cases in the United Kingdom).

103 ALBANESE, *supra* note 96, at 62.

104 Brusca, *supra* note 91, at 18.

105 *Human Trafficking: A Rights-Based Approach*, UN OHCHR (Dec. 19, 2011), http://www.ohchr.org/EN/NewsEvents/Pages/HumanTrafficking.aspx.

and Vietnam are not in full compliance with the original protection measures set forth in the UN Palermo Protocol. Even though Thailand has not ratified the UN Palermo Protocol, its government should ensure that all trafficking victims can obtain proper protection from government authorities.

a Definition of "Trafficking in Persons"

The definition of "Trafficking in Persons" includes three elements: action, means, and purpose.[106] In order to be effective, the anti-human trafficking legislation in Cambodia, Thailand and Vietnam must redress acts that contain all of these elements. Although Cambodia and Vietnam have ratified the UN Palermo Protocol, their domestic anti-trafficking law is indeed limited. While Thailand has not ratified the Protocol, its anti-human trafficking law is in compliance with it. The Cambodian and Vietnamese governments should modify their anti-human trafficking laws to adjust their qualification of trafficking in persons to cover *all* forms of human trafficking and protect *all* trafficking victims.

i *Human Trafficking Definition in Cambodia*

In February 2008, the Cambodian government enacted the *Law on the Suppression of Human Trafficking and Sexual Exploitation* (anti-human trafficking law of Cambodia).[107] The anti-human trafficking law authorizes government authorities to prosecute traffickers.[108] Even though the law itself contains many laws, this prosecutorial power is, in fact, a sign of progress in

106 U.N. Palermo Protocol, *supra* note 64, at art. 3 (defining "Action" as "the recruitment, transportation, transfer, harbouring or receipt of persons." "Means" implies "the threat or use of force or other forms of coercion, abduction, fraud or deception, the abuse of a position of vulnerability, or the giving or receiving of payments or benefits to achieve the consent of a person having control over another person." "Purpose" indicates "exploitation at a minimum—the exploitation of the prostitution of others or other forms of sexual exploitation, forced labour or services, slavery or practices similar to slavery, [or] the removal of organs").

107 Law on Suppression of Human Trafficking and Sexual Exploitation, NS/RKM/0208/005 (Cambodia) (2008), *available at* http://www.no-trafficking.org/content/Laws_Agreement/cambodia_tip_2008.pdf (last visited Dec. 12, 2012); UNITED STATES AGENCY FOR INTERNATIONAL DEVELOPMENT (UNAID), ANTI-TRAFFICKING IN PERSONS PROGRAMS IN ASIA: A SYNTHESIS 39 (2009), http://transition.usa*id*.gov/our_work/cross-cutting_programs/wid/pubs/Asia_Synthesis_Anti_Trafficking_508.pdf.

108 Law on Suppression of Human Trafficking and Sexual Exploitation (Cambodia), *supra* note 107; UNITED STATES AGENCY FOR INTERNATIONAL DEVELOPMENT (UNAID), *supra* note 107, at 39.

Cambodia.[109] The anti-human trafficking law of Cambodia defines "trafficking in persons" as:[110] the act of selling, buying or exchanging a person,[111] unlawful removal,[112] unlawful recruitment for exploitation,[113] and any form of exploitation,[114] thus admirably recognizing all forms of trafficking in persons.[115]

Although the anti-human trafficking law of Cambodia combines various forms of offences, the law does not address the condition of proof of three elements (action, means, and purpose) of trafficking in persons.[116] The vagueness of the law creates confusion when applied to trafficking cases.[117] The case relevant to this concern involves "the consensual and non-exploitative adoption of a child."[118] For instance, parents might voluntarily sell their child to a trafficker for adoption by a foreign couple. In this case, this law cannot be applied to prosecute the offender because the law does not address the key requirement to prove the three elements (action, means and purpose) of the trafficking crime.[119]

ii *Human Trafficking Definition in Thailand*

Thailand largely provides the definition of "trafficking in persons" in compliance with the UN Palermo Protocol. For instance, Section 6 of the ANTI-TRAFFICKING IN PERSONS ACT B.E. 2551 (2008)[120] (anti-human trafficking law of Thailand) presents the meaning of trafficking crimes incorporated from

---

109 Betz, *supra* note 54, at 50.

110 United Nations Inter-Agency Project on Human Trafficking (UNIAP), Human Trafficking Laws: Legal Provisions for Victims 10–11 (n.d.), *available at* http://www.no-trafficking.org/reports_docs/legal_prov_vics.pdf (last visited March 5, 2013).

111 Law on Suppression of Human Trafficking and Sexual Exploitation (Cambodia), *supra* note 107, art. 13.

112 Id. art. 8.

113 Id. art. 12.

114 Id. art. 10.

115 Betz, *supra* note 54, at 50.

116 FIONA DAVID ET AL., PROGRESS REPORT ON CRIMINAL JUSTICE RESPONSES TO TRAFFICKING IN PERSONS IN ASEAN REGION 14 (2011), *available at* http://www.artipproject.org/progress-report/Progress%20Report_Criminal%20Justice%20Responses%20to%20TIP%20in%20the%20ASEAN%20Region_2011.pdf.

117 Id.

118 Id.

119 Id.

120 ANTI-TRAFFICKING IN PERSONS ACT B.E 2551 § 4 (2008) (Thailand), *available at* http://www.no-trafficking.org/content/Laws_Agreement/laws_agreement_pdf/trafficking_in_persons_act_b.e%202551%20%28eng.%29.pdf.

the UN Palermo Protocol.[121] For that reason, the offense delineated in Section 6 composes three factors of the crime of trafficking (action, means, and purpose) as set forth in the UN Palermo Protocol.[122] In the case of adult victims, the government authorities will consider those three elements.[123] If child trafficking takes place in Thailand, the authorities take into account only action and purpose.[124] Also, this law acknowledges men, women, and children as victims.[125] Therefore, no victim should be underserved in Thailand.

iii *Human Trafficking Definition in Vietnam*

While Vietnam has not ratified the UN Palermo Protocol,[126] the President and National Assembly adopted the *Law on Prevention and Suppression against Human Trafficking* (anti-human trafficking law of Vietnam) entered into force January, 2012.[127] Article 3 of this law prescribes that "prohibited acts" as set forth in Article 119 (trafficking in women) and Article 120 (trading in, fraudulently exchanging or appropriating children) of the Vietnamese Penal Code mean "trafficking in persons."[128] Also, the anti-human trafficking law of

---

121 David et al., *supra* note 116, at 12; United Nations Inter-Agency Project on Human Trafficking (UNIAP), Strategic Information Response Network (SIREN) Human Trafficking Data Sheet: Thailand (Oct., 2008), *available at* http://www.no-trafficking.org/reports_docs/thailand/datasheet_thailand_oct2008.pdf.

122 David et al., *supra* note 116, at 12.

123 Id.

124 Id.

125 United Nations Inter-Agency Project on Human Trafficking (UNIAP), *supra* note 121.

126 U.N. Palermo Protocol, *supra* note 64, at Art. 6–8.

127 *Counter-Trafficking Action in Vietnam*, *supra* note 66; David et al., *supra* note 116, at 13.

128 Law on Prevention, Suppression against Human Trafficking (unofficial translation 2011) (Vietnam), *available at* http://www.artipproject.org/artip-tip-cjs/laws-policies/national/Vietnam/Vietnam%20Anti-trafficking%20in%20Persons%20Law%20Mar%20 2011%20final%20ENG.pdf (last visited Dec. 12, 2012) at art. 3(1) (stipulating that "The trafficking in persons as stipulated in Article 119 and Article 120 of the Penal Code." Article 119 of the Vietnamese Penal Code penalizes the offenders for committing the crime of trafficking in women in one of the following circumstances "a) Trading in women for the purpose of prostitution; b) In an organized manner; c) Being of professional characters; d) For the purpose of sending them overseas; e) Trafficking in more than one person; f) Trafficking more than once." Article 120 of the Vietnamese Penal Code imposes the offence of trafficking in children as follows "a) In an organized manner; b) Being of professional character; c) For despicable motivation; d) Trading in, fraudulently exchanging or appropriating more than one child; e) For the purpose of sending them abroad; f) For use for inhumane purposes; g) For use for prostitution purposes; h) Dangerous recidivism; i) Causing serious consequences.")

Vietnam specifies other prohibited acts,[129] which encompass the misconduct of traffickers, government officers, non-governmental organization, and persons engaged in human trafficking. Although the definitions of "sexual exploitation"[130] and "forced labour"[131] embrace the "means" element of coercion, this legislation does not address the "means" element (including force, coercion or other means) for other "inhuman purposes."[132]

b Legal Protection for Trafficking Victims[133]

The UN Palermo Protocol requires State Parties to provide legal protection for trafficking victims.[134] The privacy and identity of trafficking victims is

---

129 Law on Prevention, Suppression against Human Trafficking (unofficial translation 2011) (Vietnam), *supra* note 128, at arts. 3(5)-(1) (including the following acts: "conducting brokerage to help other persons commit any of the acts enumerated in paragraph 1, 2 and 3; Revenge or the threat of revenge of victims, witnesses, denunciators, their relatives or persons who deter the acts stipulated in this article; Misuse of the prevention, suppression against human trafficking for illegally obtaining profits or committing illegal acts; Obstruction against denunciation, notification and handling of the acts stipulated in this article; Differentiation or discrimination against victims; Disclosure of the information of victims without their consent, or their lawful representatives; Assuming false position as victims; Other acts of violation of the provision in this law.")

130 Law on Prevention, Suppression against Human Trafficking (unofficial translation 2011) (Vietnam), *supra* note 128, at art. 2.

131 Id.

132 David et al., *supra* note 116, at 13.

133 Legal protections for trafficking victims include protection of privacy and confidentiality, appropriate housing, counseling and legal rights, medical treatment, employment, education, and training, age, gender, and special needs of victims, protection and physical safety, right to remain temporarily or permanently, repatriation, non-prosecution of victims, and right to a remedy.

134 Article 6 (1)(3) (a)(b)(c)(d), (4), (15), Article 7, Article 8 (1)(2)(3)(4), (Part II: Protection of Victims of Trafficking in Persons) of the UN Palermo Protocol (providing that State Parties protect the privacy and identity of trafficking victims and maintain confidentiality in their legal proceedings. It also encourages State Parties to implement measures that provide for the physical, psychological and social recovery of victims. This includes appropriate housing, counseling about legal rights and the proceedings, medical treatment, as well as employment, education and training opportunities. The UN Palermo Protocol encourages State Parties to consider the characteristics of victims, namely their age, gender and special needs, particularly when providing housing, education and care to child victims. To ensure the physical safety of trafficking victims, the Protocol encourages State Parties to provide for the confidentiality, privacy and protection of witnesses. The protocol requires the country of destination to allow trafficking victims to remain

protected and victims are ensured confidentiality in legal proceedings. State Parties are also encouraged to implement measures providing for physical, psychological and social recovery of victims. This includes appropriate housing, counseling about legal rights and the proceedings, medical treatment, as well as employment, education and training opportunities. The UN Palermo Protocol encourages State Parties to consider the characteristics of victims, namely their age, gender and special needs, particularly when providing housing, education and care to child victims. To ensure the physical safety of trafficking victims, the Protocol encourages State Parties to provide for the confidentiality, privacy and protection of witnesses. Destination countries are required to adopt proper legislation or other measures to allow trafficking victims to remain temporarily or permanently in their territories until they can be repatriated. Regarding repatriation of trafficking victims, the State Party of nationality or permanent residence of trafficked victim is responsible for his or her return without undue or unreasonable delay. Trafficking victims should

---

temporarily or permanently in their territory by adopting proper legislation or measures. In the situation of repatriation of trafficking victims, the State Party of nationality or permanent residence of trafficked victim is responsible for his or her return without undue or unreasonable delay. The State Party should also permit trafficking victims to voluntarily return to their country of origin by considering their safety and the status of any relevant legal proceedings. The State Party, whether it is an original country or permanent residence of the trafficked victim, shall verify "without undue or unreasonable delay" the nationality or right to permanent residence of the victim. Also, this State Party shall facilitate the provision of travel documents or other authorization for the trafficked victim so that he or she can travel to or re-enter their motherland.); ANNE T. GALLAGHER, THE INTERNATIONAL LAW OF HUMAN TRAFFICKING 366 (2010) (commenting that the UN Palermo Protocol requires State parties to redress causes of trafficking, to reinforce trafficking victims' reintegration, and identify potential risks of re-victimization.); United Nations Office on Drugs and Crime (UNODC), Model Law on Trafficking in Persons (2009), Art. 28, para. 3, *available at* http://www.unodc.org/documents/human-trafficking/UNODC_Model_Law_on_Trafficking_in_Persons.pdf (viewing that victims should be compensated for physical and psychological injury, and others.); Special Rapporteur on Trafficking in Persons, *Report of the Special Rapporteur on Trafficking in Persons, Especially Women and Children, Joy Ngozi Ezeilo*, 17th Sess., Agenda Item 3, U.N. Doc A/HRC/17/35 (April 13, 2011) (by Joy Ngozi Ezeilo), para. 16, FN. 9, p. 5, *available at* http://www2.ohchr.org/english/bodies/hrcouncil/docs/17session/A-HRC-17-35.pdf (for example, the United Nations Global Plan of Action to Combat Trafficking in Persons (General Assembly resolution 64/293, annex), para. 3; U.N. Human Rights Council, *Resolution 11/3: Trafficking in Persons, especially Women and Children*, para. 1, p. 2, *available at* http://www.un.org/womenwatch/daw/vaw/humanrights/A_HRC_RES_11_3.pdf (alleging that governments should create legal procedures to facilitate trafficking victims' access to remedies.)

also be permitted to voluntarily return to their countries of origin only after their safety has been secured and the status of any relevant legal proceedings has been taken into consideration. The State Party, whether it is an original country or permanent residence of the trafficked victim, shall verify "without undue or unreasonable delay" the nationality or right to permanent residence of the victim. Also, this State Party shall facilitate the provision of travel documents or other authorization for the trafficked victim so that he or she can travel to or re-enter their motherland.[135]

This part will explore whether the anti-human trafficking laws of Cambodia, Thailand, and Vietnam do in fact provide measures for trafficking victims' primary protection by illustrating the advantages and disadvantages of these three countries' laws. The anti-human trafficking law of Cambodia fails to provide proper protection for trafficking victims such as physical and psychological treatment for trafficking victims. It is noted that the anti-human trafficking laws of Thailand and Vietnam have presented protection measures better than the Cambodian law, although both contain inadequate provisions.

i *Legal Protection for Trafficking Victims in Cambodia*

Article 49 of the anti-human trafficking law of Cambodia provides for trafficking victims' confidentiality[136] by prohibiting the media from publishing, broadcasting or otherwise circulating any data pertaining to the personal

---

135 U.N. Palermo Protocol, *supra* note 64, at arts. 6(1), 6(3)(a)-(d), 6(4), 6(15), 7, 8(1)-(4); GALLAGHER, *supra* note 134, at 366 (commenting that the UN Palermo Protocol requires State parties to redress causes of trafficking, to reinforce trafficking victims' reintegration, and identify potential risks of re-victimization); United Nations Office on Drugs and Crime (UNODC), Model Law on Trafficking in Persons art. 28(3) (2009), *available at* http://www.unodc.org/documents/human-trafficking/UNODC_Model_Law_on_Trafficking_in_Persons.pdf (viewing that victims should be compensated for physical and psychological injury, and others); Special Rapporteur on Trafficking in Persons, *Report of the Special Rapporteur on Trafficking in Persons, Especially Women and Children, Joy Ngozi Ezeilo*, 17th Sess., Agenda Item 3, U.N. Doc A/HRC/17/35 (April 13, 2011) (by Joy Ngozi Ezeilo), ¶16, 5 n.9, *available at* http://www2.ohchr.org/english/bodies/hrcouncil/docs/17session/A-HRC-17-35.pdf; United Nations Global Plan of Action to Combat Trafficking in Persons, G.A. Res. 64/293, annex ¶ 3 (Aug. 12, 2010), *available at* http://daccess-dds-ny.un.org/doc/UNDOC/GEN/N09/479/41/PDF/N0947941.pdf?OpenElement; Human Rights Council Res. 11/3, Trafficking in Persons, Especially Women and Children, ¶ 1, 27th meeting, June 17, 2009, *available at* http://www.un.org/womenwatch/daw/vaw/humanrights/A_HRC_RES_11_3.pdf (encouraging governments to create legal procedures to facilitate trafficking victims' access to remedies).

136 Law on Suppression of Human Trafficking and Sexual Exploitation (Cambodia), *supra* note 107, art. 49; UNITED NATIONS INTER-AGENCY PROJECT ON HUMAN TRAFFICKING (UNIAP), *supra* note 110, at 26.

information and identity of trafficking victims.[137] Further, the anti-human trafficking law of Cambodia provides for the right of access to remedies such as compensation or restitution for trafficking victims under Article 46 of Chapter 7 (Civil Remedy).[138] Article 46 commands any perpetrator to compensation.[139] Article 47 encourages trafficking victims to call for their damage caused by trafficking perpetrator.[140] This article provides trafficking victims the right to assets that the government forfeits.[141] Trafficking victims have the right to receive compensation, including the seized assets of trafficking offenders, through the government authorities' support by issuing the confiscation of trafficking offenders' property.

However, the anti-human trafficking law of Cambodia does not provide for confidentiality in legal proceedings.[142] The anti-human trafficking law of Cambodia has neglected to stipulate victim protection provisions such as:

- appropriate housing; counseling and information on victims' legal rights;[143]
- medical, psychological and material assistance for victims;
- employment, education and training for victims;
- consideration of the age, gender and special needs of victims of trafficking;
- protection of physical safety for victims of trafficking;

137 Law on Suppression of Human Trafficking and Sexual Exploitation (Cambodia), *supra* note 107, art. 49; United Nations Inter-Agency Project on Human Trafficking (UNIAP), *supra* note 110, at 26.

138 Law on Suppression of Human Trafficking and Sexual Exploitation (Cambodia), *supra* note 107, art. 46; United Nations Inter-Agency Project on Human Trafficking (UNIAP), *supra* note 110, at 50; David et al., *supra* note 116, at 25.

139 Law on Suppression of Human Trafficking and Sexual Exploitation (Cambodia), *supra* note 107, art. 46 (defining a perpetrator as a person, who gains "enrichment without legal cause" and *acknowledges* that the enrichment was attained from the commission of unlawful exploitation, and making such perpetrators "liable for restitution of the whole unjust enrichment" with accrued interest); United Nations Inter-Agency Project on Human Trafficking (UNIAP), *supra* note 110, at 50; David et al., *supra* note 116, at 25.

140 Law on Suppression of Human Trafficking and Sexual Exploitation (Cambodia), *supra* note 107, art. 46 (intimating that this article urges trafficking victims "to claim for damages in addition to the restitution of such unjust enrichment," including a claim for unpaid wages); David et al., *supra* note 116, at 25.

141 Law on Suppression of Human Trafficking and Sexual Exploitation (Cambodia), *supra* note 107, art. 47; David et al., *supra* note 116, at 25.

142 United Nations Inter-Agency Project on Human Trafficking (UNIAP), *supra* note 110, at 26.

143 Id. at 30, 34, 37, 41, 44, 47 53, 56, and 61; David et al., *supra* note 116, at 24; United States Agency for International Development (UNAID), *supra* note 107, at 42.

- the right to remain temporarily or permanently in the destination country; repatriation; and
- Non-prosecution of trafficking victims[144]

ii *Legal Protection for Trafficking Victims in Thailand*

Compared to the anti-Human Trafficking Law of Cambodia, the anti-human trafficking law of Thailand provides for legal protection of trafficking victims in accordance with the UN Palermo Protocol.[145] The anti-human trafficking law of Thailand provides for:

- protection of the victims' privacy and identity;[146]
- counseling and information on trafficking victims' legal rights;[147]
- medical, psychological and material assistance for victims;[148]
- employment, education and training for victims;[149]
- protection of physical safety for victims of trafficking;[150]
- the right to remain temporarily or permanently in the destination country;[151] repatriation;[152]

---

144 UNITED NATIONS INTER-AGENCY PROJECT ON HUMAN TRAFFICKING (UNIAP), *supra* note 110, at 30, 34, 37, 41, 44, 47 53, 56, and 61; DAVID ET AL., *supra* note 116, at 24.

145 ANTI-TRAFFICKING IN PERSONS ACT B.E 2551 §§ 33–41 (2008) (Thailand), *supra* note 120; UNITED NATIONS INTER-AGENCY PROJECT ON HUMAN TRAFFICKING (UNIAP), *supra* note 110, at 33, 36, 40, 43, 46, 49, 54,59, 63, 228–229.

146 ANTI-TRAFFICKING IN PERSONS ACT B.E. 2551 §§ 31, 36, 56 (2008) (Thailand), *supra* note 120; UNITED NATIONS INTER-AGENCY PROJECT ON HUMAN TRAFFICKING (UNIAP), *supra* note 110, at 28–29.

147 ANTI-TRAFFICKING IN PERSONS ACT B.E. 2551 §§ 33–34 (2008) (Thailand), *supra* note 120; UNITED NATIONS INTER-AGENCY PROJECT ON HUMAN TRAFFICKING (UNIAP), *supra* note 110, at 36.

148 ANTI-TRAFFICKING IN PERSONS ACT B.E. 2551 §§ 33 (2008) (Thailand), *supra* note 120; UNITED NATIONS INTER-AGENCY PROJECT ON HUMAN TRAFFICKING (UNIAP), *supra* note 110, at 40.

149 ANTI-TRAFFICKING IN PERSONS ACT B.E. 2551 §§ 33 (2008) (Thailand), *supra* note 120; UNITED NATIONS INTER-AGENCY PROJECT ON HUMAN TRAFFICKING (UNIAP), *supra* note 110, at 43.

150 ANTI-TRAFFICKING IN PERSONS ACT B.E. 2551 §§ 36 (2008) (Thailand), *supra* note 120; UNITED NATIONS INTER-AGENCY PROJECT ON HUMAN TRAFFICKING (UNIAP), *supra* note 110, at 49.

151 ANTI-TRAFFICKING IN PERSONS ACT B.E. 2551 §§ 37–38 (2008) (Thailand), *supra* note 120; UNITED NATIONS INTER-AGENCY PROJECT ON HUMAN TRAFFICKING (UNIAP), *supra* note 110, at 54–55.

152 ANTI-TRAFFICKING IN PERSONS ACT B.E. 2551 §§ 33, 36, 38–39 (2008) (Thailand), *supra* note 120; UNITED NATIONS INTER-AGENCY PROJECT ON HUMAN TRAFFICKING (UNIAP), *supra* note 110, at 59.

- non-prosecution of trafficking victims[153] and
- Right to a Remedy for Trafficking Victims[154]

Moreover, Section 33 of the anti-human trafficking law of Thailand requires the Ministry of Social Development and Human Security to provide appropriate housing and food for trafficking victims.[155] Competent authority can take trafficking victims to reside in either private or public shelters;[156] however, trafficking victims have no choice in these accommodations.[157] In addition, Section 29 provides for temporary custody meaning that trafficking victims will be placed in an appropriate place, not a detention cell or prison, for any

153 ANTI-TRAFFICKING IN PERSONS ACT B.E. 2551 § 41 (2008) (Thailand), *supra* note 120; UNITED NATIONS INTER-AGENCY PROJECT ON HUMAN TRAFFICKING (UNIAP), *supra* note 110, at 63; KNEEBONE & DEBELJAK, *supra* note 75, at 239; Memorandum of Understanding on Bilateral Cooperation for Eliminating Trafficking in Children and Women and Assisting Victims of Trafficking art. 7(b), Cambodia-Thai, May 31, 2003, *available at* http://www.no-trafficking.org/resources_laws_thailand.html (last visited Dec. 12, 2012) [hereinafter MOU for Eliminating Trafficking, Cambodia-Thai]; Memorandum of Understanding on Bilateral Cooperation for Eliminating Trafficking in Persons, Especially Women and Children and Assisting Victims of Trafficking art. 6(2), Vietnam-Thai, Mar. 24, 2008, *available at* http://www.no-trafficking.org/resources_laws_thailand.html (last visited Dec. 12, 2012) [hereinafter MOU for Eliminating Trafficking, Vietnam-Thai] (providing that Art. 7(b) of the MOU for Eliminating Trafficking, Cambodia-Thai, *supra* note 153, demands that parties must not arrest female and child victims).

154 ANTI-TRAFFICKING IN PERSONS ACT B.E. 2551 §§ 34–35 (2008) (Thailand), *supra* note 120; Betz, *supra* note 54, at 24 (stipulating that Article 34 of the Anti-Human Trafficking Law of Thailand authorizes compensation to victims for labor they performed while having been trafficked. The inquiry official and public prosecutor are required to notify trafficking victims of this right. Victims have the right to claim damages proscribed under article 35 free of charge. If the victim chooses to pursue the claim, the public prosecutor must file a claim for compensation on behalf of the victims. Once proceedings are final, and the offender enters a plea of guilty, the court will order compensation thus making the victim the traffickers' creditor).

155 ANTI-TRAFFICKING IN PERSONS ACT B.E. 2551 §§ 33 (2008) (Thailand), *supra* note 120; UNITED NATIONS INTER-AGENCY PROJECT ON HUMAN TRAFFICKING (UNIAP), *supra* note 110, at 33.

156 ANTI-TRAFFICKING IN PERSONS ACT B.E. 2551 §§ 33 (2008) (Thailand), *supra* note 120; UNITED NATIONS INTER-AGENCY PROJECT ON HUMAN TRAFFICKING (UNIAP), *supra* note 110, at 33.

157 ANTI-TRAFFICKING IN PERSONS ACT B.E. 2551 §§ 33 (2008) (Thailand), *supra* note 120; UNITED NATIONS INTER-AGENCY PROJECT ON HUMAN TRAFFICKING (UNIAP), *supra* note 110, at 33.

custody over twenty-four-hours.[158] But again, this law restrains the trafficking victims' freedom of choice in their residence, which may be necessary for their psychological health condition.[159]

Another way in which the anti-human trafficking law of Thailand has fallen short of the UN Palermo Protocol is in its consideration of the age, gender and special needs of trafficking victims, especially child victims.[160] Generally, Section 33 of this law commands the Ministry of Social Development and Human Security to take into account trafficking victims' age, gender, nationality, race, and culture in providing appropriate assistance. Appropriate assistance refers to food, shelter, medical treatment, physical and mental rehabilitation, education, training, legal aid, repatriation and legal proceedings to claim compensation for damages.[161] Despite these provisions, Section 33 ignores the consideration of special needs of trafficking victims, particularly children.[162]

iii *Legal Protection for Trafficking Victims in Vietnam*

The anti-human trafficking law of Vietnam provides assistance for trafficking victims such as protection of privacy and victim identification,[163] temporary or permanent immigration relief,[164] repatriation,[165] as well as employment, education and training.[166] In contrast, the law is silent on appropriate housing, the consideration of age, gender, special needs of victims, and their protection from prosecution.[167]

---

158 ANTI-TRAFFICKING IN PERSONS ACT B.E. 2551 §§ 29 (2008) (Thailand), *supra* note 120; UNITED NATIONS INTER-AGENCY PROJECT ON HUMAN TRAFFICKING (UNIAP), *supra* note 110, at 33.

159 ANTI-TRAFFICKING IN PERSONS ACT B.E. 2551 §§ 29 (2008) (Thailand), *supra* note 120; UNITED NATIONS INTER-AGENCY PROJECT ON HUMAN TRAFFICKING (UNIAP), *supra* note 110, at 33.

160 ANTI-TRAFFICKING IN PERSONS ACT B.E. 2551 §§ 33 (2008) (Thailand), *supra* note 120; UNITED NATIONS INTER-AGENCY PROJECT ON HUMAN TRAFFICKING (UNIAP), *supra* note 110, at 46.

161 ANTI-TRAFFICKING IN PERSONS ACT B.E. 2551 §§ 33 (2008) (Thailand), *supra* note 120.

162 Id.; UNITED NATIONS INTER-AGENCY PROJECT ON HUMAN TRAFFICKING (UNIAP), *supra* note 110, at 46.

163 Law on Prevention, Suppression against Human Trafficking (unofficial translation 2011) (Vietnam), *supra* note 128, arts. 3(10), 30(1)(d), 31.

164 Id. arts. 30, 33.

165 Id. art. 55.

166 Id. arts. 32(e), 37.

167 DAVID ET AL., *supra* note 116, at 23; Naparat Kranrattanasuit, Memorandum of Anti-Human Trafficking Law of Vietnam 8 (2011) (unpublished paper submitted to UNIAP) (on

The anti-human trafficking law of Vietnam articulates the right of trafficked victims to legal counseling to prevent subsequent trafficking and assistance in permanent residence or civil status registration. Also, the law enumerates claims for compensation, and participation in legal proceedings of trafficking cases.[168] However, the law does not clarify whether victims, who do not take part in criminal proceedings as witnesses, are given legal rights.[169]

Further, the anti-human trafficking law of Vietnam reflects the limitations of medical treatment.[170] This law imposes that Vietnamese citizens or stateless persons permanently residing in Vietnam; foreign victims; and minors, who accompany victims, are entitled to medical support while they reside at social welfare institutions or victim support institutions.[171] It is clear that the law neglects minors and Vietnamese citizens, who might obtain medical care.[172] Specifically, many Vietnamese women, who married to foreigners, have become stateless after renouncing their citizenship before getting citizenship from their spouse's country.[173] These women can risk becoming stateless if their marriage ends prior to their registration of citizenship in the spouse's country.[174] In an effort to rectify this problem, the Vietnamese government has modified its nationality law to provide citizenship for women

file with author) (presenting questions by Dr Lisa Rende Taylor, Counter Trafficking Technical Specialist at the United Nations Inter-Agency Project on Human Trafficking (UNIAP)).

168 Law on Prevention, Suppression against Human Trafficking (unofficial translation 2011) (Vietnam), *supra* note 128, arts. 32(1)(d).

169 Id.; Kranrattanasuit, *supra* note 167, at 8.

170 Law on Prevention, Suppression against Human Trafficking (unofficial translation 2011) (Vietnam), *supra* note 128, arts. 6(3)(c); Kranrattanasuit, *supra* note 167, at 8.

171 Id. art. 34.

172 Kranrattanasuit, *supra* note 167, at 8.

173 Alec Paxton, *Find a Country to Call Home: A Framework for Evaluating Legislation to Reduce Statelessness in Southeast Asia* 21 PAC. RIM L. & POL'Y J. 623, 628 (2012); Kitty McKinsey, *Divorce Leaves Some Vietnamese Women Broken-Hearted and Stateless*, UNCHR NEWS STORIES (Feb. 14, 2007), http://www.unhcr.org/45d324428.html; Report of the Regional Expert Roundtable on Good Practices for the Identification, Prevention and Reduction of Statelessness and the Protection of Stateless Persons in Southeast Asia, Bangkok, Oct. 28–29, 2010, *Good Practices: Addressing Statelessness in Southeast Asia* 11 (Feb. 5, 2011), *available at* http://www.unhcr.org/4d7de47f9.html.

174 Paxton, *supra* note 173, at 628 (2012); Report of the Regional Expert Roundtable on Good Practices for the Identification, Prevention and Reduction of Statelessness and the Protection of Stateless Persons in Southeast Asia, Bangkok, *supra* note 173, at 11.

who lost their citizenship because of a failed marriage with a foreign man.[175]

The anti-human trafficking law of Vietnam mentions compensation[176] in Articles 6(3) and 36(1). Per these provisions, the victims have the right to claim compensation for damages suffered by the trafficking itself.[177] The law also provides victims with the right to receive legal counseling in relation to claims for compensation of damages caused by being trafficked.[178] However, the law does not proscribe how trafficking victims can claim compensation and what kind of remedies they can receive.[179]

c Criminalization of Traffickers

This section discusses criminalization of traffickers as stipulated under Article 5 of the UN Palermo Protocol.[180] The purpose of the UN Palermo Protocol is an assurance to trafficking victims that perpetrators will be punished for committing human trafficking offences. The argument is that the anti-human trafficking laws of Cambodia, Thailand, and Vietnam have succeeded in criminalizing perpetrators; however, the Cambodian and Vietnamese laws have fallen short.

---

175 Report of the Regional Expert Roundtable on Good Practices for the Identification, Prevention and Reduction of Statelessness and the Protection of Stateless Persons in Southeast Asia, Bangkok, *supra* note 173, at 10–17.

176 David et al., *supra* note 116, at 25–26 (asserting that in addition to the anti-Human Trafficking Law of Vietnam, both the *Criminal Procedure Code* and *Civil Code* are possible mechanisms for trafficked victims to claim compensation. The Vietnamese government conducted research on human trafficking in ten provinces of Vietnam (Hanoi, Lao Cai, Quang Ninh, Lang Son, Nghe An, Thanh Hoa, HCM City, An Giang and Tay Ninh)).

177 Law on Prevention, Suppression against Human Trafficking (unofficial translation 2011) (Vietnam), *supra* note 128, art. 6(3).

178 Law on Prevention, Suppression against Human Trafficking (unofficial translation 2011) (Vietnam), *supra* note 128, art.36 (1); Kranrattanasuit, *supra* note 167, at 10.

179 Ministry of Justice of Vietnam, *supra* note 20, at 2 (giving examples of how victims and witnesses in Vietnam encounter difficulties with claiming compensation under Vietnamese Criminal Law and Criminal Procedure because when offenders allege that they have no assets, money or property, the government lacks any further methods to seize funds that can be used to compensate trafficking victims).

180 Law on Suppression of Human Trafficking and Sexual Exploitation (Cambodia), *supra* note 107, art. 5; Kelly E. Hyland, *The Impact of the Protocol to Prevent, Suppress and Punish Trafficking in Persons, Especially Women and Children*, 8 Hum. Rts. Brief, no 2, 2001, at 30 (reiterating that Article 5 mandates that State Parties penalize the acts of trafficking in persons, attempts at trafficking or complicity of this crime, and the organization and direction of such crimes).

i *Criminalization of Traffickers in Cambodia*

The anti-human trafficking law of Cambodia[181] prosecutes trafficking perpetrators depending on the classification of their criminal acts, namely unlawful removal, unlawful recruitment for exploitation, the act of selling, buying or exchanging a person, transportation, and receipt of a person, abduction, detention or confinement.[182] In addition, Article 4 criminalizes principals, accomplices, offenders merely attempting misconduct, as well as members of legal institutions,[183] and the private sector entities such as companies, associations, and charitable organizations.[184]

Those articles confirm that the anti-human trafficking law of Cambodia prescribes rigorous penalties for traffickers.[185] For that reason, this legislation progressively empowers law enforcement in the investigation and prosecution of traffickers.[186] In contrast, if government authorities are found to be involved in human trafficking businesses as accomplices, this law will also criminalize these authorities.[187]

ii *Criminalization of Traffickers in Thailand*

The Sections 6 through 9 of the anti-human trafficking law of Thailand sets forth the provisions criminalizing trafficking in Thailand.[188] Section 6 mandates

181 Law on Suppression of Human Trafficking and Sexual Exploitation (Cambodia), *supra* note 107, art. 12; DAVID ET AL., *supra* note 116, at 14–15.

182 UNITED NATIONS INTER-AGENCY PROJECT ON HUMAN TRAFFICKING (UNIAP), *supra* note 110, at 15–16 (defining criminal acts to include an offender of "unlawful removal" will be punished under Article 9, Article 10, and Article 11; an offender of "unlawful recruitment for exploitation" will be prosecuted under Article 12; an offender of "the act of selling, buying or exchanging a person" will be reprehended under Article 14, Article 15, and Article 16; an offender of "transportation" will be adjudicated under Article 17 and Article 18; an offender of "receipt of a person" will be judged under Article 19 and Article 20; an offender of "abduction, detention or confinement" will be penalized under Article 21).

183 Law on Suppression of Human Trafficking and Sexual Exploitation (Cambodia), *supra* note 107, art. 5; UNITED NATIONS INTER-AGENCY PROJECT ON HUMAN TRAFFICKING (UNIAP), *supra* note 110, at 16.

184 Law on Suppression of Human Trafficking and Sexual Exploitation (Cambodia), *supra* note 107, art. 4; DAVID ET AL., *supra* note 116, at 17.

185 *See* Law on Suppression of Human Trafficking and Sexual Exploitation (Cambodia), *supra* note 107; Betz, *supra* note 54, at 50.

186 Betz, *supra* note 54, at 50; TIP REPORT 2008, *supra* note 60, at 83.

187 Betz, *supra* note 54, at 50–51; TIP REPORT 2008, *supra* note 60, at 83.

188 ANTI-TRAFFICKING IN PERSONS ACT B.E. 2551 § 6–9 (2008) (Thailand), *supra* note 120; UNITED NATIONS INTER-AGENCY PROJECT ON HUMAN TRAFFICKING (UNIAP), *supra* note 110, at 21.

that a person, committing any trafficking act for the purpose of exploitation, is guilty of human trafficking.[189] Similar to Article 4 of the anti-human trafficking law of Cambodia, the anti-human trafficking law of Thailand criminalizes a person or a private or public entity (including companies, associations, charitable institutions), who is complicit in the commission of trafficking in persons.[190] The law also criminalizes anyone, who attempts, or conspires to, commit a human trafficking offense.[191] This law imposes a tough penalty for trafficking adults; four to ten years imprisonment and a reasonable fine. Penalties for child trafficking are even greater, sentences between six and twelve years and a higher fine may be imposed.[192]

iii *Criminalization of Traffickers in Vietnam*

Compared to Article 5 of the U.N. Palermo Protocol,[193] Article 23(1)-(2) of the anti-human trafficking law of Vietnam proscribes that any offender conducting the crime enshrined in Article 3 of the anti-human trafficking law of Vietnam will be prosecuted for criminal liability.[194] If the offender causes any damage, they are responsible for compensation.[195] In addition, if any government officer or staff commits misconduct by abusing his or her power to neglect or allow trafficking activities, he or she will be prosecuted for criminal liability.[196]

---

189 ANTI-TRAFFICKING IN PERSONS ACT B.E. 2551 § 6 (2008) (Thailand), *supra* note 120.

190 Id. § 7; DAVID ET AL., *supra* note 116, at 17.

191 ANTI-TRAFFICKING IN PERSONS ACT B.E. 2551 §§ 8–9 (2008) (Thailand), *supra* note 120.

192 Id. § 52.

193 U.N. Palermo Protocol, *supra* note 64, at Art. 5 (requiring a State Party to establish measures of criminal offences).

194 Law on Prevention, Suppression against Human Trafficking (unofficial translation 2011) (Vietnam), *supra* note 128, art.2; Kranrattanasuit, *supra* note 167, at 7; DAVID ET AL., *supra* note 116, at 14–15 (explaining that the *Penal Code* and the *Labour Code* of Vietnam both proscribe penalties for forced labor. The *Penal Code* commands a much more severe penalty than the *Labour Code*. The light penalties of the *Labour Code* apply to the maltreatment of workers and is silent on protection measure of workers with legal employment contract. The overlap between these laws can create confusion in the application of these laws).

195 Law on Prevention, Suppression against Human Trafficking (unofficial translation 2011) (Vietnam), *supra* note 128, art. 2; Kranrattanasuit, *supra* note 167, at 7.

196 Id.; Kranrattanasuit, *supra* note 167, at 7.

In short, the national anti-human trafficking laws of Cambodia, Thailand, and Vietnam have illustrated their restrictions in providing protection for human trafficking victims (*See* Comparative Table of Legal Framework of Trafficking in Persons of Cambodia, Thailand, and Vietnam, *infra*). Because of the shortcomings of their domestic anti-human trafficking laws, the goal here is to examine whether these governments have made sufficient effort to suppress human trafficking, protect victims, and convict perpetrators in order to show that it is necessary that ASEAN assists them strengthen their anti-human trafficking laws and practices through the establishment of ADTV and ACTV (Table 2).

TABLE 2 *Comparative table of legal framework of trafficking in persons of Cambodia, Thailand, and Vietnam*

Issues		Cambodia	Thailand	Vietnam
UNTOC		State Party	Signed, not ratified	State Party
UN Palermo Protocol		State Party	Signed, not ratified	State Party
Definition of "Trafficking in Persons"		Yes, but limited	Yes	Yes, but limited
Legal Protections for Trafficking Victims	***Protection of Privacy and Confidentiality***	Yes, but limited	Yes	Yes
	Appropriate Housing	No	Yes, but limited	No
	Counseling and Legal Rights	No	Yes	Yes
	Medical Treatment	No	Yes	Yes, but limited
	Employment, Education, and Training	No	Yes	Yes, but limited
	Age, Gender, and Special Needs of Victims	No	Yes, but limited	No
	Protection and Physical Safety	No	Yes	Yes, but limited
	Right to Remain Temporarily or Permanently	No	Yes	Yes
	Repatriation	No	Yes	Yes
	Non-Prosecution of Victims	No	Yes	No
	Right to a Remedy	Yes	Yes	Yes, but limited
Criminalization of Traffickers		Yes	Yes	Yes

4.2.3 *Counter-Human Trafficking Practice in Cambodia, Thailand, and Vietnam*

As previous part demonstrated, many provisions of anti-human trafficking law of Cambodia, Thailand, and Vietnam do not comply with the legal framework set forth in the UN Palermo Protocol. Nevertheless, non-implementation of the UN Palermo Protocol does not necessarily indicate that these governments lack efforts to combat human trafficking. This supports the fact that while "strong" national laws related to anti-human trafficking are crucial for all countries, the efficiency of such a law relies on the way individual countries transfer their laws into actions.[197] Therefore, it is essential to discuss whether Cambodian, Thai, and Vietnamese governments have made progress in their practical responses to prevent human trafficking, protect trafficking victims, and prosecute trafficking offenders in order to confirm that these three governments have to request ASEAN to establish a regional anti-human trafficking paradigm (ADTV) with a monitoring body (ACTV) that can address and evaluate their national anti-human trafficking law's advantages and disadvantages in order to strengthen their laws and government actions against such crime.

The governments of Cambodia, Thailand, and Vietnam have alleged efforts in suppressing human trafficking through training programs and collaboration with public and private agencies, providing protection of privacy and confidentiality and the access to compensation of trafficking victims, and criminalizing human trafficking perpetrators. However, their governments' criminal justice responses to human trafficking have demonstrated challenges, namely underserved trafficking men, deficient registration process of recruitment agencies, ineffective communication channels, improper victim identification of frontline officials, and corruption of government authorities. Therefore, ASEAN should create the ADTV to serve as a regional force against human trafficking, which can address effective counter-human trafficking strategies and methods. In addition, they should also form the ACTV to monitor and assess its member countries' domestic anti-human trafficking laws and actions in order to strengthen their government authorities' competences according to the human trafficking circumstance in individual countries.

a Strengths of Counter-Human Trafficking Responses

Even if there are much more space for these three countries to work on in order to mitigate human trafficking scourge in their countries, it is obvious that Cambodia, Thailand, and Vietnam have made progress in providing training

197 Gerald Smith, The Criminal Justice Response to Human Trafficking: Recent Developments in the Greater Mekong Sub-Region 4 (2010), *available at* http://www.no-trafficking.org/reports_docs/siren/GMS-08_eng.pdf.

programs and collaboration with public and private agencies, protection of privacy and confidentiality, and compensation.

i *Training Programs and Collaboration with Public and Private Agencies*

In response to the increasing growth of anti-human trafficking, the Cambodian government created the national anti-trafficking task force to make efforts to deter human trafficking[198] by providing law enforcement training programs to improve criminal justice responses to trafficking in persons.[199] Likewise, prior to their deployment, Cambodian military forces are required to complete a training program that covers transnational counter-trafficking in persons.[200] The government also created similar training programs for special investigators.[201]

The Thai government has established a Vocational Training Center for Women that is supervised by the Department of Social Welfare.[202] This center encourages women between the ages of fourteen and thirty five to attend free vocational training courses for six months.[203] It also includes training on the risks of human trafficking, which aim to decrease the occurrence of women and girls being subject to the commercial sex trafficking industry.[204] Additionally, the government has established a Transnational Crime Coordination Center to conduct research on the circumstances of human trafficking and create plans of action with the Office of the Attorney General's Center Against International Human Trafficking (CAHT)[205] in order to identify the root causes of human trafficking in the nation and to design effective plans to combat these causes that can mitigate the number of human trafficking victims. The Vietnamese government and other partnerships have conducted

198 Betz, *supra* note 54, at 50–51; Guy Delauney, *Trafficking Crackdown in Cambodia*, BBC NEWS (April 6, 2007, 7:49 AM), http://news.bbc.co.uk/2/hi/asia-pacific/6532181.stm.

199 Betz, *supra* note 54, at 51; TIP REPORT 2012, *supra* note 64, at 108.

200 National Plan of Action on the Suppression of Human Trafficking, Smuggling, Labour, and Sexual Exploitation of Cambodia (S.T.S.L.S.) for 2011–2013 8–9 (NCS/STLS, trans. Dec. 7, 2011), *available at* http://www.no-trafficking.org/content/pdf/CMB-National%20Plan%20of%20Action%20English2.pdf [hereinafter Cambodian National Plan of Action]; TIP REPORT 2011, *supra* note 3, at 112; TIP REPORT 2012, *supra* note 64, at 108.

201 DAVID ET AL., *supra* note 116, at 41.

202 Fiona David, *Law Enforcement Responses to Trafficking in Persons: Challenges and Emerging Good Practices*, *in* INTERNATIONAL SE TRAFFICKING OF WOMEN AND CHILDREN: UNDERSTANDING THE GLOBAL EPIDEMIC 483 (2010).

203 Id.

204 Id.

205 UNITED STATES AGENCY FOR INTERNATIONAL DEVELOPMENT (UNAID), *supra* note 107, at 56.

numerous training programs for government officials.[206] For instance, the Vietnamese Women's Union (VFU) provided vocational training courses for trafficking victims at the rehabilitation center while the MOLISA offered financial contribution.[207]

In addition to training discourses, the governments of Cambodia, Thailand, and Vietnam have reinforced collaborations with private and public sectors in preventing human trafficking. For instance, the Cambodian government has enhanced the collaboration between the Ministry of Women's Affairs (MoWA)[208] and International Organization for Migration (IOM) in safe migration campaigns.[209] These entities use radio broadcasts to promote awareness of trafficking through marriage.[210] Also, the Ministry of Labour and Vocational Training (MoLVT) adopted the *Decision on the Provision of Passports*, which issues passports for migrant workers with no fee, through this program, approximately 2531 Cambodian migrant workers received passports between 2008 and 2009.[211]

Also, the Cambodian government has attested its plan of counter-trafficking in persons through international cooperation with neighboring countries.[212] The instances of these international agreements consist of signing a *Memorandum of Understanding (MoU) with Thailand on Eliminating Trafficking in Children and Women and Assisting Victims of Trafficking* aiming to strengthen border control.[213] The second MoU with Thailand refers to *Cooperation in the Employment of Workers*.[214] The goal of this MoU is to tackle irregular migrant

206 Id. 59.

207 U.S. DEP'T OF STATE, REPORT: TRAFFICKING IN PERSONS INTERIM ASSESSMENT (April 5, 2011), *available at* http://www.state.gov/g/tip/rls/reports/2011/160017.htm.

208 Betz, *supra* note 54, at 52 (describing that the MoWA partnered with MoSVY to raise the awareness of human trafficking to trafficking victims).

209 TIP REPORT 2011, *supra* note 3, at 112.

210 Id.

211 United Nations Committee on the Elimination of Discrimination against Women, Consideration of Reports Submitted by States parties under Article 18 of the Convention on the Elimination of All Forms of Discrimination against Women, Combined Fourth and Fifth Periodic Reports of States Parties: Cambodia, ¶ 98, U.N. Doc. CEDAW/C/KHM/4-5 (Sept. 24, 2011) (prepared by the Government of Cambodia), *available at* http://daccess-ods.un.org/TMP/5445075.63114166.html (revealing that about 406 of those migrant workers were women).

212 ICSW, *supra* note 7, at 43; INTERNATIONAL LABOUR OFFICE, *supra* note 10, at 3.

213 MOU for Eliminating Trafficking, Cambodia-Thai, *supra* note 153; ICSW, *supra* note 7, at 43; INTERNATIONAL LABOUR OFFICE, *supra* note 10, at 3.

214 MOU for Eliminating Trafficking, Cambodia-Thai, *supra* note 153; ICSW, *supra* note 7, at 43; INTERNATIONAL LABOUR OFFICE, *supra* note 10, at 3.

workers by making a mutual legal framework for labor migration.[215] The third MoU with Thailand articulates *Guidelines for Cooperation between Cambodia and Thailand on the Criminal Justice Process of Trafficking-Related Crimes*.[216] This MoU has implemented the other two MoUs described above. Another MoU signed with Vietnam governs an anti-human trafficking agreement, which is applied to only women and children.[217]

The Thai government has signed several bilateral MoUs with other neighboring countries, specifically Cambodia, Laos, Vietnam, and Myanmar in relation to counter-trafficking in persons in the Greater Mekong Sub-region (GMS).[218] These bilateral agreements cover the definition of "trafficking in persons," purposes of human trafficking; preventive and protective measures; legal assistance for trafficking victims; victims' repatriation and reintegration; training programs; monitoring systems and evaluation.[219]

The Thai government has also cooperated with other organizations and NGOs.[220] The government has partnered with other regional organizations to raise awareness of safe migration practices in Southeast Asia.[221] Thailand has also established a Centre to Suppress, Arrest, and Prosecute Alien Workers Working Underground and Human Trafficking Processes in 2010.[222] They have also collaborated with NGOs and other international organizations to provide interpreters or translators for hotline callers.[223]

---

215 MOU for Eliminating Trafficking, Cambodia-Thai, *supra* note 153; ICSW, *supra* note 7, at 43; INTERNATIONAL LABOUR OFFICE, *supra* note 10, at 3.

216 ICSW, *supra* note 7, at 43.

217 Id.; KNEEBONE & DEBELJAK, *supra* note 75, at 142.

218 United Nations Children's Fund High Level Meeting on International Collaboration for Children's Rights in the Asia and Pacific Region, Beijing P.R. China, Nov. 5–7, 2010, *Thailand: Principles and Philosophy of South-South Collaboration* 6, *available at* http://www.unicef.org/eapro/Final_Thailand_HLM_Paper_1_Nov.pdf.

219 Id.

220 TIP REPORT 2011, *supra* note 3, at 354.

221 Betz, *supra* note 54, at 53; *Where We Work: Thailand*, INTERNATIONAL LABOUR ORGANIZATION, http://www.ilo.org/public/english/region/asro/bangkok/child/trafficking/wherewework-thailanddetail.htm (last visited Mar. 5, 2013).

222 TIP REPORT 2011, *supra* note 3, at 355; NATIONAL POLICY, STRATEGIES, AND MEASURES TO PREVENT AND SUPPRESS TRAFFICKING IN PERSONS (2011–2016), *available at* http://www.nocht.m-society.go.th/human-traffic/policy/download/policy_strategy_en1.pdf (last visited Dec. 12, 2012) (explaining that the plan of action addresses the application of all categories of media to promote "safe migration" and the nature of vulnerable groups to human trafficking in order to educate all migrants on the harm of human trafficking).

223 TIP REPORT 2011, *supra* note 3, at 355.

The Vietnamese government created the 2011–2015 Action Plan to address human trafficking in Vietnam, reform counter-human trafficking measures and change the perception of the Vietnamese community on deterring this crime.[224] One example of prevention includes the public awareness of human trafficking through cooperation with NGOs and other international organizations.[225] The Vietnamese Ministry of Labor Invalids, and Social Affairs (MOLISA) and the Ministry of Justice have cooperated with numerous NGOs and international organizations through a discourse on the integration of sex trafficking victims.[226] Also, Vietnam's Ministry of Public Security signed MoUs with other countries, including Chinese[227] and Laotian[228] governments to fight human trafficking.[229]

ii *Protection of Privacy and Confidentiality*

The governments of Cambodia, Thailand, and Vietnam have provided protection of privacy and confidentiality. For instance, even though the anti-human trafficking law of Cambodia does not realize the victims' right to attend and express their views during criminal proceedings against perpetrators, the national policy in Cambodia does.[230] This national policy called *Prakas on*

---

224 Vu Van Dung, *2011–2015 Action Plan for Anti-Human Trafficking in Vietnam* at the Capacity Building Workshop on Anti-Human Trafficking (Aug. 2011), *available at* http://www.google.com/url?sa=t&rct=j&q=&esrc=s&source=web&cd=1&ved=0CB4QFjAA&url=http%3A%2F%2Fjica-cb-workshop.weebly.com%2Fuploads%2F8%2F0%2F7%2F2%2F8072630%2Fvietnam_action_plan.pptx&ei=_MSTUPOZNcuz0QGp3oHoAw&usg=AFQjCNHtq8qfwOCyQcBLUo4DpNM81n7-bw&sig2=SISoYhGZUnR0ycrrsZp_4g.

225 United States Agency for International Development (UNAID), *supra* note 107, at 59.

226 U.S. Dep't of State, *supra* note 801.

227 *Counter-Trafficking Action in Vietnam, supra* note 66; Child Exploitation and Online Protection Centre (CEOP), The Trafficking of Women and Children from Vietnam 11–12 (2011), *available at* http://www.ceop.police.uk/Documents/ceopdocs/NPM_CEOP_FCO_report_-_trafficking_of_Vietnamese_women_and_children.pdf (describing that the Vietnamese baby boys have been target for Chinese parents since the Chinese government prohibits its parents to have a second child if their first child is a girl. Some Vietnamese girls, who married Chinese men for the purpose of reproducing baby boys, end up being sold in the sexual industry after her delivery).

228 *Counter-Trafficking Action in Vietnam, supra* note 66 (discussing Agreement with Lao PDR on Cooperation in Preventing and Combating Trafficking in Persons and Protection of Victims of Trafficking (2010)).

229 Id. (stating that other MoUs include Agreement with Cambodia on Cooperation to Combat Trafficking in Women and Children (2005); Agreement with Thailand on Eliminating Trafficking in Persons, Especially Women and Children and Assisting Victims of Trafficking (2008)).

230 David et al., *supra* note 116, at 116.

Minimum Standards for the Protection of the Rights of Victims of Human Trafficking allows all trafficking victims to attend proceedings and engage during the court process.[231] The relevant Cambodian laws have displayed progress in the protection of victim-witnesses' privacy at all stages.[232] For instance, the government has prohibited the press and the public access during court proceedings.[233] Trafficking victims can provide testimony (as a pre-trial statement or a deposition) without attending the court.[234]

The law in Thailand authorizes prosecutors to request specific methods (namely taking evidence or victims' testimony by video) in court to encourage trafficking victims to participate in the investigation and prosecution of perpetrators.[235] Such methods provide extra protection for trafficking victims acting as witnesses, particularly child victims.[236] For instance, prosecutors have used various methods to alleviate the confrontation between trafficking victims and the defendant,[237] such as considering victims' video recorded statements as "admissible" evidence."[238]

iii *Compensation*

Among Cambodia, Thailand, and Vietnam, Thailand has demonstrated the best practice that provides various options for trafficking victims in claiming for compensation. The Thai government has ensured that trafficking victims obtain compensation as exemplified in the *Anoma Case*.[239] In this case, two Thai employers, Mr Veerapong SaeLee and Ms. Anoma Siriyuwattananon,

---

231 Id. (mentioning Article 6 of the Cambodian *Prakas on Minimum Standards for the Protection of the Rights of Victims of Human Trafficking*).

232 Id. at 114.

233 Id. at 78.

234 Id.

235 Smith, *supra* note 197, at 11; DAVID ET AL., *supra* note 116, at 122.

236 Smith, *supra* note 197, at 11 (stating that Thailand allows child victims to testify through video recorders instead of confronting traffickers in the courtroom); DAVID ET AL., *supra* note 116, at 122–123.

237 ANTI-TRAFFICKING IN PERSONS ACT B.E. 2551 §§ 31 (2008) (Thailand), *supra* note 120 (describing that victims or witnesses have the rights to provide testimony statement before duration of trial so that victims or witnesses can be absent in court and return their original national country instead of residing in shelter in Thailand]; DAVID ET AL., *supra* note 116, at 122.

238 Smith, *supra* note 197, at 11 (mentioning § 172 of the CRIMINAL PROCEDURE CODE OF THAILAND B.E. 2477 (1934) (Thai)).

239 *The Public Prosecutor of Sumutsakorn v. Mr Veerapong SaeLee and Ms. Arnoma Siriyuwattananon*, First Ct. Dika No. 7314/2552, Nov. 26 2009 (unofficial translation on file with author).

hired 206 illegal migrant workers including 73 women and children, eleven of those children were under the age of 15 and fourteen of children were over 15, but under 18 years old.[240] They worked in a factory called *Long Kung Anoma*.[241] On Sept 10, 2008, a prosecutor filed a complaint in the Court of the First Instance in Criminal Cases with predicate offenses based on Immigration Act; the Penal Code; Measures in Prevention and Suppression of Trafficking in Women and Children Act; Labor Protection Act; Anti-Trafficking in Persons Act; and Working of Aliens Act.[242] On November 26, 2009, the Court of the First Instance in Criminal Case found the defendants guilty of human trafficking. The court sentenced the first defendant to 5-years imprisonment and a fine for 1,054,000 baht (approximately US$35,133), and the second defendant to imprisonment to 8 years imprisonment and a fine for 2,084,000 baht (approximately US$69,466).[243] The defendants appealed to the Appeal Court and on July 27, 2011, the Court of Appeal upheld the decision of the Court of the First Instance in Criminal Case.[244] Later, the defendants bailed themselves out and appealed to the Supreme Court.[245]

Based on the *Anoma* case, there are several ways for these trafficking victims to make compensation claims.[246] First, victims can make a claim based on Section 44/1 of Criminal Procedure Code, which regards the offence of civil prosecution. The law allows trafficking victims to file a petition for criminal prosecution, which includes a remedy of compensation.[247] Trafficking victims must file a criminal complaint before the Court of the First Instance and Criminal Case makes the decision.[248] The advantages of this option are the facts that: (1) trafficking victims do not have to pay application fees; and (2) trafficking victims have the right to receive compensation as soon as the

240 Id.

241 Id.

242 Id.

243 Id.

244 Id.

245 *The Public Prosecutor of Sumutsakorn v. Mr Veerapong SaeLee and Ms. Arnoma Siriyuwattananon*, *supra* note 239.

246 CRIMINAL PROCEDURE CODE, B.E. 2477 § 44(1) (1934) (Thai), *available at* http://web.krisdika.go.th/data/law/law4/%bb05/%bb05-20-9999-update.pdf; ANTI-TRAFFICKING IN PERSONS ACT B.E. 2551 § 35 para. 2 (2008) (Thailand), *supra* note 120; DAMAGES FOR THE INJURED PERSON AND COMPENSATION AND EXPENSE FOR THE ACCUSED IN THE CRIMINAL CASE ACT, B.E. 2544 §§ 3, 17 (2001) (Thai), *available at* http://www.thailawforum.com/laws/Damages%20for%20the%20injured%20person.pdf.

247 CRIMINAL PROCEDURE CODE, B.E. 2477 § 44(1) (1934) (Thailand), *supra* note 246.

248 Id.

Court of the First Instance in Criminal Case orders to compensate for compensation.[249]

The second option is a claim for compensation based on the offense of criminal case embodied in Section 35, paragraph 2 of the Anti-Trafficking in Persons Act of Thailand.[250] This law provides a right to compensation for damages as a result of the commission of trafficking in persons.[251] Victims can express their intention to claims for compensation to the Permanent Secretary for Social Development and Human Security.[252] On behalf of the victims, the Public Prosecutor will make a claim for compensation and file it with the criminal prosecution or filing at any time during the trial of the criminal case in the Court of the First Instance.[253] If ordered by the court, trafficking victims have the right to obtain compensation.[254] This normally takes longer than the first option because the Ministry of Social Development and Human Security has to evaluate the most reasonable amount of compensation. The advantage of this option is that the trafficking victims do not have to pay for an application fee. In fact, this was the option that the trafficking victims of the *Anoma* chose to claim compensation under this option.[255]

The third option is a claim of compensation based on tort law, namely physical abuse, sexual exploitation, etc.[256] If trafficking victims miss filing the application for compensation before the Court of the First Instance in Criminal Prosecution, trafficking victims, by themselves, can claim for compensation to the Court of the First Instance in Civil Prosecution at any time within 10 years after the tort offense occurred.[257] The disadvantage of this option is that the victims have to pay a filing fee. The diagram below displays the three options for a claim for compensation in order to better understand the Thai laws on the right to a remedy (Figure 4).

Furthermore, trafficking victims can request financial contribution from the Thai Government Agencies, namely the Anti-Trafficking in Persons Fund

249 Id.

250 ANTI-TRAFFICKING IN PERSONS ACT B.E. 2551 §§ 35(2) (2008) (Thailand), *supra* note 120.

251 Id.

252 Id.

253 Id.

254 Id.

255 *The Public Prosecutor of Sumutsakorn v. Mr Veerapong SaeLee and Ms. Arnoma Siriyuwattananon*, *supra* note 239.

256 CIVIL CODE B.E. 2535 § 424 (1992) (Thailand), *available at* http://web.krisdika.go.th/data/law/law4/%bb03/%bb03-20-9999-update.pdf.

257 Id.

Option 1: Victim Initiated Petition

- Victims file petition for compensation with criminal compensation with criminal prosecution (Sec. 44/1)

Option 2: Prosecution Intitated Petition

- On behalf of the victim, the prosecutor may file a claim for compensation. (Sec. 35, para 2)

Option 3: Civil Prosecution Petition

- In the absence of filing the petion for compensation before the Court of 1st instance in Criminal Prosecution, the victims can file a petition for compensation to the Court of the 1st instance in Civil Prosection

Must be effectuated within 10 years of Criminal Prosecution

FIGURE 4 *Three ways to make a claim for compensation in Thailand*

and Ministry of Justice Fund.[258] The Anti-Trafficking in Persons Fund proscribes that trafficking victims have the right to be given assistance based on Section 44 (1) of the Anti-Trafficking in Persons including legal proceedings to claim compensation.[259] The Ministry of Justice Fund stipulates that physically abused victims can apply for compensation from this fund according to Section 3 and Section 17 of Damages for the Injured Person and Compensation and Expense for the Accused in the *Criminal Case Act*.[260] Figure 4 shows that trafficking victims can also expect to receive financial contribution from outside Thai government agencies as well.

258 TRAFFICKING IN PERSONS ACT B.E. 2551 § 44(1) (2008) (Thailand), *available at* http://www.no-trafficking.org/content/Laws_Agreement/laws_agreement_pdf/trafficking_in_persons_act_b.e%202551%20%28eng.%29.pdf; DAMAGES FOR THE INJURED PERSON AND COMPENSATION AND EXPENSE FOR THE ACCUSED IN THE CRIMINAL CASE ACT, B.E. 2544 §§ 3, 17 (2001) (Thailand), *available at* http://www.thailawforum.com/laws/Damages%20for%20the%20injured%20person.pdf.

259 ANTI-TRAFFICKING IN PERSONS ACT B.E. 2551 §§ 44(1) (2008) (Thailand), *supra* note 120.

260 DAMAGES FOR THE INJURED PERSON AND COMPENSATION AND EXPENSE FOR THE ACCUSED IN THE CRIMINAL CASE ACT, B.E. 2544 §§ 3, 17 (2001) (Thailand), *supra* note 258.

Despite the strengths of these governments' protection measures, the anti-human trafficking laws of Cambodia, Thailand, and Vietnam have applied to all women, children, and men,[261] these three countries have prioritized the protection of women and children victims rather than male victims because the sex trafficking industry has made these problems more pervasive.[262] For instance, the Cambodian government created the Cambodian National Council for Children to strengthen *Guideline for the Protection of the Rights of Trafficked Children for the Kingdom of Cambodia* in 2007.[263] This guideline contains provisions for child victims' care and support, special rights (including rights to non-discrimination, information, confidentiality, and respect for view and identity).[264] In instances, where child victims have to confront their traffickers, screens are put between the victim and defendant during the court proceedings.[265]

The Cambodian government also actively supports female victims. For instance, the government has supported non-governmental organizations to help female trafficking victims with repatriation to their native Vietnam.[266] In addition, the Ministry of Social Affairs, Veterans and Youth Rehabilitation (MoSAVY) provided primary and temporary housing for 1096 trafficking victims referred by local and foreign authorities,[267] treatment for 3028 sex trafficking victims in women,[268] repatriation and reintegration for 4723 victims trafficked to other countries.[269] Also, MoSAVY cooperated with UNICEF to

---

261 Law on Suppression of Human Trafficking and Sexual Exploitation (Cambodia), *supra* note 107; ANTI-TRAFFICKING IN PERSONS ACT B.E. 2551 (2008) (Thailand), *supra* note 120; UNITED STATES AGENCY FOR INTERNATIONAL DEVELOPMENT (UNAID), *supra* note 107, at 59 (revealing that the Vietnamese government presented a proposal to strengthen the definition of "trafficking in persons" enshrined in Article 119–120 of the *Penal Code* to cover male trafficking victims over 16 years old); DAVID ET AL., *supra* note 116, at 13 (explaining evidence confirming that human trafficking offenses embodied in the *Penal Code* apply to male, female and child victims alike).

262 United Nations Technical Working Group on Human Trafficking, Factsheet on Combatting Human Trafficking (May, 2012), *available at* http://www.un.org.vn/en/publications/doc_details/192-factsheet-on-combating-human-trafficking.html.

263 DAVID ET AL., *supra* note 116, at 103.

264 Id.

265 Id. at 78.

266 TIP REPORT 2011, *supra* note 3, at 111.

267 Id.

268 U.N. Convention on the Elimination of All Forms of Discrimination against Women, *supra* note 211, at ¶ 102(a).

269 Id.

operate a transit center in Poipet for 119 trafficking victims deported from Thailand.[270]

b Challenges of Counter-Human Trafficking Responses

Even though the governments of Cambodia, Thailand, and Vietnam have attempted to make progress in criminal justice responses as discussed above, these governments still need to advance promotion of forced labour, protection of trafficking men, lawful registration process of recruitment agencies, communication channels with various dialects, and anti-corruption.

i *Insufficient Focus on Forced Labour*

Cambodia, Thailand, and Vietnam should be praised for their anti-human trafficking laws, which have prohibited all forms of human trafficking (sexual and forced labour exploitation).[271] All of these governments have enhanced various training programs for judges, prosecutors, and law enforcement authorities in order to strengthen their exercises. For instance, the government of Cambodia has made significant progress by designing training courses for prosecutors and judges to better understand the anti-human trafficking law of Cambodia.[272] Vietnamese prosecutors take immediate action to police requests for warrants and detention orders by assigning a prosecutor to work closely with investigators at provincial police stations.[273]

Further, the Vietnamese government's effort has encompassed cross-border cooperation with other neighboring countries, namely Cambodia, China, and Thailand, to rescue trafficking victims and capture perpetrators.[274] The Vietnamese government remains in a partnership with other international organizations to train relevant competent authorities and social workers on human trafficking.[275] In Thailand, the Central Investigation Bureau of Thailand has advanced its authorities' investigative operations by sponsoring their

270 TIP REPORT 2011, *supra* note 3, at 111.

271 Law on Suppression of Human Trafficking and Sexual Exploitation (Cambodia), *supra* note 107; ANTI-TRAFFICKING IN PERSONS ACT B.E. 2551 (2008) (Thailand), *supra* note 120; Law on Prevention, Suppression against Human Trafficking (unofficial translation 2011) (Vietnam), *supra* note 128.

272 DAVID ET AL., *supra* note 116, at 75.

273 Id. at 76.

274 UNITED STATES AGENCY FOR INTERNATIONAL DEVELOPMENT (UNAID), *supra* note 107, at 59 (2009.

275 TIP REPORT 2011, *supra* note 3, at 385.

attendance at training programs in Britain and Canada.[276] The bureau of Thailand has also collaborated with the United Nations Office on Drugs and Crime to tackle human trafficking proliferation.[277]

Despite these efforts, there are still opportunities and areas that these three governments need to address in order to strengthen their authorities' knowledge and competence in battling human trafficking. For instance, Vietnamese officials have highlighted sexual commercial trafficking more than other forms of human trafficking such as forced labour exploitation.[278] The Cambodian government has neglected to create measures to prosecute traffickers of labor exploitation.[279] In Thailand, even though the Court of Justice of Thailand confirmed the increasing number of human trafficking investigations and prosecutions,[280] the government has not provided justice for many trafficking victims subject labor exploitation, in particular the thousands in the fishing industry.[281] Therefore, these three governments should maintain these training courses for their government official, including front-line authorities on victim identification[282] because these front-line authorities' working conditions have given them opportunities to meet human trafficking victims as other officials.

ii *Inadequate Protection of Trafficking Men*

While the governments of Cambodia, Thailand, and Vietnam have concentrated on providing protection and assistance for trafficked women and children, they have underserved trafficked men, particularly through arbitrary deportation of male victims without proper identification procedures and a dearth of shelter for male victims.

Despite these three governments' efforts in preventing human trafficking, the governments of Cambodia, Thailand, and Vietnam have fallen short in repressing forced labour male trafficking, controlling recruitment agencies'

---

276 Thachayan Waharak, *Thailand Remains Major Centre for Human Trafficking*, THE NATION [THAILAND] (June 28, 2012, 1:00 AM), http://www.nationmultimedia.com/national/Thailand-remains-major-centre-for-human-traffickin-30185065.html.

277 Id.

278 *Counter-Trafficking Action in Vietnam*, *supra* note 66.

279 Betz, *supra* note 54, at 53; TIP REPORT 2010, *supra* note 282, at 83.

280 TIP REPORT 2011, *supra* note 3, at 353.

281 Betz, *supra* note 54, at 60; Pennapa Hongthong, *New Law on Trafficking*, THE NATION [Thailand] (Oct. 1, 2007, 12:00 AM), http://www.nationmultimedia.com/2007/10/01/national_30050827.php; TIP REPORT 2011, *supra* note 3, at 353; TIP REPORT 2010, *supra* note 282, at 340.

282 TIP REPORT 2010, *supra* note 282, at 340.

human trafficking activities, and providing communication channels with various dialects. Statistics show that although the anti-human trafficking law of Cambodia recognizes *all* forms of trafficking offenses, the government has been deficient in providing proper attention to preventing labor trafficking and exploitation, particularly amongst Cambodian men in Thailand.[283] The government barely criminalizes labor traffickers and focuses most of its efforts on sex trafficking amongst women.[284]

It is important that governments provide protection for women and children as a vulnerable group; however, the government must also ensure that all human trafficking victims, including men, receive sufficient protection and aid. The government should not leave any victims underserved just because they are men. Until now, the governments in Thailand, Cambodia, and Vietnam have failed to provide these kinds of protections.

Recently the Vietnamese government modified the *Criminal Penal Code* to focus on trafficking in persons instead of only trafficking involving women and children.[285] This law was enacted as an impetus to victim assistance groups to acknowledge males as trafficking victims through forced labour.[286] However, the general Vietnamese law does not concentrate on assisting men as victims.[287] It is clear from this legislation that Vietnam seems to construe human trafficking as a narrow concept that does not contemplate forced labour exploitation or men as trafficking victims. It is clear that the Vietnamese government needs to modify these laws in order to ensure that trafficked men and boys are given services just as their female counterparts.[288] There seems to be much more room for the Vietnamese government to improve protection and assistance for trafficking victims.[289]

Further, these three governments have failed to identify trafficking victims, which can cause unsuccessful prosecution because of a lack of adequately

---

283 Human Trafficking Datasheet: Cambodia, *supra* note 8, at 2.

284 Betz, *supra* note 54, at 53; tip Report 2010, *supra* note 282, at 83.

285 Child Exploitation and Online Protection Centre (ceop), *supra* note 227, at 11; *Vietnam Marks One-Year of the "Shelter Self Improvement Project,"* United Nations Inter-Agency Project on Human Trafficking (uniap) (Sept. 2010), http://www.no-trafficking.org/story_vn_shelteranniversary.html (explaining that the Vietnamese government modified its Criminal Code to protect all trafficking victims, including men since January 2010).

286 *Vietnam Marks One-Year of the "Shelter Self Improvement Project," supra* note 285.

287 Child Exploitation and Online Protection Centre (ceop), *supra* note 227, at 9.

288 United Nations Technical Working Group on Human Trafficking, *supra* note 262.

289 United States Agency for International Development (unaid), *supra* note 107, at 59.

trained government officials. For instance, Cambodia has adopted *Agreement on Guidelines for Practices and Cooperation between the Relevant Government Institutions and Victim Support Agencies in Cases of Human Trafficking* to promote collaboration between Government Institutions and Victim Support Agencies on victim identification and victim protection.[290] However, the Cambodian government has struggled to implement these guidelines because it lacks sufficient training courses and resources for its agencies.[291] Also, there has been no sign of improvement in identification or protection of trafficking victims in that country.[292]

The Vietnamese government ensures that all government authorities acknowledge the significance of victim identification by creating the *Guidelines on Process and Procedures of Identification and Reception of Trafficked Women and Children from Abroad*.[293] The government laid out procedures for identification, verification, and reception of Vietnamese women and children subject to human trafficking in other countries.[294] These guidelines mandate that the Department of Labour, Invalids, and Social Affairs provide medical care and psycho-social counseling for trafficking victims, in particular women and children.[295] These guidelines are not emphasized on the assistance and support for trafficking victims in Vietnam or for adult male or foreign victims.[296]

In addition to the creation of those guidelines, the government has collaborated with NGOs and other international organizations to offer training programs for victim identification and basic assistance for trafficking victims.[297] However, the evidence reveals that the government has not conducted

---

290 ECPAT INTERNATIONAL, CAMBODIA: COUNTRY PROGRESS CARD 14 (2010), *available at* http://www.ecpat.net/TBS/PDF/2010_Cambodia_Progress_Card.pdf.

291 Agreement on Guidelines for Practices and Cooperation between the Relevant Government Institutions and Victim Support Agencies in Cases of Human Trafficking, Phnom Penh, Feb. 6, 2007, *translated at* http://www.no-trafficking.org/content/pdf/guidelines%20for%20victims%20support%20agencies.pdf (last visited Dec. 12, 2012); ECPAT INTERNATIONAL, *supra* note 290, at 14.

292 TIP REPORT 2011, *supra* note 3, at 111.

293 SOCIALIST REPUBLIC OF VIETNAM, GUIDELINES ON PROCESS AND PROCEDURES OF IDENTIFICATION AND RECEPTION OF TRAFFICKED WOMEN AND CHILDREN FROM ABROAD (Inter-Ministerial Circular 03/2008/TTLC-MPS-MOD-MOLISA) (May 8, 2008), *available at* http://www.no-trafficking.org/reports_docs/legal/vietnam/vn_imc_vic*id*.pdf.

294 DAVID ET AL., *supra* note 116, at 60.

295 Id. at 102–103.

296 Id. at 103.

297 UNITED STATES AGENCY FOR INTERNATIONAL DEVELOPMENT (UNAID), *supra* note 107, at 59.

adequate training courses on victim identification and case management for Vietnamese border guards and law enforcement officials at the district and provincial levels.[298] This lack of sufficient training has caused ineffective investigations and prosecutions leading up to the trafficking victims' loss of cases.[299]

The Thai government has designed and published the *Preliminary Checklist for Identifying Trafficked Persons*, which is a set of instructions to accelerate the process of victim identification.[300] This checklist contains the fundamental description of trafficking victims' characteristics and the methods for assistance of trafficking victims.[301] The government has disseminated this checklist to law enforcement, government agencies, and NGOs in Thailand.[302]

In practice, the Thai government's performance has been deficient in identifying and providing legal protections for trafficking victims.[303] The report disclosed the low number of trafficking victims given public shelter.[304] This report also reveals that even though counseling services are provided, legal aid, and medical treatment are limited.[305] While the government has concentrated on identifying more victims among vulnerable groups at its national and international airports and cross-borders, immigration detention center staff has identified a low number of trafficking victims actually in those centers.[306]

Because of the inefficiency of victim identifications, the Thai government has arbitrarily deported many human trafficking victims without recognizing them as victims. Based on the statistics, there are currently over 100,000 Cambodian migrant workers unlawfully residing in Thailand.[307] In addition, in

298 TIP REPORT 2011, *supra* note 3, at 385–386.

299 Id.

300 OFFICE OF ANTI-TRAFFICKING IN PERSONS COMMITTEE, SCOPE AND ELEMENTS OF IDENTIFICATION OF TRAFFICKED PERSONS, *available at* http://www.no-trafficking.org/reports_docs/legal/thailand/se_vicid_pamph_en.pdf; DAVID ET AL., *supra* note 116, at 100.

301 OFFICE OF ANTI-TRAFFICKING IN PERSONS COMMITTEE, *supra* note 300; DAVID ET AL., *supra* note 116, at 100.

302 OFFICE OF ANTI-TRAFFICKING IN PERSONS COMMITTEE, *supra* note 300; DAVID ET AL., *supra* note 116, at 100.

303 TIP REPORT 2011, *supra* note 3, at 354 (positing that Thailand must do more to combat human trafficking effectively and protect the rights of migrant workers who are increasingly vulnerable to forced and exploitative labor); Press Release, Office of the High Commissioner for Human Rights, *supra* note 31.

304 TIP REPORT 2011, *supra* note 3, at 354.

305 TIP REPORT 2012, *supra* note 64, at 341.

306 TIP REPORT 2011, *supra* note 3, at 354.

307 Rachel Vandenbrink, *Trafficking Victims Return Home*, RADIO FREE ASIA (July 5, 2012), http://www.rfa.org/english/news/cambodia/trafficking-07052012182450.html/.

2011 there were more than 100 Cambodian men were subject to forced labour on Thai fishing boats, who were either able to flee their traffickers or received help from government authorities.[308] Most employment companies have typically recruited workers through unofficial procedures.[309] Many traffickers have used forged working agreements to deceive male victims into thinking that they have received legitimate jobs.[310]

According to the International Organization for Migration report, the Thai government has not provided efficient protection and aid for the victims from Cambodia and Myanmar, who fled from this fishing boat.[311] In addition, they also seem to have deficient procedures for victim identification and repatriation.[312] Hundreds of victims from Cambodia and Myanmar have escaped the Thai fishing industry, but they have lacked access to the proper legal evidence or methods to go back to their country of origins. Others can access their home countries, but they have not obtained proper reintegration assistance.[313]

Based on the Thai government, the silence of these victims has prevented the country from making changes regarding fishing boat trafficking.[314] These fishing boat victims have refrained from reporting trafficking to Thai authorities for a variety of reasons, including the fact that they fear of retaliation by both traffickers and detention by authorities, their own incompetence of Thai language and overall unfamiliarity with their rights.[315]

According to Human Rights Watch, the Thai government authorities have been complicit in men's forced labour. According to Phil Robertson, many Thai law enforcements have not made serious commitment to protect migrant workers, but they tend to transfer these workers to immigration office as

---

308 Id.

309 Nurul Qoiriah, *Fishing Industry in South-East Asia Rife with Human Trafficking*, 11 Global Eye on Human Trafficking, March 2012, at 4, *available at* http://www.iom.int/jahia/webdav/shared/shared/mainsite/projects/showcase_pdf/Global-Eye-Issue11-Mar2012.pdf.

310 Id.

311 International Organization for Migration, Trafficking of Fishermen in Thailand 30 (Jan. 14, 2011), *available at* http://publications.iom.int/bookstore/index.php?main_page=product_info&cPath=41_7&products_id=720.

312 Id.

313 Id.

314 *Cambodia-Thailand: Men Trafficked into "Slavery" at Sea*, Integrated Regional Information Networks (irin) (Aug. 29, 2011), *available at* http://www.irinnews.org/Report/93606/.

315 Id.

unlawful migration.[316] According to the former Marine Police Commander of Thailand, Surapol Thuangthong, criticizes that many Thai law enforcements have obtained money from unlawful migrant workers and business owners.[317]

While the Thai government's inefficient identification process has been condemned by the international community, so has Cambodia's. Advocates of migrant's rights in that country have complained about the Cambodian government's inefficient protections. Generally speaking women and children are more often victims of human trafficking, but many unrecognized Cambodian men have also been exploited and subject to forced labour in various industries including, the fishing boats of Malaysia and Thailand.[318] Accordingly, there will be more trafficking of men in forced labour because of the deficiency of anti-human trafficking laws and implementation of laws of the Cambodian government.[319]

In addition to ineffective victim identification, the governments of Cambodia, Thailand, and Vietnam have provided inadequate shelter for male victims. For instance, the Cambodian government has not provided an "official" shelter plan for any class of trafficking victims,[320] particularly males.[321] Their approach has been silent on shelter for male victims and they fail to separate adults and children in shelters.[322]

---

316 Shannon Service and Becky Palmstrom, *Confined to a Thai Fishing Boat, For Three Years*, NPR ASIA (June 19, 2012, 3:06 AM), http://www.npr.org/2012/06/19/155045295/confined-to-a-thai-fishing-boat-for-three-years (reporting Phil Robertson's comment that "[m]ost of the time when migrants are arrested, the police aren't planning to make a sense or hand them over to immigration, as they're required to do.")

317 Id. (discussing the assertion by Surapol Thuangthong that "[e]very part of the Thai officers will benefit from this—the province, police, labor officers...[t]hey all get bribes from illegal migrants and related businesses").

318 *See* Robert Carmichael, *Young Cambodian Men at Risk of Being Trafficked and Sold into Labor*, VOICE OF AMERICA (May 11, 2010, 7:00 AM), http://www.voacambodia.com/content/young-cambodian-men-at-risk-of-being-trafficked-and-sold-into-labor-93402399/1356531.html (explaining that the Mekong Ministerial Initiative Against Trafficking (COMMIT) contends that "[m]ore and more men are falling victim" to human trafficking, which is a "genuine concern of the Cambodian government" because "it's not just women and children anymore."); *see also Cambodia-Thailand: Men Trafficked into "Slavery" at Sea, supra* note 314

319 Carmichael, *supra* note 318.

320 KNEEBONE & DEBELJAK, *supra* note 75, at 138.

321 TIP REPORT 2012, *supra* note 64, at 108.

322 Cambodian National Plan of Action, *supra* note 200, at 14–16.

In Thailand, the Ministry of Social Development and Human Security has built four shelters to house trafficked men.[323] In addition to these accommodations, they offer other assistance including food, physical and psychological treatment, health education, and transportation for medical services.[324] However, it appears that space is insufficient for such a large scale of trafficking victims.[325]

Similar to Cambodia and Thailand, the Vietnamese government designed the national plan of action that promotes the building of protection for victims to provide proper protection for all victims,[326] all men victims as women and children victims.[327] However, the government has failed to provide adequate shelter and assessment centers,[328] specifically shelter for male victims.[329]

iii *Deficient Registration Process of Recruitment Agencies*

Another concern of the governments of Cambodia, Thailand, and Vietnam is the constraint of managing recruitment agencies' activities that may cause human trafficking. For instance, the Thai government has granted irregular migrant workers work permits under the Nationality Verification and Granting an Amnesty to Remain in the Kingdom of Thailand.[330] The evidence revealed that in the year 2011 there were 851,830 migrants participating in the registration process.[331] This registration ensures that these migrant workers can

323 International Organization for Migration, *supra* note 311, at 31 (alleging that the male shelters are located in Chiang Rai, Pathum Thani, Ranong, and Songkhla provinces).

324 Id.

325 Id.; International Organization for Migration, *The Causes and Consequences of Re-Trafficking*, 2 Global Eye on Human Trafficking, Mar. 2008, at 1, 6, *available at* http://www.iom.int/jahia/webdav/site/myjahiasite/shared/shared/mainsite/projects/showcase_pdf/global_eye_2nd_issue.pdf (asserting that while Thai officials have placed women and children trafficking victims in public shelters, they have tended to exclude most trafficked men from such services because they are more prone to illegal migration).

326 Van Dung, *supra* note 224.

327 Id.

328 United States Agency for International Development (unaid), *supra* note 107, at 59.

329 tip Report 2012, *supra* note 64, at 373.

330 Yongyuth Chalamwong, *Management of Cross-Border Low-Skilled Workers in Thailand: An Update* 26 tdri Quarterly Rev., no. 4, 2011, at 3, 12, 17–18, *available at* http://tdri.or.th/publications/tdri-quarterly-review-december-2011; tip Report 2012, *supra* note 64, at 342.

331 tip Report 2012, *supra* note 64, at 342.

continually work in Thailand. Critics have questioned the fiscally discriminatory application fees of this program and have found that employers and irregular migrant workers have not been fully acknowledged this program.[332]

It is likely that unregistered recruitment agencies may deceive migrant workers into labor exploitation because Thai government has rarely focused on examining the legal status of recruitment firms.[333] In order to curtail debt bondage and other forms of human trafficking, the Thai government should consider registering labor brokers. Such a registration process would help migrant workers connect with only lawful and qualified labor agencies, where the government has compiled their business background (namely trademark number, accountability, reliability, recruitment achievement) and employees (such as identification number and criminal record). Otherwise, migrant workers may be trapped by human traffickers' deception of overcharging recruitment fees and loans for travel expenses.[334] Many victims have also succumbed to debt bondage and are forced to provide monthly payment for these traffickers because traffickers coerce victims to pay interest of original loan.[335]

Even though the governments of Cambodia and Vietnam have endeavored to ensure safe migration and recruitment, they have been incapable in convicting illicit conduct of these recruitment agencies. For instance, the Vietnamese Ministry of Foreign Affairs (MFA) initiated an online migration website to eradicate unlawful recruitment of unlicensed employment agencies, particularly marriage brokers.[336] Yet, the Vietnamese government has been silent on creating a regulation to control these agencies.[337] Even though the government has penalized some recruitment companies for overcharging employment application fees, there has been no evidence of criminal prosecution against illegal labor brokers.[338] Consequently, trafficking victims in Vietnam cannot fully find justice because the government has allowed recruitment agencies to operate with impunity. Similarly, Cambodian laws on the recruitment, placement, and protection of migrant labor show restriction and obsolescence.[339] This relevant legislation does not impose legal liability on

---

332 Chalamwong, *supra* note 330, at 12, 17.

333 Id.; TIP REPORT 2012, *supra* note 64, at 342.

334 *Bonded Labour*, ANTI-SLAVERY, http://www.antislavery.org/english/slavery_today/bonded_labour.aspx (last visited Mar. 5, 2013).

335 Id.

336 tip Report 2012, *supra* note 64, at 374.

337 Id.

338 Id.

339 TIP REPORT 2011, *supra* note 3, at 111.

recruitment agencies[340] or a monitoring system to punish unlawful recruitment agencies.[341]

iv *Ineffective Communication Channels*

The next concern of Cambodian, Thai, and Vietnamese governments' efforts in preventing human trafficking is the awareness-raising inefficiency of communication channels with various dialects. To diminish the growth of human trafficking victims, these three governments should provide knowledge of human trafficking to people through various media channels with different dialects so that all nationals can understand and recognize this harmful crime. In practice, even though Thailand created the anti-human trafficking hotline number 1300 to raise awareness of human trafficking, this service does not employ interpreters to respond to foreign victims, particularly those speaking the Khmer language.[342] With these constraints, local authorities may not be able to provide proper suggestions or assistance for non-Thai callers.[343] The Thai government needs to ensure that trafficking victims or reporters can access this service and other media options so that they have opportunities to compile information about trafficking victims and enhance their efforts at victim identification.[344]

While the Social Services Division and the National Council for Children of Thailand has set up two call numbers to support children, the CRC Committee has found that these hotlines may confuse child victims.[345] In order for this mechanism to be effective, the government should only have *one* line that

340 Id.; TIP REPORT 2012, *supra* note 64, at 108.

341 TIP REPORT 2011, *supra* note 3, at 111.

342 Id. at 355.

343 ANDRÉ OLIVIE, IDENTIFYING CAMBODIAN VICTIMS OF HUMAN TRAFFICKING AMONG DEPORTEES FROM THAILAND 37 (Dec. 2008), *available at* http://www.no-trafficking.org/reports_docs/commit/commit_cambodia%20deportees.pdf.

344 Id.

345 United Nations Committee on the Rights of the Child, Consideration of Reports Submitted by States Parties under Article 44 of the Convention Concluding Observations: Thailand, U.N. Doc. CRC/C/TH/A/CO/3-4, para. 78 (Feb. 17, 2012), *available at* http://www2.ohchr.org/english/bodies/crc/docs/co/CRC_C_THA_CO_3-4.pdf [hereinafter CRC Consideration of Reports under Art. 44]; United Nations Committee on the Rights of the Child, Consideration of Reports Submitted by States Parties under Article 12, para. 1, of the Optional Protocol to the Convention on the Rights of the Child on the Sale of Children, Child Prostitution and Child Pornography: Concluding Observations: Thailand, U.N. Doc. CRC/C/OPSC/THA/CO/1, para 35 (Feb. 21, 2012), *available at* http://daccess-ods.un.org/TMP/7597856.52160645.html [hereinafter CRC Consideration of Reports under Art. 12].

provides 24-hour-service for *everyone* in Thailand, which is staffed with knowledgeable receivers that can provide effective support for all trafficking victims, including children.[346]

Likewise, the national action plan illuminates the human trafficking situation in Vietnam through a variety of reporting channels mechanisms, including books, movies, and a website to raise awareness of the problem.[347] However, these materials are in English rather than the various different dialects of the victims of human trafficking.[348] While this information will obviously benefit English-Speaking customers, it does little to assist victims. Therefore, the Vietnamese government should ensure that it creates materials that can communicate with all groups of people through various languages so that they can learn how to protect themselves and their family members from human traffickers.

v *Corruption of Government Authorities*

Even though the Cambodian, Thai, and Vietnamese governments have strived to convict human traffickers, the inefficient capacity of law enforcement officials and the epidemic corruption of government authorities have obstructed the effectiveness of these three governments' exercises against human trafficking.

From the research presented here, it is obvious that the corrupt government authorities in Cambodia, Thailand, and Vietnam have decelerated human trafficking responses of these three countries. For instance, even though the Cambodian government ratified United Nations Convention against Corruption[349] and enacted a domestic corruption law and proclaimed a "zero-tolerance" policy for corrupt government authorities to illustrate its vigorous political will to counter-human trafficking,[350] the non-corruption policy has not curtailed corruption.[351] Law enforcement officials provide labor

346 CRC Consideration of Reports under Art. 44, *supra* note 345, para. 78; CRC Consideration of Reports under Art. 12, *supra* note 345 para. 35, *available at* http://www2.ohchr.org/english/bodies/crc/docs/co/CRC_C_OPSC_THA_CO_1.pdf.

347 Van Dung, *supra* note 224.

348 Id.

349 *United Nations Convention against Corruption: Signature and Ratification Status as of Dec. 24, 2012*, UNITED NATIONS OFFICE ON DRUGS AND CRIME (UNODC), http://www.unodc.org/unodc/en/treaties/CAC/signatories.html (last visited Mar. 1, 2013) (describing that "score below five on a scale of 0 (highly corrupt) to 10 (very clean)").

350 TIP REPORT 2011, *supra* note 3, at 111.

351 Laura Cohen, *A Policy Memo: Human Trafficking as a Human Security Threat—The Cambodian Context*, PERSPECTIVES ON GLOBAL ISSUES (Aug. 7, 2012), http://

recruitment agents with early warning notices of inspections,[352] which allow the agents to conceal evidence of human trafficking.[353] According to Transparency International's world ranking of corruption,[354] it evaluated Cambodia at 2.1 out of 10 points or a rank 164 out of 183 countries, showing that Cambodia is extremely corrupt.[355]

In Thailand, there is endemic corruption of Thai law enforcement authorities, including "low-cadre law enforcement officers," who are involved in human trafficking businesses such as seafood factories and brothels.[356] Such corruption has not only exacerbated the problem and delayed implementation of the anti-human trafficking policies and action plans as Transparency International's world ranking of corruption has assessed Thailand at 3.4 out of 10 points or 80 of 183 countries rank, which refers to highly corrupt in Thailand (Table 3).[357]

While the Vietnamese government has expressed a no tolerance policy for corruption by government authorities, a number of non-government organizations have disclosed that many local authorities have been involved in human

---

www.perspectivesonglobalissues.com/archives/spring-2010-security/cambodia/ (explaining that although Article 31 of Cambodia's national constitution acknowledges the Universal Declaration for Human Rights (UDHR) to ensure the rights of women and children, government authorities' corruption in human trafficking business has ravaged their rights); TIP REPORT 2011, *supra* note 3, at 111.

352 *Cambodia: Trafficking Domestic Workers to Malaysia*, INTEGRATED REGIONAL INFORMATION NETWORKS (IRIN) (Mar. 17, 2011), http://www.irinnews.org/Report/92210/CAMBODIA-Trafficking-domestic-workers-to-Malaysia (insisting that although the Cambodian government has planned to abolish unlawful employment recruiters, and has established an anti-human trafficking law, many government authorities have in fact been complicit in human trafficking); TIP REPORT 2011, *supra* note 3, at 111.

353 TIP REPORT 2011, *supra* note 3, at 111.

354 *Corruption Perceptions Index 2011*, TRANSPARENCY INTERNATIONAL (2011), http://cpi.transparency.org/cpi2011/results/ (explaining that "Transparency International is the global civil society organisation leading the fight against corruption. The Corruption Perceptions Index ranks countries/territories based on how corrupt their public sector is perceived to be. A country/territory's score indicates the perceived level of public sector corruption on a scale of 0–10, where 0 means that a country is perceived as highly corrupt and 10 means that a country is perceived as very clean. A country's rank indicates its position relative to the other countries/territories included in the index").

355 Id.

356 *Cambodia-Thailand: Men Trafficked into "Slavery" at Sea*, *supra* note 314; TIP REPORT 2012, *supra* note 64, at 340.

357 *Corruption Perceptions Index 2011*, *supra* note 354.

TABLE 3 *Inefficient approaches to anti-human trafficking laws by the governments of Cambodia, Thailand and Vietnam*

Measures	Inefficient Approaches by the Governments of Cambodia, Thailand & Vietnam
Prevention	Insufficient focus on forced labour, inadequate protection of trafficking men, deficient registration process of recruitment agencies, and ineffective communication channels
Protection	Arbitrary deportation of male victims without proper identification procedures and dearth of shelter for male victims
Prosecution	Inefficient capacity of law enforcement officials and the epidemic corruption of government authorities

trafficking.[358] Authorities arrested a local government official in Can Tho for registering marriages between Vietnamese women and foreign men without monitoring whether these women had been forced into these marriages.[359] Several NGOs have reported more corruption in cross-border areas of Vietnam.[360] In Transparency International's world ranking of corruption, Vietnam was assessed at 2.9 out of 10 points or 112 of 183 countries rank, which amounts highly corrupt in Vietnam.[361]

Conclusion

The governments of Cambodia, Thailand, and Vietnam have strived to suppress human trafficking, protect trafficking victims, and penalize trafficking offenders set forth in the UN Palermo Protocol. However, due to the insufficient implementation of these three governments, this research suggests that these three countries should reinforce ASEAN to establish ADTV that stipulates specific requirements of preventing human trafficking, protecting trafficking victims, and prosecuting trafficking offenders that Cambodia, Thailand, and Vietnam, including all ASEAN member countries, can meet and apply to their particular root causes of human trafficking problem in their ASEAN region.

358 TIP REPORT 2011, *supra* note 3, at 385; TIP REPORT 2012, *supra* note 64, at 372.
359 TIP REPORT 2011, *supra* note 3, at 385.
360 Id.
361 *Corruption Perceptions Index 2011*, *supra* note 354.

Also, this research believes that the Cambodian, Thai, and Vietnamese governments need to enhance ASEAN to form ACTV in order to address and instruct them into the best practices through ACTV's monitoring, evaluating, collecting data on achievements and challenges of their laws as enshrined in the ADTV (discussed both ADTV and ACTV in Chapter 5). The ADTV can serve as the regional anti-human trafficking models of Cambodia, Thailand, Vietnam and other ASEAN member countries while ACTV can help ASEAN bridge the gap between national and international anti-human trafficking law in order to meet international anti-human trafficking norms by encouraging its member countries to at least comply with ADTV that contains key measures of preventing human trafficking, protecting trafficking victims, and prosecuting trafficking perpetrator that rapidly need to be addressed and tackled in the ASEAN region.

The proposal of establishing ADTV and ACTV can help the governments of Cambodia, Thailand, Vietnam, and other ASEAN member countries to tackle national and regional human trafficking dilemmas that require multi-collaborations among neighboring countries. In order to support this proposal, it is critical that the next chapter discusses the necessity of creating ADTV and its fundamental provisions against human trafficking, and of forming ACTV and its qualifications as a monitoring mechanism that this research believes that they can help ASEAN strengthen its anti-human trafficking strategies.

CHAPTER 5

A Proposal for ASEAN Regional Reform

The Establishment of ASEAN Declaration of the Promotion and Protection of Trafficking Victims (ADTV) and ASEAN Commission on the Promotion and Protection of Trafficking Victims (ACTV)

This chapter makes two proposals, which can draw attention to strengthening ASEAN counter-human trafficking methods and strategies. First, it is proposed that the ASEAN Declaration on the Promotion and Protection on the Rights of Trafficking Victims (ADTV) should be established because the existing ASEAN counter-human trafficking laws are insufficient, and there is no specific anti-human trafficking law, which emphasizes victim-centered approaches or equal protection for all victims. The second proposal is formation of the ASEAN Commission on the Promotion and Protection of Trafficking Victims (ACTV) because ASEAN lacks anti-human trafficking body that specializes in preventing human trafficking, promoting equal protection of all trafficking victims, and prosecuting human traffickers. Its attributes can help its member countries monitor, evaluate, and compile data on the strengths and weaknesses of national laws, policies, and actions against human trafficking. The extent of these proposals relies upon the urgent needs of ASEAN member countries, particularly Cambodia, Thailand, and Vietnam, in decelerating human trafficking enlargement in their countries.

In order to affirm the significance of the creation of ADTV, the first section assesses the needs of reforming ASEAN's role in drafting ADTV by illustrating the existing regional and national legal deficiencies. This section also looks at the feasibility of establishing the ADTV and ACTV. ASEAN itself lacks a specific anti-human trafficking law providing equal protection for all trafficking victims. In addition, Cambodia, Thailand, and Vietnam all have insufficient anti-human trafficking laws (namely non-prosecution of trafficking victims, appropriate housing, age, gender, and special needs of trafficking victims) and actions (including protection of male victims, victim identification, and criminalization of human trafficking perpetrators). It is clear that these countries and the region as a whole should strive towards more cohesive norms to fight human trafficking.

ASEAN lacks a human rights body, which specializes in countering human trafficking and focuses on the promotion and equal protection of all human trafficking victims. In order to help its member countries strengthen their laws and practices, the region should adopt the attributes of the ACTV,

 | DOI 10.1163/9789004265189_006

which will be based on the Council of Europe (CoE)'s monitoring mechanisms, specifically the Group of Experts on Action against Trafficking in Human Beings (GRETA). GRETA requires high ethics, counter-human trafficking specialization, and monitoring authority, which in turn can help ASEAN provide better directions against human trafficking to its member countries (including Cambodia, Thailand, and Vietnam) by ensuring the equal protection of all trafficking victims of women, children, and men through monitoring power.

5.1 Recommendations of the Selective Measures of ASEAN Declaration on the Promotion and Protection of the Rights of Trafficking Victims (ADTV)

To confirm the needs of reforming ASEAN's role in the establishment of ADTV, this section revisits the disadvantages of counter-human trafficking laws and the practices of ASEAN and the three ASEAN member countries (Cambodia, Thailand, and Vietnam), namely the deficiency of existing ASEAN laws against human trafficking. For this reason, it is suggested that ASEAN should consider the establishment of ADTV. Even though ASEAN has not announced its approval of ADTV, ASEAN has considered doing research on the feasibility of the creation of ADTV.

5.1.1 *Necessity of Creating ADTV: Deficiency of Existing ASEAN Regional and National Anti-Human Trafficking Laws*

Since not all ASEAN member parties have ratified the U.N. Palermo Protocol, there are no common counter-human trafficking norms in the ASEAN region.[1]

1 Fiona David et al., Progress Report on Criminal Justice Responses to Trafficking in Persons in ASEAN Region 10 (2011), *available at* http://www.artipproject.org/progress-report/Progress%20Report_Criminal%20Justice%20Responses%20to%20TIP%20in%20the%20ASEAN%20Region_2011.pdf; United Nations Convention against Transnational Organized Crime and the Protocol Thereto, Nov. 15, 2000, 2225 U.N.T.S. 209, G.A. Res. 55/25, Annex I, U.N. Doc. A/RES/55/25, Ch. 18: Penal Matters, *available at* http://www.unodc.org/documents/treaties/UNTOC/Publications/TOC%20Convention/TOCebook-e.pdf [hereinafter UNTOC], at Chapter 18: Penal Matters; Protocol to Prevent, Suppress and Punish Trafficking in Persons, especially Women and Children, supplementing the United Nations Convention against Transnational Organized Crime, Nov. 15, 2000, 2237 U.N.T.S. 319, Annex II (entered into force Dec. 25, 2003), *available at* http://www.unodc.org/documents/treaties/UNTOC/Publications/TOC%20Convention/TOCebook-e.pdf [hereinafter the U.N. Palermo Protocol], at Chapter 18: Penal Matters (reiterating that seven ASEAN member countries have ratified to the U.N. Palermo Protocol, except Brunei, Singapore, and Thailand).

The member countries that have not ratified the U.N. Palermo Protocol are not bound by provisions (such as the definition of "trafficking in persons") as set forth in the U.N. Palermo Protocol.[2]

Because ASEAN prefers soft law over hard law, most of its laws dealing with counter-human trafficking consist of non-legally binding agreements.[3] Even though member countries have no obligation to implement these laws, ASEAN has encouraged its member countries to make a serious commitment in the fight against human trafficking as mentioned in Chapters 2 and 3.

However, the contents of these laws contain numerous drawbacks illustrating the reason ASEAN needs to create the ADTV. For instance, the ASEAN Practitioner Guidelines on Effective Criminal Justice Responses to Trafficking in Person (ASEAN Practitioner Guidelines), which is a non-legally binding law that enumerates the responsibility of ASEAN member countries in the fight against human trafficking,[4] are silent on defining the term "trafficking victim" and providing for the non-prosecution of trafficking victims.[5] Also, the ASEAN Practitioner Guidelines lack provisions on shelter conditions, which can lead member countries to place trafficking victims in inappropriate housing conditions. And the 2007 ASEAN Declaration on the Rights of Migrant Workers[6] does not provide protection for trafficking victims, who are undocumented migrant workers, even on the ground of humanitarian purposes.[7]

Although ASEAN has placed its efforts to fight human trafficking by creating numerous anti-human trafficking laws,[8] this regional legislation does contain

---

2 David et al., *supra* note 1, at 12 (exemplifying that Singapore lacks an anti-human trafficking law, and has neglected to enact other domestic laws in compliance with the U.N. Palermo Protocol).

3 Sunsanee Sutthisunsanee, Response of ASEAN to Human Rights Violations in Southeast Asia: Case Studies of Cambodia and East Timor 25 (2006).

4 ASEAN, Criminal Justice Responses to Trafficking in Persons: ASEAN Practitioner Guidelines pt. 1(A) (2007), *available at* http://www.artipproject.org/artip-tip-cjs/tip-cjr/recent_developments/ASEAN-PG_Web_English_Final.pdf [hereinafter ASEAN Practitioner Guidelines].

5 *See* id.

6 Susan Kneebone, *ASEAN: Setting the Agenda for the Rights of Migrant Workers?*, *in* Human Rights in the Asia-Pacific Region: Towards Institution Building *160*–161(Hitoshi Nasu & Ben Saul eds., 2011).

7 Id.

8 ASEAN Declaration on Transnational Crime, Paragraph 8, Manila, Dec. 20, 1997, *available at* http://cil.nus.edu.sg/rp/pdf/1997%20ASEAN%20Declaration%20on%20Transnational%20Crime-pdf.pdf [hereinafter ADTC]; ASEAN Declaration against Trafficking in Persons, Particularly Women and Children, Vientiane, Nov. 29, 2004, *available at* http://www.asean.org/communities/asean-political-security-community/item/asean-declaration-against-trafficking-in-persons-particularly-women-and-children-2 [hereinafter ADTC]; Cheah Wuiling,

deficiencies, which can prevent all trafficking victims from enjoying their rights and protection because of their inadequate contents. Specifically, most of the ASEAN agreements[9] have only prioritized awareness-raising campaigns and the protection of women and children[10] even though it is not just women and children affected by human trafficking,[11] men have also been trafficked in the ASEAN region's construction, food service, manufacturing, agriculture, begging, and commercial sex industries.[12] Therefore, ASEAN needs to broaden its understanding and attitude by addressing prevention and equal protection of all trafficking victims through a specific anti-trafficking law in order to alleviate all forms of human trafficking and protect all trafficking of women, children, and men.

Even though the results of criminal justice response against human trafficking of Cambodia, Thailand, and Vietnam reveal that these countries have made

---

Assessing Criminal Justice and Human Rights Models in the Fight Sex Trafficking: A case Research of ASEAN Region, 3 Essex Hum. Rts. Rev 46, 56 (2006); Ralf Emmers, Beth Greener-Barcham & Nicholas Thomas, *Institutional Arrangements to Counter Human Trafficking in the Asia Pacific*, 28 Contemp. S.E. Asia 490, 495 (2006); Olivia Khoo, *Regional Approaches to Trafficking in Women in South-East Asia: the Role of National Human Rights Institutions and the New ASEAN Human Rights Body*, 15 Austl. J. of Hum. Rts., no. 2, 2010, at 59, 69, *available at* http://www.austlii.edu.au/au/journals/AJHR/2010/3.pdf; David et al., *supra* note 1, at 1 (concluding that the instances of these ineffective anti-human trafficking laws include the 1997 ASEAN Declaration on Transnational Crime and the 2004 ASEAN Declaration against Trafficking in Persons, Particularly Women and Children).

9 ADTC, *supra* note 8; ADTC, *supra* note 8; *Initiatives: Support to Underserved Victims*, United Nations Inter-Agency Project on Human Trafficking (UNIAP), http://www.no-trafficking.org/init_underserved.html (citing several agreements including ASEAN declaration on Transnational Crime and ASEAN Declaration against Human Trafficking, Particularly Women and Children that tend to direct member countries' government authorities to understand that only women and children are vulnerable to human trafficking and should therefore be protected by the officials).

10 ASEAN Declaration on Transnational Crime, Paragraph 8, Manila, Dec. 20, 1997, *available at* http://cil.nus.edu.sg/rp/pdf/1997%20ASEAN%20Declaration%20on%20Transnational%20Crime-pdf.pdf [hereinafter ADTC]; ASEAN Declaration against Trafficking in Persons, Particularly Women and Children, Vientiane, Nov. 29, 2004, *available at* http://www.asean.org/communities/asean-political-security-community/item/asean-declaration-against-trafficking-in-persons-particularly-women-and-children-2 [hereinafter ADTC].

11 Victoria E. Kalu, *Issues in Human Trafficking and Migrant Smuggling in the Context of Illegal Migration*, 1 Int'l Legal Stud. Program J. 27 (2009).

12 *See* Kelly Hyland Heinrich, *Ten Years After the Palermo Protocol: Where are Protections for Human Trafficking Victims?*, 18 Hum. Rts Brief, no. 1, 2010, at 2, 4.

several efforts on the prevention, protection, and prosecution measures, these three countries have numerous challenges.[13] Specifically, the Cambodian, Thai, and Vietnamese governments have made it a priority to provide protection for victims of women and children while overlooking the need for prevention and protection of male victims (Chapter 4). For instance, even though the government of Vietnam modified the *Penal Code* to be practical for all individuals, including men, women, and children,[14] most Vietnamese measures and policies have focused on the assistance and support for women and children, not adult male victims (Chapter 4). And even if the Cambodia, Thai, and Vietnamese laws impose penalties on traffickers, these three governments need to advance their government authorities' competence and knowledge on identifying trafficking victims, especially male victims (Chapter 4).

5.1.2 *The Selective Measures of ADTV*

Because of ASEAN's deficient laws and action plans against human trafficking, ASEAN needs to create a specific anti-human trafficking law that can strengthen the prevention of human trafficking, protection of trafficking victims, and prosecution of trafficking offenders in order to decrease the volume of human trafficking in its region. ASEAN should advocate for cooperation among government offices as well as between public and private sectors in awareness-raising campaign against human trafficking to diminish the expansion of human trafficking. ASEAN should also address the fundamental protection of all trafficking victims in order to ensure that not only women and children, but also men will be protected. ASEAN needs to maximize the number of human trafficking offenders through strengthening government officials' intelligence and punishing everyone involved in human trafficking.

a Discussion on the Prevention of Trafficking in Persons: Lawful Registration Process of Recruitment Agencies

In order to alleviate the growth of human trafficking in the ASEAN region, there are certain preventive measures that ASEAN should stipulate in the ADTV. Even if their current legal instruments and guidelines have stipulated measures to deter human trafficking, there are other preventive measures and action plans that ASEAN should consider to advance its strategies and methods. It is important that ASEAN focuses on minimizing the number of

---

13 David et al., *supra* note 1.

14 Id. at 13.

trafficking victims[15] through the registration of recruitment agencies by engaging private sector in awareness-raising campaign of counter-human trafficking[16] and a campaign targeting potential migrant workers, which would strengthen their competence in protecting themselves from the cycle human trafficking perpetuated through the registration of recruitment agencies.

Demand drives human trafficking; so ASEAN should ensure that ADTV addresses the registration of the recruitment agencies in order to alleviate their risk of human trafficking. ASEAN should require the origin country to be responsible for investigating the creditability of employment companies in order to eradicate the illegal businesses and representatives engaged in human trafficking.[17]

ASEAN has partnered with MTV Exit, which is a "campaign" aiming to raise awareness of anti-human trafficking and prevention of human trafficking through online social networking websites, television programs, and other events such as musical concerts in its region.[18] This exemplifies ASEAN's efforts to engage other sectors in order to counter-human trafficking.[19] However, ASEAN still needs to involve more private groups (such as tourism companies)

15 *See* Anne T. Gallagher, *Recent Legal Developments in the Field of Human Trafficking: A Critical Review of the 2005 European Convention and Related Instruments*, 8 Eur. J. Migration & L.163, 184.

16 *See* Special Rapporteur on Trafficking in Persons, *Summary of Regional and Sub-Regional Structures and Initiatives to Counter Trafficking in Persons* 13 (Dec., 2010), *available at* http://www.ohchr.org/EN/Issues/Trafficking/Pages/DakarConsultationoct2010.aspx [hereinafter OHCHR] (stating that based on submissions received from regional mechanisms in response to questionnaire of the U.N. Special Rapporteur on Trafficking in Persons, Especially Women and Children, the Special Rapporteur's 2010 Report to the Human Rights Council and more recent submissions).

17 Group of Experts on Action against Trafficking in Human Beings, Second General Report on GRETA's Activities Covering the Period from 1 August 2011 to 31 July 2012, GRETA (2012)13 para. 33 (Oct. 4, 2012), *available at* http://www.coe.int/t/dghl/monitoring/trafficking/Docs/Gen_Report/GRETA_2012_13_2ndGenRpt_en.pdf; *see, e.g.*, *Rantsev v. Cyprus and Russia*, App. No. 25965/04, 51 Eur. H.R. Rep. 1, 21–22 (Jan. 7, 2010), *available at* http://www.coe.int/t/dghl/cooperation/economiccrime/corruption/Projects/CAR_Serbia/ECtHR%20Judgements/English/RANTSEV%20v%20CYPRUS%20%20RUSSIA%20-%20ECHR%20Judgment%20_English_.pdf.

18 *About mtv Exit*, MTV Exit: End Exploitation & Trafficking, http://mtvexit.org/about/ (last visited Mar. 5, 2013) (explaining that "MTV EXIT is a campaign about freedom – about our rights as human beings to choose where we live, where we work, who our friends are, and who we love. Most of us take these freedoms for granted, but hundreds of thousands of people throughout the world have had these basic human rights taken away").

19 Id.

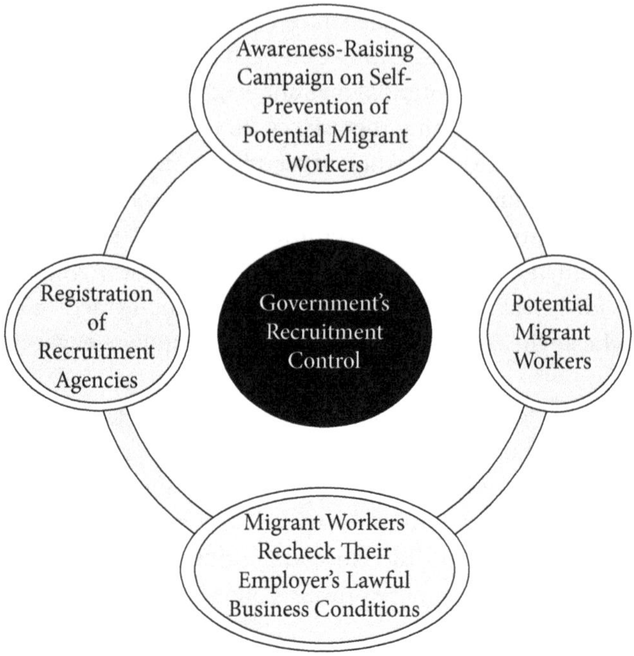

FIGURE 5 *The prevention of trafficking in persons: lawful registration processes for recruitment agencies*

in awareness-raising campaigns against this crime. Because of ASEAN's insufficient preventive laws and measures, most ASEAN member countries, particularly Cambodia, Thailand, and Vietnam, have not concentrated in decreasing the demand of forced labour and commercial sexual exploitation through cooperation between public and private groups (Figure 5).[20]

Apart from partnerships between the public and private sectors through a prevention- focused, awareness-raising ASEAN should encourage member countries to control recruitment in two ways. First, ASEAN urges its member countries to regulate the registration of recruitment agencies in order to keep records on the legal status of businesses and to permit public background checks. Second, a "self-prevention" campaign should be carried out through mutual data exchange amongst the ASEAN member countries, which can provide information about legal recruitment agencies in order to protect them from unlawful employment activities. This can allow potential migrant workers to check their employers' legitimacy and business background

20 The author views that ASEAN needs to encourage its member countries to improve training program of the specialist investigation units, prosecutorial and judicial response.

before engaging in work. This designed cycle at least has the potential to alleviate the expansion in the number of trafficked migrant workers if ASEAN can persuade its member countries to require all employment companies to verify the legitimacy of their businesses. In addition, ASEAN member countries should ensure that potential migrant workers will be able to find out about these recruitment agencies before seeking employment in order to decrease their risk of being trafficked by illegal employment companies, which may be involved in human trafficking.

b Analysis of the Protection for Trafficking Victims

While ASEAN has concentrated on criminal justice responses rather than a victim-centered approach, which emphasizes the protection of all trafficking victims (Chapter 3), the governments of Cambodia, Thailand, and Vietnam have not sufficiently provided protection for all trafficking victims through their laws and actions against human trafficking (Chapter 4). In particular, these three countries' laws have demonstrated failures in providing immunity for trafficking victims, appropriate housing, and taking into account age, gender, and special needs of trafficking victims when providing assistance. Their governments' performances have illustrated the deficiencies in victim identification and criminalization of human trafficking perpetrators. ASEAN has to address these issues specifically as fundamental provisions under ADTV in order to help strengthen the anti-human trafficking criterions of ASEAN member countries (particularly these three countries). Therefore, ASEAN needs to ensure that ADTV stipulates primary provisions of victim protection applicable to all trafficking victims.[21]

i *Victim Identification*

The various ASEAN guidelines instituted to battle human trafficking still lack a specific method of identifying trafficking victims.[22] It appears that no ASEAN legal instruments set out an efficient victim identification process to direct the member countries. Also, even if most ASEAN member countries have made efforts to improve victim identification, the evidence reveals that several ASEAN member countries have not appropriately identified many trafficking

21 *See* Council of Europe, Directorate General of Human Rights Equality Division: Council of Europe Convention on Action against Trafficking in Human Beings, Aug. 2005, *available at* http://www.coe.int/t/dg3/children/pdf/PDF_FS_TrafConv_E_Aug05.pdf; *See also Initiatives: Support to Underserved Victims, supra* note 9.

22 *See*, e.g., ASEAN Practitioner Guidelines, *supra* note 4.

victims in ASEAN region.[23] Vietnamese law, for instance, requires that enforcement authorities not identify victims unless there is evidence demonstrating that a "trafficker" was in fact engaged in human trafficking.[24] This means that trafficking victims may not be identified by Vietnamese government authorities if these authorities are incompetent in demonstrating human trafficking conduct of traffickers through ample evidence compilation against these offenders. It is likely that trafficking victims will not be given justice in Vietnam if the Vietnamese government officials lack competence and skill in identification of human traffickers and trafficking victims. Therefore, ASEAN should take into account creation of a training program to advance government authorities' knowledge of victim identification in order to ensure that they properly precede this process.

ASEAN has acknowledged the victim identification process through training programs for competent authorities; however, all ASEAN member countries need to strengthen the identification process by creating a concise and mutual knowledge of human trafficking for all competent authorities.[25] Numerous ASEAN training curriculums on trafficking in persons consist of ASEAN training programs[26] that aim to develop their member countries' government

---

23 *See* Press Release, Office of the High Commissioner for Human Rights, Thailand Must Do More to Combat Human Trafficking Effectively and Protect the Rights of Migrant Workers Who are Increasingly Vulnerable to Forced and Exploitative Labor, Says Special Rapporteur on Trafficking in Persons, Especially Women and Children, Joy Ngozi Ezeilo (Aug. 19, 2011), http://www.ohchr.org/en/NewsEvents/Pages/DisplayNews.aspx?NewsID=11319&LangID=E.

24 Susan Kneebone and Julie Debeljak, Transnational Crime and Human Rights: Responses to Human Trafficking in the Greater Mekong Subregion 234–235, 237 (2012) (explaining that the COMMIT encourages its member countries to ensure that their authorities identify victim status and provide services on the basis of age and gender for their "best interest," although, Kneebone and Debeljak have raised concern on the member countries' implementation of the COMMIT Process on victim identification); COMMIT, Sub-Regional Plan of Action (SPA_III 2011–2013) 23 (Jan. 2011), *available at* http://www.no-trafficking.org/reports_docs/commit/commit_resources/commit_spaiii_en.pdf (explaining that SPA_III requires the member countries to make sure that trafficking victims are "identified and offered individualized, gender and age-appropriate assistance after determining the best interests of the victim").

25 David et al., *supra* note 1, at 65.

26 Association of Southeast Asian Nations, ASEAN Responses to Trafficking in Persons: Ending Impunity for Traffickers and Securing Justice for Victims 40–49 (2006), *available at* http://www.artipproject.org/artip-tip-cjs/resources/specialised_publications/ASEAN%20Responses%20to%20TIP_2006.pdf (describing that the Work Plan to Implement ASEAN Declaration Against Trafficking in Persons, Particularly Women and Children

authorities' knowledge and competence to battle human trafficking.[27] Nevertheless, none of these training programs indicate the involvement of victim support agencies[28] that should be instructed on how to identify victims so that they can report government officials and provide indispensable assistance. NGOs tend to have a better understanding of the human trafficking phenomena than the governments of ASEAN member countries. Their competence and skill in victim identification can provide effective methods and strategies of victim identification for ASEAN. ASEAN should encourage its member countries to uphold the partnership between the government and victim support agencies to strengthen the identification process.[29] Specifically, ASEAN should reinforce its member countries to learn the efficient techniques of victim identification from these NGOs.

Misidentification of victims of national competent authorities can lead to arrest, detention, and deportation of trafficking victims,[30] particularly irregular migrant workers. Thailand exemplifies the high risk of misidentification of victims, particularly males.[31] To address the millions of migrant workers from Cambodia and Myanmar trafficked in the fishing factories in Thailand, the U.N. Special Rapporteur Joy Ngozi has recommended that the Thai government authorizes the marine police to oversee and investigate the risk of human

---

elaborates the significance of regional and international cooperation, law enforcement cooperation in the investigation of trafficking cases, prosecution and adjudication of trafficking cases, and victim protection and support. The work plan indicates strengthening victim identification to protection and support trafficking victims. Nonetheless, the work plan neglects to determine the feasibility of the cooperation between government and victim support agencies); David et al., *supra* note 1, at 153–154.

27 David et al., *supra* note 1, at 153–154.

28 Association of Southeast Asian Nations, *supra* note 26, at 48–49.

29 Secretariat to the Conference of the Parties to the United Nations Convention against Transnational Organized Crime, *Victims of Trafficking in Persons, with Particular Emphasis on Identification*, U.N. Doc. CTOC/COP/WG.4/2011/4 (Aug. 10, 2011), *available at* http://www.unodc.org/documents/treaties/organized_crime/2011_CTOC_COP_WG4/2011_CTOC_COP_WG4_4/CTOC_COP_WG4_2011_4_E.pdf; *See also*, e.g., Directive 2011/36/EU, of the European Parliament and of the Council of 5 April 2011 on preventing and combating trafficking in human beings and protecting its victims, and replacing Council Framework Decision 2002/629/JHA, 2011, (L 101), *available at* http://ec.europa.eu/anti-trafficking/download.action?nodeId=9c9ba3cd-794b-4a57-b534-ad89effac575&fileName=Directive+THB+L+101+15+april+2011.pdf&fileType=pdf (requiring the CoE member countries to collaborate with support victim agencies to create proper mechanisms for rapid victim identification and protection for trafficking victims).

30 Ezeilo, *supra* note 23.

31 Id.

trafficking on fishing boats.[32] The Thai government should also allow the marine police to attend a training program on the victim identification process for its capacity building.[33]

Regardless of existing ASEAN training programs for government authorities, ASEAN should ensure that its member countries provide adequate training programs for all stages of government authorities[34] to understand the same level of the identification process. The Task Force on ASEAN Migrant Workers (TF-AMW)[35] is correct in insisting that ASEAN enhances its member countries to rapidly and efficiently identify these irregular migrant workers' status on whether they are human trafficking victims and to provide them protection as other trafficking victims on the basis of humanitarian reason[36] instead of arbitrarily deport them without proper identification.[37]

After the first round of the training program, ASEAN should urge its member countries to review their training programs for all government officials in order to strengthen their knowledge and competence in identification of human trafficking victims.[38] ASEAN member countries should also assess investigative

---

32 Id.

33 Id.

34 David et al., *supra* note 1, at 49.

35 South East Asia Regional Cooperation in Human Development (SEARCH), *Promoting a Process of Change: The Task Force on ASEAN Migrant Workers, available at* http://www.docstoc.com/docs/74046970/Task-Force-on-ASEAN-Migrant-Workers-Civil-Society---Trade-Union-Consultation-Process-Towards-an-ASEAN-FRAMEWORK-INSTRUMENT-FOR-THE-PROTECTION-AND-PROMOTION-OF-THE-RIGHTS-OF-T (last visited Mar. 2, 2013) (describing that "The Task Force on ASEAN Migrant Workers (TF-AMW) is a regional platform comprised of key regional and national civil society organizations, trade unions, human rights and migrant rights NGOs, and migrant worker associations. The Task Force is engaged in both regional and national consultation processes that are "bottom-up" and aimed at forging cooperation and common ground among key stakeholders to protect and promote the rights of migrant workers in the region. TF-AMW activities have been supported by SEARCH since early 2006, through provision of funding and technical assistance for policy development and advocacy for the protection of migrant workers").

36 Task Force on ASEAN Migrant Workers, Civil Society Proposal: ASEAN Framework Instrument on the Protection and Promotion of the Rights of Migrant Workers 26 (2009), *available at* http://www.workersconnection.org/resources/Resources_72/book_tf-amw_feb2010.pdf.

37 *Foreign Domestic Workers' Recommendations to the ASEAN Intergovernmental Commission on Human Rights*, Asia Pacific Mission for Migrants (APMM) (Oct. 24, 2011), *available at* http://www.apmigrants.org/home/item/55-foreign-domestic-workers-recommendations-to-the-asean-intergovernmental-commission-on-human-rights.

38 David et al., *supra* note 1, at 49.

shortcomings of previous training programs in order to improve training methods of the next program.[39]

ii Non-Prosecution of Trafficking Victims

ASEAN created ASEAN Practitioner Guidelines[40] aiming to assist its member countries to provide justice for victims and to stop impunity of human traffickers[41] through substances that instruct criminal justice responses to law enforcement officials, specialist investigators, prosecutors, and judges.[42] However, these guidelines are silent on the non-prosecution of trafficking victims,[43] which can attract trafficking victims to cooperate with authorities in investigating and prosecuting trafficking offenders.

Without regional anti-human trafficking law on non-punishment of trafficking victims, half of ASEAN member countries, including Cambodia and Vietnam, have criminalized trafficking victims on the grounds of illicit activities because of being forced by traffickers.[44] ASEAN legal instruments should require member countries to establish provisions for immunity from prosecution for trafficking victims in order to increase the rate of victims' collaboration with competent authorities in investigation, prosecution, and adjudication. Such collaboration has the potential to be increased in the member countries, including Cambodia and Vietnam because these victims are not concerned with whether they will be criminalized for unlawful acts while being trafficked.

Criminalizing trafficking victims contradicts the rights-based approach[45] because trafficking victims cannot enjoy their rights to protection as victims when they are prosecuted.[46] In addition, they are doubly traumatized by the initial injury caused by traffickers and then the further strife of being prosecuted and possibly punished by the government.[47]

---

39 Id.

40 ASEAN Practitioner Guidelines, *supra* note 4.

41 Id.

42 Id.

43 Id. at pt. 1(A).

44 David et al., *supra* note 1, at 23 (finding that on the other hand, Indonesia, Malaysia, Myanmar, Philippines, and Thailand support non-prosecution of trafficking victims).

45 Anne T. Gallagher & Nicole Karlebach, *Prosecution of Trafficking in Persons Cases: Integrating a Human Rights-Based Approach in the Administration of Criminal Justice* 6 (OHCHR Background Paper, No. 4, July 2011), available at http://www.ohchr.org/Documents/Issues/Trafficking/Geneva2011BP_GallagherAndKarlebach.pdf.

46 Id.

47 Id.

Several best practices underscore non-prosecution of human trafficking victims. For instance, Guideline two of the *OHCHR Recommended Principles and Guidelines on Human Rights and Human Trafficking* stresses that States, intergovernmental and non-governmental organizations should not punish trafficking victims for the violations of immigration laws or for the activities as subjected to human trafficking.[48] Article 26 of the CoE Convention reinforces its member countries to take into account the possibility of non-prosecution of trafficking victims if they are forced to commit illegal activities by human trafficking offenders.[49] The *2011 European Trafficking Directive* recommends its member countries to authorize domestic government officials to protect trafficking victims by not criminalizing trafficking victims for unlawful conduct if trafficking victims are coerced by traffickers.[50] Therefore, ASEAN should require its member countries to reinforce the non-prosecution of trafficking victims through ADTV. Non-prosecution can allow trafficking victims to recover their physical and psychological health without being primarily concerned by the illicit activities they were coerced in to committing by traffickers. In addition, it also has the potential to strengthen the investigation and prosecution of traffickers because it is an incentive for victim cooperation in the proceedings.

Rather than target the victims for their immigration and labor violations, prosecutorial efforts to prevent trafficking should focus on the criminalization of the traffickers themselves. Criminalization implies the State's obligation to deter human trafficking and protect trafficking victims.[51] The failure of traffickers' criminalization can impact the investigation, prosecution, and adjudication of human trafficking cases.[52] Consequently, ASEAN should consider the implementation of non-prosecution of trafficking victims in its regional legal framework.

iii *Appropriate Housing*

The ASEAN Practitioner Guidelines stipulate that member countries should promptly provide victims with protection, but the guidelines fail to detail

48 United Nations Office of the High Commissioner for Human Rights, *Recommended Principles and Guidelines on Human Rights and Human Trafficking*, U.N. Doc. E/2002/68/Add.1, 6–7 (May 20, 2002), *available at* http://daccess-dds-ny.un.org/doc/UNDOC/GEN/N02/401/68/PDF/N0240168.pdf?OpenElement [hereinafter *Recommended Principles and Guidelines on Human Rights and Human Trafficking*].

49 Council of European Convention on Action against Trafficking in Human Beings and its Explanatory Report, May 16, 2005, C.E.T.S No. 197, para. 272–274, *available at* http://www.coe.int/T/E/human_rights/trafficking/PDF_conv_197_trafficking_e.pdf.

50 Directive 2011/36/EU, *supra* note 29, at art. 8; Gallagher & Karlebach, *supra* note 45, at 7.

51 Gallagher & Karlebach, *supra* note 45, at 4.

52 Id.

stipulations for shelter conditions.[53] Because there is no common regional law on appropriate housing, Cambodia, and Vietnam have neglected to prescribe provisions for appropriate housing.[54] This failure may also lead ASEAN member countries to perceive that they can place trafficking victims in any place, including the inconvenient and improper environment.[55] Likewise, the U.N. Special Rapporteur raised concern on improper shelter in Thailand and suggested that the Thai government should ensure a secure atmosphere of shelter for trafficking victims.[56] The Ministry of Social Development and Human Security of Thailand should provide physical and psychological treatment for trafficking victims' recovery, linguistic services for trafficking victims.[57] And the shelter should reflect a friendly accommodation for child victims by providing foster care.[58]

Both international and regional agreements have confirmed that governments should provide appropriate housing, but not detention. For instance, the CoE Convention emphasizes that the shelter program aims to comfort and recover trafficking victims' physical and psychological health because of human trafficking crisis.[59] The "appropriate" shelter refers to proper and safe environment, physical and psychological services and assistance.[60]

---

53 ASEAN Practitioner Guidelines, *supra* note 4.

54 United Nations Inter-Agency Project on Human Trafficking (UNIAP), Human Trafficking Laws: Legal Provisions for Victims 30 (n.d.), *available at* http://www.no-trafficking.org/reports_docs/legal_prov_vics.pdf (last visited March 5, 2013); David et al., *supra* note 1, at 23–24, 119 (explaining that the Vietnamese government has emphasized the protection of women and children, practically excluding men, and not sufficiently providing shelter for them); United States Agency for International Development (UNAID), Anti-Trafficking in Persons Programs in Asia: A Synthesis 42 (2009), http://transition.usa*id*.gov/our_work/cross-cutting_programs/wid/pubs/Asia_Synthesis_Anti_Trafficking_508.pdf.

55 David et al., *supra* note 1, at 118–119 (describing that some ASEAN member countries' domestic laws do not equally provide protection for all trafficking victims. For instance, Singapore's domestic law neglects to provide security and protection of adult male victims if they need a safety and temporary shelter).

56 Ezeilo, *supra* note 23.

57 Id.

58 Id.

59 Convention on Action against Trafficking in Human Beings and its Explanatory Report, *supra* note 49, at, Art. 12.1(a); U.S. Dep't of State, Trafficking in Persons Report 2010 8 (2010), *available at* http://www.state.gov/documents/organization/142979.pdf [hereinafter TIP Report 2010].

60 Convention on Action against Trafficking in Human Beings and its Explanatory Report, *supra* note 49, at art. 12.1(a).

The shelter facilitates trafficking victims to access an emergency medical treatment,[61] translation and interpretation assistance,[62] and legal counseling and assistance.[63] Also, the shelter should help child victims to access education.[64]

Regarding the extent of protection, recovery and reintegration, Part III of the Coordinated Mekong Ministerial Initiative Against Trafficking in Persons (the COMMIT Process)[65] provides that Cambodia, Thailand, and Vietnam have made an additional commitment to strengthen their laws by joining the COMMIT Process (concentrating on the promotion and protection of women, children, and men)[66] recommends that government officials in its member countries should not detain trafficking victims.[67] The Task Force on ASEAN Migrant Workers calls ASEAN for "a safe dignified manner and in human conditions" of housing, detention, and deportation of migrants.[68]

As a result, it is imperative that ASEAN should encourage its member countries to provide a safe and proper housing environment through ADTV. Even though ASEAN member countries, like Cambodia and Vietnam, have

---

61 Id.

62 Id.

63 Id.

64 Id.

65 Special Rapporteur on Trafficking in Persons, *Summary of Regional and Sub-Regional Structures and Initiatives to Counter Trafficking in Persons* 11 (Dec., 2010), *available at* http://www.ohchr.org/EN/Issues/Trafficking/Pages/DakarConsultationoct2010.aspx [hereinafter OHCHR] (intoning that the United Nations Inter-Agency Project on Human Trafficking (UNIAP) serves as Secretariat); Kneebone & Debeljak, *supra* note 24, at 203; United Nations Inter-Agency Project on Human Trafficking (UNIAP), The COMMIT Sub-Regional Plan of Action (COMMIT SPA): Achievements in Combating Human Trafficking in the Greater Mekong Sub-Region, 2005–2007 29, 38, and 40 (Dec. 2007), *available at* http://www.no-trafficking.org/reports_docs/commit/commit_spa1_achievements.pdf [hereinafter COMMIT SPA] (explaining that COMMIT has underscored the necessity of providing protecting to all women, children, and men victims of all kinds of human trafficking. The process has adopted labour policies and monitoring system of employment recruitment agencies to combat the crime and exemplifies "a mutually shared framework for cooperation.").

66 Gerald Smith, The Criminal Justice Response to Human Trafficking: Recent Developments in the Greater Mekong Sub-Region 13 (2010), *available at* http://www.no-trafficking.org/reports_docs/siren/GMS-08_eng.pdf (explaining that the COMMIT MoU on TIP paves a way with guidance of national and sub-regional coordination).

67 *See* Kneebone & DebeljAk, *supra* note 24, at 239; *see also* COMMIT, *supra* note 24, at art. 16.

68 Task Force on ASEAN Migrant Workers, *supra* note 36, at 28.

experienced financial constraint; they can provide clean rooms and trainings of handicraft or other activities for trafficking victims to loosen up their tension and fear. More importantly, ASEAN member countries can recruit volunteers (retired professionals or apprentices of social work) specializing in nurturing trafficking victims to assist well-trained social workers to create effective, secure and friendly shelter conditions for all trafficking victims. The appropriate housing atmosphere with sufficient treatment and career training program can strengthen trafficking victims' physical and mental health conditions to be prepared for other problems after their reintegration, particularly societal stigma.

iv *Right to Remedy*

ASEAN encourages its member countries to consider the feasibility of providing varied options for trafficking victims to obtain compensation.[69] The ASEAN Practitioner Guidelines enhance ASEAN member countries to ensure victims' rights to compensation by undertaking actions, namely "identify, trace and freeze or seize proceeds of crime derived from trafficking in persons for the purpose of eventual confiscation."[70] Likewise, the ASEAN Mutual Legal Assistance Treaty (ASEAN MLAT) requires ASEAN member countries to reinforce the joint collaboration in "the identification, seizure, confiscation and return of proceeds of trafficking in persons and related crimes."[71] However, ASEAN needs to require this provision as its member countries' responsibility to inform this right and to guarantee sufficient compensation for trafficking victims.[72] The remedy symbolizes justice for trafficking victims[73] and allows them to proceed with their lives in the way they prefer.[74]

---

69 *See*, e.g., ASEAN Practitioner Guidelines, *supra* note 4, at pt. 1(A)(6).

70 ASEAN Practitioner Guidelines, *supra* note 4, at pt. 2(D)(6).

71 Treaty on Mutual Legal Assistance in Criminal Matters among Like-Minded ASEAN Member Countries, Nov. 29, 2004, *available at* http://www.agc.gov.my/images/pdf/int/emam/mlatdoc/mutuallegalassisttreaty.pdf, at Art. 1(2)(i), 22.

72 *Foreign Domestic Workers' Recommendations to the ASEAN Intergovernmental Commission on Human Rights*, *supra* note 37 (listing the migrant domestic workers groups, NGOs and regional networks request AICHR ensure that trafficked migrant workers can access to sufficient remedies); Wolfgang Benedek et al., The Role of Regional Human Rights Mechanisms, European Parliament, EXPO/B/DROI/2009/25, 20 (Nov. 2010), *available at* http://www.europarl.europa.eu/committees/en/droi/studiesdownload.html?languageDocument=EN&file=33385.

73 *See* Convention on Action against Trafficking in Human Beings and its Explanatory Report, *supra* note 49, at Art. 15(197) (addressing the right to a remedy in its legal framework to encourage its member countries to recognize such right, trafficking victims in ASEAN region will be able to cover their suffering caused by traffickers).

74 Benedek, *supra* note 72, at 20.

Most ASEAN member countries do not recognize the right to remedies for trafficking victims.[75] Only Cambodia, Indonesia, Philippines,[76] Thailand, and Vietnam[77] elaborate this right in their internal laws.[78] However, Vietnam lacks seizure measures against trafficking offenders to compensate trafficking victims when the offenders allege the absence of asset, property, or money.[79]

As a result, ASEAN should ensure that trafficking victims recognize their right to compensation and receive adequate amount of the proceeds to cover suffering caused by traffickers. Various sources[80] have addressed a victims' right to remedies (particularly compensation) that ASEAN should set out in ADTV. For instance, Joy Ngozi Ezeilo, Special Rapporteur on Trafficking in Persons, especially Women and Children, addresses that trafficking victims should have the right to remedies, including data access, safe repatriation, and recovery treatment.[81] Ivan Simonović, Assistant Secretary-General for Human Rights adds that governments should not only provide "financial compensation,"[82] but also medical and psychological treatment, vocational training program, and other assistances such as legal advice and interpretation and translation

75 David et al., *supra* note 1, at 24–25.

76 Id. (addressing Section 14 of the Trafficking in Persons Law of Philippine that the law of Philippines exemplifies a well-written provision that allows trafficking victims to claim compensation for all damages from human trafficking offenders. Also, the law guarantees compensation by providing confiscated and forfeited assets for trafficking victims if human trafficking offenders cannot afford to compensate for all damages).

77 Law on Prevention, Suppression against Human Trafficking of Vietnam art. 6(3) (unofficial translation 2011) (Vietnam), *available at* http://www.artipproject.org/artip-tip-cjs/laws-policies/national/Vietnam/Vietnam%20Anti-trafficking%20in%20Persons%20Law%20Mar%202011%20final%20ENG.pdf (last visited Dec. 12, 2012).

78 David et al., *supra* note 1, at 24–25.

79 Ministry of Justice of Vietnam, (Draft) Report: Survey Findings on the Enforcement of Laws and Regulations on Investigation, Prosecution, and Trial of Criminals in Women and Children Trafficking 21 (Report Draft Project 4-CT 130/CP, June 2008).

80 TIP Report 2010, *supra* note 59; U.N. Palermo Protocol, *supra* note 1, at Art. 6(6) (explaining that the U.S. Department of State reiterates that a good anti-trafficking law should accommodate trafficking victims to claim compensation); Convention on Action against Trafficking in Human Beings and its Explanatory Report, *supra* note 49, at Art. 15(197) (acknowledging the right to access effective legal remedies, including compensation for trafficking victims by the Palermo Protocol and CoE Convention).

81 *Human Trafficking: A Rights-Based Approach*, U.N. OHCHR (Dec. 19, 2011), http://www.ohchr.org/EN/NewsEvents/Pages/HumanTrafficking.aspx.

82 Id.

assistance.[83] These remedies enable trafficking victims to strengthen not only their economic status, but they also help recover their physical and psychological conditions before repatriation.

While most trafficking victims do not know about these rights, they lack an opportunity to claim their right as a result of human trafficking.[84] ASEAN should require its member countries to inform victims of all relevant procedures in order to ensure that all trafficking victims will realize their right to claim compensation in their destination countries.[85] These relevant procedures include access to court and administrative proceedings in trafficking victims' native language.[86] The destination country should ensure the feasibility of a residence permit approval for trafficking victims because trafficking victims need to remain in the State to claim their rights.[87] Also, ASEAN should demand that its member countries are accountable for reporting trafficking victims' right to compensation in the dialect of victims so that they can acknowledge their right.

Even though the criminal courts in the destination country have no authority to adjudicate civil liability for trafficking victims, the civil courts dealing with compensation for damages can determine trafficking victims' claims for all damages.[88] ASEAN should address the fact that traffickers are liable for compensation.[89] If traffickers disappear or cannot afford to award compensation, the destination country should assure compensation for trafficking victims, namely by establishing a compensation fund in order to guarantee that trafficking victims will receive their compensation from the government of destination country even though trafficking perpetrators neglect or allege that they have no assets or proceeds that have frequently taken place in Vietnam.[90] In this extent, ASEAN can leave its member countries to determine their most convenient means of awarding compensation to trafficking victims in order to accelerate this process.[91]

---

83 Id.

84 *See* Convention on Action against Trafficking in Human Beings and its Explanatory Report, *supra* note 49, at Art. 15(192).

85 *See* id. at Art. 15(191).

86 *See* id. at Art. 15(192).

87 *See* id.

88 *See* id. at Art. 15(197).

89 *See* id.

90 *See* Convention on Action against Trafficking in Human Beings and its Explanatory Report, *supra* note 49, at Art. 15(198).

91 *See* id.

v Special Protection for Child Victims

While the growing number of trafficking victims in the ASEAN region is children,[92] the laws of Cambodia and Vietnam are silent in their consideration of age, gender and special needs for trafficking victims; and the laws of Thailand have demonstrated the limitation of the protection for child trafficking victims.[93] Therefore, ASEAN should detail the special protection for child victims under ADTV in order to fulfill their needs.

ASEAN has failed to indicate the exact age of a "child."[94] The lack of the definition can create inappropriate assistance and treatment for a person victimized while still a child, but was subsequently rescued by law enforcement officers once turning an adult. Particularly, in the case of male victims, there will be further problems because ASEAN does not have a specific anti-trafficking law and mechanism, which expedites effective protection of male victims. Likewise, ASEAN member countries have not paid adequate attention to identify male victims, who are nearly eighteen years old as child victims. For instance, the anti-human trafficking laws of Cambodia and Vietnam have failed to consider the age, gender, or special needs of trafficking victims.

Therefore, it is very imperative that ASEAN addresses the necessity of the sensitivity of age, gender, and special needs of trafficking victims in ADTV. For instance, while competent authorities cannot identify the age of the trafficking victim and the authorities assume that victim is a child, the authorities should provide special protection and assistance for an unaccompanied child.[95] Also, ASEAN should require its member countries to provide a representative for the unaccompanied child, to verify the child's identity and

---

92 *See* United Nations Children's Fund, Progress for Children: A Report Card on Child Protection 17, no. 8, U.N. Sales No. E.09.XX.14 (Sept., 2009), *available at* http://www.childinfo.org/files/Progress_for_Children-No.8_EN.pdf.

93 ANTI-TRAFFICKING IN PERSONS ACT B.E. 2551 § 33 (2008) (Thailand) , *available at* http://www.no-trafficking.org/content/Laws_Agreement/laws_agreement_pdf/trafficking_in_persons_act_b.e%202551%20%28eng.%29.pdf; United Nations Inter-Agency Project on Human Trafficking (UNIAP), *supra* note 54, at 44, 46; David et al., *supra* note 1, at 23.

94 *See*, e.g., ASEAN Practitioner Guidelines, *supra* note 4.

95 Secretariat to the Conference of the Parties to the United Nations Convention against Transnational Organized Crime, *Victims of Trafficking in Persons, with Particular Emphasis on Identification*, U.N. Doc. CTOC/COP/WG.4/2011/4, 8 (Aug. 10, 2011), *available at* http://www.unodc.org/documents/treaties/organized_crime/2011_CTOC_COP_WG4/2011_CTOC_COP_WG4_4/CTOC_COP_WG4_2011_4_E.pdf; Convention on the Rights of the Child 11, entered into force Sept. 2, 1990, 15 U.N.T.S. 3, Art. 20, http://www.ohchr.org/EN/ProfessionalInterest/Pages/CRC.aspx.

nationality, and locate their family.[96] The proper identification process of child victims, including male children at the age near eighteen years old, can receive their rights and protection as child victims. Specifically, ASEAN should ensure that its member countries provide "appropriate accommodation" that facilitates the child victims' sufficient needs (namely security from traffickers),[97] but not their detention.[98]

Due to insufficient protection for child victims in Cambodia, Thailand, and Vietnam,[99] ASEAN must ensure that its member countries recognize child victims' special needs because of their vulnerability of age, education, and experience. For instance, the substantive provisions of prevention and promotion of anti-trafficking in persons that can apply to all individuals, but the protection measures between adults and children need to be divided into different categories because children have different special needs and assistances from adults. The CoE Convention completely elaborates the special protection for child victims.[100] There are seven provisions of the children's specific rights and protection[101] based on the child victims' best interests in the extents of victim identification, residence permit, repatriation and return of victims; protection of victims, witnesses and collaborators with the judicial authorities.[102]

---

96 U.N. Conference of the Parties to the United Nations Convention against Transnational Organized Crime, *supra* note 29, at 8.

97 *See* Convention on Action against Trafficking in Human Beings and its Explanatory Report, *supra* note 49, at Art. 12(1), para. 153.

98 *See* id. at Art. 12(1), para. 155.

99 *See* Asian Human Rights Commission, Asian Human Rights Charter: A Peoples' Charter 19 (Mar. 30, 1998), *available at* http://material.ahrchk.net/charter/pdf/charter-final.pdf.

100 Gallagher, *supra* note 15, at 178.

101 Id.

102 Convention on Action against Trafficking in Human Beings and its Explanatory Report, *supra* note 49, at Art. 10(3)–(4), para. 136–137 (stating that "…while children need special protection measures, it is sometimes difficult to determine whether someone is over or under 18. Paragraph 3 consequently requires Parties to presume that a victim is a child if there are reasons for believing that to be so and if there is uncertainty about their age. Parties must provide for the representation of the child by a legal guardian, organi[z]ation or authority which is responsible to act in the best interests of that child (a); take the necessary steps to establish his/her identity and nationality (b); and make every effort to locate his/her family when this is in the best interests of the child. The family of the child should be found only when this is in the best interests of the child given that sometimes it is his/her family who is at the source of his/her trafficking."); Art. 14(2) (Residence permit), p. 52, para. 186 (providing that "the child's best interests take precedence over the above two requirements: the Convention provides that residence permits for child victims are to be "issued in accordance with the best interests of the child and, where

ASEAN should also require its member countries to reinforce the children's capacity-building and knowledge of human trafficking in ADTV in order to prevent further victimization or re-victimization of children. To accomplish this goal, ASEAN requires its member countries to design a "protective environment" for children to decrease their vulnerability to human trafficking.[103] The main elements of a "protective environment," including the strength of children's life skills, knowledge, and involvement in anti-human trafficking; of activities of recovery and reintegration of trafficking children; of monitoring and reporting of human trafficking cases; and of government's attention to promote and protect children's rights.[104] Consequently, ASEAN should stimulate its member countries to reduce the risk of child trafficking by instructing practical activities and events related to human trafficking characteristics and elements such as groups of involvement (including family members, relatives, and friends). ASEAN should particularly stress disseminating contact information of government agencies, where children can contact if children face a risk of human trafficking.

c Examination of the Prosecution of Traffickers

Even though ASEAN has encouraged its member countries to penalize human trafficking perpetrators, ASEAN member countries, particularly Cambodia, Thailand, and Vietnam have all had low conviction rates for trafficking crimes (Chapter 4). ASEAN should encourage member countries to maximize prosecutions of traffickers[105] through two methods. First, ASEAN should reinforce the improvement of training programs for government authorities[106] in order to strengthen their competence and knowledge of human trafficking. Second, ASEAN should focus on punishing everyone, who engages in human trafficking

---

appropriate, renewed under the same conditions" (Article 14(2)).'); Art. 16(7) (Repatriation and return of victims), p. 56, para. 207 (stipulating that "When the authorities take a decision regarding the repatriation of a child victim, the best interests of the child must be the primary consideration. According to this provision, the authorities must undertake an assessment of the risks which could be generated by the return of the child to a State as well as on its security, before implementing any repatriation measure."); Art. 28(3) (Protection of victims, witnesses and collaborators with the judicial authorities), p. 65, para. 286 ("a child victim shall be afforded special protection measures taking into account the best interests of the child.")

103 Convention on Action against Trafficking in Human Beings and its Explanatory Report, *supra* note 49, at Art. 5, para. 106.

104 Id. at Art. 5, para. 106.

105 *See* Gallagher, *supra* note 15, at 184.

106 *See* Gallagher & Karlebach, *supra* note 45, at 14.

(namely companies, associations, or organizations), in its legal framework in order to discourage human trafficking offenders for committing human trafficking activities. And third, ASEAN should accelerate the promotion of zero-tolerance of corruption in order to strengthen the government officials' anti-human trafficking action in convicting human trafficking offenders.

i *Regular Training Program for Government Authorities*

In terms of the development of training programs of government authorities, most international and regional agreements have reflected that well-trained and knowledgeable government authorities can take effective actions against human trafficking.[107] ASEAN has established various guidelines and training programs for the government authorities of its member countries, and have illustrated the need to improve the training programs on the victim identification, investigation, prosecution, and adjudication of human trafficking cases.[108] For instance, the U.N. Special Rapporteur Joy Ngozi commented that Thailand has not made progress in the prosecution of traffickers[109] and recommended that Thailand develops the training programs to advance victim identification and thus addresses traffickers' impunity. Further, ASEAN should require its member countries to advance policies and action plans on criminal justice responses to human trafficking and border controls,[110] including regular training programs for all competent authorities, including front line authorities (that have more opportunities to have the first contact with human trafficking victims) because ASEAN Practitioner Guidelines are silent on the training course of front line officers.[111]

ASEAN Practitioner Guidelines articulate the significance of effective cooperation between government authorities, namely prosecutors and investigators and prosecutors and judges, in responding to human trafficking cases.[112] However, these guidelines fail to emphasize cooperation between the front

107 U.N. Palermo Protocol, *supra* note 1, at Art. 10 (2); Council of Europe Convention on Action Against Trafficking in Human Beings, May 16, 2005, C.E.T.S. No. 197, 2569 U.N.T.S. 45795, art. 29(3) [hereinafter CoE Convention]; Directive 2011/36/EU, *supra* note 29, at art. 18(3).

108 The author suggests that ASEAN needs to encourage its member countries to improve training program of the specialist investigation units, prosecutorial and judicial response.

109 Ezeilo, *supra* note 23.

110 *See* Gallagher, *supra* note 15, at 184–185.

111 Smith, *supra* note 66, at 7.

112 *See* ASEAN Practitioner Guidelines, *supra* note 4, at pt. 1(B)(6)(7), 1(C)(1), 1(F)(1)(5).

line law enforcement officers[113] and specialist investigators.[114] It is imperative that ASEAN encourages collaboration between front line law enforcement authorities and special investigators because in the first 24 hours of the revelation of human trafficking case, national front line law enforcement authorities find trafficking victims and investigate the key elements of trafficking in persons.[115] If the front line law enforcement authorities are unable to identify victims, they should be encouraged by ASEAN to consult with special investigators, which can prevent arbitrary deportation without proper identification of trafficking victims. The evidence discloses the weaknesses of the front line law enforcement officials' performance in most ASEAN member countries.[116]

ii *Criminalization of Trafficking Offenders, Accomplices and Clients*

To the extent of human trafficking criminalization, it is vital to recognize that if an anti-human trafficking law proscribes only sexual exploitation, or only trafficking of women and children, the law will contain loopholes[117] for prevention, protection, and prosecution of all traffickers, especially labor traffickers. Government authorities have to implement laws and punish all groups of trafficking perpetrators that involve in any form of trafficking for all trafficking victims in order to suppress the volume of trafficking and provide justice.[118]

Even though most ASEAN member countries have acknowledged the criminalization of traffickers,[119] some ASEAN member countries, especially Vietnam, have failed to criminalize companies, organizations, and other legal people participating in human trafficking.[120] Also, many ASEAN member countries, particularly Cambodia, Thailand, and Vietnam, have been lax in investigating and prosecuting traffickers and their accomplices while trafficking victims have been criminalized on the basis of violations of immigration and labor laws (Chapter 4). These victims are refused justice and remain unprotected by government authorities (Chapter 4).

---

113 Smith, *supra* note 66, at 7 (illustrating that the front line law enforcement officers refer to "general duties police, border guards, and immigration and customs officials").

114 ASEAN Practitioner Guidelines, *supra* note 4.

115 David et al., *supra* note 1, at 55.

116 David et al., *supra* note 1, at 65–66.

117 *See* Gallagher & Karlebach, *supra* note 45, at 5.

118 Id. at 3 (commenting that victims barely are given justice and protection from danger affecting their security).

119 David et al., *supra* note 1, at 17–18.

120 Id. at 18.

As a result, ASEAN should consider penalizing clients who demand labor based on human trafficking.[121] Punishment has the potential to address both supply and demand of human trafficking services.[122] ASEAN should require member countries to address the demand for human trafficking, which has caused its growth. Therefore, apart from criminalizing traffickers and complicities, ASEAN can mitigate the problem by criminalizing the demand. Demand underpins all forms of human trafficking, by targeting those that use services as a result of human trafficking and inflicting more stringent penalties, including imprisonment and mandatory financial compensation for victims.[123]

Effective anti-human trafficking criminalization requires practice at all levels of law enforcement (namely front line officers, investigators, prosecutors, and judges victim identification, investigation, and prosecution), which can increase expenditures on counter-human trafficking training programs.[124] Well-trained government officials have the potential to both reinforce zero-tolerance policies and raise awareness in learning and comprehending the human trafficking situation through authorities' actions against human trafficking. While these training costs may demand regional and internal funds, they also can provide justice and proper protection for all trafficking victims.

ASEAN should recognize that increased penalties such as fines and fees can provide compensation for trafficking victims and proceeds for human trafficking suppression and protection of trafficking victims.[125] ASEAN should encourage their member countries to strengthen their law enforcement authorities' performance in order to effective tackle trafficking in persons and bring justice to trafficking victims.

---

121 CoE Convention, *supra* note 1077, at Art. 18(4); Gallagher & Karlebach, *supra* note 45, at 5–6.

122 Directive 2011/36/EU, *supra* note 29, at preambular para. 26; Gallagher & Karlebach, *supra* note 45, at 5–6.

123 *See Recommended Principles and Guidelines on Human Rights and Human Trafficking*, *supra* note 48, at para. 4; *see also* CoE Convention, *supra* note 1077, at Arts. 4, 18.

124 *See*, e.g., California Attorney General, Proposition 35 Human Trafficking. Penalties. Initiative Statute: Official Title and Summary 42–45 (Nov. 6, 2012), *available at* http://vig.cdn.sos.ca.gov/2012/general/pdf/35-title-summ-analysis.pdf (analyzing that the Federal Trafficking Victims Protection Act containing increased punishment can cause higher expenses, including maintenance of prison detaining longer term imprisonment of trafficking victims that can enlarge regional and internal costs of ASEAN and its member countries).

125 *See*, e.g., id. at 45.

iii *Promotion of Zero-Tolerance of Corruption*

ASEAN also should address the punishment of corrupt government authorities because this low rate of prosecution because it implies a great deal of impunity towards traffickers.[126] In order to prosecute offenders, ASEAN should focus on "effective" investigation and prosecution of human trafficking.[127] In addition, as the U.N. Special Rapporteur has suggested, the government also needs to reinforce the law enforcement authorities' professionalism, encouragement, and promotion for their position.[128] Also, the government should boost the awareness-raising campaign of zero-tolerance for corruption by government authorities engaging in human trafficking[129] because their involvement has weakened the investigation, prosecution, and adjudication of human trafficking cases.

In order to carry out this zero-tolerance campaign, ASEAN should address in ADTV on the establishment of the incentives and positive attitude of being professional of their government authorities, including the reinforcement of career advancement and salary.[130] ADTV should emphasize the high moral character of law enforcement authorities, special investigators, prosecutors, and judges to intensify these government officials' criminal justice responses to human trafficking and to construct public's attitude towards those officials.[131] In order to achieve this goal, ASEAN should enact a media campaign to promote ethics and morals for characteristics of government officials because media group can help ASEAN and its member countries rapidly and efficiently convey this message to public.

5.1.3 *Feasibility of ASEAN's Acceptance of ADTV*

ASEAN has at least acknowledged the need to establish a specific anti-human trafficking law. For instance, since 2007, ASEAN leaders have authorized the ASEAN Ministerial Meeting on Transnational Crimes (AMMTC) to assign Senior Officials Meeting on Transnational Crime (SOMTC) to study the possibility of

126 *See* Ezeilo, *supra* note 23.

127 *See* Kneebone & Debeljak, *supra* note 24, at 180; *see also* Ezeilo, *supra* note 23; Convention on Action against Trafficking in Human Beings and its Explanatory Report, *supra* note 49.

128 Ezeilo, *supra* note 23.

129 Ezeilo, *supra* note 23.

130 *See*, e.g., United Nations Office of the High Commissioner for Human Rights, *Recommended Principles and Guidelines on Human Rights and Human Trafficking: Commentary*, U.N. Doc. HR/PUB/10/2, U.N. Sales No. E.10.XIV.1, 24–26 (2010), *available at* http://www.ohchr.org/Documents/Publications/Commentary_Human_Trafficking_en.pdf. [hereinafter OHCHR Commentary].

131 Id.

drafting an "ASEAN Convention on Trafficking in Persons."[132] Even though the resolution has yet to be promulgated, its consideration shows that ASEAN has valued the significance of a specialized anti-human trafficking law that can address and tackle trafficking of all men, women, and children in its region.

Likewise, half of ASEAN member countries (Cambodia, Lao PDR, Myanmar, Thailand, and Vietnam)[133] have illustrated their attention in creating the efficient counter-human trafficking strategies by participating in the Coordinated Mekong Ministerial Initiative against Human Trafficking (COMMIT Process).[134] This process has provided specific anti-human trafficking directions and action plans that apply to all trafficking victims.[135] Since human trafficking is affected at both the national and transnational levels, these five ASEAN member countries will need to collaborate with ASEAN and other member countries to draft the ADTV and articulate equal protection for all victims in order to truly alleviate the situation. However, these five ASEAN member countries will not be able to alleviate human trafficking without the collaboration with ASEAN and other member countries in drafting the ADTV articulating equal protection for all trafficking victims because human trafficking originates at both the national and transnational stages. These five member countries also need ASEAN to consider creating a specialized anti-human trafficking law and monitoring body to address trafficking in general, without any discrimination based on gender, just as the COMMIT Process's member countries have provided for.

Despite the efforts of the other organizations with which ASEAN member countries have joined to mitigate human trafficking, these countries have

---

132 Joint Communiqué of the Sixth ASEAN Ministerial Meeting on Transnational Crime (AMMTC), Nov. 6, 2007, http://www.asean.org/news/item/joint-communique-of-the-6th-ammtc-bandar-seri-begawan-6-november-2007 [hereinafter Sixth Joint Communiqué]; ASEAN Leaders' Joint Statement in Enhancing Cooperation against Trafficking in Persons in Southeast Asia, May 8, 2011, http://www.asean.org/archive/Joint_Statement_TIP.pdf.

133 *Where We Work*, United Nations Inter-Agency Project on Human Trafficking (UNIAP), http://www.no-trafficking.org/where.html (last visited Mar. 1, 2013).

134 OHCHR, *supra* note 16, at 10–11 (explaining that the COMMIT Process is the first regional instrument with a sub-regional approach that attempts to urge its member countries to take rigorous actions); Ahmad Shah Pakeer Mohamad et al., *The Phenomenon of Human Trafficking Activities in Southeast Asia*, 1 Int'l J. Human. & Soc. Sci. 13, 168, 173 (2011) (finding that although the COMMIT MoU on TIP is the only one sub-regional MoU of the GMS member countries, the COMMIT MoU on TIP has influenced ASEAN member countries' bilateral agreements on the fight human trafficking).

135 South East Asia National Human Rights Institutions Forum (SEANF) Paper on Migrant Workers 14 (2010), *available at* http://www.aseannhriforum.org/attachments/059_SEANF_Paper_on_Migrant_Workers_-_Final.pdf.

expressed their trust and confidence in ASEAN to help fight battle. For instance, the Cambodian government has adhered to the ASEAN plan to enhance regional cooperation to combat trafficking in persons even though their government had already created its own comprehensive anti-Trafficking law and established the National Taskforce on Human Trafficking, in charge of counter-trafficking policy and collaboration, prevention, criminal justice, protection, rehabilitation and reintegration.[136] The government admits that membership in ASEAN has allowed the government to collaborate with other Member States struggling with human trafficking and that this regional organization has been supportive of these activities.[137]

The Thai government has admitted that if ASEAN had not been established, the driven cooperation among the Thai Parliament, social, community and civil society groups, and non-governmental organizations would not become as well-built as it is now.[138] The Thai Parliament has intentionally invested its times and budget to attend a variety of ASEAN conferences and activities.[139] Furthermore, Thailand has been one of the most active stakeholders that support diverse ASEAN plans of action and strategies.[140]

Even though the Vietnamese government still needs to improve its efforts at promoting and protecting male victims, it recently enacted the anti-human trafficking law, which applies to all trafficking victims.[141] Creation of this law shows that the Vietnamese government has made efforts in countering human trafficking based on ASEAN's encouragement. The Vietnam Academy of Social

136 Sriprapha Petcharamesree et al., Towards an ASEAN Commission on the Promotion and Protection of the Rights of Women and Children 16 (2008).

137 *See* Sakada Chun, *Cambodia Joins ASEAN to Combat Human Trafficking*, Voice of Am. | Khmer, (Nov. 17, 2005, 7:00 AM), http://www.voacambodia.com/content/a-40 -2005-11 -17-voa2-90146237/1357440.html.

138 Pradap Pibulsonngram, *The Thai Perspective*, *in* The Making of ASEAN Charter 81(Tommy Koh, Rorario G Manalo, & Walter Woon eds., 2009).

139 Id. at 80–81.

140 Id. at 81.

141 *See*, e.g., Law on Suppression of Human Trafficking and Sexual Exploitation, NS/RKM/0208/005 (Cambodia) (2008), *available at* http://www.no-trafficking.org/content/Laws_Agreement/cambodia_tip_2008.pdf (last visited Dec. 12, 2012); ANTI-TRAFFICKING IN PERSONS ACT B.E. 2551 (2008) (Thailand), http://www.no-trafficking.org/content/Laws_Agreement/laws_agreement_pdf/trafficking_in_persons_act_b.e%202551 %20%28eng.%29.pdf; Law on Prevention, Suppression against Human Trafficking of Vietnam art. 6(3) (unofficial translation 2011) (Vietnam), *available at* http://www .artipproject.org/artip-tip-cjs/laws-policies/national/Vietnam/Vietnam%20 Anti-trafficking%20in%20Persons%20Law%20Mar%202011%20final%20ENG.pdf (last visited Dec.12, 2012).

Sciences and the associate professor, Dr. Dang Nguyen Anh, have confirmed the necessity of the government to cooperate with other ASEAN member countries by sharing and addressing the human trafficking phenomenon.[142]

While the three respective countries have accepted that ASEAN has influenced the human rights development in their countries, the governments of Cambodia, Thailand, and Vietnam have admitted that their governments alone cannot afford to address and combat against human trafficking scourge by their own countries.[143] These three countries seem to have great respect and trust for ASEAN, thus paving the way for the establishment of the ADTV as a common regional anti-human trafficking norm.

5.2 Recommendations of the Selective Qualification and Power of ASEAN Commission on the Promotion and Protection of the Rights of Trafficking Victims (ACTV)

Due to the absence of regional anti-human trafficking expert, this section affirms the importance of creating a regional human rights monitoring body specializing in fighting trafficking in persons, providing equal protection for all trafficking victims, and prosecuting trafficking perpetrators that can help its member countries advance their domestic laws and actions through its recommendations. For this reason, it is suggested that ASEAN should consider the formation of ACTV in order to fulfill its regional and national needs in the battle against human trafficking.

Since ASEAN lacks a regional anti-human trafficking human rights body with monitoring power, this section examines what character and power of ASEAN Commission on the Promotion and Protection of Trafficking victims (ACTV) ASEAN should form. It is clear that the international community (namely Global Alliance Against Traffic in Women and the U.N. Special Rapporteur)[144] has praised the Group of Experts on Action against Trafficking

142 *ASEAN–Vietnam Emphasises ASEAN Cooperation to Combat Human Trafficking*, Disabled Peoples' International Asia-Pacific Region (Apr. 3, 2010), http://www.dpiap.org/resources/article.php?id=0000472&genreid=15&genre=ASEAN (reporting Dr Dang Nguyen Anh's statement that "human trafficking is a problem that needs to be addressed quickly to ensure human security in Asia").

143 *See* Rizal Sukma, ASEAN and Non-Traditional Security 1 (Dec. 3, 2010), *available at* http://www.waseda-giari.jp/sysimg/imgs/20101203_2c_sukuma_research.pdf.

144 Gallagher, *supra* note 15, at 186; Caroline Hames et Al., Feeling Good About Feeling Bad: A Global Review of Evaluation in Anti-Trafficking Initiatives 18 (2010), *available at* http://www.gaatw.org/publications/GAATW_Global_Review.FeelingGood

in Human Beings (GRETA) as the most effective human rights mechanism with high attributes of ethics and monitoring competence of the Council of Europe[145] even though GRETA is a brand new monitoring mechanism.[146] ASEAN should learn from the best practices and lessons of GRETA and create a monitoring system that can help its member countries address and assess the strengths and weaknesses of their anti-human trafficking laws and measures in order to advance their future responses.

ASEAN should model its monitoring mechanisms after GRETA and include some of its characteristics and monitoring powers. This section evaluates this mechanism and scrutinizes its stipulations. It also advises selective qualifications and the monitoring role of ACTV in order to ensure that ACTV can play a significant monitoring role in strengthening ASEAN member countries' anti-human trafficking laws and actions aiming to promote and protect the rights of all trafficking victims. This research believes that even though the CoE monitoring system has demonstrated several shortcomings, ASEAN should learn its challenges and accomplishments in order to create ACTV with sufficient monitoring authorities.

.AboutFeelingBad.pdf; Group of Experts on Action against Trafficking in Human Beings (GRETA), *Questionnaire for the Evaluation of the Implementation of the Council of Europe Convention on Action against Trafficking in Human Beings by the Parties: First Evaluation Round* 4, 8, 10, GRETA (2010)1 rev2, Feb. 1, 2010, *available at* http://www.coe.int/t/dghl/monitoring/trafficking/Source/GRETA_2010_1_rev3_en.pdf (the instances of its approach include "Section I. Q 4. Please indicate if, in your internal law, THB is considered as a HR violation; Q 5. Please indicate what special legal protection exists under your internal law (including case law if any) in cases of violations of human rights, which would apply in cases of THB; II.1. Q 23 Please describe the social and economic empowerment measures for disadvantaged groups vulnerable to THB which have been implemented or planned; Section II.Q 55 Please describe the measures taken in your internal law to protect the identity and safety of victims before, during and after investigations and legal proceedings").

145 Gallagher, *supra* note 15, at 186; Hames et Al., *supra* note 144, at 18; Group of Experts on Action against Trafficking in Human Beings (GRETA), *Questionnaire for the Evaluation of the Implementation of the Council of Europe Convention on Action against Trafficking in Human Beings by the Parties: First Evaluation Round*, *supra* note 144, at 4, 8, 10.

146 Regional and Sub-Regional Cooperation in Promoting a Human Rights-Based Approach to Combating Trafficking in Persons especially in Women and Children, Dakar, Oct. 4–5, 2010, *Discussion Paper: Consultation of the Special Rapporteur on Trafficking in Persons, especially Women and Children* (2010), *available at* http://www.ohchr.org/Documents/Issues/Trafficking/Dakar_discussion_paper_en.pdf.

5.2.1 *Need for Forming ACTV*

Even though ASEAN has dealt with numerous transnational security crimes, human trafficking has been one of the most challenges of ASEAN and all ASEAN member countries.[147] The International Labour Organization has declared that the Asia-Pacific region contains the first highest volume of forced laborers or 56 percent of the global sum.[148] It is clear from these statistics that the scourge of human trafficking has tremendously affected ASEAN member countries and that they should rapidly tackle this dilemma. However, none of the existing ASEAN human rights mechanisms fully specializes in promoting anti-human trafficking, equal protection for all trafficking victims, and prosecution of people involved in human trafficking (Chapter 4). They also lack the power to monitor, evaluate, and compile information on accomplishments and challenges that can assist ASEAN and its member countries in addressing the root causes of human trafficking, both regionally and nationally (Chapter 3).

The ASEAN Intergovernmental Commission on Human Rights (AICHR) deals with numerous human rights issues (including human trafficking) and scarcely discusses counter-human trafficking methods based on its experiences.[149] While the ASEAN Commission on the Promotion and Protection of Women and Children (ACWC) is in charge of promoting and protecting the rights of women and children (including human trafficking), it has been assigned to prioritize the promotion and protection of women and children rather than male victims.[150] In addition, the ASEAN Committee on the Implementation of the ASEAN Declaration on the Protection and Promotion of the Rights of Migrant Workers (ACMW) is assigned to concentrate on the implementation of the Declaration and the cooperation in fighting human trafficking more than the promotion and protection of the rights of migrant

147 Evolving towards ASEAN 2015: ASEAN Annual Report 2011–2012, 31–32 (2012), *available at* http://www.aseansec.org/documents/annual%20report%202011-2012.pdf.

148 *Summary of the ILO 2012 Global Estimate of Forced Labour: Executive Summary*, International Labour Organization, *available at* http://www.ilo.org/wcmsp5/groups/public/---ed_norm/---declaration/documents/publication/wcms_181953.pdf [hereinafter *2012 ilo Global Estimate*].

149 Five-Year Work Plan of the ASEAN Intergovernmental Commission on Human Rights (2010–2015), *available at* http://aichr.org/documents/?doing_wp_cron=1356371613.7076230049133300781250 (last visited Dec. 24, 2012) (Scroll down to.PDF link for AICHR Five-Year Work Plan 2010–2015).

150 *Summary Notes of cs-acwc Meeting: Work Plan*, Human Rights Working Group – Indonesia (Sept 8, 2011), *available at* http://www.hrwg.org/en/asean/acwc/document/item/3278-summary-notes-of-cs-acwc-meeting-pt-8-2011 (scroll down to link to "download attachment") (summarizing the meeting between civil society organizations and ACWC).

workers.[151] This means that ACMW has not concentrated on protecting migrant workers from human trafficking. Even worse is that ACMW has not been assigned to protect illegal migrant workers even though they have been trafficked according to the Declaration on the Protection and Promotion of the Rights of Migrant Workers. The deficiencies of these human rights mechanisms illustrate that it is imperative to establish ACTV in order to ensure that its member countries provide equal protection for all trafficking victims.

Without a regional anti-human trafficking body with monitoring power focusing on equal protection of all trafficking victims, ASEAN member countries individually have to encounter human trafficking without effective anti-human trafficking instruction of regional human rights expert like ACTV. The establishment of a specialized human rights mechanism can demonstrate ASEAN's political will and serious commitment against human trafficking of ASEAN regional leaders to the international community.[152] If ASEAN wants to help member countries strengthen their laws and actions, ASEAN should consider creation of the ACTV (Figure 6).

The creation of ACTV will not overlap with other ASEAN existing human rights mechanisms' authorities. While AICHR is an overarching human rights institution accountable for counter-human trafficking under the Political-Security Community, ACWC (focusing on trafficking of women and children) and ACMW (cooperating body to battle against trafficking of migrant workers)[153] are structured under Socio-Cultural Community (Chapter 3). Even though ASEAN envisioned the separation of ACWC and ACMW from AICHR that cannot fully promote and protect all human trafficking victims (Chapter 3). ASEAN should assign ACTV to supplement AICHR's anti-human trafficking section under the Political-Security Community, which is designed to guarantee that all people in ASEAN member countries live in peace and in the atmosphere of justice, democracy, and coherence in ASEAN region.[154]

Specifically, this community is directly in charge of all human rights issues, including counter-human trafficking (a transnational crime) that can impact

---

151 Vitit Muntarbphorn, Development of ASEAN Human Rights Mechanism 13, EXPO/B/DROI/2012/05 (Sep. 25, 2012), *available at* http://www.europarl.europa.eu/committees/en/droi/studiesdownload.html?languageDocument=EN&file=76531.

152 Petcharamesree, *supra* note 136, at 110, 112–113.

153 Muntarbphorn, *supra* note 151, at 13.

154 *See* ASEAN, Roadmap for an ASEAN Community 2009–2015, 5 (2009), *available at* http://www.asean.org/images/2012/publications/RoadmapASEANCommunity.pdf; Yuyun Wahyuningrum, *Understanding ASEAN: Its Systems and Structure* (Dec. 2009), *available at* http://www.scribd.com/doc/81600447/ASEAN-Structures-Mechanisms-Yuyun-10-03-04-Copy.

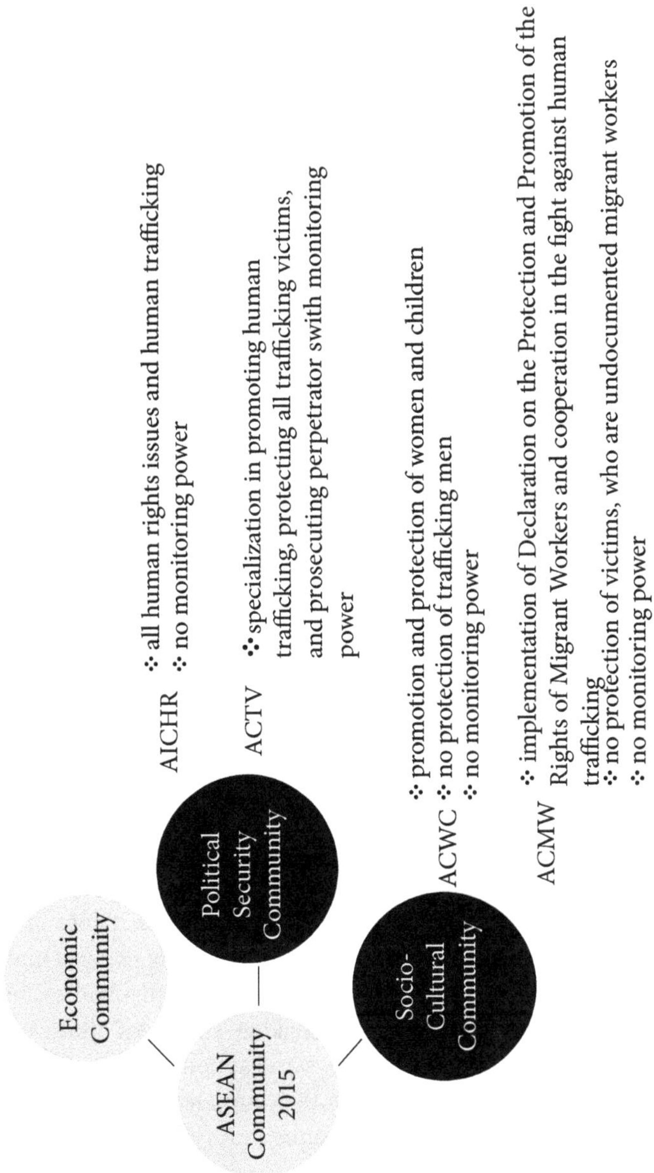

FIGURE 6 *The selective anti-human trafficking structure of* ASEAN

more than one countries' national sovereignty. While ASEAN has envisioned human trafficking as political insecurity, it has also moved toward political conflict avoidance among its member countries in counter-human trafficking management. It is presumed that ASEAN requires its member countries to tackle this crime under political security community without violation of individual sovereignty on the basis of the collaboration of their mutual criminal justice response.

The deficiencies of the existing ASEAN human rights mechanisms (AICHR, ACWC, and ACMW) and the growth in human trafficking exhibit a dire need for creating an anti-human trafficking bureaucracy like ACTV that can help bridge the loopholes of all existing human rights bodies' counter-human trafficking methods by addressing the promotion and equal protection of all trafficking victims without discrimination based on gender or legal status.

Based on its specialization in the fight against human trafficking, ACTV can help AICHR, ACWC, and ACMW strengthen their work plans by contributing data relevant to regional and national counter-human trafficking situation through monitoring system through a regular anti-human trafficking meeting of all human rights bodies (Chapter 3). Also, ACTV can help ASEAN member countries strengthen their national anti-human trafficking laws[155] and urge member countries to implement international counter-human trafficking laws by bridging the space between the national and international norm. As a result, apart from creating the sufficient provisions of ADTV, the efficient monitoring power of ACTV can assist both ASEAN and its member countries (particularly Cambodia, Thailand, and Vietnam) advance their anti-human trafficking methods and practices that help minimize the number of human trafficking victims in the ASEAN region. Therefore, the creation of ACTV encompassing counter-human trafficking experts and monitoring power will not be redundant over other human rights bodies. In order to accelerate ASEAN counter-human trafficking strategies that can assist its member countries strengthen their laws and actions, ASEAN should consider the creation of ACTV separating from other human rights bodies so that these anti-human trafficking experts can concentrate on this particular crime without distraction of other issues that AICHR, ACWC, and ACMW have been in charge of.

---

155 *See* U.N. Centre for Human Rights, National Human Rights Institutions: A Handbook on the Establishment and Strengthening of National Institutions for the Promotion and Protection of Human Rights 3, U.N. Doc. No. HR/P/PT/4, U.N. Sales No. E.95.XIV.2 (1995), *available at* http://www.asiapacificforum.net/members/international-standards/downloads/best-practice-for-nhris/NHRIs_a_handbook.pdf.

5.2.2 *Analysis of Selective Qualification and Monitoring Power of* ACTV

It should be acknowledged that regional mechanisms can contribute their organizations to promote and protect human rights in its region by mobilizing its member countries[156] and encouraging other non-compliant member countries to implement their adhered international and regional legal framework.[157] If the organization escalates the mechanism's competence in monitoring system, the mechanism can strengthen its organization's human rights development.[158] Therefore, in order to promote and protect the rights of all trafficking victims, this research insists that ASEAN should form ACTV with efficient and sufficient attributes by learning and adopting better human rights mechanism specializing in the promotion and protection of trafficking victims' fundamental rights.

Compared to other regional human rights systems, the Council of Europe is the only system, which has created a monitoring mechanism comprised of the Group of Experts on Action against Trafficking in Human Beings (GRETA) and the Committee of the Parties.[159] GRETA exemplifies the qualifications of independence and counter-human trafficking specialization while the Committee of the Parties represents a political body[160] examining and approving GRETA's recommendations after GRETA's monitoring system. Their authorities have highlighted the promotion and protection of all trafficking victims' rights by requiring member countries to undertake measures in suppressing all forms of human trafficking and providing equal protection for all groups of trafficking victims.[161]

---

156 Kathryn Hay, *A Pacific Human Rights Mechanism: Specific Challenges and Requirements*, 40 Victoria U. Wellington L. Rev. 195, 195 n.1 (2010); Carole J. Petersen, *Bridging the Gap?: The Role of Regional and National Human Rights Institutions in the Asia Pacific*, 13 Asian-Pac. L. & Policy J. 174, 184 (2011); Submission on the Inquiry into Human Rights Mechanisms and the Asia-Pacific 35 (Dec. 2008), *available at* http://www.hrlrc.org.au/files/FLRI3TIBW4/HRLRC_Submission__Asia_Pacific.pdf (mentioning the report of the Human Rights Law Resource Centre that addresses that the 1993 Vienna Declaration and Programme of Action's confirmation on the advantage of establishing a regional human rights mechanism that "regional arrangements play a fundamental role in promoting and protecting human rights. They should reinforce universal human rights standards, as contained in international human rights instruments and their protection").

157 Petersen, *supra* note 156, at 184.

158 Hay, *supra* note 156, at 213; Dave Peebles, Pacific Regional Order 2 (2005).

159 Convention on Action against Trafficking in Human Beings and its Explanatory Report, *supra* note 49, at 76.

160 *Action against Trafficking in Human Beings*, Council of Europe Human Rights and Rule of Law, http://www.coe.int/t/dghl/monitoring/trafficking/Docs/Monitoring/Monitoring_en.asp#TopOfPage (last visited Dec. 12, 2012).

161 *See* Benedek et al., *supra* note 72, at 21–22.

In order to respond whether ASEAN should adopt GRETA monitoring model, it is worth acknowledging the distinction between European and ASEAN systems although both European and ASEAN systems represent intergovernmental organizations.[162] For instance, while GRETA is authorized to implement a legally binding instrument (Council of Europe Convention on Action against Trafficking in Human Beings), ASEAN human rights bodies are assigned to implement non-binding tools. Since ASEAN prefers to undertake a soft law to human rights, it is anticipated that ASEAN can strengthen counter-human trafficking strategies and methods coupled with a monitoring expert body. Because this body focuses on the promotion and equal protection of all trafficking victims, ASEAN needs to strengthen its counter-human trafficking tactics in order to ensure that all trafficking victims will be given their justice and basic rights through effective monitoring process (Chapter 3).

Another distinction between European and ASEAN systems is that ASEAN tends to strictly embrace the principle of non-interference in the internal affairs of member countries (ASEAN Way) greater than the European system.[163] The non-interference principle can in fact interfere with ASEAN's counter-human trafficking efforts. Human trafficking represents a transnational crime that requires serious criminal justice responses and collaboration among all member countries affected by this crime; ASEAN should encourage its member countries to relent their claim of national sovereignty during the investigation and prosecution procedure in order to achieve mutual cooperation against human trafficking among member countries concerned.

Even though there are differences between the CoE and ASEAN counter-human trafficking systems, it is anticipated that ASEAN should learn and apply the GRETA monitoring model to the ASEAN Commission on the Promotion and Protection of Trafficking Victims (ACTV). This monitoring power can strengthen ASEAN counter trafficking efforts through a better approach to trafficking victim protection and mutual collaboration among monitoring human rights body, member countries, and civil society organizations in compiling human trafficking information, areas in which ASEAN has been deficient.

Even though it is premature to evaluate the accomplishment of the CoE monitoring mechanism, especially GRETA as a counter-human trafficking

162 *See* The Academic Association for Contemporary European Studies, The European Union and the Council of Europe: Difference, Duplication or Delegation? 1 (2008), *available at* http://www.uaces.org/pdf/papers/0801/2008_Bond.pdf; David Camroux, The European Union and ASEAN: Two to Tango? 7 (2008), *available at* http://www.notre-europe.eu/media/Etude65EU-ASEAN-en.pdf.

163 *See* id. at 8.

expert body, its monitoring system has moved toward effective methods against transnational crime.[164] Its current practices have also confirmed the efficiency of its monitoring process through the requirements of trafficking victims' rights approach and data collection from member countries' government organizations and various reliable resources, including civil society organizations,[165] which has not been concentrated in the context of ASEAN.

Further, it is critical that ASEAN undertakes GRETA's effective qualifications of high ethics, counter-human trafficking specialization, and monitoring powers in order to assist member countries enact or modify better anti-human trafficking laws and actions because ASEAN existing human rights bodies lack these indispensable qualifications that can help strengthen counter-human trafficking strategies. Therefore, this section analyzes the realm of the selective characteristics and monitoring authority of ACTV applied based on the GRETA model.

a Selective Qualifications of ACTV

It should be acknowledged that regional mechanisms can contribute their organizations to promote and protect human rights in its region by mobilizing its member countries[166] and encouraging other non-compliant member countries to implement their adhered international and regional legal framework.[167] If the organization escalates the mechanism's competence in monitoring system, the mechanism can strengthen its organization's human rights development.[168] Therefore, in order to promote and protect the rights of all trafficking victims, this research insists that ASEAN should form ACTV with efficient and sufficient attributes by learning and adopting better human rights mechanism specializing in the promotion and protection of trafficking victims' fundamental rights.

Compared to other regional human rights systems, the Council of Europe is the only system, which has created a monitoring mechanism comprised of the Group of Experts on Action against Trafficking in Human Beings (GRETA) and

---

164 Gallagher, *supra* note 15, at 186.

165 Group of Experts on Action against Trafficking in Human Beings (GRETA), *Rules of Procedure for evaluating implementation of the Council of Europe Convention on Action against Trafficking in Human Beings by the Parties* 7, THB-GRETA (2009)3, June 17, 2009, *available at* http://www.coe.int/t/dghl/monitoring/trafficking/Source/THB-GRETA (2009)3_en.pdf.

166 Hay, *supra* note 156; Petersen, *supra* note 156, at 184; Submission on the Inquiry into Human Rights Mechanisms and the Asia-Pacific, *supra* note 156, at 35.

167 Petersen, *supra* note 156, at 184.

168 Hay, *supra* note 156, at 213; Peebles, *supra* note 158, at 2.

the Committee of the Parties.[169] GRETA exemplifies the qualifications of independence and counter-human trafficking specialization while the Committee of the Parties represents a political body[170] examining and approving GRETA's recommendations after GRETA's monitoring system. Their authorities have highlighted the promotion and protection of all trafficking victims' rights by requiring member countries to undertake measures in suppressing all forms of human trafficking and providing equal protection for all groups of trafficking victims.[171]

In order to respond whether ASEAN should adopt GRETA monitoring model, it is worth acknowledging the distinction between European and ASEAN systems although both European and ASEAN systems represent intergovernmental organizations.[172] For instance, while GRETA is authorized to implement a legally binding instrument (Council of Europe Convention on Action against Trafficking in Human Beings), ASEAN human rights bodies are assigned to implement non-binding tools. Since ASEAN prefers to undertake a soft law to human rights, it is anticipated that ASEAN can strengthen counter-human trafficking strategies and methods coupled with a monitoring expert body. Because this body focuses on the promotion and equal protection of all trafficking victims, ASEAN needs to strengthen its counter-human trafficking tactics in order to ensure that all trafficking victims will be given their justice and basic rights through effective monitoring process (Chapter 3).

Another distinction between European and ASEAN systems is that ASEAN tends to strictly embrace the principle of non-interference in the internal affairs of member countries (ASEAN Way) greater than the European system.[173] The non-interference principle can in fact interfere with ASEAN's counter-human trafficking efforts. Human trafficking represents a transnational crime that requires serious criminal justice responses and collaboration among all member countries affected by this crime; ASEAN should encourage its member countries to relent their claim of national sovereignty during the investigation and prosecution procedure in order to achieve mutual cooperation against human trafficking among member countries concerned.

169 Convention on Action against Trafficking in Human Beings and its Explanatory Report, *supra* note 49, at 76.

170 *Action against Trafficking in Human Beings*, *supra* note 160.

171 *See* Benedek et al., *supra* note 72, at 21–22.

172 *See* The Academic Association for Contemporary European Studies, *supra* note 162, at 1; Camroux, *supra* note 162, at 7.

173 *See* Camroux, *supra* note 162, at 8.

ASEAN should apply the GRETA monitoring model to the ASEAN Commission on the Promotion and Protection of Trafficking Victims (ACTV). This monitoring power can strengthen ASEAN counter trafficking efforts through a better approach to trafficking victim protection and mutual collaboration among monitoring human rights body, member countries, and civil society organizations in compiling human trafficking information, areas in which ASEAN has been deficient.

Even though it is premature to evaluate the accomplishment of the CoE monitoring mechanism, especially GRETA as a counter-human trafficking expert body, its monitoring system has moved toward effective methods against transnational crime.[174] Its current practices have also confirmed the efficiency of its monitoring process through the requirements of trafficking victims' rights approach and data collection from member countries' government organizations and various reliable resources, including civil society organizations,[175] which has not been concentrated in the context of ASEAN.

Further, it is critical that ASEAN undertakes GRETA's effective qualifications of high ethics, counter-human trafficking specialization, and monitoring powers in order to assist member countries enact or modify better anti-human trafficking laws and actions because ASEAN existing human rights bodies lack these indispensable qualifications that can help strengthen counter-human trafficking strategies. Therefore, this section analyzes the realm of the selective characteristics and monitoring authority of ACTV applied based on the GRETA model.

i *Requirement and Capacity*

GRETA commissioners are comprised of expert independent from their governments' control so that the commission can provide effective determination through monitoring human trafficking circumstance from various reliable resources and member countries' responses to GRETA's questionnaire.[176] However, both AICHR and ACWC (existing human rights bodies of ASEAN) are dependable inter-governmental representatives without monitoring systems.[177] It is possible that they can be influenced by their governments and

174 Gallagher, *supra* note 15, at 186.

175 Group of Experts on Action against Trafficking in Human Beings (GRETA), *Rules of Procedure for evaluating implementation of the Council of Europe Convention on Action against Trafficking in Human Beings by the Parties* 7, *supra* note 165, at 7.

176 *See* Benedek et al., *supra* note 72.

177 *See*, e.g., ASEAN Commission on the Promotion and Protection of the Rights of Women and Children (ACWC), Terms of Reference (Feb. 2010), *available at* http://www.asean.org/images/2012/publications/TOR%20of%20ACWC%201.pdf [hereinafter ACWC Terms of

other public institutions in the exercise of their powers in defining and implementing anti-human trafficking policies.[178] The Terms of Reference for these human rights bodies underline their members' capacity and knowledge of integrity and gender equality.[179] ACWC should specialize in the rights of women and children while the AICHR should expertise in the human rights.[180] Neither the ACWC TOR nor the AICHR TOR addresses their personalities of high ethics, independence and neutrality, and the competence in counter-trafficking specialization.[181]

ASEAN should address the ACTV's characters of high ethics and anti-human trafficking specialization as embodied in the CoE Convention. The representatives' qualifications would assist ASEAN to reduce enormous expenditures of anti-human trafficking control and management, as well as trafficking victims' protection. For instance, these representatives with high moral personality would exercise their conduct against corruption while their anti-human trafficking competence would contribute ASEAN with providing effective performance and technical plans of action to prevent human trafficking, protect trafficking victims, and implement investigation and prosecution.

Even though ASEAN did select the ACWC and the AICHR representatives from its member countries' government members, ASEAN should ensure that ACTV representatives will be independent and impartial in order to allow these representatives to focus on the benefits of trafficking victims rather than individual country. If ASEAN envisions progress in the political-security community dealing with anti-human trafficking, then ASEAN should allow ACTV to exercise their duties with decision-making power; and the government should not involve in ACTV's decision-making resolutions. Given its full decision -making authority, with its high morality and anti-human trafficking expertise,

---

Reference] para. 4; *see also*, e.g., ASEAN Intergovernmental Commission on Human Rights (AICHR), Terms of Reference § 3 (Oct. 2009), *available at* http://www.asean.org/images/2012/publications/Terms%20of%20Reference%20of%20ASEAN%20Intergovernmental%20Commission%20on%20Human%20Rights.pdf [hereinafter AICHR Terms of Reference]; Khoo, *supra* note 8, at 68–69.

178 *See* Council of Europe, Resolution CM/Res (2008)7 on Rules on the Election Procedure of the Members of the Group of Experts on Action against Trafficking in Human Beings (GRETA) adopted by the Committee of Minister on 11 June 2008 at the 1029th meeting of the Ministers' Deputies, R. 3(2), *available at* https://wcd.coe.int/ViewDoc.jsp?Ref=CM/Res%282008%297&Language=lanEnglish&Ver=original&Site=CM&BackColorInternet=9999CC&BackColorIntranet=FFBB55&BackColorLogged=FFAC75.

179 *See*, e.g., AICHR Terms of Reference, *supra* note 177, at Art. 6.4 and Art. 5.3.

180 *See*, e.g., id.

181 *See*, e.g., id.

ACTV could make progress in the fight against human trafficking because it focuses on the promotion and protection the rights of trafficking victims instead of the benefit of government.

It seems that ASEAN would appoint a high moral personality with specialization in human rights, protection and support of trafficking victims, anti-human trafficking.[182] ASEAN however selects dependent and partial representatives because its member countries prefer to be involved in their representatives' decision-making process in order to ensure that their implementation will not affect their national sovereignty. Consequently, ASEAN should encourage its member countries to compromise their principle of non-intervention in the battle against human trafficking in order to achieve mutual collaboration on criminal justice responses against such crime.

ii *Composition*

The current GRETA members include fifteen[183] professionals with diverse backgrounds, namely lawyer, U.N. Special Rapporteur, professor, law enforcement officials, judge, legal consultant, and immigration officials.[184] In addition, approximately five of the members have worked or cooperated with non-governmental organizations (NGOs).[185] The recruitment of NGO representatives as GRETA memberships reflects the CoE's recognition of civil society organization's roles and influences.

According to the number of ASEAN member countries, ACTV may consist of ten independent and impartial experts in human trafficking or relevant to this crime. Even with ASEAN's preference of governmental representatives, ASEAN should ensure that at least three members of ACTV have worked or interacted with civil society organizations. These members can lay out data of human trafficking flow and the needs of trafficking victims.

The evidence reveals that non-governmental organizations have taken a vital role in human security advocacy,[186] and ASEAN has admitted civil society

182 *See* Council of Europe, Group of Experts on Action Against Trafficking in Human Beings (GRETA): *List of Items Discussed and Decision Taken*, THB-GRETA (2010)LD5, 5th meeting of GRETA (Strasbourg, 16–19 March 2010), Mar. 19, 2010, para. 10, *available at* http://www.coe.int/t/dghl/monitoring/trafficking/docs/GRETA_MeetingDocs/Lists%20of%20decisions/THB-GRETA%282010%29LD5_en.pdf.

183 Convention on Action against Trafficking in Human Beings and its Explanatory Report, *supra* note 49, at Art. 36, para. 355.

184 *Action against Trafficking in Human Beings, supra* note 160.

185 Id.; Resolution CM/Res (2008)7. *supra* note 178, at Rule 3.

186 Sorpong Peou, *Critical Challenges for Globalism in Human Security Studies, in* Human Security in East Asia: Challenges for Collaborative Action 21 (Sorpong Peou ed., 2009).

organizations' competence.[187] For instance, the Working Group for an ASEAN Human Rights Mechanism have involved in the evolution of ASEAN human rights issues since 1993,[188] specifically, the engagement in the draft of ASEAN Charter.[189] Also, many domestic non-governmental organizations have played an integral role in countering and ending the consequences of non-traditional security dilemmas.[190]

ASEAN civil society organizations have demonstrated "best practices" that envision establishing a regional human rights mechanism, including human trafficking.[191] Navanethem Pillay, United Nations High Commissioner for Human Rights, asserted civil society organization's influence in human rights development in ASEAN that the Solidarity for Asian People's Advocacy Task Force on ASEAN and Human Rights have created to mobilize the advancement of AICHR.[192] The fact that ASEAN would never move toward human rights approach without the civil society organizations' attempts to value this significant affair through a variety of their involvements should be addressed.[193] The evidence reveals that ASEAN initially identified human rights in the Vientiane Action Programme in 2004.[194]

The NGOs in the ASEAN region have influenced in counter-human trafficking through global engagement with various international, regional, and local

---

187 Seng Tan, *ngos in Conflict Management in Southeast Asia, in* U.N. Peace Operations and Asian Security 41–55 (Mely Caballero-Anthony & Amitav Acharya eds., 2005).

188 Yukiko Nishikawa, Human Security in Southeast Asia 97 (2010).

189 Id. (reprinting a memo distributed at ASEAN People's Forum at Chulalongkorn University on 21 February 2009).

190 Mely Caballero-Anthony, *Non-Traditional Security Challenges, Regional Governance, and the ASEAN Political Security Community* (*APSC*), in ASEAN and the Institutionalization of East Asia 40 (Ralf Emmers, ed., 2012).

191 Navanethem Pillay, U.N. High Commissioner for Human Rights, Keynote Speech at the 4th Regional Civil Society Consultation on ASEAN and Human Rights (Nov. 27, 2011), *available at* http://bangkok.ohchr.org/news/press/keynote-speech-4th-regional-civil-society-consultation-asean-and-human-rights.aspx (reiterating that "...we need to encourage the two ASEAN human rights mechanisms to entrench the principle of broad consultation with all of civil society, as a requirement in their work. An effective ASEAN human rights system that is responsive to civil society can play a vital role in addressing human rights problems common to all countries of the region, including in relation to discrimination, freedom of expression, torture and impunity, migration and human trafficking").

192 Id.

193 Tan Hsien-Li, The ASEAN Intergovernmental Commission on Human Rights: Institutionalising Human Rights in Southeast Asia 249 (2011).

194 Id.

dialogue partners to mobilize their implementation of international laws against human trafficking.[195] Also, NGOs have educated most governments on traffickers' behavioral patterns over trafficking victims, namely confiscation of trafficking victims' passports, identifications, and personal documents; infringement of labor contract; deprivation of trafficking victims' communication; physical and psychological harm; and other human rights violations.[196] Several government authorities confirm the vital roles of civil society organizations. Police Lieutenant Colonel Chachvan Bunmee, the Department of Special Investigation (DSI) of the Ministry of Justice of Thailand, admitted that the

---

195 Anne Gallagher, The International Law of Human Trafficking 493 and 499 (2010) (commenting that their impetus has strengthened "the capacity of transnational human rights networks to promote accountability, as well as to contribute, more directly, to improving compliance with international rules and standards" and illustrating NGOs' influential role that "Interights and the AIRE Centre were third party interveners in *Rantsev v. Cyprus and Russia, supra* note 17 (referring that their submissions were quoted extensively in the judgment. The Litigation Director of Interights was co-counsel in a case involving consideration of slavery before the ECOWAS Court. The epilogue presents this case that "In January 2010, the European Court of Human Rights found that Cyprus and Russia had incurred international legal responsibility with respect to the death, in Cyprus, of a Russian national and probable victim of trafficking, and that they were therefore liable in damages. Although the victim's death and likely exploitation were not attributed to Cyprus or Russia, both States were held to have violated related human rights obligations, specifically through failure to regulate employment and through inaction in the face of private conduct. These violations arose through failure to carry out an effective investigation into the death (including securing the relevant evidence from overseas as well as domestically, and investigating whether there had been any trafficking-related corruption); failure to ensure that the migration regime itself afforded protection against trafficking; and failure to investigate trafficking. The Court held that "national legislation must be adequate to ensure the practical and effective protection of the rights of victims or potential victims of trafficking." It explained that in addition to criminal law measures to punish traffickers, Member States are also required to "put in place adequate measures regulating businesses often used as a cover for human trafficking," and to ensure their immigration rules "address relevant concerns relating to encouragement, facilitation or tolerance of trafficking." In reaching its decision, the Court went beyond the European Convention on Human Rights to examine the provisions of a range of specialist instruments including the Trafficking Protocol, the European Trafficking Convention, and the European Convention on Mutual Assistance in Criminal Matters."); Luningning G. Camoying, *Establishing an ASEAN Human Rights Mechanism: Developments and Prospects*, FSI Insights, no. 1, Mar. 2005, at 13 (explaining that the civil society organizations' active role and contribution can reinforce ASEAN to establish competent human rights mechanism).

196 Kelly E. Hyland, *The Impact of the Protocol to Prevent, Suppress and Punish Trafficking in Persons, Especially Women and Children*, 8 Hum. Rts. Brief, no 2, 2001, at 30.

engagement of the NGOs representatives and social workers has contributed the law enforcement authorities in raids and investigations of human trafficking cases.[197] Mr. Chhuon Vibol of LICADHO, Cambodian human rights NGO, addressed that NGOs and social workers have pointed out the essential protection and assistance of trafficking victims because these groups understand trafficking victims' vulnerability and needs.[198]

While most trafficking victims fear to inform and invoke for protection and assistance from competent authorities, trafficking victims believe in the NGO representatives' trust and the best protection because these NGO representatives mostly understand victims' vulnerability.[199] The law enforcement authorities have identified the low number of trafficking victims because of trafficking victims' distrust against law enforcement authorities.[200] In contrast, trafficking victims tend to inform their trafficking damages to credited NGO representatives.[201]

The roles of civil society organizations have influenced the establishment of international, regional, and national laws and policies; ASEAN has inadequately engaged representatives of civil society organizations in the decision-making process or in the involvement as a membership of human rights mechanism.[202] For example, even though ASEAN has aimed to move forward to strengthen relationships with various public and private actors, including civil society organizations, ASEAN has not transformed this goal into action.[203] The core reason is because the civil society sector has frequently proposed different perspectives from ASEAN member countries.[204] Consequently, these member countries have been reluctant to reinforce civil society engagement in decision-making process.[205]

197 Press Release, United Nations Inter-Agency Project on Human Trafficking, Mekong Countries Build Regional Capacity to Combat Transnational Human Trafficking (June 19, 2009), *available at* http://www.no-trafficking.org/reports_docs/news/press_releases/rtp_press_release_eng.pdf.

198 Id.

199 Fiona David, *Law Enforcement Responses to Trafficking in Persons: Challenges and Emerging Good Practices, in* International Se Trafficking of Women and Children: Understanding the Global Epidemic 279 (2010).

200 Heinrich, *supra* note 12, at 4.

201 Id.

202 *South East Asia Regional Office (2008–2009): Human Rights Context*, OHCHR, http://www.ohchr.org/EN/Countries/AsiaRegion/Pages/SouthEastAsiaSummary0809.aspx (last visited Mar. 1, 2013); Caballero-Anthony, *supra note* 190, at 31.

203 Caballero-Anthony, *supra* note 190, at 40.

204 Id.

205 Id.

In practice, most AICHR members do not have much experience in human rights affairs.[206] ASEAN appointed two of ten members, who are civil society representatives from Indonesia and Thailand, Rafendi Djamin and Dr. Sriprapha Petcharamesree[207] to the AICHR.[208] ASEAN has barely recruited representatives from civil society organizations to comply with their existing human rights mechanisms, namely AICHR and ACWC. Particularly, ASEAN selected the ACWC members with dependence and partiality that perhaps allow the ACWC members' governments to instruct their responsibilities as the ACWC membership.[209] The dependence of the ACWC can create a conflict of interest[210] with the ACWC's working transparency as the ACWC memberships.

According to the preferences of ASEAN member countries, it is more likely that they will prefer to appoint their government staff rather than representatives of non-governmental organizations as members of ACTV. However, ASEAN should follow the best practices of GRETA that it should acknowledge the necessity of the strong collaboration with civil society organizations of human rights if ASEAN envisions strengthening its capacity of human rights,[211] including anti-human trafficking. In addition to the number and competence of ACTV, ASEAN should ensure that ACTV is comprised of both female and male representatives in order to ensure that all victims have been represented their fundamental needs based on their genders and ages. A combination of diverse representatives can allow them to share different perspectives and to empower all victims' rights by designing sufficient anti-human trafficking

---

206 Hsien-Li, *supra* note 193, at 160; Asian Forum for Human Rights and Development (Forum-Asia), *Faces of the ASEAN Intergovernmental Commission on Human Rights*, 5 Asian Hum. Rts. Defender, no. 3, 2009, at 4, 16–17.

207 Working Group for an ASEAN Human Rights Mechanism, *Dr Sriprapha Petcharamesree: On Being a Member of the aichr*, Hum. Rts. Herald, Jan. 2010, at 2, *available at* http://www.aseanhrmech.org/downloads/Human_Rights_Herald_Jan2010_Issue.pdf; Asian Forum for Human Rights and Development (Forum-Asia), *supra* note 206, at 16–17; Interview with Ms Sriprapha Petcharamesree, Professor at Mahidol University, Thailand (June 17, 2011) (reiterating her role as AICHR representative as same as her quotation. In response to the ASEAN's appointment to the AICHR, Dr Sriprapha Petcharamesree elaborated that "I should be able to bridge the gap between civil society and the governments. I really hope so").

208 Hsien-Li, *supra* note 193, at 160.

209 *See* Justin Lo, *ASEAN Human Rights Commission: Why Is It Important to Stay Relevant and Credible in Today's Global Environment?* 3 CSR Asia Weekly, no. 32, Aug. 8, 2007, at 4–5, http://storage.canalblog.com/18/13/273060/15902769.pdf; *see also* Khoo, *supra* note 8, at 71.

210 Council of Europe, Resolution CM/Res (2008)7 *supra* note 178, at Rule 3, para. 3.

211 Camoying, *supra* note 195, at 13.

methods and strategies applicable for all trafficked women, men, and children.

iii Meeting Frequency

Designing practical policies and plans of action against human trafficking would require ACTV for more than ten days a year to accomplish these plans as ACWC and AICHR have spent. Even if ASEAN has not often assigned its existing human rights bodies[212] to convene a meeting, ASEAN should encourage ACTV to arrange mutual regular meetings with these mechanisms as many as they could. For instance, ASEAN may take into account three-time meeting annually instead of two-time meeting, and each time could take maximum five days. The annual fifteen-day meeting would allow ACTV to deliberately create efficient strategic means and activities.

In addition, ASEAN may apply GRETA's meeting rule in order to accelerate the suppression of human trafficking. GRETA's internal rules of procedure require GRETA to convene meetings as many as needed to conduct their duties.[213] GRETA has actually held quarterly meetings since 2009 to develop effective prevention, protection, and prosecution measures to battle human trafficking.[214]

If ASEAN aims to hasten counter-human trafficking strategies, ACTV may convene its meeting via camera on the grounds of urgent issues, time and financial constraint.[215] Even though ASEAN has not convened a long-distance meeting, such a meeting *in camera* should enhance time management of all ACTV members because the geographic and time differences of ACTV representatives' countries can facilitate them to access these meetings without travel and additional expenses. Therefore, ACTV should take into consideration this method in order to be in a position to address urgent issues that take place

---

212 *See,* e.g., ACWC Terms of Reference, *supra* note 177, at para. 7.2; *See,* e.g., AICHR Terms of Reference, *supra* note 177, at Art. 6.2 (providing the instance that the ACWC TOR and the AICHR TOR have two regular meetings a year, and each meeting takes no longer than five days).

213 Group of Experts on Action against Trafficking in Human Beings (GRETA), *Rules of Procedure for evaluating implementation of the Council of Europe Convention on Action against Trafficking in Human Beings by the Parties* 7, *supra* note 165, at Rule 13.

214 *Action against Trafficking in Human Beings, supra* note 160.

215 *See* Group of Experts on Action Against Trafficking in Human Beings (GRETA), *Integral Rules of Procedure of the Group of Experts on Action Against Trafficking in Human Beings* (*GRETA*) Rule 17, THB-GRETA (2009)1, Feb. 24, 2009, *available at* http://www.coe.int/t/dghl/monitoring/trafficking/Source/THB-GRETA%282009%291_en.pdf (compared to GRETA, it may meet in camera for the purpose of privacy).

for its mutual resolution. Since this long-distance meeting can represent economical brainstorming that can allow the ACTV representatives to share their mutual human trafficking concerns and enhance their cooperation against human trafficking with lower cost than regular physical gathering, it is feasible that ASEAN will encourage the ACTV to hold online meeting as frequently as it could.

iv *Terms of Office*

While the ACWC TOR and the AICHR TOR stipulate that each representative serves three years a term, which is renewable once,[216] the GRETA terms are four years in length with a one-time reappointment.[217] GRETA has not been in place long enough to fully exercise its functions, including monitoring and evaluation of the performance of the counter-trafficking mechanisms of approximately forty seven member countries. The ACTV can maintain their three-year terms because there are only ten ASEAN member countries.

b Selective Monitoring Power of ACTV

The role of regional organizations role in the promotion of prosecutorial and judicial responses includes establishment of a monitoring system to ensure efficient implementation of laws and policies and indicate drawbacks in order to strengthen national criminal justice responses to human trafficking.[218] The CoE Convention deliberately draws the workflow of the monitoring mechanism involving several steps of the evaluation procedure[219] to ensure accurate data collection. The CoE Convention classifies the evaluation procedure into cycles.[220]

216 *See*, e.g., ACWC Terms of Reference, *supra* note 177, at para. 6.5; *see also*, e.g., AICHR Terms of Reference, *supra* note 177, at Art. 5.5.

217 Council of Europe, Resolution CM/Res (2008)7 *supra* note 178, at Rule 16, para. 1.

218 Special Rapporteur on Trafficking in Persons, Especially Women and Children, *Report on Agenda Item 3: Promotion and Protection of all Human Rights, Civil, Political, Economic, Social and Cultural Rights, including the Right to Development*, U.N. Human Rights Council, U.N. Doc. A/HRC/14/32 (May 4, 2010) (by Joy Ngozi Ezeilo), *available at* http://daccess-dds-ny.un.org/doc/UNDOC/GEN/G10/132/11/PDF/G1013211.pdf?OpenElement [hereinafter U.N. Doc. A/HRC/14/32], at 22, para. 133 (recommending advancement in the training program of government officials).

219 Convention on Action against Trafficking in Human Beings and its Explanatory Report, *supra* note 49, at Art. 38, para. 363–369.

220 Group of Experts on Action against Trafficking in Human Beings (GRETA), First General Report on GRETA's Activities: Covering the Period from February 2009 to July 2011 para. 25, Public GRETA (2011)11, Sep. 1, 2011, *available at* http://www.coe.int/t/dghl/monitoring/trafficking/Docs/Gen_Report/GRETA_2011_11_GenRpt_en.pdf.

The evaluation procedure includes selecting the provisions to be monitored,[221] designing the methods of the assessment,[222] and submitting a questionnaire for the CoE member countries to complete.[223] To complete its assessment, GRETA considers the replies of member countries, responses of civil society organizations, and country visits.[224]

Though ASEAN created human rights mechanisms (namely AICHR and ACWC), ASEAN does not authorize these mechanisms to monitor the implementation of national anti-human trafficking laws.[225] As a result, ASEAN should empower ACTV to examine national anti-human trafficking laws in order to address achievements and challenges of these laws that can address and guide its member countries into the right direction through legal reform and effective responses against human trafficking.

ASEAN has preferred the principle of non-interference principle over sovereignty; however, they will potentially accept a monitoring system on the grounds of no "naming and shaming techniques."[226] Five ASEAN member countries have engaged in the monitoring and evaluating system of the COMMIT process[227] while all of them have cooperated in regional activities based upon "trust and confidence" among its member countries.[228] Therefore, it is likely that ASEAN can undertake monitoring function of GRETA into action. Because ASEAN has never assigned any human rights body to conduct this monitoring process to counter-human trafficking, this part focuses on analyzing scope of questionnaire, country visit, and evaluation of ACTV and responses of ASEAN member countries in order to evaluate whether ASEAN can apply the entire GRETA's monitoring process through ACTV's operation.

---

221 Convention on Action against Trafficking in Human Beings and its Explanatory Report, *supra* note 49, at Art. 38(1), para. 364.

222 Id. at Art. 38(2), para. 365.

223 Id.

224 Group of Experts on Action against Trafficking in Human Beings (GRETA), *Rules of Procedure for evaluating implementation of the Council of Europe Convention on Action against Trafficking in Human Beings by the Parties* 7, *supra* note 165, at Rule 2; Julia Planitzer, *GRETA's First Years of Work: Review of the Monitoring of Implementation of the Council of Europe Convention on Action against Trafficking in Human Beings*, Anti-Trafficking Rev., no. 1, June 2012, at 31, 33, http://www.antitraffickingreview.org/images/documents/issue1/Anti-Traficking_Review_Issue1_06.2012.pdf.

225 AICHR Terms of Reference, *supra* note 177; ACWC Terms of Reference, *supra* note 177.

226 Kneebone & Debeljak, *supra* note 24, at 210.

227 Id.

228 Id.

i Scope of Questionnaire

The role of regional organizations in the promotion of prosecutorial and judicial responses should include establishment of a monitoring system to ensure efficient implementation of laws and policies and indicate drawbacks in order to strengthen national criminal justice responses to human trafficking.[229] The CoE Convention deliberately draws the workflow of the monitoring mechanism involving several steps of the evaluation procedure[230] to ensure accurate data collection. The CoE Convention classifies the evaluation procedure into cycles.[231] The evaluation procedure includes selecting the provisions to be monitored,[232] designing the methods of the assessment,[233] and submitting a questionnaire for the CoE member countries to complete.[234] To complete its assessment, GRETA considers the replies of member countries, responses of civil society organizations, and country visits.[235]

Though ASEAN created human rights mechanisms (namely AICHR and ACWC), ASEAN does not authorize these mechanisms to monitor the implementation of national anti-human trafficking laws.[236] As a result, ASEAN should empower ACTV to examine national anti-human trafficking laws in order to address achievements and challenges of these laws that can address and guide its member countries into the right direction through legal reform and effective responses against human trafficking.

ASEAN has preferred the principle of non-interference principle over sovereignty; however, they will potentially accept a monitoring system on the grounds of no "naming and shaming techniques."[237] Five ASEAN member

229 U.N. Doc. A/HRC/14/32, *supra* note 218, at 22, para. 133 (recommending to advance the training program of government officials).

230 Convention on Action against Trafficking in Human Beings and its Explanatory Report, *supra* note 49, at Art. 38, para. 363–369.

231 Group of Experts on Action against Trafficking in Human Beings (GRETA), First General Report on GRETA's Activities: Covering the Period from February 2009 to July 2011, para. 25, Public GRETA (2011)11, Sep. 1, 2011, *available at* http://www.coe.int/t/dghl/monitoring/trafficking/Docs/Gen_Report/GRETA_2011_11_GenRpt_en.pdf.

232 Convention on Action against Trafficking in Human Beings and its Explanatory Report, *supra* note 49, at Art. 38 (1), para. 364.

233 Id. at Art. 38(2), para. 365.

234 Convention on Action against Trafficking in Human Beings and its Explanatory Report, *supra* note 49, at Art. 38(2), para. 365.

235 Group of Experts on Action against Trafficking in Human Beings (GRETA), *Rules of Procedure for evaluating implementation of the Council of Europe Convention on Action against Trafficking in Human Beings by the Parties* 7, *supra* note 165, at Rule 2; Planitzer, *supra* note 224, at 33.

236 AICHR Terms of Reference, *supra* note 177; ACWC Terms of Reference, *supra* note 177.

237 Kneebone & Debeljak, *supra* note 24, at 210.

countries have engaged in the monitoring and evaluating system of the COMMIT process[238] while all of them have cooperated in regional activities based upon "trust and confidence" among its member countries.[239] Therefore, it is likely that ASEAN can undertake monitoring function of GRETA into action. Because ASEAN has never assigned any human rights body to conduct this monitoring process to counter-human trafficking, this part focuses on analyzing scope of questionnaire, country visit, and evaluation of ACTV and responses of ASEAN member countries in order to evaluate whether ASEAN can apply the entire GRETA's monitoring process through ACTV's operation.

ii *Country Visit*

The exercise of country visits and capacity of obtaining relevant data not only from member countries, but also civil society organizations have illustrated "effective" authorities of GRETA because they provide various perspectives and impacts of its member countries' laws and actions against human trafficking.[240] ACTV has to organize country visits to keep track of the human trafficking problems in member countries and provide relevant recommendations on the prevention of human trafficking, protection of all trafficking victims, and investigation and prosecution of human trafficking cases to member countries.[241]

If ASEAN takes into consideration the development of security in ASEAN region, ASEAN should persuade its member countries to participate in addressing human trafficking scourge and reporting technical problem in anti-human trafficking laws and agreements. The exchange of such information can render ASEAN and its member countries in order to fully understand the main root causes of human trafficking in ASEAN region. The exchange of information between the government and ACTV illustrates ASEAN's support of mutual legal assistance (Chapter 3).

ASEAN should assign the contact person to serve as a coordinator, facilitators, and dialogue carrier of ACTV and ASEAN member countries' government agencies.[242] The contact person should be primarily responsible for receiving

---

238 Id.

239 Id.

240 Gallagher, *supra* note 195, at 476–477.

241 *See Special Rapporteur on Trafficking in Persons, Especially in Women and Children: Country Visits*, U.N. Office of the High Commissioner on Human Rights (OHCHR), http://www.ohchr.org/EN/Issues/Trafficking/Pages/Visits.aspx (last visited Mar. 1, 2013); *see also* Convention on Action against Trafficking in Human Beings and its Explanatory Report, *supra* note 49, at 14.

242 *See* Group of Experts on Action against Trafficking in Human Beings (GRETA), First General Report on GRETA's Activities: Covering the Period from February 2009 to July 2011, *supra* note 231, at para. 27.

and circulating the questionnaire from ACTV to ASEAN member countries' government agencies requested, as well as submitting the government response from the government agencies to ACTV.[243] Second, the contact person should also be in charge of other anecdotal tasks in the extent of evaluating process.[244] Lastly, this contact person can assist both ACTV and ASEAN member countries to accelerate the process of data collection by checking on their work submission timeline.[245]

In addition, in order to examine ASEAN member countries' information, ACTV should continually value them as dialogue stakeholders during their country visits in order to collect various dimensions of human trafficking circumstances that lead to effective national counter-human trafficking laws and strategies. Therefore, ACTV should cooperate with civil society organizations to assessing these member countries' domestic laws and responses against human trafficking through their individual evaluation report.

iii *Evaluation of ACTV and Responses of ASEAN Member Countries*

GRETA's evaluation reports reflect proficient and neutral international information[246] and the transparency of the evaluation process even though the main source of information derives from the government concerned. Prior to evaluating the first draft of evaluation report, GRETA scrutinizes all analytical data obtaining from various public and private sectors.[247] Subsequently, GRETA submits its first draft of the evaluation report to the government concerned for responses.[248] GRETA examines the government's responses to draft the final evaluation report.[249]

After completing the final report, it is submitted to the government for comments again.[250] They then have one month to respond the final report so that GRETA publishes its final report with the government's attached comments and submit them to the Committee of the Parties based upon the dateline.[251]

243 *See* id.

244 *See* id.

245 *See* id.

246 Group of Experts on Action against Trafficking in Human Beings (GRETA), First General Report on GRETA's Activities: Covering the Period from February 2009 to July 2011, *supra* note 231, at para. 31.

247 Id.

248 Id. at para. 32.

249 Id.

250 Id.

251 Id.

The Committee of the Parties might reinforce GRETA's conclusion by recommending GRETA's proposed measures to the relevant government for its appropriate implementation of the CoE Convention.[252]

Subsequent to completing the final draft report and receiving the government's comments on final report, GRETA integrates them in publication.[253] Though GRETA has only exercised its monitoring function this first time, the GRETA's first round of evaluation reports represents the collaboration between GRETA and the CoE member countries evaluated and GRETA's commitment to help the countries strengthen their criminal justice responses to human trafficking.[254] GRETA launched the first evaluation round by sending its questionnaire to the first ten CoE member countries in February 2010.[255]

It is clear that GRETA's qualifications and actions contain best practices and deficiencies that ACTV should learn from. Its best practices include the independence and impartiality of its expert body, member countries' commitment in submitting a report to GRETA, GRETA's obligation on providing advices to its member countries, and country visit of GRETA without its member countries' consent.[256] On the other hand, GRETA does not consider individual petitions for its evaluation because the CoE Convention does not stipulate this individual complaints procedure.[257]

It is anticipated that if ACTV permits ASEAN member countries to respond its first and final drafts of report, these interacting opportunities can satisfy ASEAN member countries because ACTV empowers them to correct or argue other information resources compared to the TIP Report that focuses on naming and shaming through ranking that causes the disappointment of ASEAN member countries, particularly Thailand (Chapter 4). Several reasons support this assumption.

The rational interactions between GRETA and the governments concerned are applicable for ASEAN and its member countries. It is feasible because ASESAN member countries' governments will have two opportunities to

252 Convention on Action against Trafficking in Human Beings and its Explanatory Report, *supra* note 49, at Art. 38(3), para. 369.

253 Group of Experts on Action against Trafficking in Human Beings (GRETA), *Rules of Procedure for evaluating implementation of the Council of Europe Convention on Action against Trafficking in Human Beings by the Parties* 7, *supra* note 165, at Rule 14.

254 Group of Experts on Action against Trafficking in Human Beings (GRETA), First General Report on GRETA's Activities: Covering the Period from February 2009 to July 2011, *supra* note 231, at para. 31.

255 Id. at para. 35.

256 Planitzer, *supra* note 224, at 34.

257 Id. at 35.

discuss their agreements and disagreements of ACTV's first and final drafts of report. Also, ACTV could learn ASEAN member countries' obstacles of anti-human trafficking that may suggest ACTV how to provide contribution for ASEAN member countries. The contribution may include the request to national, regional, and international organizations for human resources of training programs, legal experts of counter-human trafficking, and financial supports.

Just as in the GRETA practices, if ASEAN member countries fail to provide adequate information, ACTV should acknowledge and address deficient reports.[258] Even though the CoE member countries have neglected to respond

---

258 Group of Experts on Action against Trafficking in Human Beings, Second General Report on GRETA's Activities Covering the Period from 1 August 2011 to 31 July 2012, *supra* note 17, at para. 32; Group of Experts on Action against Trafficking in Human Beings (GRETA), Report Concerning the Implementation of the Council of Europe Convention on Action against Trafficking in Human Beings by Cyprus: First Evaluation Round para 213 (2011)8, Sep. 12, 2011, *available at* http://www.coe.int/t/dghl/monitoring/trafficking/Docs/Reports/GRETA_2011_8_FGR_CYP_en_final.pdf [hereinafter GRETA 2011 Cyprus Report]; Group of Experts on Action against Trafficking in Human Beings (GRETA), Report Concerning the Implementation of the Council of Europe Convention on Action against Trafficking in Human Beings by the Slovak Republic: First Evaluation Round (2011)9, Sep. 19, 2011, para 149–150, *available at* http://www.coe.int/t/dghl/monitoring/trafficking/Docs/Reports/GRETA_2011_9_FGR_SVK_en.pdf [hereinafter GRETA 2011 Slovak Republic First Evaluation Round Report]; Group of Experts on Action against Trafficking in Human Beings (GRETA), Report Concerning the Implementation of the Council of Europe Convention on Action against Trafficking in Human Beings by Austria: First Evaluation Round (2011)10, (2011), Sep. 15, 2011, paras. 160–161, *available at* http://www.coe.int/t/dghl/monitoring/trafficking/Docs/Reports/GRETA_2011_10_FGR_AUT_en.pdf [hereinafter GRETA 2011 Austrian First Evaluation Report]; Group of Experts on Action against Trafficking in Human Beings (GRETA), Report Concerning the Implementation of the Council of Europe Convention on Action against Trafficking in Human Beings by Bulgaria: First Evaluation Round (2011)19, Dec. 14, 2011, paras. 231, 233, *available at* http://www.coe.int/t/dghl/monitoring/trafficking/Docs/Reports/GRETA_2011_19_FGR_BGR_en.pdf [hereinafter GRETA 2011 Bulgarian First Round Report]; Group of Experts on Action against Trafficking in Human Beings (GRETA), Report Concerning the Implementation of the Council of Europe Convention on Action against Trafficking in Human Beings by Denmark: First Evaluation Round, GRETA (2011)21, Dec. 20, 2011, para. 219, p. 44, *available at* http://www.coe.int/t/dghl/monitoring/trafficking/Docs/Reports/GRETA_2011_21_FGR_DNK_en.pdf (summarizing that the human rights approach includes victim identification, protection and assistance for trafficking victims including foreign victims, non-prosecution of trafficking victims for the involvement of any illicit activities if they are forced, special attention to trafficked children and men, coordination, collaboration and partnerships among governmental agencies, NGOs, and other active civil society organizations to tackle human

to any questions,[259] GRETA has called them for additional data and reiterated them to modify their laws and measures through their final evaluation report

trafficking, advancement of training course of all relevant government authorities, including prosecutors and judges, on victim identification and other protection of trafficking victims); Group of Experts on Action against Trafficking in Human Beings (GRETA), Report Concerning the Implementation of the Council of Europe Convention on Action against Trafficking in Human Beings by Georgia: First Evaluation Round, GRETA (2011)24, Feb. 7, 2012, para. 224, *available at* http://www.coe.int/t/dghl/monitoring/trafficking/Docs/Reports/GRETA_2011_24_FGR_GEO_en.pdf; Group of Experts on Action against Trafficking in Human Beings (GRETA), Report Concerning the Implementation of the Council of Europe Convention on Action against Trafficking in Human Beings by Moldova: First Evaluation Round, GRETA (2011)25, Feb. 22, 2012, para. 165, *available at* http://www.coe.int/t/dghl/monitoring/trafficking/Docs/Reports/GRETA_2011_25_FGR_MDA_en.pdf; Group of Experts on Action against Trafficking in Human Beings (GRETA), Report Concerning the Implementation of the Council of Europe Convention on Action against Trafficking in Human Beings by Romania: First Evaluation Round, GRETA (2012)2, May 31, 2012, para. 205, *available at* http://www.coe.int/t/dghl/monitoring/trafficking/Docs/Reports/GRETA_2012_2_FGR_ROU_en.pdf (summarizing that even though the replies of all ten CoE member countries have illustrated their responsibility to implement the CoE Convention, GRETA has raised several concerns about its member countries' insufficient laws and practices against human trafficking such as failure of "human rights-based" and "victim-centred approach" in the prevention of human trafficking, protection for trafficking victims, and prosecution of traffickers); Group of Experts on Action against Trafficking in Human Beings (GRETA), Report Concerning the Implementation of the Council of Europe Convention on Action against Trafficking in Human Beings by Croatia: First Evaluation Round, GRETA (2011)20, Nov. 30, 2011, para. 140, *available at* http://www.coe.int/t/dghl/monitoring/trafficking/Docs/Reports/GRETA_2011_20_FGR_HRV_en.pdf; Group of Experts on Action against Trafficking in Human Beings (GRETA), Report Concerning the Implementation of the Council of Europe Convention on Action against Trafficking in Human Beings by Albania: First Evaluation Round, GRETA (2011)22, Dec. 2, 2011, paras. 164–165, 182, *available at* http://www.coe.int/t/dghl/monitoring/trafficking/Docs/Reports/GRETA_2011_22_FGR_ALB_en.pdf [hereinafter GRETA 2011 Albanian First Evaluation Round Report].

259 GRETA 2011 Slovak Republic First Evaluation Round Report, *supra* note 258, at para.17; GRETA 2011 Cyprus Report, *supra* note 258, at para. 73 (questioning Cyprus as to whether or not there "have been any cases of confiscation regarding THB-related activities" because of Cyprus' silence and unwillingness to provide the number of court decisions on confiscation); GRETA 2011 Austrian First Evaluation Report, *supra* note 258, at para. 23 (explaining that "GRETA considers that the Austrian authorities should take measures to assess the implementation by the judicial and other relevant authorities of the principle of non-punishment of victims of THB for their involvement in unlawful

before publication.[260] This request demonstrates best practices that should be applied by ACTV because the supplementary document and information can exhibit whether member countries have sufficiently provided anti-human trafficking legal instruments and actions.[261] These facts can help ACTV assess and recommend proper instruction how to strengthen these member countries as they support GRETA in the evaluation process.[262]

GRETA submits this publication to the Committees of the Parties[263] to determine whether the government concerned should undertake the measures GRETA recommends.[264] This process gives ACTV an opportunity to present its opinions and advice to the Senior Officials Meeting on Transnational Crime (SOMTC) that responds to work plans against eight crimes, including

---

activities, to the extent that they were compelled to do so, as contained in Article 26 of the Convention. They should be prepared to readjust on the basis of such an assessment the content and/or the application of the relevant provisions with a view to addressing any shortcoming identified"); GRETA 2011 Albanian First Evaluation Round Report, *supra* note 258, at paras. 182, 183; GRETA 2011 Cyprus Report, *supra* note 258, at para 213; GRETA 2011 Bulgarian First Round Report, *supra* note 258, at para. 86.

260 Planitzer, *supra* note 224, at 38.

261 Id. at 39–40 (commenting that not only does GRETA highlight specific information, it also scrutinizes whether anti-human trafficking laws and strategies are adequate).

262 *See*, e.g., GRETA 2011 Slovak Republic First Evaluation Round Report, *supra* note 258, at para. 67 (mentioning that "GRETA considers that more systematic and robust economic, social and educational measures should be taken by the Slovak authorities vis-à-vis groups vulnerable to THB. These measures should be based on the identified structural causes of THB (economic and social conditions, poverty, inadequate education, absence of employment opportunities, etc.) and should consist of actions aiming to eliminate these causes"); Group of Experts on Action against Trafficking in Human Beings, Report Concerning the Implementation of the GRETA 2011 Austrian First Evaluation Report, *supra* note 258, at para. 71 (addressing that "GRETA considers that the Austrian authorities should take further measures to raise awareness on the problem of THB, in particular as regards child trafficking and trafficking for the purpose of labour exploitation. Awareness-raising campaigns should target among others foreign nationals coming to work in Austria, employers and employers' associations, trade unions, social workers, recruitment agencies and other intermediaries, as well as labour and tax inspectors").

263 *See* Convention on Action against Trafficking in Human Beings and its Explanatory Report, *supra* note 49, at Art. 37(1) (describing that the Committee of the Parties include representatives of the Committee of Ministers of the Council of Europe of the member countries to the Convention and representatives of the Parties to the Convention).

264 *See* Group of Experts on Action against Trafficking in Human Beings (GRETA), *Rules of Procedure for evaluating implementation of the Council of Europe Convention on Action against Trafficking in Human Beings by the Parties* 7, *supra* note 165, at Rule 14.

anti-human trafficking.[265] This is because while the CoE Convention requires the Committee of the Parties to take into account the implementation of GRETA's conclusion,[266] ASEAN tasks the SOMTC to strengthen ASEAN regional performances in enhancing ASEAN Declaration on Transnational Crime and other regional agreements related to transnational crimes (Chapter 3).[267] It is imperative to acknowledge that the Committee of the Parties and the SOMTC conduct the same functions by advancing the member countries' actions against human trafficking. It is practical that ACTV could submit its report and conclusion to the SOMTC to endorse and persuade ASEAN member countries evaluated to adopt ACTV's recommendations.

The Committee of Parties seems to support GRETA's suggestions to member countries.[268] The Committee of Parties may call member countries for more data that enhances GRETA's advices "if necessary."[269] The Committee of Parties tends to require member countries to submit information on the implementation of GRETA's advices within two years.[270]

Based on the analysis and evaluation of selective qualification and monitoring power of ACTV, this research believes that ASEAN should consider the creation of ACTV by learning from and applying effective monitoring system of GRETA that ASEAN lacks in order to assist its member countries advance their responses against human trafficking by addressing both strengths and weaknesses of their national anti-human trafficking measures of prevention, protection, and prosecution through the monitoring process. (*See the Workflow of the Monitoring Mechanism of ACTV Imitated from the Council of Europe Convention on Action against Trafficking in Human Beings below*) (Figure 7).

---

265 Evolving Towards ASEAN 2015, *supra* note 147, at 31–32 (describing that eight crimes refer to drug and human trafficking, anti-terrorism, sea piracy, money laundering, arms smuggling, international economic crime, and cyber crime).

266 *See* Convention on Action against Trafficking in Human Beings and its Explanatory Report, *supra* note 49, at Art. 38(7).

267 ASEAN in the Global Community: Annual Report 2010–2011, 23 (2011), *available at* http://www.asean.org/images/2012/publications/Annual%20Report%202010_2011.pdf.

268 Planitzer, *supra* note 224, at 40.

269 Convention on Action against Trafficking in Human Beings and its Explanatory Report, *supra* note 49, at Art. 38(7) (stipulating that "...the Committee of the Parties may adopt, on the basis of the report and conclusions of GRETA, recommendations addressed to this Party (a) concerning the measures to be taken to implement the conclusions of GRETA, if necessary setting a date for submitting information on their implementation").

270 Planitzer, *supra* note 224, at 40.

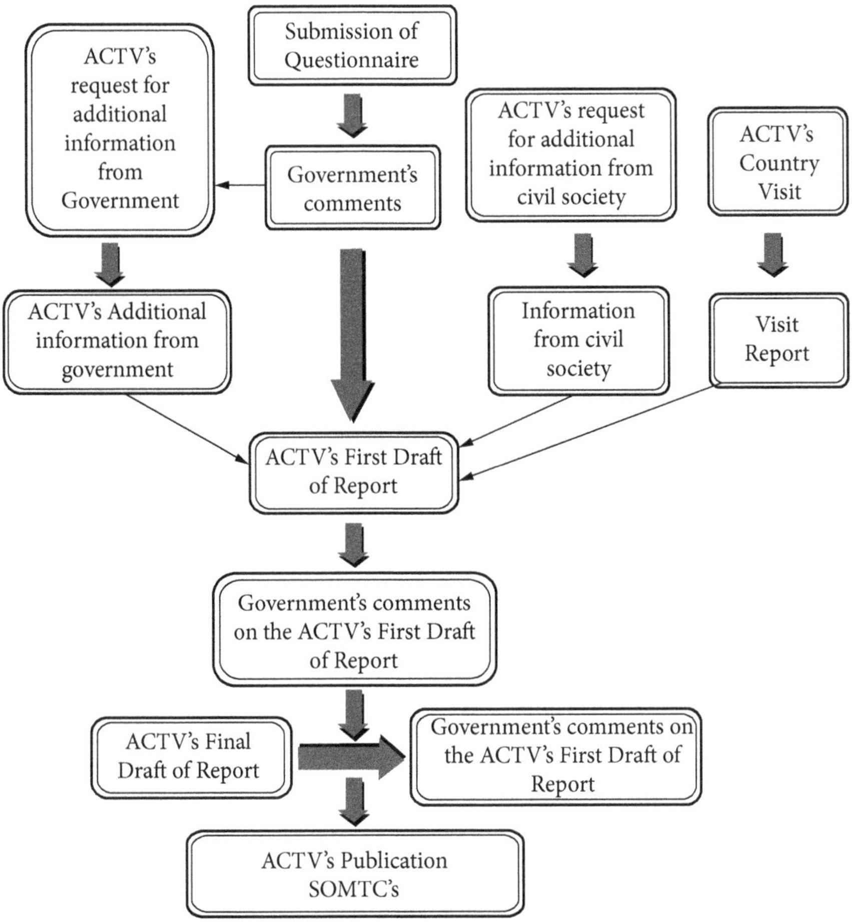

FIGURE 7 *Workflow of the monitoring mechanism of* ASEAN *Commission on the Promotion and Protection of the Rights of Trafficking Victims* (ACTV) *(reproduced from the CoE Convention* [CETS *No. 197*] *© Council of Europe)*[271]

5.2.3 *Possibility of* ASEAN*'s Admission of* ACTV

Typically, ASEAN has formed human rights bodies to encourage implementation of regional laws. For instance, ASEAN established the ASEAN Declaration against Trafficking in Persons, particularly Women and Children[272] and

271 Group of experts on action against trafficking in human beings (GRETA), *rules of procedure for evaluating implementation of the council of europe convention on action against trafficking in human beings by the parties* 7, *supra* note 16,565, at 7.

272 ADTC, *supra* note 8.

assigned ASEAN Commission on the Promotion and Protection of the Rights of Women and Children to be responsible for persuading its member countries in order to promote and protect the rights of women and children.[273] Therefore, it is reasonable that if ASEAN establishes the ADTV, they will also create the corresponding ACTV in order to help member countries address and tackle human trafficking in their countries by guiding them towards best practices, including sufficient domestic anti-human trafficking initiatives and measures applicable for them.

Despite the ACTV's designation, ASEAN may allow its member countries to select representatives influenced by their governments based on the attributes of AICHR and ACWC commissioners (Chapter 3). It is feasible that the qualifications of ACTV delegates will not present independence and impartiality from its member countries' governments that mostly can be influenced by their governments. If ACTV members focused on mutual security against human trafficking in the ASEAN region instead of their individual government's interest, their government positions need not be concerned. However, according to the work progress of AICHR and ACWC, they tend to make efforts in promoting more than protecting human rights as their governments' preferences that cause the insufficiencies of providing assistances and services for trafficking victims, especially the priority of only the promotion of the rights of women and children (Chapter 3 and 4). Consequently, the influence of governments towards the action of ACTV delegates comprising of their government authorities can affect human rights approach, including counter-human trafficking.

Another challenge ASEAN may struggle with is that since ASEAN lacks a human rights body with a monitoring duty, ACTV will have to concentrate on friendly interaction with all ASEAN member countries in order to encourage them to fully collaboration in data submission. In the case of country visits, it is predictable that ASEAN will prefer ACTV to obtain permission from its member countries because ASEAN member countries have enhanced non-interference principle. However, these member countries probably allow ACTV to visit their countries if ACTV presents its intention of learning and monitoring procedure with respectful manners, not a censorious process.

Both ASEAN and the CoE lack individual complaint procedures, and it is expected that ACTV will not include individual petitions as witnesses in its evaluation process as same as GRETA.[274] Despite no individual complaint admission, ASEAN can assess its member countries' counter-human trafficking

273 ACWC Terms of Reference, *supra* note 177.

274 Planitzer, *supra* note 224, at 35.

responses by considering civil society organizations' diverse views because these institutions have routinely appealed the rights on behalf of all trafficking victims.

Conclusion

The deficiency of a regional anti-human trafficking law has demonstrated the need for designing the ADTV by providing fundamental contents that ASEAN and its member countries insufficient stipulate and implement them, particularly victim identification, non-prosecution of trafficking victims, appropriate housing, right to remedy, and special protection for child victims. ASEAN should address these provisions in ADTV in order to instruct its member countries into adequate counter-human trafficking means that aim to deter all forms of human trafficking, to protect all trafficking victims (including men), and to prosecute human traffickers.

In order to achieve implementation of ADTV, ASEAN should form ACTV that has a monitoring power that evaluates ASEAN member countries' anti-human trafficking laws and policies in order to address the strengths and challenges of their laws and responses against human trafficking that can mitigate human trafficking growth in their region. The monitoring system of the CoE Convention has exemplified the best practices that ASEAN should learn from because it can enhance ASEAN and its member countries, particularly Cambodia, Thailand, and Vietnam, intensify their efforts to address and deter human trafficking scourge, and to protect all trafficking victims without discrimination of age, gender, and nationality. Also, ACTV can help ASEAN bridge the gap between national and international anti-human trafficking laws by enhancing ASEAN member countries to implement ADTV stipulating core measures applicable for them that are based on various international anti-human trafficking laws.

CHAPTER 6

Conclusion

This book recognizes ASEAN's efforts to tackle the scourge trafficking in persons in its region and acknowledges all challenges that ASEAN has faced through its regional agreements and mechanisms. ASEAN's achievements and struggles in the battle against trafficking in persons suggest that ASEAN should strengthen its counter-human trafficking strategies by enacting the ASEAN Declaration on the Promotion and Protection of the Rights of Trafficking Victims (ADTV), which will contain adequate mechanisms for preventing human trafficking, protecting victims, and prosecuting of offenders. The creation of the ASEAN Commission on the Promotion and Protection of the Rights of Trafficking Victims (ACTV) is also supported as a special mechanism to battle trafficking of all men, women and children in the region.

ASEAN emerged from the desire of its founding member countries to enhance the internal relations amongst its member countries and protect their sovereignty from external invasion by other powerful countries. The growth of ASEAN's memberships represents the increasing collaboration among its member countries. Also, the growth of ASEAN illustrates its strong commitment to maintaining peace and solidarity among its member countries through numerous agreements even though ASEAN has encountered internal and external political conflicts (Chapter 2).

At its formation ASEAN persuaded its member countries to concentrate on an economic approach to community building. Herein, other dimensions of ASEAN's purpose have been traced and its multiple approaches considered, namely political-security and socio-cultural affairs. However, ASEAN has neglected to empower itself through the use of military force (Chapter 2).

ASEAN's expansion of external relations through its regional discussions, especially the ASEAN Regional Forum, and the growing number of its dialogue partners illustrate that ASEAN can play a crucial role in both internal and external communities. Its dialogue forums serve member countries and external partners as a central venue to share their experiences and advise each other on various concerns, including responding natural disasters and infectious diseases, and implementing counter-terrorism and anti-human trafficking measures. The success of these dialogues signals ASEAN's expansion from regional to global collaboration. However, ASEAN should draw on its commitment to the flexibility of its principles, namely non-interference,

 | DOI 10.1163/9789004265189_007

consensus decision-making and consultation, to expand its counter-human trafficking legal frameworks and enforce mechanisms to protect all trafficking victims (Chapter 2).

Since ASEAN has undertaken a variety of laws and measures against human trafficking, they should be able to convince their member countries to control the growth of human trafficking in the region. The research presented here evaluates whether ASEAN's existing laws are sufficient. In fact, ASEAN has preferred to adopt non-legally binding laws or soft law to deal with trafficking in persons. It is proposed here that ASEAN establish soft laws such as ADTV to ensure that all trafficking victims in the region have the right to receive assistance and protection from their respective governments (Chapter 3).

Despite the creation of various regional laws in the ASEAN region, there are several challenges, namely unequal gender sensitivity, ambiguous and insufficient content, and lack of protection for trafficking victims (Chapter 3). In addition, ASEAN has deferred its responsibility for anti-human trafficking efforts across political-security and socio-cultural communities. However, after thorough research, it is clear the best approach for ASEAN would be to combine human trafficking and migration issues in the same division because they are interconnected. For instance, anti-human trafficking laws and policies may affect migrant workers' freedom of movement. ASEAN should consolidate human trafficking and labour migration issues in its regular agenda among human rights bodies (AICHR, ACWC, and ACMW) with ACTV so that the best strategies and methods in the fight human trafficking and the safe migration are considered in the same light (Chapter 3).

ASEAN's existing human rights body, the ACWC, was also evaluated in an effort to assess its effectiveness at dealing with human trafficking. Accordingly, ACWC lacks monitoring, evaluation, and data collection on achievements and challenges of the national and regional policies. These mechanisms have been proven to help strengthen anti-human trafficking mechanisms. As a result, ASEAN should consider the creation of a specialized human trafficking body with sufficient monitoring powers, akin to the ACTV (Chapter 3).

ASEAN member countries, specifically Cambodia, Thailand, and Vietnam, have been affected by the deficiencies in the regional agreements and human rights bodies. This chapter assesses these three countries' anti-human trafficking and related laws because they all represent the advantages and disadvantages of other ASEAN member countries. The human trafficking phenomenon in each of these countries was explored to understand its root causes. It was found that in Cambodia and Vietnam the sheer lack of job opportunity was the cause of their trafficking problem. In Thailand, the problem could be attributed to the economic boom taking place in that country, which has attracted many migrant workers from neighboring countries to seek jobs, but some of these migrant workers fail to reach their career goal as a result of human trafficking. In addition the war in Vietnam ignited the demands of human trafficking *vis-a-vis* Thailand and Vietnam (Chapter 4).

Even though most ASEAN member countries have ratified the U.N. Palermo Protocol as a minimum standard of counter-human trafficking, governments of Cambodia, Thailand, and Vietnam have illustrated their insufficient national counter-human trafficking laws because they contain consistent and inconsistency of the U.N. Palermo Protocol. For instance, these countries assign different meanings of "trafficking in persons," while the anti-human trafficking law of Thailand defines this terms in accordance with the treaty, the anti-human trafficking law of Vietnam has an unclear description of the "means" element of human trafficking (Chapter 4).

As regards the impunity of traffickers, Vietnam does not recognize corporate liability while Thailand and Cambodia include this provision to stop impunity of perpetrators as required in the treaty. These respective countries' laws lack major responses, including provisions for appropriate housing and consideration of age, gender, and special needs of victims. Cambodia and Vietnam fail to incorporate provisions of protecting trafficking victims from prosecution. Although the governments of Cambodia, Thailand, and Vietnam have strived to prevent human trafficking crime by highlighting awareness-raising campaign and conducting training for government authorities, these three governments all should focus on decreasing the growing demand for child sex trafficking (Chapter 4).

These three governments have failed to implement these provisions. While the Thai government provides remedies for trafficking victims, the Vietnamese government does not. One recommendation is that the Thai government ensures effective identification of victims before deporting them. The evidence suggests that it is necessary for the governments of all three countries to increase prosecutions for human trafficking related crimes and implement zero tolerance policies for corruption (Chapter 4).

The inadequacies of the regional and national anti-human trafficking laws mentioned above and the lack of a regional anti-human rights body support the need for the establishment of the ADTV. This mechanism would contain fundamental measures for the prevention of human trafficking, protection of trafficking victims, and prosecution of offenders and the establishment of the ACTV and ensures a body, which specializes in tackling human trafficking. This mechanism would assist ASEAN and these three countries in strengthening regional and national strategies through sufficient counter-human trafficking provisions and monitoring powers (Chapter 5).

The ADTV should include preventive measures, aimed at decreasing the growing number of trafficking victims through an awareness-raising campaign for safe migration and collaboration with the private sector to implement plans of action for addressing human trafficking and forced labour migration. The ASEAN region in general, but more specifically the countries under review have a poor track record in providing legal protection and assistance for their trafficking victims. As a result, ASEAN should strengthen victim identification, immunity for trafficking victims, provisions for appropriate housing, rights to remedies, special protection for child victims, and prosecution of traffickers. Even though most ASEAN member countries have addressed the punishment of traffickers, the laws of Cambodia and Vietnam have failed to criminalize perpetrators. By imposing a severe penalty on consumers, in tandem with that of traffickers, ASEAN would be able to further decrease the demand for trafficking in person, which in turn may lead to an increase in the prosecution of perpetrators (Chapter 5).

The research articulates an ambitious goal of combating human trafficking scourge in its region. Recently, ASEAN has expressed its strong intention to fight human trafficking by considering the possibility of the establishment of the ADTIP. This means that ASEAN has acknowledged the need of a common anti-human trafficking norm in the region (Chapter 5).

Because of the lack of monitoring human rights bodies specializing in the fight against human trafficking and the epidemic of the crime of human trafficking in the ASEAN region, it is critical that ASEAN forms the ACTV to guide effective counter-human trafficking to its member countries. The requirements and capacity of the ACTV in comparison to GRETA's qualification were analyzed to determine its efficacy at dealing with human trafficking and the feasibility that such a mechanism would be accepted in the region. The research highlights the importance of ethical performance, independence and neutrality, as well as competence in anti-human trafficking of the ACTV. Since ASEAN lacks a human rights body specializing in combating human trafficking, the research suggests that ASEAN should select the members of the ACTV for that purpose. The members of the ACTV should consist of civil society members and other professionals, who have experience in anti-human trafficking so that they can provide the best strategies and methods to strengthen national and regional laws in ASEAN region. In order to design effective measures for ASEAN and its member countries, ACTV should convene meetings three times a year for a total of at least fifteen days to design effective measures for ASEAN and ASEAN member countries. In addition, in order to conduct duties such as monitoring and evaluating workflow, they should also appoint members to serve three-year terms, which should be renewable only once. These limited six-year terms could allow the ACTV to investigate and share information about strengths and weaknesses of the ten ASEAN member countries' laws (Chapter 5).

Last but not least, the research underscores the ACTV's monitoring power based on the GRETA's workflow and the human trafficking problems in Cambodia, Thailand, and Vietnam. This analysis includes the scope of a questionnaire that the ACTV should request from its member countries. The questions should cover three major parts: measures to prevent human trafficking, measures to promote and protect trafficking victims' rights, and measures to investigate and prosecute traffickers (Chapter 5).

In the monitoring process, the ACTV may conduct country visits to collect information pertaining to anti-human trafficking laws and policies of ASEAN member countries. ASEAN member countries should designate the contact person, who is knowledgeable about all government counter-human trafficking measures and serves as a coordinator between ACTV and ASEAN member country. For different perspectives on ASEAN member country's actions, the ACTV may request for additional information from civil society (Chapter 5).

It is clear that evaluation process should be collaborative. Proper exchanges between the ACTV and ASEAN member countries have the potential to alleviate suspicion and allow for discussion of the findings of anti-human trafficking. The member country would have the opportunity to agree or disagree with the ACTV's first and final drafts of the report. Therefore, that country can benefit from the ACTV's findings of strengths and weaknesses of their laws and policies. At the same time, that member country would also have the opportunity to correct any misunderstanding by the ACTV. ASEAN member countries could research each other's evaluations to strengthen their anti-human trafficking and related laws and policies (Chapter 5).

It is unlikely that while the present research is going ton, that either the ADTV and ACTV will be established, but it is posited that this anti-human trafficking law coupled with monitoring anti-human trafficking body can help ASEAN provide more sufficient methods and strategies. If ASEAN desires to respond this proposal, there is no doubt that ASEAN[1] will be eligible to influence its member countries to take serious commitments and actions through sufficient provisions of ADTV and anti-human trafficking competence of ACTV.

1 Martin Löffelholz & Danilo A. Arao, The ASEAN Guide: A Journalist's Handbook to Regional Integration in Southeast Asia 7 (2010); Kofi Annan on March 4, 2010 at the ASEAN Secretariat in Jakarta (explaining that the former Secretary-General of the United Nations Kofi Annan remarked that "ASEAN is one of the most successful organisations which I look up to and admire.").

APPENDIX A

Comparative Table of Trafficking Law Provisions of the UN Palermo Protocol and the National Anti-Human Trafficking Laws of Cambodia, Thailand and Vietnam

Issues	The UN Palermo Protocol	Cambodia	Thailand	Vietnam
Definition of Trafficking in Persons	**Art. 3** **Act** The recruitment, transportation, transfer, harbouring or receipt of persons **Means** the threat or use of: · force or other forms of coercion; · abduction; · fraud or deception; · the abuse of a position of vulnerability; or · the giving or receiving of payments/benefits to	**Article 13 defines "the act of selling, buying or exchanging a person"** "The act of selling, buying or exchanging a person shall mean to unlawfully deliver the control over a person to another, or to unlawfully receive the control over a person from another, in exchange for anything of value including any services and persons."	**Section 6 defines "trafficking in persons"** Trafficking in persons means committing any of the following acts for the purpose of exploitation: "(1) procuring, buying, selling, vending, bringing from or sending to, detaining or confining, harboring, or receiving any persons, by means of the threat or use of force, abduction, fraud, deception, abuse of power, or of the giving [of] money or	**Art. 3 – Prohibited Acts** 1. The trafficking in persons as stipulated in Art. 119 and Art. 120 of the Penal Code. Human trafficking is generally held to be: · for the purpose of prostitution; · in an organized manner; · of professional character; · for the purpose of organ removal; · for the purpose of sending the victim overseas;

 | DOI 10.1163/9789004265189_008

Issues	The UN Palermo Protocol	Cambodia	Thailand	Vietnam
	achieve the consent of a person having control over another person. **Purpose** **Exploitation** – **This includes at a minimum:** · the exploitation of the prostitution of others or other forms of sexual exploitation; · forced labour or services; · slavery or practices similar to slavery; the removal of organs	**Article 8 defines "unlawful removal"** "The act of unlawful removal means to: 1. remove a person from his/her current place of residence to a place under the actor's or a third person's control by means of force, threat, deception, abuse of power, or enticement, or 2. without legal authority or any other legal justification to do. So, take a minor or a person under general custody or curatorship or legal custody away from the legal custody of the parents, care taker or guardian."	benefits to achieve the consent of a person having control over another person in allowing the offender to exploit the person under his control; or (2) procuring, buying, selling, vending, bringing from or sending to, detaining or confining, harboring, or receiving a child."	· where it involves more than one victim, or · where trafficking occurs more than once. 2. The transfer or receipt of persons for sexual exploitation, forced labor, the removal or organs, or for other inhuman purposes. 3. The recruitment, transportation, harboring of persons for sexual exploitation, forced labors, the removal of organs or for other inhuman purposes, or for the commission of the acts as stipulated in paragraph 1 and 2 of this article.

Article 12 defines "unlawful recruitment for exploitation" "The act of unlawful recruitment…shall mean to induce, hire or employ a person to engage in any form of exploitation with the use of deception, abuse of power, confinement, force, threat or any coercive means." **Article 10 defines "any form of exploitation"** · Any form of exploitation "shall include the exploitation of the prostitution of others, pornography, commercial sex acts, forced labor or services, slavery or	4. Coercion of persons to commit any of the acts stipulated in paragraphs 1, 2 and 3 of this article. 5. Conducting brokerage to help other persons commit any of the acts stipulated in paragraph 1, 2 and 3 of this article. 6. Revenge or the threat of revenge of victims, witnesses, denunciators, their relatives or persons who deter the acts stipulated in this article. (*Means*) 7. Misuse of the prevention, suppression against human trafficking for illegally obtaining profits or committing illegal acts.

Issues	The UN Palermo Protocol	Cambodia	Thailand	Vietnam
		practices similar to slavery, debt bondage, involuntary servitude, child labor or removal of organs".		8. Obstruction against denunciation, notification and handling of the acts stipulated in this article. 9. Differentiation or discrimination against victims. 10. Disclosure of the information of victims without their consent, or their lawful representatives. (*protection of victims' privacy*) 11. Assuming false position as victims. 12. Other acts of violation of the provisions in this law.
Definitions of other terms			**Section 4 defines "exploitation"** "Exploitation means seeking benefits from the	**Art. 2 – Use of Terms** *Sexual exploitation* means the coercion of persons for prostitution, for being subject

prostitution, production or distribution of pornographic materials, other forms of sexual exploitation, slavery, causing another person to be a beggar, forced labor or service, coerced removal of organs for the purpose of trade, or any other similar practices resulting in forced extortion, regardless of such person's consent." "Forced Labor or Service means compelling the other person to work or provide service by putting such person in fear of injury to life, body, liberty, reputation or property, of such person or another person, by means of intimidation, use of force, or any other means causing such person to be in a state of being unable to resist."	matters for the production of pornographic materials, for erotic performance, or for sexual slavery. *Sexual slave* means persons who, under dependent situation, are forced to serve other persons for the latter's sexual demands. *Forced labor* means the use of force or the threat of use of force, or other means to coerce persons to work against their will. *Victim* means a person who is infringed upon by the acts stipulated in paragraph 1, 2 and 3, Article 3 of this Law.

Issues	The UN Palermo Protocol	Cambodia	Thailand	Vietnam
Criminalization of Trafficking	**Art. 5** 1. Each State Party shall adopt such legislative and other measures as may be necessary to establish as criminal offences the conduct set forth in article 3 of this Protocol, when committed intentionally. 2. Each State Party shall also adopt such legislative and other measures as may be necessary to establish criminal offences: Subject to the basic concepts of its legal system, attempting to commit an offence established in (a) accordance with paragraph 1 of this article; (b) Participating as an accomplice in an offence	Circumstances and facts of the trafficking act are applied to determine the category of offence and the penalty. • Unlawful removal – Article 9, 10, 11. • Unlawful recruitment for exploitation – Article 12. • The act of selling, buying or exchanging a person – Article 14, 15, and 16. • Transportation – Article 17 and 18. • Receipt of a person – Article 19 and 20. • Abduction, detention or confinement – Article 21. • Article 4 of the law also criminalizes the following: • Attempts to commit an offence;	Trafficking in persons is criminalized under Section 6 of the Anti-Trafficking in Persons Act 2008. Its section 6 provides that "[w]hoever, for the purpose of exploitation, does any of the following acts: (1) Procuring, buying, selling, vending, bringing from or sending to, detaining or confining, harboring, or receiving any persons, by means of the threat or use of force, abduction, fraud, deception, abuse of power, or of the giving [of] money or benefits to achieve the consent of a person having control over another person in	**Art. 23** (1) Any person who commits the acts stipulated in Article 3 of this Law shall, depending on the nature and extent of the violation, be disciplined or prosecuted for criminal liability... (2) Any person who abuses his/her power or position to shield, ignore wrongly handle, or not to handle the acts stipulated in Article 3 of this Law shall, depending on the nature and extent of the violation, be disciplined or prosecuted for criminal liability... -Offenders will be penalized under Art. 119 and Art. 120 of Penal Code.

established in accordance with paragraph 1 of this article; and (c) Organizing or directing other persons to commit an offence established in accordance with paragraph 1 of this article.	• Acting as an accomplice or instigator, which includes but is not limited to organizing or directing another to commit an offence; and • Offences committed by representatives, agents or employees of a legal entity or principal done in the scope of its business or in the interest of the legal entity or principal.	allowing the offender to exploit the person under his control; or (2) Procuring, buying, selling, vending, brining from or sending to, detaining or confining, harboring, or receiving a child; is guilty of 'trafficking in persons.'" Section 7 also criminalizes supporting the commission of an offence of trafficking in persons, aiding by contributing property, procuring a meeting place or lodge for the offender, assisting an offender to evade arrest, demanding, accepting or agreeing to accept property or any other benefit so an offender will not be punished and

Issues	The UN Palermo Protocol	Cambodia	Thailand	Vietnam
			inducing, suggesting or contracting a person to become a member of an organized criminal group, for the purpose of committing an offence of trafficking in persons. Section 8 criminalizes preparing to commit a trafficking offence. Section 9 criminalizes conspiracy to commit an offence of trafficking in persons	
Definition of a Minor	Under 18	Chapter 1, Article 7 of the 2008 Law on the Suppression of Human Trafficking and Sexual Exploitation defines a minor as a person less than 18 years of age. However,	Section 4 defines a child as any person less than eighteen years of age. However note when considering penalties under Chapter 6, section 52 provides that for offences of	The law does not indicate this term. However, the Vietnamese legal expert, Ms. Nguyễn Hải Anh, confirms that the term "minor" implies any person under 18.

		that Chapter 6 Specifically deals with indecency with minors under the age of 15 years.	trafficking in persons against a child not over the age of 15 years, the punishment shall be higher than for offences of trafficking in persons against a child between the ages of 16 and 18 years.	
Protection of Privacy and Confidentiality	Art. 6 (1) In appropriate cases and to the extent possible under its domestic law, each State Party shall protect the privacy and identity of victims of trafficking in persons, including, inter alia, by making legal proceedings relating to such trafficking confidential.	Chapter 8, Article 49 of the 2008 Law on the Suppression of Human Trafficking and Sexual Exploitation prevents the media from publishing, broadcasting or disseminating any information that could reveal the identity of a trafficked person to the public. This is not a comprehensive protection when considering the requirements of the Protocol as the Cambodian law does not make legal proceedings relating to trafficking confidential.	Section 56 makes it an offence for any individual to take, publish or disseminate, via whatever type of information communication media, pictures, voice recordings, and any information arising out of an inquiry or court hearing that could reveal the identity of a trafficking victim. This section prohibits disclosure of the first or last name, family members, history, residence, workplace and place of education of a trafficked person.	Art. 3 (10) Prohibited Acts – Disclosure or discrimination against victims Art. 30 Protection of the Safety of Victims, the Relatives of Victims (1) Measures to protect the safety of victims and their relatives shall include: (b) Keeping secret the places of residence, work or research of victims and their relatives... Art. 31Protection of the Personal Information Secret of Victims (1) Agencies, organizations or individuals shall have the responsibility to

Issues	The UN Palermo Protocol	Cambodia	Thailand	Vietnam
			Section 31 establishes a process for prompt testimony (the last paragraph of section 31 indicates that such testimony may be taken prior to the indictment of a defendant for an offence in Chapter 1 of the Anti-Trafficking in Persons Act 2008) and extracting pre-trial oral testimony by the Court from the trafficked person. Such testimony is admissible as evidence, thus avoiding the need for the victim to appear physically in court. Requests to cross-examine by interested people will only be granted by the court where appropriate.	keep secret the information of victims, unless otherwise as provided for by law. (2) At the request of victims or their lawful representative, courts shall consider and/or decide the commencement of closed court sessions on human trafficking cases.

				Section 36 provides that where a trafficked person will make a statement or testify as a witness in a trafficking in persons case, he/she will be afforded protection according to the law on the protection of witnesses in a criminal case in all respects (Under Section 44 money and property of the Anti-Trafficking in Persons Fund shall be used for the purpose of providing safety protection of the trafficked person under Section 36).	
Appropriate Housing	Art. 6 (3) (a) Each State Party shall consider implementing measures to provide for the physical, psychological and social recovery of victims of trafficking in persons,	Silent		Section 33 indicates that the Ministry of Social Development and Human Security shall consider providing assistance as appropriate to a trafficked person on food and shelter.	Art. 33 Support for Essential Needs and Traveling Expenses: In case of necessity, victims shall be provided with temporary housing, clothing, food and other necessary person tools on basis of actual

Issues	The UN Palermo Protocol	Cambodia	Thailand	Vietnam
	including, in appropriate cases, in cooperation with non-governmental organizations, other elements of civil society, and, in particular, the provision of Appropriate housing		A competent official may place the trafficked person in the care of primary shelter or other government or private welfare centers. The opinion of the trafficked person is to be sought in connection with the right to receive protection. Section 29 allows a competent official to take a person into temporary custody when there is reasonable ground to believe that person has been trafficked. Temporary custody is not to exceed 24 hours. Additionally, the trafficked person must be placed in an appropriate place which shall not be a detention cell or prison.	conditions, and according to their sex, age, health characteristics. If victims are willing to return their places of residence but are unable to pay their fares and foods during their traveling, they shall be provided with such expenses. Art. 40 (1)(a) Social Welfare Institutions, Victim Supporting Institutions: (1) Public-run social welfare institutions shall perform the following duties to support victims: (a) Receiving and providing shelter for victims.

Counseling and Legal Rights	Art. 6 (3) (b) Each State Party shall consider implementing measures to provide for the physical, psychological and social recovery of victims of trafficking in persons, including, in appropriate cases, in cooperation with non-governmental organizations, other elements of civil society, and, in particular, the provision of: Counseling and information, in particular as regards their legal rights, in a language that the victims of trafficking in persons can understand.	Silent	Section 33 requires the Ministry of Social Development and Human Security to consider providing assistance as appropriate to a trafficked person in mental rehabilitation, in legal aid and in legal proceedings to claim compensation. Section 34 requires the inquiry official or public prosecutor to inform the trafficked person of his/her right to compensation for damages resulting from the commission of trafficking in persons and the right to legal *aid.* Section 35 requires the Public Prosecutor to claim compensation for a trafficked person, where that	Art. 32 (1)(d) Eligible Persons and Supportive Regimes – (1) Victims who are Vietnamese citizens or stateless persons permanently residing in Vietnam shall,…, are entitled to the following supportive regimes: (d) Legal aid… Art. 36 Psychological Support – Psychological support shall be provided to victims to help them have their psychology stabilized during their stay in social welfare institutions or victim supporting institutions.

Issues	The UN Palermo Protocol	Cambodia	Thailand	Vietnam
			trafficked person has a right to compensation and has expressed his/her intention to make a claim.	
Medical Treatment	Art. 6 (3) (c) Each State Party shall consider implementing measures to provide for the physical, psychological and social recovery of victims of trafficking in persons, including, in appropriate cases, in cooperation with non-governmental organizations, other elements of civil society, and, in particular, the provision of: Medical, psychological and material assistance…	Silent	Section 33 requires the Ministry of Social Development and Human Security to consider providing assistance as appropriate to a trafficked person on medical treatment, and physical and mental rehabilitation.	Art. 32 (1) (b) Eligible Persons and Supportive Regimes – (1) Victims who are Vietnamese citizens or stateless persons permanently residing in Vietnam shall,…, are entitled to the following supportive regimes: (b) Medical support- Art. 34 Medical Support – During victims' stay in social welfare institutions or victim supporting institutions, provision of health care and/or medical treatment expenses to victims shall be taken into consideration if they are in need of health care for health recovery.

Employment, Education and Training	Art. (6) (3) (d) victims of trafficking in persons, including, in appropriate cases, in cooperation with non-governmental organizations, other elements of civil society, and, in particular, the provision of: Employment, educational and training opportunities…	Silent		Section 33 requires the Ministry of Social Development and Human Security to consider providing assistance as appropriate as appropriate to a trafficked person on education and training.	Art. 32 (e) Eligible Persons and Supportive Regimes – (1) Victims who are Vietnamese citizens or stateless persons permanently residing in Vietnam shall,…, are entitled to the following supportive regimes: (e) Support for educational training, vocational training. Art. 37 Support of Educational Training and Vocational Training – (1) Victims who are minors in poor household families shall be provided with tuition fees, and expenses for purchase of textbooks and school items for their first school year if they continue their schooling. (2) Provision of vocational training to victims shall be taken into consideration when they return their areas if they are poor household family members.

Issues	The UN Palermo Protocol	Cambodia	Thailand	Vietnam
Age, Gender and Special Needs of Victims	Art. 6 (4) Each State Party shall take into account, in applying the provisions of this article, the age, gender and special needs of victims of trafficking in persons, in particular the special needs of children, including appropriate housing, education and care.	Silent	Section 33, Chapter 4 requires the Ministry of Social Development and Human Security to provide assistance as appropriate to trafficked persons. In providing this assistance (Assistance includes on food, shelter, medical treatment, physical and mental rehabilitation, education, training, legal aid, repatriation and compensation claims in court) the difference in sex, age, nationality, race, and culture of the trafficked person is required to be taken into account. However, the Thai law does not have any provisions that relate to the special needs of	Art. 33 Support for Essential Needs and Traveling Expenses: In case of necessity, victims shall be provided with temporary housing, clothing, food and other necessary person tools on basis of actual conditions, and according to their sex, age, health characteristics. If victims are willing to return their places of residence but are unable to pay their fares and foods during their traveling, they shall be provided with such expenses. Art. 40 (1) (b) Social Welfare Institutions, Victim Supporting Institutions: (1) Public-run social welfare institutions shall perform the following duties to support

				victims or to the needs of child victims in particular.	victims: (b) Providing support for essential needs, health care and psychological support to the victims according to their sex, age and will, and on basis of the institutions' availability (providing essential needs according to sex, age, health characteristics, But no provision of victims' *special* needs),
Protection and Physical Safety	Art. 6 (5) Each State Party shall endeavour to provide for the physical safety of victims of trafficking in persons while they are within its territory.	Silent		Section 36 requires the competent official to provide for the safety protection of the trafficked person under his care. This safety protection is to be provided regardless of where such person stays (The length and purpose of the stay is not elaborated in the law). and is	Art. 30 Protection of the Safety of Victims, the Relatives of Victims (1) Measures to protect the safety of victims and their relatives shall include: (a) Provision of temporary shelter in case the life or health of victims or their relatives is likely to be threatened;

Issues	The UN Palermo Protocol	Cambodia	Thailand	Vietnam
			to be provided prior to, during or after proceedings. Safety protection of the family members of the trafficked person is also to be taken into account. Section 36 further requires the competent official to coordinate with the relevant authorities for continuous safety protection for the trafficked person and family members once they have returned to their country of residence or domicile.	(b) Keeping secret the places of residence, work or research of victims and their relatives; (c) Measures to prevent acts of infringement upon or threatening to infringe upon the life, health, honor, dignity or property of victims or their relatives in accordance with law; (d) Other protective measures as stipulated by criminal procedure law. (2) The Government shall specify the protection of the safety of victims, their relatives.
Compensation	Art. 6 (6) Each State Party shall ensure that its domestic legal system contains measures that offer victims of trafficking in persons the possibility of obtaining compensation for damage suffered.	Article 46 under Chapter 7 Civil Remedy of the Law on the Suppression of Human Trafficking and Sexual Exploitation indicates that a person who obtains enrichment without a legal cause knowing that the	Section 33 indicates that the Ministry of Social Development and Human Security shall consider providing assistance as appropriate to a trafficked person in the legal proceedings to claim compensation	Art. 6 Rights and Obligations of Victims – (3) To be entitled to compensation in accordance with law. Art. 36 Legal Aid (1) Victims shall be provided with legal counseling for the purpose of prevention of re-trafficking,

enrichment has been obtained from the act of selling/buying or exchanging a person or sexual exploitation shall be liable for restitution of the whole unjust enrichment along with accrued interest. An aggrieved person (a person being exploited) may claim for damages in addition to the restitution of such unjust enrichment. Article 47, victims shall have preference over property confiscated by the state for their compensation and restitution.	according to the regulations prescribed by the Minister. Section 34 for the benefit of the assistance to a trafficked person, the inquiry official or public prosecutor shall, in the first chance, inform the trafficked person of his right to compensation for damages resulting from being trafficked. Section 35 indicates that where the trafficked person has the right to compensation for damages as a result of being trafficked and expresses his intention to claim compensation thereof, the Public Prosecutor, shall, on behalf of the trafficked person, claim for compensation thereof.	and with legal aid to apply for permanent residence registration, civil status registration, entitlement to supportive regimes, to claim compensation, and to participate in litigation and other legal procedures in connection with the human trafficking cases.

Issues	The UN Palermo Protocol	Cambodia	Thailand	Vietnam
Right to Remain Temporarily or Permanently	Art. 7 (1) In addition to taking measures pursuant to article 6 of this Protocol, each State Party shall consider adopting legislative or other appropriate measures that permit victims of trafficking in persons to remain in its territory, temporarily or permanently, in appropriate cases.	Silent	Chapter 4, Section 38 states that trafficked persons will be returned to their country of residence unless they are allowed permanent residence under immigration law or have exceptional circumstances necessitating relief from the Minister of Interior. Evidence and documents under the law on census registration or the law on alien registration are required. Section 37 allows a trafficked person to obtain permission to reside temporarily and temporarily be allowed to work in accordance with the law where that person is taking proceedings against an	Art. 33 Support for Essential Needs and Traveling Expenses: In case of necessity, victims shall be provided with temporary housing, clothing, food and other necessary person tools on basis of actual conditions, and according to their sex, age, health characteristics. If victims are willing to return their places of residence but are unable to pay their fares and foods during their traveling, they shall be provided with such expenses.

				offender under the Anti-Trafficking in Persons Act. (2008), obtaining medical treatment or rehabilitation or claiming compensation. Section 38 indicates that in exceptional cases, where a person is not eligible for permanent residence, the Minister of the Interior can grant relief for the person to stay in Thailand	
Repatriation	Art. 8 The State Party of which a victim of trafficking in persons is a national or in which the person had the right of permanent residence at the time of entry into the territory of the receiving State party shall facilitate and accept, with due regard for the safety of that person, the return of	Silent		Section 33 requires the Ministry of Social Development and Human Security to consider providing assistance as appropriate to a trafficked person to return to the country of his/her origin or domicile. Section 36 requires the competent official to	Art. 55 Co-operation of Rescue and Repatriation of Victims – (2) The State of Vietnam shall create favorable conditions for the repatriation of victims who are foreigners to the countries where they hold the nationalities or their last places of residence are; apply appropriate measures for the repatriation of victims

Issues	The UN Palermo Protocol	Cambodia	Thailand	Vietnam
	that person without undue or unreasonable delay.		coordinate with the appropriate agency in the origin country to provide continuous safety protection for trafficked persons returning to their country of residence. Section 38 requires that the competent official shall undertake to have the trafficked person who is an alien return to his/her country of residence or domicile without delay except where the person is allowed permanent residence according to immigration law or has been granted relief by the Minister of the Interior. In undertaking the return of the person, the security and	in accordance with the prescribed procedures and the agreements between Vietnam and foreign countries, and protect the life, health, honor and dignity of victims.

welfare of such a person shall be taken into account (Section 38 is subject to section 37, which relates to the institution of legal proceedings, provision of medical treatment, rehabilitation and claims for compensation).

Section 39 requires that where a Thai national is in another country and wants to return to Thailand, the competent official shall undertake to clarify whether such a person is Thai. Where the person is Thai, the competent official shall undertake to have that person returned to Thailand without delay, and to do so with consideration to the safety and welfare of the person. This section also

Issues	The UN Palermo Protocol	Cambodia	Thailand	Vietnam
			contains provisions in relation to a trafficked person in a foreign country who is an alien being allowed residence in Thailand and in relation to a trafficked person in a foreign country as an alien and without identity documentation (Under Section 44 money and property of the Anti-Trafficking in Persons Fund shall be used for the purpose of providing assistance to the trafficked person in a foreign country to return to Thailand Section 39).	
Protection from Prosecution	Art. 4 This Protocol shall apply, except as otherwise stated herein, to the prevention, investigation and	Silent	Section 41 unless the Minister of Justice grants permission in writing, the inquiry official is barred	Silent

prosecution of the offences established in accordance with article 5 of this Protocol, where those offences are transnational in nature and involve an organized criminal group, as well as to the protection of victims of such offences.	from taking criminal proceedings against any trafficked person for the offence of entering, leaving or residing in the Kingdom without permission under the law on immigration, for giving false information to the official, forging or using forged travel document under the Penal code, for an offence under the law. · on prevention and suppression of prostitution, particularly on contacting, persuading, introducing and soliciting a person for the purpose of prostitution and assembling together in the place of prostitution for the

Issues	The UN Palermo Protocol	Cambodia	Thailand	Vietnam
			purpose of prostitution, or the offence of being an alien working without permission under the law on working of the alien.	

Sources: Law on Suppression of Human Trafficking and Social Exploitation 2008 of Cambodia; Anti-Trafficking in Persons Act B.E 2551 (2008) (Thailand); Anti-Trafficking in Persons Act 2008 of Thailand; Law on Prevention, Suppression against Human Trafficking (unofficial translation, 2011) (Vietnam), *available at* http://www.artipproject.org/artip-tip-cjs/laws-policies/national/Vietnam/Vietnam%20Anti-trafficking%20in%20Persons%20Law%20Mar%202011%20final%20ENG.pdf (last visited Dec. 12, 2012); United Nations Inter-Agency Project on Human Trafficking (UNIAP), Human Trafficking Laws: Legal Provisions for Victims, *available at* http://www.no-trafficking.org/reports_docs/legal_prov_vics.pdf (last visited March 5, 2013); David, Fiona et al., Progress Report on Criminal Justice Responses to Trafficking in Persons in ASEAN Region, 10-123 (July 2011).

APPENDIX B

ASEAN Member Countries on Corruption

ASEAN Member Countries Corruption Scores

ASEAN Member Countries	UNCAC	Corruption Score (of 10 score)
Brunei	2 Dec. 2008	5.2
Cambodia	5 Sep. 2007	2.1
Indonesia	19 Sep. 2006	3.0
Lao PDR	25 Sep. 2009	2.2
Malaysia	24 Sep. 2008	4.3
Myanmar	2 Dec. 2005 (signature)	1.5
Philippines	8 Nov. 2006	2.6
Singapore	6 Nov. 2009	9.2
Thailand	1 Mar. 2011	3.4
Vietnam	19 Aug. 2009	2.9

Corruption Score = The Perceived Levels of Public-Sector Corruption ["score below five on a scale of 0 (highly corrupt) to 10 (very clean)"]
Sources: *United Nations Convention against Corruption: Signature and Ratification Status as of 24 December 2012*, UNITED NATIONS OFFICE ON DRUGS AND CRIME (2013), *available at* http://www.unodc.org/unodc/en/treaties/CAC/signatories.html; *Corruption Perceptions Index 2011*, TRANSPARENCY INTERNATIONAL (2012), *available at* http://cpi.transparency.org/cpi2011/results/.

 | DOI 10.1163/9789004265189_009

Bibliography

Domestic Laws and Documents

Cambodia

Agreement on Guidelines for Practices and Cooperation between the Relevant Government Institutions and Victim Support Agencies in Cases of Human Trafficking, Phnom Penh, Feb. 6, 2007, *translated at* http://www.no-trafficking.org/content/pdf/guidelines%20for%20victims%20support%20agencies.pdf (last visited Dec. 12, 2012).

Law on Suppression of Human Trafficking and Sexual Exploitation, NS/RKM/0208/005 (Cambodia) (2008), *available at* http://www.no-trafficking.org/content/Laws_Agreement/cambodia_tip_2008.pdf (last visited Dec. 12, 2012).

National Plan of Action on the Suppression of Human Trafficking, Smuggling, Labour, and Sexual Exploitation of Cambodia (S.T.S.L.S.) for 2011–2013 (NCS/STLS, trans. Dec. 7, 2011), *available at* http://www.no-trafficking.org/content/pdf/CMB-National%20Plan%20of%20Action%20English2.pdf.

Thailand

Anti-trafficking in Persons Act B.E. 2551 (2008) (Thailand), *available at* http://www.no-trafficking.org/content/Laws_Agreement/laws_agreement_pdf/trafficking_in_persons_act_b.e%202551%20%28eng.%29.pdf.

Civil Code, B.E. 2535 (1992) (Thai), *available at* http://web.krisdika.go.th/data/law/law4/%bb03/%bb03-20-9999-update.pdf.

Criminal Procedure Code, B.E. 2477 (1934) (Thai), *available at* http://web.krisdika.go.th/data/law/law4/%BB05/%BB05-20-9999-update.pdf.

Damages for the Injured Person and Compensation and Expense for the Accused in the Criminal Case Act, B.E. 2544 (2001) (Thai), *available at* http://www.thailawforum.com/laws/Damages%20for%20the%20injured%20person.pdf.

National Policy, Strategies, and Measures to Prevent and Suppress Trafficking in Persons (2011–2016), *available at* http://www.nocht.m-society.go.th/human-traffic/policy/download/policy_strategy_en1.pdf (last visited Dec. 12, 2012).

The Public Prosecutor of Sumutsakorn v. Mr. Veerapong SaeLee and Ms. Arnoma Siriyuwattananon, First Ct. Dika No. 7314/2552, Nov. 26 2009 (unofficial translation on file with author).

Vietnam

Law on Child Protection, Care and Education, No. 25/2004/QH11 (June 15, 2004) (Vietnam), *available at* https://docs.google.com/viewer?a=v&q=cache:RCoGyArRV

UcJ:www.hsph.harvard.edu/population/trafficking/vietnam.child.04.doc+&hl=en&gl=us&pid=bl&srcid=ADGEESh8XXn7M0OWkRJNIolJ_VwYnM4-OXpQlclT5I10pCrKogaSINgmXh6n6DmcCRMLio6AOsPXBJkYGRUjG7-SBdQqfj0DN-XtQ770fpYW5C08MkZ1i7Ukg8sXo62ozpZyP5iKlavm&sig=AHIEtbSbVcVVfFRPTgJqFDcXzLODJfh_Gw.

Law on Prevention, Suppression against Human Trafficking (unofficial translation, 2011) (Vietnam), *available at* http://www.artipproject.org/artip-tip-cjs/laws-policies/national/Vietnam/Vietnam%20Anti-trafficking%20in%20Persons%20Law%20Mar%202011%20final%20ENG.pdf (last visited Dec. 12, 2012).

Ministry of Justice of Vietnam, (Draft) Report: Survey Findings on the Enforcement of Laws and Regulations on Investigation, Prosecution, and Trial of Criminals in Women and Children Trafficking (Report Draft Project 4-CT 130/CP, June 2008).

Socialist Republic of Vietnam, Guidelines on Process and Procedures of Identification and Reception of Trafficked Women and Children from Abroad (Inter-Ministerial Circular 03/2008/TTLC-MPS-MOD-MOLISA) (May 8, 2008), *available at* http://www.no-trafficking.org/reports_docs/legal/vietnam/vn_imc_vic*id*.pdf.

United States

United States Reports

U.S. Agency for Int'l Development (UNAID), Anti-Trafficking in Persons Programs in Asia: A Synthesis (2009), *available at* http://transition.usa*id*.gov/our_work/cross-cutting_programs/wid/pubs/Asia_Synthesis_Anti_Trafficking_508.pdf.

U.S. Dep't of State Office to Monitor and Combat Trafficking in Persons, Addressing Modern Slavery in the ASEAN Region (Nov. 20, 2012), *available at* http://www.state.gov/documents/organization/201097.pdf.

U.S. Dep't of State, Trafficking in Persons Report (2006), *available at* http://www.state.gov/documents/organization/66086.pdf.

U.S. Dep't of State, Trafficking in Persons Report (2007), *available at* http://www.state.gov/documents/organization/82902.pdf.

U.S. Dep't of State, Trafficking in Persons Report (2008), *available at* http://www.state.gov/documents/organization/105501.pdf.

U.S. Dep't of State, Trafficking in Persons Report (2009), *available at* http://www.state.gov/documents/organization/123357.pdf.

U.S. Dep't of State, Trafficking in Persons Report 2010 (2010), *available at* http://www.state.gov/documents/organization/142979.pdf.

U.S. Dep't of State, Trafficking in Persons Report 2011 (2011), *available at* http://www.state.gov/j/tip/rls/tiprpt/2011/index.htm.

U.S. Dep't of State, Trafficking in Persons Report 2012 (2012), *available at* http://www.state.gov/documents/organization/192594.pdf.

U.S. Dep't of State, Report: Trafficking in Persons Interim Assessment (April 5, 2011), *available at* http://www.state.gov/g/tip/rls/reports/2011/160017.htm.

U.S. Dep't of State, *Tier Placements*, Trafficking in Persons Report 2011 (Dec. 10, 2012), http://www.state.gov/j/tip/rls/tiprpt/2011/164228.htm.

U.S. Dep't of State, Trafficking in Persons Report 2012 (Dec. 6, 2012), *available at* http://www.state.gov/j/tip/rls/tiprpt/.

European Union Materials

European Court of Human Rights

Rantsev v. Cyprus and Russia, App. No. 25965/04, 51 Eur. H.R. Rep. 1, 2010 Eur. Ct. H.R. __ (Jan. 7, 2010), *available at* http://www.coe.int/t/dghl/cooperation/economiccrime/corruption/Projects/CAR_Serbia/ECtHR%20Judgements/English/RANTSEV%20v%20CYPRUS%20%20RUSSIA%20-%20ECHR%20Judgment%20_English_.pdf.

Council of Europe

Council of Europe Official Documents

Group of Experts on Action against Trafficking in Human Beings (GRETA), First General Report on GRETA's Activities: Covering the Period from February 2009 to July 2011, Public GRETA (2011) 11, Sep. 1, 2011, *available at* http://www.coe.int/t/dghl/monitoring/trafficking/Docs/Gen_Report/GRETA_2011_11_GenRpt_en.pdf.

Group of Experts on Action Against Trafficking in Human Beings (GRETA), *Integral Rules of Procedure of the Group of Experts on Action Against Trafficking in Human Beings* (*GRETA*), THB-GRETA (2009) 1, Feb. 24, 2009, *available at* http://www.coe.int/t/dghl/monitoring/trafficking/Source/THB-GRETA%282009%291_en.pdf.

Group of Experts on Action Against Trafficking in Human Beings (GRETA), *List of Items Discussed and Decision Taken*, THB-GRETA (2010) LD5, 5th meeting of GRETA (Strasbourg, 16–19 March 2010), Mar. 19, 2010, *available at* http://www.coe.int/t/dghl/monitoring/trafficking/docs/GRETA_MeetingDocs/Lists%20of%20decisions/THB-GRETA%282010%29LD5_en.pdf.

Group of Experts on Action against Trafficking in Human Beings (GRETA), *Questionnaire for the Evaluation of the Implementation of the Council of Europe Convention on Action against Trafficking in Human Beings by the Parties: First Evaluation Round*, GRETA(2010)1 rev2, Feb. 1, 2010, *available at* http://www.coe.int/t/dghl/monitoring/trafficking/Source/GRETA_2010_1_rev3_en.pdf.

Group of Experts on Action against Trafficking in Human Beings, Reply from Denmark to the Questionnaire for the evaluation of the implementation of the Council of Europe Convention on Action against Trafficking in Human Beings by the Parties, GRETA (2011) 01, *available at* http://www.coe.int/t/dghl/monitoring/trafficking/Source/Public_R_Q/GRETA_2011_01_R_Q_DNK_en.pdf.

Group of Experts on Action against Trafficking in Human Beings (GRETA), Report Concerning the Implementation of the Council of Europe Convention on Action against

Trafficking in Human Beings by Albania: First Evaluation Round, GRETA (2011) 22, Dec. 2, 2011, *available at* http://www.coe.int/t/dghl/monitoring/trafficking/Docs/Reports/GRETA_2011_22_FGR_ALB_en.pdf.

Group of Experts on Action against Trafficking in Human Beings (GRETA), Report Concerning the Implementation of the Council of Europe Convention on Action against Trafficking in Human Beings by Austria: First Evaluation Round, GRETA (2011) 10, Sep. 15, 2011, *available at* http://www.coe.int/t/dghl/monitoring/trafficking/Docs/Reports/GRETA_2011_10_FGR_AUT_en.pdf.

Group of Experts on Action against Trafficking in Human Beings (GRETA), Report Concerning the Implementation of the Council of Europe Convention on Action against Trafficking in Human Beings by Bulgaria: First Evaluation Round, GRETA (2011) 19, Dec. 14, 2011, *available at* http://www.coe.int/t/dghl/monitoring/trafficking/Docs/Reports/GRETA_2011_19_FGR_BGR_en.pdf.

Group of Experts on Action against Trafficking in Human Beings (GRETA), Report Concerning the Implementation of the Council of Europe Convention on Action against Trafficking in Human Beings by Croatia: First Evaluation Round, GRETA (2011) 20, Nov. 30, 2011, *available at* http://www.coe.int/t/dghl/monitoring/trafficking/Docs/Reports/GRETA_2011_20_FGR_HRV_en.pdf.

Group of Experts on Action against Trafficking in Human Beings, Report Concerning the Implementation of the Council of Europe Convention on Action against Trafficking in Human Beings by Cyprus: First Evaluation Round, GRETA (2011) 8, Sep. 12, 2011, *available at* http://www.coe.int/t/dghl/monitoring/trafficking/Docs/Reports/GRETA_2011_8_FGR_CYP_en_final.pdf.

Group of Experts on Action against Trafficking in Human Beings (GRETA), Report Concerning the Implementation of the Council of Europe Convention on Action against Trafficking in Human Beings by Denmark: First Evaluation Round, GRETA (2011) 21, Dec. 20, 2011, *available at* http://www.coe.int/t/dghl/monitoring/trafficking/Docs/Reports/GRETA_2011_21_FGR_DNK_en.pdf.

Group of Experts on Action against Trafficking in Human Beings (GRETA), Report Concerning the Implementation of the Council of Europe Convention on Action against Trafficking in Human Beings by Georgia: First Evaluation Round, GRETA (2011) 24 , Feb. 7, 2012, *available at* http://www.coe.int/t/dghl/monitoring/trafficking/Docs/Reports/GRETA_2011_24_FGR_GEO_en.pdf.

Group of Experts on Action against Trafficking in Human Beings (GRETA), Report Concerning the Implementation of the Council of Europe Convention on Action against Trafficking in Human Beings by Moldova: First Evaluation Round, GRETA (2011) 25, Feb. 22, 2012, *available at* http://www.coe.int/t/dghl/monitoring/trafficking/Docs/Reports/GRETA_2011_25_FGR_MDA_en.pdf.

Group of Experts on Action against Trafficking in Human Beings (GRETA), Report Concerning the Implementation of the Council of Europe Convention on Action against Trafficking in Human Beings by Romania: First Evaluation Round, GRETA (2012) 2,

May 31, 2012, *available at* http://www.coe.int/t/dghl/monitoring/trafficking/Docs/Reports/GRETA_2012_2_FGR_ROU_en.pdf.

Group of Experts on Action against Trafficking in Human Beings (GRETA), Report Concerning the Implementation of the Council of Europe Convention on Action against Trafficking in Human Beings by the Slovak Republic: First Evaluation Round (2011) 9, Sep. 19, 2011, *available at* http://www.coe.int/t/dghl/monitoring/trafficking/Docs/Reports/GRETA_2011_9_FGR_SVK_en.pdf.

Group of Experts on Action against Trafficking in Human Beings (GRETA), *Rules of Procedure for evaluating implementation of the Council of Europe Convention on Action against Trafficking in Human Beings by the Parties, THB-GRETA (2009) 3*, June 17, 2009, *available at* http://www.coe.int/t/dghl/monitoring/trafficking/Source/THB-GRETA(2009)3_en.pdf.

Group of Experts on Action against Trafficking in Human Beings (GRETA), Second General Report on GRETA's Activities Covering the Period from 1 August 2011 to 31 July 2012, GRETA (2012) 13, Oct. 4, 2012, *available at* http://www.coe.int/t/dghl/monitoring/trafficking/Docs/Gen_Report/GRETA_2012_13_2ndGenRpt_en.pdf.

Council of Europe Resolution

Council of Europe, Resolution CM/Res (2008)7 on Rules on the Election Procedure of the Members of the Group of Experts on Action against Trafficking in Human Beings (GRETA) adopted by the Committee of Minister on 11 June 2008 at the 1029th meeting of the Ministers' Deputies, *available at* https://wcd.coe.int/ViewDoc.jsp?Ref=CM/Res%282008%297&Language=lanEnglish&Ver=original&Site=CM&BackColorInternet=9999CC&BackColorIntranet=FFBB55&BackColorLogged=FFAC75.

Council of Europe Recommendations

Action against Trafficking in Human Beings for the Purpose of Sexual Exploitation: Recommendation No. R (2000) 11 of the Committee of Ministers and Explanatory Memorandum, (May 19, 2000), *available at* http://www.coe.int/T/E/human_rights/trafficking/PDF_Rec%282000%2911_E.pdf.

Committee of the Parties to the Council of Europe Convention on Action against Trafficking in Human Beings, *Recommendation CP (2011)2 on the implementation of the Council of Europe Convention on Action against Trafficking in Human Beings by Cyprus* (Sept. 26, 2011), *available at* http://www.coe.int/t/dghl/monitoring/trafficking/docs/CommitteeParties/Recommendations/CP_2011_2_en.pdf.

Council of Europe, *Recommendation CP (2012)2 on the implementation of the Council of Europe Convention on Action against Trafficking in Human Beings by Bulgaria*, (June 30, 2012), *available at* http://www.coe.int/t/dghl/monitoring/trafficking/docs/CommitteeParties/Recommendations/CP_2012_2_BGR_en.pdf.

Council of Europe Factsheet

Council of Europe, Directorate General of Human Rights Equality Division: Council of Europe Convention on Action against Trafficking in Human Beings, Aug. 2005, *available at* http://www.coe.int/t/dg3/children/pdf/PDF_FS_TrafConv_E_Aug05.pdf.

European Parliament

Directive 2011/36/EU, of the European Parliament and of the Council of 5 April 2011 on preventing and combating trafficking in human beings and protecting its victims, and replacing Council Framework Decision 2002/629/JHA, 2011, (L 101), *available at* http://ec.europa.eu/anti-trafficking/download.action?nodeId=9c9ba3cd-794b-4a57-b534-ad89effac575&fileName=Directive+THB+L+101+15+april+2011.pdf&fileType=pdf.

Treaties & Other International Agreements

Council of Europe Treaties & Agreements

Council of Europe Convention on Action Against Trafficking in Human Beings, May 16, 2005, C.E.T.S. No. 197, 2569 U.N.T.S. 45795.

European Convention for the Protection of Human Rights and Fundamental Freedoms, Nov. 4, 1950, C.E.T.S. No. 5, 213 U.N.T.S. 221.

Memorandums of Understanding

Memorandum of Understanding on Bilateral Cooperation for Eliminating Trafficking in Children and Women and Assisting Victims of Trafficking, Cambodia-Thai, May 31, 2003, *available at* http://www.no-trafficking.org/resources_laws_thailand.html (last visited Dec. 12, 2012).

Memorandum of Understanding on Bilateral Cooperation for Eliminating Trafficking in Persons, Especially Women and Children and Assisting Victims of Trafficking, Vietnam-Thai, Mar. 24, 2008, *available at* http://www.no-trafficking.org/resources_laws_thailand.html (last visited Dec. 12, 2012).

Memorandum of Understanding on Bilateral Cooperation on Cooperation in the Employment of Workers, Cambodia-Thai, May 31, 2003, *available at* http://www.no-trafficking.org/content/pdf/mou_cambodiathailand_on_cooperation_in_the_employment_of_wo.pdf.

United Nations Treaties

Convention on the Rights of the Child (CRC), Nov. 20, 1989, 1577 U.N.T.S. 3.

Protocol to Prevent, Suppress and Punish Trafficking in Persons, especially Women and Children, supplementing the United Nations Convention against Transnational Organized Crime (Palermo Protocol), Nov. 2, 2000, 2237 U.N.T.S. 319.

United Nations Convention against Transnational Organized Crime, Nov. 15, 2000, 225 U.N.T.S. 209.

United Nations Convention against Transnational Organized Crime and the Protocol Thereto, Nov. 15, 2000, 2225 U.N.T.S. 209.

United Nations Convention on the Elimination of All Forms of Discrimination against Women (CEDAW), Dec. 18, 1979, 1249 U.N.T.S. 13.

Treaty of Amity and Cooperation (TAC) in Southeast Asia, Feb. 24, 1976, 1025 U.N.T.S. 316.

United Nations Sources

United Nations Resolutions

World Summit Outcome, G.A. Res. 60/1, U.N. Doc. A/RES/60/1 (Oct. 24, 2005), *available at* http://unpanl.un.org/intradoc/groups/public/documents/un/unpan021752.pdf.

G.A. Res. 34/22, U.N. Doc. A/RES/34/22 (Nov. 14, 1979), *available at* http://www.un.org/documents/ga/res/34/a34res22.pdf.

Human Rights Council Res. 11/3, Rep. of the Human Rights Council, 11th Sess. Oct. 16, 2009, U.N. Doc. A/HRC/11/37, *available at* http://daccess-dds-ny.un.org/doc/UNDOC/GEN/G09/167/66/PDF/G0916766.pdf?OpenElement.

Improving the Coordination of Efforts against Trafficking in Persons, G.A. Res. 64/178, U.N. Doc. A/RES/64/178 (Mar 26, 2010), *available at* http://www.un.org/ga/search/view_doc.asp?symbol=A/RES/64/178.

United Nations Global Plan of Action to Combat Trafficking in persons, G.A. Res. 64/293, U.N. Doc. A/RES/64/293 (Aug. 12, 2010).

United Nations Documents

Secretariat to the Conference of the Parties to the United Nations Convention against Transnational Organized Crime, *Victims of Trafficking in Persons, with Particular Emphasis on Identification*, U.N. Doc. CTOC/COP/WG.4/2011/4 (Aug. 10, 2011), *available at* http://www.unodc.org/documents/treaties/organized_crime/2011_CTOC_COP_WG4/2011_CTOC_COP_WG4_4/CTOC_COP_WG4_2011_4_E.pdf.

Special Rapporteur on Trafficking in Persons, Especially Women and Children, *Report on Agenda Item 3: Promotion and Protection of all Human Rights, Civil, Political, Economic, Social and Cultural Rights, including the Right to Development*, U.N. Human Rights Council, U.N. Doc. A/HRC/14/32 (May 4, 2010) (by Joy Ngozi Ezeilo), *available at* http://daccess-dds-ny.un.org/doc/UNDOC/GEN/G10/132/11/PDF/G1013211.pdf?OpenElement.

Special Rapporteur on Trafficking in Persons, *Report of the Special Rapporteur on Trafficking in Persons, Especially Women and Children, Joy Ngozi Ezeilo*, 17th Sess., Agenda Item 3, U.N. Doc A/HRC/17/35 (April 13, 2011) (by Joy Ngozi Ezeilo), *available at* http://www2.ohchr.org/english/bodies/hrcouncil/docs/17session/A-HRC-17-35.pdf.

Special Rapporteur on Violence Against Women its Causes and Consequences, *Integration of the Human Rights of Women and the Gender Perspective: Violence against Women*, U.N. Eco. & Soc. Council, U.N. Doc. E/CN.4/2001/73/Add.2 (Feb. 6, 2001) (by Radhika Coomaraswamy, *available at* http://daccess-dds-ny.un.org/doc/UNDOC/GEN/G01/108/65/PDF/G0110865.pdf?OpenElement.

United Nations Centre for Human Rights, National Human Rights Institutions: A Handbook on the Establishment and Strengthening of National Institutions for the Promotion and Protection of Human Rights, U.N. Doc. No. HR/P/PT/4, U.N. Sales No. E.95.XIV.2 (1995), *available at* http://www.asiapacificforum.net/members/international-standards/downloads/best-practice-for-nhris/NHRIs_a_handbook.pdf.

United Nations Children's Fund, Progress for Children: A Report Card on Child Protection, no. 8, U.N. Sales No. E.09.XX.14 (Sept., 2009), *available at* http://www.childinfo.org/files/Progress_for_Children-No.8_EN.pdf.

United Nations Committee on the Elimination of Discrimination against Women, Consideration of Reports Submitted by States parties under Article 18 of the Convention on the Elimination of All Forms of Discrimination against Women, Combined Fourth and Fifth Periodic Reports of States Parties: Cambodia U.N. Doc. CEDAW/C/KHM/4-5 (Sept. 24, 2011) (prepared by the Government of Cambodia), *available at* http://daccess-ods.un.org/TMP/5445075.63114166.html.

United Nations Committee on the Rights of the Child, Consideration of Reports Submitted by States Parties under Article 12, para. 1, of the Optional Protocol to the Convention on the Rights of the Child on the Sale of Children, Child Prostitution and Child Pornography: Concluding Observations: Thailand, U.N. Doc. CRC/C/OPSC/THA/CO/1 (Feb. 21, 2012), *available at* http://daccess-ods.un.org/TMP/7597856.52160645.html.

United Nations Committee on the Rights of the Child, Consideration of Reports Submitted by States Parties under Article 44 of the Convention Concluding Observations: Thailand, U.N. Doc. CRC/C/TH/A/CO/3-4 (Feb. 17, 2012), *available at* http://www2.ohchr.org/english/bodies/crc/docs/co/CRC_C_THA_CO_3-4.pdf.

United Nations Office of the High Commissioner for Human Rights, *Recommended Principles and Guidelines on Human Rights and Human Trafficking*, U.N. Doc. E/2002/68/Add.1 (May 20, 2002), *available at* http://daccess-dds-ny.un.org/doc/UNDOC/GEN/N02/401/68/PDF/N0240168.pdf?OpenElement.

United Nations Office of the High Commissioner for Human Rights, *Recommended Principles and Guidelines on Human Rights and Human Trafficking: Commentary*, U.N. Doc. HR/PUB/10/2, U.N. Sales No. E.10.XIV.1 (2010), *available at* http://www.ohchr.org/Documents/Publications/Commentary_Human_Trafficking_en.pdf.

U.N. Secretary-General, *In Larger Freedom: Towards Development, Security and Human Rights for All Report of the Secretary-General: Explanatory Note of the Secretary-General,*

U.N. Doc. A/59/2005/Add.1 (May 23, 2005), *available at* http://daccess-ods.un.org/TMP/1690984.36832428.html.

United Nations Publications

Regional and Sub-Regional Cooperation in Promoting a Human Rights-Based Approach to Combating Trafficking in Persons especially in Women and Children, Dakar, Oct. 4–5, 2010, *Discussion Paper: Consultation of the Special Rapporteur on Trafficking in Persons, Especially Women and Children* (2010), *available at* http://www.ohchr.org/Documents/Issues/Trafficking/Dakar_discussion_paper_en.pdf.

Regional Expert Roundtable on Good Practices for the Identification, Prevention and Reduction of Statelessness and the Protection of Stateless Persons in Southeast Asia, Bangkok, Oct. 28–29, 2010, *Good Practices: Addressing Statelessness in Southeast Asia* (Feb. 5, 2011), *available at* http://www.unhcr.org/4d7de47f9.html.

Special Rapporteur on Trafficking in Persons, *Summary of Regional and Sub-Regional Structures and Initiatives to Counter Trafficking in Persons* (Dec., 2010), *available at* http://www.ohchr.org/EN/Issues/Trafficking/Pages/DakarConsultationoct2010.aspx (scroll down to "Summary of Regional Structures and Initiatives").

UNDP Asia Pacific Regional Centre & OHCHR Regional Office for Southeast Asia, *Report on Regional Dialogue on UN Engagement with ASEAN Human Rights System* (Sept. 6, 2010), *available at* http://bangkok.ohchr.org/files/Regional_Dialogue_ASEAN_Report.pdf.

United Nations Children's Fund High Level meeting on International Collaboration for Children's Rights in the Asia and Pacific Region, Beijing P.R. China, Nov. 5–7, 2010, *Thailand: Principles and Philosophy of South-South Collaboration*, *available at* http://www.unicef.org/eapro/Final_Thailand_HLM_Paper_1_Nov.pdf.

United Nations Development Programme, Human Development Report: New Dimensions of Human Security (1994), *available at* http://hdr.undp.org/en/reports/global/hdr1994/chapters/.

United Nations Inter-Agency Project on Human Trafficking, Human Trafficking Laws: Legal Provisions for Victims (n.d.), *available at* http://www.no-trafficking.org/reports_docs/legal_prov_vics.pdf (last visited March 5, 2013).

United Nations Inter-Agency Project on Human Trafficking, The COMMIT Sub-Regional Plan of Action (COMMIT SPA): Achievements in Combating Human Trafficking in the Greater Mekong Sub-Region, 2005–2007 (Dec. 2007), *available at* http://www.no-trafficking.org/reports_docs/commit/commit_spa1_achievements.pdf.

United Nations Inter-Agency Project on Human Trafficking, Human Trafficking Sentinel Surveillance: Poipet, Cambodia 2009–2010 (2010), *available at* http://www.no-trafficking.org/reports_docs/2009-2010_UNIAP_sentinel_surveillance_Poipet.pdf.

United Nations Inter-Agency Project on Human Trafficking (UNIAP), Strategic Information Response Network (SIREN) Human Trafficking Data Sheet: Cambodia (Mar. 2008), *available at* http://www.no-trafficking.org/reports_docs/cambodia/datasheet_cambodia_march08.pdf.

United Nations Inter-Agency Project on Human Trafficking (UNIAP), Strategic Information Response Network (SIREN) Human Trafficking Datasheets: Mekong Region (Sept. 2010), *available at* http://www.no-trafficking.org/reports_docs/siren/uniap_2010ht_datasheets.pdf.

United Nations Inter-Agency Project on Human Trafficking (UNIAP), Strategic Information Response Network (SIREN) Human Trafficking Data Sheet: Thailand (Oct., 2008), *available at* http://www.no-trafficking.org/reports_docs/thailand/datasheet_thailand_oct2008.pdf.

United Nations Office on Drugs and Crime (UNODC), Global Report on Trafficking in Persons (2009), *available at* http://www.unodc.org/documents/human-trafficking/Global_Report_on_TIP.pdf.

United Nations Office on Drugs and Crime (UNODC), Model Law on Trafficking in Persons (2009), *available at* http://www.unodc.org/documents/human-trafficking/UNODC_Model_Law_on_Trafficking_in_Persons.pdf.

United Nations Technical Working Group on Human Trafficking, Factsheet on Combatting Human Trafficking (May, 2012), *available at* http://www.un.org.vn/en/publications/doc_details/192-factsheet-on-combating-human-trafficking.html.

United Nations News and Press Releases

Press Release, Office of the High Commissioner for Human Rights, Thailand Must Do More to Combat Human Trafficking Effectively and Protect the Rights of Migrant Workers Who are Increasingly Vulnerable to Forced and Exploitative Labor, Says Special Rapporteur on Trafficking in Persons, Especially Women and Children, Joy Ngozi Ezeilo (Aug. 19, 2011), http://www.ohchr.org/en/NewsEvents/Pages/DisplayNews.aspx?NewsID=11319&LangID=E.

Press Release, United Nations Inter-Agency Project on Human Trafficking, Mekong Countries Build Regional Capacity to Combat Transnational Human Trafficking (June 19, 2009), *available at* http://www.no-trafficking.org/reports_docs/news/press_releases/rtp_press_release_eng.pdf.

Press Release. United Nations Office of the High Commissioner for Human Rights, Address by the UN High Commissioner for Human Rights on the 7th Official Meeting of the ASEAN Intergovernmental Commission on Human Rights (Nov. 28, 2011), *available at* http://bangkok.ohchr.org/news/press/address-high-commissioner-asean-intergovernmental-commission-human-rights.aspx.

United Nations Internet Sources

Cambodia—Background, United Nations Children's Fund (UNICEF), http://www.unicef.org/infobycountry/cambodia_2190.html (last updated Feb. 26, 2003).

COMMIT: The Coordinated Mekong Ministerial Initiative Against Trafficking, United Nations Inter-Agency Project on Human Trafficking (UNIAP), http://www.no-trafficking.org/commit.html (last visited Mar. 1, 2013).

Counter-Trafficking Action in Vietnam, United Nations Inter-Agency Project on Human Trafficking (UNIAP), http://www.no-trafficking.org/vietnam_action.html (last visited Mar. 1, 2013).

Human Trafficking: A Rights-Based Approach, United Nations Office of the High Commissioner for Human Rights (Dec. 19, 2011), http://www.ohchr.org/EN/NewsEvents/Pages/HumanTrafficking.aspx.

Initiatives: Support to Underserved Victims, United Nations Inter-Agency Project on Human Trafficking (UNIAP), http://www.no-trafficking.org/init_underserved.html (last visited Mar 1, 2013).

South East Asia Regional Office (2008–2009): Human Rights Context, United Nations Office of the High Commissioner for Human Rights, http://www.ohchr.org/EN/Countries/AsiaRegion/Pages/SouthEastAsiaSummary0809.aspx (last visited Mar. 1, 2013).

Special Rapporteur on Trafficking in Persons, Especially in Women and Children: Country Visits, United Nations Office of the High Commissioner for Human Rights, http://www.ohchr.org/EN/Issues/Trafficking/Pages/Visits.aspx (last visited Mar. 1, 2013).

UNIAP Thailand, United Nations Inter-Agency Project on Human Trafficking, http://www.no-trafficking.org/thailand_who.html (last visited Mar. 1, 2013).

United Nations Convention against Corruption: Signature and Ratification Status as of Dec. 24, 2012, United Nations Office on Drugs and Crime, http://www.unodc.org/unodc/en/treaties/CAC/signatories.html (last visited Mar. 1, 2013).

Where We Work, United Nations Inter-Agency Project on Human Trafficking, http://www.no-trafficking.org/where.html (last visited Mar. 1, 2013).

ASEAN Documents

ASEAN Agreements

Charter of the Association of Southeast Nations [ASEAN Charter], Nov. 20, 2007, *available at* http://www.asean.org/archive/publications/ASEAN-Charter.pdf.

Treaty on Mutual Legal Assistance in Criminal Matters among Like-Minded ASEAN Member Countries, Nov. 29, 2004, *available at* http://www.agc.gov.my/images/pdf/int/emam/mlatdoc/mutuallegalassisttreaty.pdf.

Treaty on the Southeast Asia Nuclear Weapon-Free Zone, Dec. 15, 1995, *available at* http://www.asean.org/asean/asean-summit/item/treaty-on-the-southeast-asia-nuclear-weapon-free-zone.

ASEAN Terms of Reference

ASEAN Commission on the Promotion and Protection of the Rights of Women and Children (ACWC), Terms of Reference (Feb. 2010), *available at* http://www.asean.org/images/2012/publications/TOR%20of%20ACWC%201.pdf.

ASEAN Intergovernmental Commission on Human Rights (AICHR), Terms of Reference, (Oct. 2009), *available at* http://www.asean.org/images/2012/publications/Terms%20of%20Reference%20of%20ASEAN%20Intergovernmental%20Commission%20on%20Human%20Rights.pdf.

ASEAN Declarations

ASEAN Declaration (Bangkok Declaration), Thailand, Aug. 8, 1967, 6 I.L.M. 1223, *available at* http://www.asean.org/component/zoo/item/the-asean-declaration-bangkok-declaration.

ASEAN Declaration against Trafficking in Persons, Particularly Women and Children, Vientiane, Nov. 29, 2004, *available at* http://www.asean.org/communities/asean-political-security-community/item/asean-declaration-against-trafficking-in-persons-particularly-women-and-children-2.

ASEAN Declaration on the Protection and Promotion of the Rights of Migrant Workers, Cebu, Jan. 13, 2007, *available at* http://www.asean.org/communities/asean-political-security-community/item/asean-declaration-on-the-protection-and-promotion-of-the-rights-of-migrant-workers-3.

ASEAN Declaration on the South China Sea, Manila, July 22, 1992, *available at* http://cil.nus.edu.sg/rp/pdf/1992%20ASEAN%20Declaration%20on%20the%20South%20China%20Sea-pdf.pdf.

ASEAN Declaration on Transnational Crime, Manila, Dec. 20, 1997, *available at* http://cil.nus.edu.sg/rp/pdf/1997%20ASEAN%20Declaration%20on%20Transnational%20Crime-pdf.pdf.

Declaration of ASEAN Concord II (Bali Concord II), Oct. 7, 2003, *available at* http://www.asean.org/news/item/declaration-of-asean-concord-ii-bali-concord-ii-2.

Declaration on the Conduct of Parties in the South China Sea, Phnom Peh, Nov. 4, 2002, *available at* http://www.asean.org/news/item/declaration-on-the-conduct-of-parties-in-the-south-china-sea-2.

The Bangkok Declaration on Irregular Migration, *International Symposium on Migration: Towards Regional Cooperation on Irregular/Undocumented Migration* (Apr. 21–23, 1999) *available at* http://www.iom.int/jahia/webdav/site/myjahiasite/shared/shared/mainsite/policy_and_research/rcp/APC/BANGKOK_DECLARATION.pdf.

The Cebu Declaration on the Blueprint of ASEAN Charter, Cebu, Jan. 13, 2007, *available at* http://www.asean.org/asean/asean-summit/item/cebu-declaration-on-the-blueprint-of-the-asean-charter-cebu-philippines-13-january-2007.

Zone of Peace, Freedom and Neutrality Declaration, Kuala Lumpur, Nov. 27, 1971, *available at* http://cil.nus.edu.sg/rp/pdf/1971%20Zone%20of%20Peace%20Freedom%20and%20Neutrality%20Declaration-pdf.pdf.

ASEAN Statements

ASEAN Leaders' Joint Statement in Enhancing Cooperation against Trafficking in Persons in Southeast Asia, May 8, 2011, http://www.asean.org/archive/Joint_Statement_TIP.pdf.

ASEAN Regional Forum Vision Statement, July 23, 2009, http://aseanregionalforum.asean.org/files/library/ARF%20Chairman%27s%20Statements%20and%20Reports/The%20Sixteenth%20ASEAN%20Regional%20Forum,%202008-2009/ARF_Vision_Statement.pdf.

Chairman's Statement of the 11th ASEAN Summit, *One Vision, One Identity, and One Community Statement*, Dec. 12, 2005, http://www.asean.org/asean/asean-summit/item/chairman-s-statement-of-the-11th-asean-summit-one-vision-one-identity-one-community.

Chairman's Statement of the 13th ASEAN Summit, *One ASEAN at the Heart of Dynamic Asia*, Nov. 20, 2007, http://www.asean.org/asean/asean-summit/item/chairman-s-statement-of-the-13th-asean-summit-one-asean-at-the-heart-of-dynamic-asia-singapore-20-november-2007.

Chairman's Statement of the Twelfth Meeting of the ASEAN Regional Forum (ARF), July 29 2005, http://www.asean.org/communities/asean-political-security-community/item/chairman-s-statement-of-the-twelfth-meeting-of-the-asean-regional-forum-arf-vientiane-29-july-2005-2.

Co-chairs' Statement of the Fourth Bali Regional Ministerial Conference on People Smuggling, Trafficking in Persons and Related Transnational Crime, Bali, Indonesia, Mar. 29–30, 2011, http://www.asean.org/communities/asean-political-security-community/item/co-chairs-statement-of-the-fourth-bali-regional-ministerial-conference-on-people-smuggling-trafficking-in-persons-and-related-transnational-crime-bali-indonesia-29-30-march-2011.

Joint Statement of the Fifth ASEAN Plus Three Ministerial Meeting on Transnational Crime (5th AMMTC+3) Consultation, Oct. 12, 2011, http://www.asean.org/news/asean-statement-communiques/item/joint-statement-of-the-fifth-asean-plus-three-ministerial-meeting-on-transnational-crime-5th-ammtc3-consultation-2.

Statement on the Establishment of ASEAN Committee on the Implementation of ASEAN Declaration on the Protection and Promotion of the Rights of Migrant Workers, July 13, 2007, http://www.asean.org/communities/asean-political-security-community/item/statement-of-the-establishment-of-the-asean-committee-on-the-implementation-of-the-asean-declaration-on-the-protection-and-promotion-of-the-rights-of-migrant-workers.

ASEAN Plans of Action

ASEAN Plan of Action for Cooperation on Immigration Matters, *available at* http://www.asean.org/communities/asean-political-security-community/item/asean-plan-of-action-for-cooperation-on-immigration-matters (last visited Dec. 12, 2012).

ASEAN Plan of Action to Combat Transnational Crime, June 23, 1999, *available at* http://www.asean.org/communities/asean-political-security-community/item/asean-plan-of-action-to-combat-transnational-crime.

Five-Year Work Plan of the ASEAN Intergovernmental Commission on Human Rights (2010–2015), *available at* http://aichr.org/documents/?doing_wp_cron=1356371613.7076230049133300781250 (last visited Dec. 24, 2012) (Scroll down to .PDF link for AICHR Five-Year Work Plan 2010–2015).

Vientiane Action Programme 2004–2010, Nov. 29, 2004, *available at* http://cil.nus.edu.sg/rp/pdf/2004%20Vientiane%20Action%20Programme%202004-2010-pdf.pdf.

ASEAN Joint Communiqués

Joint Communiqué issued by the 37th ASEAN Ministerial Meeting Jakarta, June 29–30, 2004, http://www.asean.org/communities/asean-political-security-community/item/joint-communique-of-the-37th-asean-ministerial-meeting-jakarta-29-30-june-2004-3.

Joint Communiqué of the Sixth ASEAN Ministerial Meeting on Transnational Crime (AMMTC), Nov. 6, 2007, http://www.asean.org/news/item/joint-communique-of-the-6th-ammtc-bandar-seri-begawan-6-november-2007.

ASEAN Reports and Publications

Association of Southeast Asian Nations, ASEAN Documents on Combating Transnational Crime and Terrorism: A Compilation of ASEAN Declarations, Joint Declarations, and Statements on Combating Transnational Crime and Terrorism (2012), *available at* http://www.asean.org/resources/publications/asean-publications/item/asean-documents-on-combating-transnational-crime-and-terrorism?category_id=382.

Association of Southeast Asian Nations, ASEAN Handbook on International legal Cooperation in Trafficking in Persons Cases (2010), *available at* http://www.asean.org/archive/publications/ASEAN%20Handbook%20on%20International%20Legal%20Cooperation%20in%20TIP%20Cases.pdf.

Association of Southeast Asian Nations, Vision 2020, Dec. 15, 1997, *available at* http://www.asean.org/asean/asean-summit/item/asean-vision-2020.

Association of Southeast Asian Nations, ASEAN in the Global Community: Annual Report 2010–2011 (2011), *available at* http://www.asean.org/images/2012/publications/Annual%20Report%202010_2011.pdf.

Association of Southeast Asian Nations, ASEAN Political-Security Community Blueprint (2009), *available at* http://www.asean.org/archive/5187-18.pdf.

Association of Southeast Asian Nations, ASEAN Regional Forum: Annual Security Outlook-2011, 12 ARF ASO (2011), *available at* http://aseanregionalforum.asean.org/files/ARF-Publication/ARF-Annual-Security-Outlook/ARF%20Annual%20Security%20Outlook%202011.pdf.

Association of Southeast Asian Nations, ASEAN Regional Forum: Documents Series 2006–2009 (2010), *available at* http://www.google.com/url?sa=t&rct=j&q=&esrc=s&source=web&cd=1&ved=0CDAQFjAA&url=http%3A%2F%2Fwww.asean.org%2Fresources%2Farchives%3Ftask%3Dcallelement%26format%3Draw%26item_id%3D5239%26element%3Da0c6d315-bb76-42c6-9ecf-c287d406937b%26method%3Ddownload&ei=NWe_UNScDaqQ0QHR24CgBQ&usg=AFQjCNELpftOR9t-G7LplLBG1zMGPfy6yw&sig2=TBgL-hHksuO-ux70b-OT_Q (last visited Dec. 12, 2012).

Association of Southeast Asian Nations, ASEAN Responses to Trafficking in Persons (Supp. & Update 2008), *available at* http://www.artipproject.org/artip-tip-cjs/resources/specialised_publications/ASEAN%20Responses%20to%20TIP_2006.pdf.

Association of Southeast Asian Nations, ASEAN Responses to Trafficking in Persons: Ending Impunity for Traffickers and Securing Justice for Victims (Supp. & Update 2007), *available at* http://www.artipproject.org/artip-tip-cjs/resources/specialised_publications/ASEAN%20Responses%20to%20TIP%20Study_Supplement_2007.pdf.

Association of Southeast Asian Nations, ASEAN Socio-Cultural Community Blueprint (2009), *available at* http://www.asean.org/images/archive/5187-19.pdf.

Association of Southeast Asian Nations, Criminal Justice Responses to Trafficking in Persons: ASEAN Practitioner Guidelines (2007), *available at* http://www.artipproject.org/artip-tip-cjs/tip-cjr/recent_developments/ASEAN-PG_Web_English_Final.pdf.

Association of Southeast Asian Nations, Evolving towards ASEAN 2015: ASEAN Annual Report 2011–2012 (2012), *available at* http://www.asean.org/resources/publications/asean-publications/item/asean-annual-report-2011-2012.

Association of Southeast Asian Nations, Roadmap for an ASEAN Community 2009–2015 (2009), *available at* http://www.asean.org/images/2012/publications/RoadmapASEANCommunity.pdf.

Association of Southeast Asian Nations, The First ASEAN Regional Forum (Bangkok, Thailand, July 25, 1994), *available at* http://aseanregionalforum.asean.org/files/ARF-Publication/ARF-Document-Series-1994-2006/01_Bangkok2006.pdf.

Association of Southeast Asian Nations, The Ninth ASEAN Regional Forum (Bandar Seri Begawan, Brunei Darussalam, July 31, 2002), *available at* http://aseanregionalforum.asean.org/files/ARF-Publication/ARF-Document-Series-1994-2006/09_Brunei2006.pdf.

Association of Southeast Asian Nations, The Second ASEAN Regional Forum (Bandar Seri Begawan, Brunei Darussalam , Aug. 1, 1995), *available at* http://aseanregionalforum.asean.org/files/ARF-Publication/ARF-Document-Series-1994-2006/02_Brunei 2006.pdf.

Association of Southeast Asian Nations, The Tenth ASEAN Regional Forum (Phnom Penh, Cambodia, June 18, 2003), *available at* http://aseanregionalforum.asean.org/files/ARF-Publication/ARF-Document-Series-1994-2006/10_Cambodia2006.pdf.

Johannah, Wegerdt & Mark, Siu Sue, Post-Nargis Needs Assessment and Monitoring: ASEAN's Pioneering Response (2010), *available at* http://www.asean.org/images/2012/publications/Post-Nargis%20Needs%20Assessment%20and%20Monitoring%20ASEAN's%20Pioneering%20Response.pdf.

ASEAN Periodicals

Dr. Sriprapha Petcharamesree: On Being a Member of the AICHR, Hum. Rts. Herald, Jan. 2010, at 2, *available at* http://www.aseanhrmech.org/downloads/Human_Rights_Herald_Jan2010_Issue.pdf.

Working Group for an ASEAN Human Rights Mechanism, *Terms of Reference of the ACWC completed at the 15th ASEAN Summit*, Hum. Rts. Herald, Jan. 2010, *available at* http://www.aseanhrmech.org/downloads/Human_Rights_Herald_Jan2010_Issue.pdf.

ASEAN News

ASEAN News Desk, *Highlights of the 4th ASEAN-U.S. JCC*, Zambotimes, June 22, 2012, http://www.zambotimes.com/archives/48745-Highlights-of-the-4th-ASEAN-U.S.-JCC.html.

Press Release, Assoc. of Southeast Asian Nations (ASEAN), Press Release of the Seventh Meeting of the ASEAN Intergovernmental Commission in Human Rights (AICHR) (Dec. 2, 2011), *available at* http://www.asean.org/news/asean-secretariat-news/item/press-release-of-the-seventh-meeting-of-the-asean-intergovernmental-commission-in-human-rights-aichr.

Press Release, Assoc. of Southeast Asian Nations (ASEAN), Third Press Release of the ASEAN Commission on the Promotion and Protection of the Rights of Women and Children (AWC) (Feb. 18, 2012), *available at* http://www.asean.org/news/asean-secretariat-news/item/third-press-release-of-the-asean-commission-on-the-promotion-and-protection-of-the-rights-of-women-and-children-acwc.

UN High Commissioner for Human Rights Boosts Human Rights Development in ASEAN, ASEAN Secretariat News, Nov. 29, 2011, *available at* http://www.asean.org/news/asean-secretariat-news/item/un-high-commissioner-for-human-rights-boosts-human-rights-development-in-asean.

Yuhoyoo, Susilo Bambang, On Building ASEAN Community: The Democratic Aspect, Lecture on the occasion of the Thirty-Eighth Anniversary of the Association of Southeast Asian Nations, ASEAN Secretariat News (Aug. 8, 2005) http://www.asean.org/resources/2012-02-10-08-47-56/leaders-view/item/on-building-the-asean -community-the-democratic-aspect.

ASEAN Internet Sources

About ASEAN: Overview, Association of Southeast Asian Nations, http://www.asean.org/asean/about-asean (last visited Dec. 12, 2012).

About the ASEAN Regional Forum, ASEAN Regional Forum (ARF), http://aseanregional-forum.asean.org/about.html (last visited Dec. 12, 2012).

About Us, Working Group for an ASEAN Human Rights Mechanism, http://www.aseanhrmech.org/aboutus.html (last visited Dec. 12, 2012).

ASEAN Member States, Association of Southeast Asean Nations (ASEAN), http://www.asean.org/asean/asean-member-states (last visited Dec. 12, 2012).

ASEAN to Proceed with Commission on the Promotion and Protection of the Rights of Women and Children, Working Group for an ASEAN Human Rights Mechanism, http://www.aseanhrmech.org/news/asean-to-proceed-with-commission.html (last visited Dec. 12, 2012).

Chalermpalanupap, Termsak, *10 Facts about ASEAN Human Rights Cooperation,* http://www.asean.org/images/archive/HLP-OtherDoc-1.pdf (last visited Dec. 12, 2012).

Secondary Sources

Books

Acharya, Amitav, Constructing a Security Community in Southeast Asia: ASEAN and the Problem of Regional Order (2d ed., 2009).

Acharya, Amitav, Promoting Human Security: Ethical, Normative and Educational Frameworks in South-East Asia (2007).

Acharya, Amitav, The Quest for Identity: International Relations of Southeast Asia (2000).

Albanese, Jay S., Transnational Crime and the 21st Century: Criminal Enterprise, Corruption, and Opportunity (2011).

Andreas, Peter, Border Games: Policing the US-Mexico Divide (2000).

Anh, Dang Nguyen, A Review of Literature and Information on the Current Situation of Human Trafficking in Vietnam (2006).

Anh, Dang Nguyen, Forced Migration in Vietnam: Historical and Contemporary Perspectives (2004).

Ankumah, Evelyn A., The African Commission on Human and Peoples' Rights: Practice and Procedures (1996).

Beeson, Mark, Institutions of the Asia-Pacific: ASEAN, APEC, and Beyond (2009).

Buzan, Barry, People, States and Fear: An Agenda for International Security Studies in the Post-Cold War Era (1991).

Caballero-Anthony, Mely, Regional Security in Southeast Asia: Beyond ASEAN Way (2005).

Crafting Cooperation: Regional International Institutions in Comparative Perspective (Amitav Acharya and Alastair Iain Johnston eds., 2007).

Derks, Annuska, Combating Trafficking in South-East Asia: Review of Policy and Programme Response (2000).

Dunoff, Jeffrey L., Ratner, Steven R., and Wippman, David, International Law: Norms, Actors, Process: A Problem-Oriented Approach (3d ed. 2010).

Freeman, Mark & Ert, Gibran Van, International Human Rights Law (2004).

Gallagher, Anne T., The International Law of Human Trafficking (2010).

Gordon, John Brown, Dimension of Conflict (1966).

Haacke, Jűrgen, ASEAN's Diplomatic Culture: Origins, Development, and Prospects (2003).

Haas, Michael, The Asian Way to Peace: A Story of Regional Cooperation (1989).

Hsien-Li, Tan, The ASEAN Intergovernmental Commission on Human Rights: Institutionalising Human Rights in Southeast Asia (2011).

Human Security Centre, Human Security Report 2005: War and Peace in the 21st Century (2005).

International Commission on Intervention and State Sovereignty (ICISS), The Responsibility to Protect (2002).

Kneebone, Susan and Debeljak, Julie, Transnational Crime and Human Rights: Responses to Human Trafficking in the Greater Mekong Subregion (2012).

Leifer, Michael, ASEAN Regional Forum: Extending ASEAN's Model of Regional Security (Adelphi Research, No. 302, 1996).

Leifer, Michael, Singapore's Foreign Policy: Coping with Vulnerability (2000).

Löffelholz, Martin and Arao, Danilo A., The ASEAN Guide: A Journalist's Handbook to Regional Integrationi in Southeast Asia (2010).

MacFarlane, S. Neil & Khong, Yuen Foong, The UN and Human Security: A Critical History (2006).

Narine, Shaun, Explaining ASEAN: A Regionalism in Southeast Asia (2002).

Nishikawa, Yukiko, Human Security in Southeast Asia (2010).

Non-Traditional Security Issues in Southeast Asia (Andrew T.H. Tan & J.D. Kenneth Boutin eds., 2001).

O'Grady, Ron, The Child and the Tourist (1992).

Peebles, Dave, Pacific Regional Order (2005).

Petcharamesree, Sriprapha et al., Towards an ASEAN Commission on the Promotion and Protection of the Rights of Women and Children (2008).

Rajang, Ramkishen S. et al., Singapore and Free Trade Agreements: Economic Relations with Japan and the United States (2001).

Severino, Rudolfo C., Toward in ASEAN Security Community (2004).

Shelley, Louise, Human Trafficking: A Global Perspective (2010).

Shelton, Dinah L., Regional Protection of Human Rights (2008).

Smith, Rhona K. M., International Human Rights (2003).

The Making of ASEAN Charter (Tommy Koh, Rorario G Manalo, and Walter Woon eds., 2009).

Wunderlich, Jens-Uwe, Regionalism, Globalisation and international Order: Europe and Southeast Asia (2007).

Yuzawa, Takeshi, Japan's Security Policy and the ASEAN Regional Forum: The Search for Multilateral Security in the Asia-Pacific (2007).

Book Chapters

Abbott, Kenneth W. & Snidal, Duncan, *Pathways to International Cooperation*, *in* The Impact of International Law on International Cooperation: Theoretical Perspectives (Eyal Benvenisti & Moshe Hirsch eds., 2004).

Anwar, Dewi Fortuna, *Human Security: An Intractable Problem in Asia*, *in* Asian Security Order (Multhiah Algappa ed., 2003).

Archarya, Amitav & Johnston, Alastair Iain, *Comparing Regional Institutions: An Introduction*, *in* Crafting Cooperation: Regional International Institutions in Comparative Perspective (Amitav Archarya & Alastair Iain Johnston eds., 2007).

Ba, Alice D., *ASEAN Centrality Imperiled? ASEAN Institutionalism and the Challenges of Major Power Institutionalization*, *in* ASEAN and the Institutionalization of East Asia (Ralf Emmers ed., 2012).

Baviera, Aileen S. P., *Introduction*, *in* Regional Security in East Asia: Challenges to Cooperation and Community Building (Aileen S. P. Baviera ed., 2008).

Braaten, Daniel B., *Human Rights and Soft Law: Alternative Paths for New Challenges*, *in* Negotiating Sovereignty and Human Rights: Actors and Issues in Contemporary Human Rights Politics (Noha Shawki & Michaelene Cox eds., 2009).

Buzan, Barry, *Is International Security Possible?*, *in* New Thinking about Strategy and International Security (Bjorn Hettne, Andras Inotai & Osvaldo Sunkel eds., 1991).

Caballero-Anthony, Mely, *Nontraditional Security and Multilateralism in Asia: Reshaping the Contours of Regional Security Architecture*, *in* Asia's New Multilateralism: Cooperation, Competition, and the Search for Community (Michael J. Green & Bates Gill eds., 2009).

Caballero-Anthony, Mely, *Non-Traditional Security Challenges, Regional Governance, and the ASEAN Political Security Community (APSC)*, *in* ASEAN and the Institutionalization of East Asia (Ralf Emmers ed., 2012).

Caballero-Anthony, Mely, *UN Peace Operations and Asian Security, in* UN Peace Operations and Asian Security (Mely Caballero-Anthony & Amitav Acharya eds., 2005).

Callabero-Anthony, Mely and Emmers, Ralf, *Understanding the Dynamics of Securitizing Non-Traditional Security, in* Non-Traditional Security in Asia: Dilemma in Securitization (Mely Callabero-Anthony, Ralf Emmers, & Amitav Acharya eds., 2006).

Choi, Young Jong & Caporaso, James A., *Comparative Regional Integration, in* Handbook of International Relations (W. Carlsnaes, T. Risse & B. Simmons eds., 2002).

Chongkittavorn, Kavi, *Covering ASEAN for Three Decades, in* ASEAN Matters!: Reflecting on the Association of Southeast Asian Nations (Lee Yoong Yoong ed., 2011).

Collins, Alan, *Non-Traditional Security, in* Routledge Handbook of Asian Regionalism (Mark Beeson and Richard Stubbs ed., 2012).

Dammen, Nicholas T., *Relevance of ASEAN in Forging Regional Peace, Security, and Prosperity, in* ASEAN Matters!: Reflecting on the Association of Southeast Asian Nations (Lee Yoong Yoong ed., 2011).

David, Fiona, *Law Enforcement Responses to Trafficking in Persons: Challenges and Emerging Good Practices, in* International Sex Trafficking of Women and Children: Understanding the Global Epidemic (2010).

Emmers, Ralf & Tan, See Seng, *Conclusion: Trends and Driving Forces in East Asian Regionalism, in* ASEAN and the Institutionalization of East Asia (Ralf Emmers ed., 2012).

Emmers, Ralf & Tan, See Seng, *The ASEAN Regional Forum and Preventive Diplomacy: A Review Essay, in* ASEAN and the Institutionalization of East Asia (Ralf Emmers ed., 2012).

Frost, Frank, *Introduction: ASEAN Since 1967–Origins, Evolution and Recent Developments, in* ASEAN into the 1990s (Alison Broinowski ed., 1990).

Fukushima, Okiko, *East versus West? Debate and Convergence on Human Security, in* Human Security in East Asia: Challenges for Collaborative Action (Sorpong Peou ed., 2009).

Goodey, Jo, *Compensating Victims of Violent Crime in the European Union: The Case for State Restitution, in* Reparation and Victim-Focused Social Work (Brian Williams ed., 2002).

Hsien-Li, Tan, *Persistent Engagement and Insistent Persuasion: The Role of the Working Group for an ASEAN Human Rights Mechanism in Institutionalizing Human Rights in the Region, in* Human Rights in the Asia-Pacific Region: Towards Institution Building (Hitoshi Nasu & Ben Saul eds., 2011).

Huxley, Tim, *International Relations, in* An Introduction to Southeast Asian Studies (Mohammed Halib & Tim Huxley eds., 1996).

Jetschke, Anja, *ASEAN, in* Routledge Handbook of Asian Regionalism (Mark Beeson & Richard Stubbs eds., 2012).

Johnston, Alastair Iain, *Socialization in International Institutions: ASEAN Way and International Relations Theory, in* International Relations Theory and the Asia-Pacific (G. John Ikenberry & Michael Mastanduno eds., 2003).

Khong, Yuen Foong, *ASEAN and the Southeast Asian Security Complex, in* Regional Orders: Building Security in a New World (David A. Lake & Patrick Morgan eds., 1997).

Kim, Jina, *Development of Regional Human Rights Regime: Prospects for and Implications to Asia, in* The SYLFF 2007 Regional Forum Selected Papers on Human Rights and Creative Leadership (2009).

Kneebone, Susan, *ASEAN: Setting the Agenda for the Rights of Migrant Workers?, in* Human Rights in the Asia-Pacific Region: Towards Institution Building (Hitoshi Nasu & Ben Saul eds., 2011).

Kneebone, Susan & Debeljak , Julie, *Combating Transnational Crime in the Greater Mekong Subregion: the Cases of Laos and Cambodia, in* Trafficking and Human Rights: European and Asia-Pacific Perspectives (Leslie Holmes ed., 2010).

Koh, Tommy, *Foreword, in* ASEAN Matters!: Reflecting on the Association of Southeast Asian Nations (Lee Yoong Yoong ed., 2011).

Lee, Maggy, *Introduction: Understanding Human Trafficking, in* Human Trafficking (Maggy Lee ed., 2007).

Lingliang, Zeng, *ASEAN-China Relations: An International Law Perspective, in* China-ASEAN Relations: Economic and Legal Dimensions (Zou Keyuan, John Wong, & Zeng Huaqun eds., 2006).

Malik, Adam, *Regional Cooperation in International Politics, in* Regionalism In Southeast Asia (1975).

Morada, Noel M., *The ASEAN Regional Forum: Origins and Evolution, in* Cooperation Security in the Asia-Pacific: The ASEAN Regional Forum (Jurgen Haacke ed., 2010).

Narine Shaun, *Asia, ASEAN and the Question of Sovereignty: the Persistence of Non-Intervention in the Asia-Pacific, in* The Routledge Handbook of Asian Regionalism (Mark Beeson & Richard Stubbs eds., 2012).

Peou, Sorpong, *Critical Challenges for Globalism in Human Security Studies, in* Human Security in East Asia: Challenges for Collaborative Action (Sorpong Peou ed., 2009).

Pibulsonngram, Pradap, *The Thai Perspective, in* The Making of ASEAN Charter (Tommy Koh, Rorario G Manalo, & Walter Woon eds., 2009).

Pietropaoli, Irene, *Challenges for ASEAN Human Rights Mechanisms: the Case of Lao PDR from a Gender Perspective, in* Human Rights in the Asia-Pacific Region: Towards Institution Building (Hitoshi Nasu & Ben Saul eds., 2011).

Prebensen, Soren C., *Inter-State Complaints under Treaty Provisions-The Experience under the European Convention on Human Rights, in* International Human Rights Monitoring Mechanisms: Essays in Honour of Jakob Th. Möller (Gudmundur Alfredsson et al., 2d Revised ed., 2009).

Razak, Tan Sri Ahmad Fuzi bin Abdul, *Facing Unfair Criticisms, in* The Making of ASEAN Charter (Tommy Koh, Rorario G Manalo, & Walter Woon eds., 2009).

Roberts, Christopher B., *State Weakness and Political Values: Ramifications for the ASEAN Community, in* ASEAN and the Institutionalization of East Asia (Ralf Emmers ed., 2012).

Rozman, Gilbert, *East Asian Regionalism, in* Routledge Handbook of Asian Regionalism (Mark Beeson & Richard Stubbs ed., 2012).

Sakamoto, Shigeki, *Challenges to a Human Rights Mechanism in the Asia-Pacific Region: the Experience of the Universal Periodic Review of the UN Human Rights Council, in* Human Rights in the Asia-Pacific Region: Towards Institution Building (Hitoshi Nasu & Ben Saul eds., 2011).

Severino, Rodolfo C., *ASEAN: What It Cannot Do, What It can and Should Do, in* ASEAN Matters!: Reflecting on the Association of Southeast Asian Nations (Lee Yoong Yoong ed., 2011).

Shearer, Ivan, and Hart, Naomi, *The Engagement of Asia-Pacific States with the UN Human Rights Committee: Reporting and Individual Petitions, in* Human Rights in the Asia-Pacific Region: Towards Institution Building (Hitoshi Nasu & Ben Saul eds., 2011).

Shelley, Louise, *Human Security and Human Trafficking, in* Human Trafficking and Human Security (Anna Jonsson ed., 2009).

Shelley, Louise, *International Trafficking: An Important Component of Transnational Crime, in* Human Security, Transnational Crime and Human Trafficking: Asian and Western Perspectives (Shiro Okubo & Louise Shelly eds., 2011).

Söderbaum, Fredrik, *Theories of Regionalism, in* The Routledge Handbook of Asian Regionalism (Mark Beeson & Richard Stubbs eds., 2012).

Sovannasam, Un, *ASEAN Efforts in Dealing with Transnational Crime, in* ASEAN Matters!: Reflecting on the Association of Southeast Asian Nations (Lee Yoong Yoong ed., 2011).

Storey, Ian, *The Institutionalization of ASEAN-China Relations: Managing the South China Sea Dispute, in* ASEAN and the Institutionalization of East Asia (Ralf Emmers ed., 2012).

Sukma, Rizal, *ASEAN Charter: Neither Bold Nor Visionary, in* The Road to Ratification and Implementation of ASEAN Charter (Pavin Chachavalpongpun ed., 2009).

Tan, See Seng, *NGOs in Conflict Management in Southeast Asia, in* UN Peace Operations and Asian Security (Mely Caballero-Anthony and Amitav Acharya ed., 2005).

Tiwari, Sivkant, *ASEAN's Perception Problem, in* ASEAN Matters!: Reflecting on the Association of Southeast Asian Nations (Lee Yoong Yoong ed., 2011).

Tow, William T. & Trood, Russell, *Linkage between Traditional Security and Human Security, in* Asia's Emerging Regional Order: Reconciling Traditional and Human Security (William T. Tow, Ramesh Thakur, & In-Taek Hyun eds., 2000).

Villacorta Wilfrido V., *Strengthening the Foundation for an ASEAN Community*, *in* ASEAN Matters!: Reflecting on the Association of Southeast Asian Nations (Lee Yoong Yoong ed., 2011).

Young, Ong Keng, *At Close Quarters with the Drafting of ASEAN Charter*, *in* The Making of ASEAN Charter (Tommy Koh, Rorario G Manalo & Walter Woon eds., 2009).

Yuzawa Takeshi, *The ASEAN Regional Forum: Challenges and Prospects*, *in* The Routledge Handbook of ASIAN Regionalism (Mark Beeson & Richard Stubbs ed., 2012).

Periodicals & News Sources

Scholarly Journals

Acharya, Amitav, *Arguing about ASEAN: What Do We Disagree About?* 22 Cambridge Rev. Int'l Aff. 493 (2009).

Acharya, Amitav, *Human Security: East versus West*, 3 Int'l J. 442 (2001).

Acharya, Amitav, *Ideas, Identity and Institution-Building: From the 'ASEAN Way' to the 'Asia-Pacific Way?'*, 10 Pac. Rev. 3 (1997).

Acharya, Amitav, *Regional Military-Security Cooperation in the Third World: A Conceptual Analysis of the Relevance and Limitations of ASEAN* (Association of Southeast Asian Nations) 29 J. of Peace Research 7 (1992).

Alagappa, Muthiah, *The Dynamics of International Security in Southeast Asia: Change and Continuity*, 45 Austl. J. Int'l Aff. 1 (1991).

Amador III, Julio Santiago, *ASEAN in the Asia Pacific: Central or Peripheral?* 2 Asian Politics & Policy 601 (2010).

Asian Forum for Human Rights and Development (Forum-Asia), *Faces of the ASEAN Intergovernmental Commission on Human Rights*, 5 Asian Hum. Rts. Defender, no. 3, 2009, at 4.

Ba, Alice, *ASEAN Regional Forum: Maintaining the Regional Idea in Southeast Asia*, 52 Int'l J. 635 (1997).

Berkofsky, Axel, *Can the EU Play a Meaningful Role in Asian Security through ASEAN Regional Forum?* 3 EIAS Pol'y Brief 1 (2003).

Boister, Neil, *New Directions for Regional Cooperation in the Suppression of Transnational Crime in the Southeast Pacific*, 9 J. S. Pac. L. 2 (2005).

Brusca, Carol S., *Palermo Protocol: The First Ten Years after Adoption*, 2 Global Security Stud., no. 3, 2011, at 8, *available at* http://globalsecuritystudies.com/Brusca%20Palermo%20Final%20One.pdf.

Buszynski, Leszek, *Thailand and Myanmar: The Perils of "Constructive Engagement"*, 11 Pac. Rev. 290 (1998).

Caballero-Anthony, Mely, *Non-Traditional Security and Infectious Diseases in ASEAN: Going Beyond the Rhetoric of Securitization to Institutionalization*, 2 Pac. Rev. 507 (2008).

Camoying, Luningning G., *Establishing an ASEAN Human Rights Mechanism: Developments and Prospects*, FSI Insights, no. 1, Mar. 2005.

Caplin, Jessica, *Mirage in the Desert Oasis: Forced Labor in Dubai and the United Arab Emirates*, Harvard Int'l Rev., Mar. 21, 2009, http://hir.harvard.edu/rethinking-finance/mirage-in-the-desert-oasis.

Chalamwong, Yongyuth, *Management of Cross-Border Low-Skilled Workers in Thailand: An Update* 26 TDRI Quarterly Rev., no. 4, 2011, at 3, *available at* http://tdri.or.th/publications/tdri-quarterly-review-december-2011.

Chiam, Sou, *Asia's Experience in the Quest for a Regional Human Rights Mechanism*, 40 Victoria U. of Wellington L. Rev. 127 (2009).

Chuang Janie, *Beyond a Snapshot: Preventing Human Trafficking in the Global Economy*, 13 Ind. J. Global Legal Stud. 137 (2006).

Cohen, Laura, *A Policy Memo: Human Trafficking as a Human Security Threat—The Cambodian Context*, Perspectives on Global Issues (Aug. 7, 2012), http://www.perspectivesonglobalissues.com/archives/spring-2010-security/cambodia/.

Collins Alan, *Forming a Security Community: Lessons from ASEAN*, 7 Int'l Rel. Asia-Pac. 203 (2007).

Curley Melissa, Human Security's Future in Regional Cooperation and Governance?, 66 Ausl. J. Int'l Aff. 527 (2011).

D'Aspremont, Jean, *Softness in International Law: A Self-Serving Quest for New Legal Materials*, 19 Eur. J. of Int'l L. 1075 (2008), *available at* http://www.ejil.org/pdfs/19/5/1700.pdf.

Dijk, Jan J.M. Van, *Empowering Victims of Organized Crime: on the Concurrence of the Palermo Convention with the UN Declaration on Basic Principles of Justice for Victims*, 9 Int'l Rev. of Victimology 15 (2002).

Dosch, Jörn, *The Concept and Management of Non-Traditional Security in the Southeast Asia*, 24 Security & Peace, no. 4, 2006, at 179, *available at* http://www.security-and-peace.de/archiv/PDF/2006-4/SuF_2006_04_2.pdf.

Duxbury, Alison, ASEAN Features: Moving Towards or Turning Away from Institutions? The Future of International Organizations in Asia and the Pacific, 11 Singapore Y.B. Int'l L. & Contributors 177 (2007), *available at* http://law.nus.edu.sg/sybil/downloads/articles/SYBIL-2007/SYBIL-2007-177.pdf.

Emmer, Ralf, Greener-Barcham, Beth & Thomas, Nicholas, *Institutional Arrangements to Counter Human Trafficking in the Asia Pacific*, 28 Contemp. S.E. Asia 490 (2006).

Gallagher Anne T., *Human Rights and the New UN Protocols on Trafficking and Migrant Smuggling - a Preliminary Analysis*. 23 Hum. Rts Q. 975–1004 (2001).

Gallagher Anne T., *Recent Legal Developments in the Field of Human Trafficking: A Critical Review of the 2005 European Convention and Related Instruments*, 8 Eur. J. Migration & L. 163 (2006).

Ginbar Yuval, *Human Rights in ASEAN—Setting Sail or Treading Water?*, 10 Hum. Rts L. Rev. 504 (2010).

Goldmann Matthias, *We Need to Cut off the Head of the King: Past, Present, and Future Approaches to International Soft Law*, 25 Leiden J. of Int'l L. 335 (2012).

Gordon Bernard, *Problems of Regional Cooperation in Southeast Asia*, 16 World Pol. 222 (1964).

Green, David Jay, *The Role of ASEAN Economic Community as a Commitment to Policy Certainty*, 25 ASEAN Econ. Bull. 209 (2008).

Guzman, Andrew T. & Meyer, Timothy L., *International Soft Law*, 2 J. Legal Analysis 171 (2010).

Haacke, Jurgen, *The ASEAN Regional Forum: From Dialogue to Practical Security Cooperation?*, 22 Cambridge Rev. of Int'l Studies 427 (2009).

Hay Kathryn, *A Pacific Human Rights Mechanism: Specific Challenges and Requirements*, 40 Victoria U. Wellington L. Rev. 195 (2010).

Heinrich, Kelly Hyland, *Ten Years After the Palermo Protocol: Where are Protections for Human Trafficking Victims?*, 18 Hum. Rts Brief, no. 1, 2010, at 2.

Hillgenberg Hartmut, *A Fresh Look at Soft Law*, 10 Eur. J. Int'l L. 499 (1999).

Hsien-Li, Tan, *The ASEAN Human Rights Body: Incorporating Forgotten Promises for Policy Coherence and Efficacy*, 12 Singapore Y.B. Int'l L. & Contributors 239 (2008), *available at* http://law.nus.edu.sg/sybil/downloads/articles/SYBIL-2008/SYBIL-2008-239.pdf.

Huong, Le Thu, *Many Faces and One Identity? ASEAN in the Case of Human Rights Regime*, Asia-Pacific J. Soc. Sci., Special Issue No. 1, 2010, at 56.

Hyland Kelly E., *The Impact of the Protocol to Prevent, Suppress and Punish Trafficking in Persons, Especially Women and Children*, 8 Hum. Rts. Brief, no 2, 2001, at 30.

International Organization for Migration, *The Causes and Consequences of Re-Trafficking*, 2 Global Eye on Human Trafficking, Mar. 2008, at 1, *available at* http://www.iom.int/jahia/webdav/site/myjahiasite/shared/shared/mainsite/projects/showcase_pdf/global_eye_2nd_issue.pdf.

A Regional Human Rights Mechanism for The Pacific?: Lessons Learnt from Developments in other Regions, 3 Hum. Rts. Monitor Q., no. 3, 2010, at 32.

Jones Lee, *ASEAN's Unchanged Melody? The Theory and Practice of "Non-Interference" in Southeast Asia*, 23 Pac. Rev. 479 (2010).

Kalu Victoria E., *Issues in Human Trafficking and Migrant Smuggling in the Context of Illegal Migration*, 1 Int'l Legal Stud. Program J. 27 (2009).

Khoo Olivia, *Regional Approaches to Trafficking in Women in South-East Asia: the Role of National Human Rights Institutions and the New ASEAN Human Rights Body*, 15 Austl. J. of Hum. Rts., no. 2, 2010, at 59.

Leviter Lee, *The ASEAN Charter: ASEAN Failure or Member Failure?*, 43 Int'l L. & Pol. 159 (2010).

Lo, Justin, *ASEAN Human Rights Commission: Why Is It Important to Stay Relevant and Credible in Today's Global Environment?* 3 CSR Asia Weekly, no. 32, Aug. 8, 2007, at 4–5, http://storage.canalblog.com/18/13/273060/15902769.pdf.

Loke Beverly, *The 'ASEAN Way': Towards Regional Order and Security Cooperation*? 30 Melbourne J. of Politics, 2005.

Macabuag, Ma. Lorena, *ASEAN Committee on Migrants Workers, in* 49 FOCUS Asia -Pacific, Sept. 2007, *available at* http://www.hurights.or.jp/asia-pacific/049/focus49 .pdf.

Mohamad, Ahmad Shah Pakeer et al., *The Phenomenon of Human Trafficking Activities in Southeast Asian,* 1 Int'l J. Human. & Soc. Sci. 13 (Sept. 2011).

Narine Shaun, *ASEAN and the Management of Regional Security*, 71 Pac. Aff. 195 (1998).

Ollus, Natalia, *Protocol against the Smuggling of Migrants by Land Air and Sea supplementing the United Nations Convention against Transboundary Organized Crime: A Tool for Criminal Justice Personnel*, 1 Int'l Legal Stud. Program L. J., 1, 1 (2000), *available at* http://www.wcl.american.edu/journal/ilsp/v1/1/ilsplj_v1_1.pdf?rd=1.

Patterson, David et al., *Use of Soft Law to Address HIV/AIDS in Southeast Asia*, 12 HIV/AIDS Policy & L. Rev., no. 2/3, 2007, at 18, *available at* http://www.aidslaw.ca/publications/interfaces/downloadFile.php?ref=1277.

Paxton Alec, *Find a Country to Call Home: A Framework for Evaluating Legislation to Reduce Statelessness in Southeast Asia* 21 Pac. Rim L. & Pol'y J. 623 (2012).

Petersen Carole J., *Bridging the Gap?: The Role of Regional and National Human Rights Institutions in the Asia Pacific*, 13 Asian-Pac. L. & Policy J. 174 (2011).

Piotrowicz Ryszard, *The UNHCR's Guidelines on Human Trafficking*, 20 Int'l J. Refugee L. 242 (2008).

Piper Nicola, *A Problem by a Different Name? A Review of Research on Trafficking in South-East Asia and Oceania* 43 Int'l Migration, no. 1–2, at 203, 2005.

Planitzer, Julia, *GRETA's First Years of Work: Review of the Monitoring of Implementation of the Council of Europe Convention on Action against Trafficking in Human Beings*, Anti-Trafficking Rev., no. 1, June 2012, at 31, http://www.antitraffickingreview.org/images/documents/issue1/Anti-Traficking_Review_Issue1_06.2012.pdf.

Qoiriah, Nurul, *Fishing Industry in South-East Asia Rife with Human Trafficking*, 11 Global Eye on Human Trafficking, March 2012, at 4, *available at* http://www.iom .int/jahia/webdav/shared/shared/mainsite/projects/showcase_pdf/Global-Eye -Issue11-Mar2012.pdf.

Ramcharan Robin, *ASEAN's Human Rights Commission: Policy Considerations for Enhancing Its Capacity to Protect Human Rights*, 3 UCL Human Rts. Rev. 199 (2010).

Rees Nicholas, *EU and ASEAN: Issues of Regional Security*, 47 Int'l Pol. 402 (2010).

Segrave Marie, *Human Trafficking and Human Rights*, 14 Austl. J. of Hum. Rts. 2, 71 (2009).

Severino Rodolfo C., *Will There Be a New ASEAN in the 21st Century?*, 2 Asia Eur. J. 184 (2004).

Shen Jianming, *China's Sovereignty over the South China Sea Islands: A Historical Perspective*, 1 Chinese J. Int'l L 94 (2002).

Sucharitkul Sompong, *ASEAN Society, A Dynamic Experiment for South-East Asian Regional Co-Operation*, 1 Asian Y.B. Int'l 113 (1991).

Supancana I.B.R., *Special Note: The Roadmap toward the Creation of ASEAN Security Community in 2015: Legal Perspectives*, 1 J. E. Asia & Int'l 323 (2008).

Tan, Eugene K.B., *ASEAN Charter as "Legs To Go Places": Ideational Norms and Pragmatic Legalism in Community Building in Southeast Asia*, 12 Singapore Y.B. Int'l L. & Contributors 171 (2008), *available at* http://law.nus.edu.sg/sybil/downloads/articles/SYBIL-2008/SYBIL-2008-171.pdf.

Taran Patrick, *Human Rights of Migrants: Challenges of the New Decade*, 38 Int'l Migration 7 (2000).

Vandystadt, Nathalie, *Justice and Home Affairs Commission to Revise EU Action Against Human Trafficking*, Europolitics (Oct. 17, 2008), *available at* http://www.europolitics.info/commission-to-revise-eu-action-against-human-trafficking-artr151215-10.html.

Wahyuningrum Yuyun, *Can AICHR Promote and Protect Human Rights?* in 5 Asian Hum. Rts. Defender 2, 2009, at 4.

Woo, Misun, *Voicing Women's Concerns to ASEAN*, 22 Asia Pac. F. Women L. & Dev., no. 1, 2009, *available at* http://apwld.org/pdf/ForumNews/APWLD-Forum-News-june-09-22-1.pdf.

Wuiling Cheah, *Assessing Criminal Justice and Human Rights Models in the Fight against Sex Trafficking: A case Research of ASEAN Region*, 3 Essex Hum. Rts. Rev. 46 (2006).

Yuzawa Takeshi, *The Evolution of Preventive Diplomacy in the ASEAN Regional Forum: Problems and Prospects*, 46 Asian Survey 790 (2006).

News Sources

Acharya, Amitav, *ASEAN at 40: Mid-Life Rejuvenation?*, Foreign Aff. (Aug. 15, 2007), http://www.foreignaffairs.com/print/64249?page=show.

American Shadow over South China Sea, Global Times (July 26, 2010), http://www.globaltimes.cn/opinion/editorial/2010-07/555723.html.

ASEAN: The ASEAN Foreign Ministers' Meeting with High Level Panel on an ASEAN Human Rights Body (HLP), Thai Press Reports (Mar. 2, 2009).

ASEAN Body to Address Rights of Women and Children, Inquirer.net (Apr. 7, 2010, 07:43 PM), http://newsinfo.inquirer.net/breakingnews/world/view/20100407-262920/ASEAN-body-to-address-rights-of-women-and-children.

ASEAN Makes Public Anti-Human Trafficking Report, VietnamPlus (Aug. 24, 2011, 11:15 AM), http://en.vietnamplus.vn/Utilities/PrintView.aspx?ID=20456.

Bacalla, Tess, *ASEAN Urged to Set Up Mechanism for Migrant Rights*, Vera Files (Sept. 10, 2012), http://oppenheimer.mcgill.ca/ASEAN-urged-to-set-up-mechanism.

Berger, Matthew, *Rights: Govts Pledge to Renew Fight against Human Trafficking*, Inter Press Service (May 14, 2009), http://www.ipsnews.net/2009/05/rights-few-govts-serious-about-human-trafficking-un-finds/.

Cambodia: Trafficking Domestic Workers to Malaysia, Integrated Regional Information Networks (IRIN) (Mar. 17, 2011), http://www.irinnews.org/Report/92210/CAMBODIA-Trafficking-domestic-workers-to-Malaysia.

Cambodia-Thailand: Men Trafficked into "Slavery" at Sea, Integrated Regional Information Networks (IRIN) (Aug. 29, 2011), *available at* http://www.irinnews.org/Report/93606/.

Carmichael, Robert, *Young Cambodian Men at Risk of Being Trafficked and Sold into Labor*, Voice of America (May 11, 2010, 7:00 AM), http://www.voacambodia.com/content/young-cambodian-men-at-risk-of-being-trafficked-and-sold-into-labor-93402399/1356531.html.

Chalermpalanupap, Termsak, *ASEAN Charter Is a New Commitment to Rights*, The Nation [Thailand] (Dec. 19, 2008), http://www.nationmultimedia.com/2008/12/19/opinion/opinion_30091372.php.

Chalermpalanupap, Termsak, *ASEAN Is Working to Promote and Protect Human Rights*, The Nation [Thailand] (Dec. 18, 2008), http://www.nationmultimedia.com/2008/12/18/opinion/opinion_30091288.php.

China-ASEAN Cooperation: 1991–2011, China Daily (Nov. 16, 2011, 08:03 AM), http://www.chinadaily.com.cn/cndy/2011-11/16/content_14101968.htm.

Chun, Sakada, *Cambodia Joins ASEAN to Combat Human Trafficking*, Voice of Am. | Khmer, (Nov. 17, 2005, 7:00 AM), http://www.voacambodia.com/content/a-40-2005-11-17-voa2-90146237/1357440.html.

Compromising - Even on Human Rights, AsiaViews (July 25, 2009), http://www.asiaviews.org/index.php?option=com_content&view=article&id=5302:colcomalias1266&catid=3:column-a-commentaries&Itemid=10.

Cook, Alistair D.B. & Bhalla, Priyanka, *Regional Champions – Examining the Comparative Advantages of AICHR and ACWC*, Centre for Non-Traditional Security Studies Insight, Issue 1 (June 2010), *available at* http://www.rsis.edu.sg/nts/HTML-Newsletter/Insight/NTS-Insight-jun-1001.html.

Dairiam, Shanthi, *Failing Women: Why We Need a New Approach to Human Trafficking*, 6 Global Asia 3 (Sept. 2011), http://www.globalasia.org/V6N3_Fall_2011/Shanthi_Dairiam.html.

Delauney, Guy, *Trafficking Crackdown in Cambodia*, BBC News (April 6, 2007, 7:49 AM), http://news.bbc.co.uk/2/hi/asia-pacific/6532181.stm.

Foreign Domestic Workers' Recommendations to the ASEAN Intergovernmental Commission on Human Rights, Asia Pacific Mission for Migrants (APMM) (Oct. 24, 2011), *available at* http://www.apmigrants.org/home/item/55-foreign-domestic-workers-recommendations-to-the-asean-intergovernmental-commission-on-human-rights.

Hongthong, Pennapa, *New Law on Trafficking*, The Nation [Thailand] (Oct. 1, 2007, 12:00 AM), http://www.nationmultimedia.com/national/New-law-on-trafficking-30050827.html.

Kon, James, *ASEAN Body on Rights of Women, Children Established*, Sultanate (Apr. 8, 2010), http://www.sultanate.com/news_server/2010/8_apr_4.html.

Macan-Markar, Marwaan, *Human Trafficking Exposes ASEAN's Underbelly*, Inter Press Service (June 17, 2010), http://ipsnews.net/news.asp?idnews=51857.

McKinsey, Kitty, *Divorce Leaves Some Vietnamese Women Broken-Hearted and Stateless*, UNCHR News Stories (Feb. 14, 2007), http://www.unhcr.org/45d324428.html.

NNT, *Cabinet Approves Addendum to ASEAN-EU Financing Agreement*, Pattaya Mail (May 16, 2012), http://www.pattayamail.com/business/cabinet-approves-addendum-to-asean-eu-financing-agreement-12718.

Salaverria, Leila, *Toothless Rights Body Would Hurt ASEAN Group*, Philippine Daily Inquirer (June 30, 2009, 2:58 AM), http://newsinfo.inquirer.net/inquirerheadlines/nation/view/20090630-213089/Toothless-rights-body-would-hurt-ASEAN-group.

Service, Shannon & Palmstrom, Becky, *Confined to a Thai Fishing Boat, For Three Years*, NPR ASIA (June 19, 2012, 3:06 AM), http://www.npr.org/2012/06/19/155045295/confined-to-a-thai-fishing-boat-for-three-years.

Storey, Ian, *Implementing CBMS in the 2002 DOC: A Roadmap to Managing the South China Sea Dispute*, East SEA (South China Sea) Studies (Aug. 2, 2011, 8:20 AM), http://nghiencuubiendong.vn/en/conferences-and-seminars-/second-international-workshop/602-602-.

Trafficking of Men Appears in Border Provinces, Human Trafficking Blog (Oct. 1, 2007), http://humantrafficking21.blogspot.com/2007/10/trafficking-of-men-appears-in-border.html.

Vandenbrink, Rachel, *Trafficking Victims Return Home*, Radio Free Asia (July 5, 2012), http://www.rfa.org/english/news/cambodia/trafficking-07052012182450.html/.

Vietnam Marks One-Year of the 'Shelter Self Improvement Project,' United Nations Inter-Agency Project on Human Trafficking (UNIAP) (Sept. 2010), http://www.no-trafficking.org/story_vn_shelteranniversary.html.

Waharak, Thachayan, *Thailand Remains Major Centre for Human Trafficking*, The Nation [Thailand] (June 28, 2012, 1:00 AM), http://www.nationmultimedia.com/national/Thailand-remains-major-centre-for-human-traffickin-30185065.html.

Wanandi, Jusuf, *ASEAN's Problem with Myanmar*, The Jakarta Post (July 13, 2005, 7:13 AM) http://www.thejakartapost.com/news/2005/07/13/ASEAN039s-problem-myanmar.html.

Ye, Shiwei, *Migrant Workers in Southeast Asia Need Stronger Protection*, Asia Catalyst (May 19, 2010,12:38 PM), http://asiacatalyst.org/blog/2010/05/migrant-workers-in-southeast-asia-need-stronger-protection.html.

Reports & Publications

ASEAN and Trafficking in Persons: Using Data as a Tool to Combat Trafficking in Persons, International Organization for Migration (Fiona David ed., 2008), *available at* http://www.iom.or.id/publications/pdf/16_MIL6010112_ASEAN_lo.pdf.

Asian Human Rights Commission, Asian Human Rights Charter: A Peoples' Charter (Mar. 30, 1998), *available at* http://material.ahrchk.net/charter/pdf/charter-final.pdf.

California Attorney General, Proposition 35 Human Trafficking. Penalties. Initiative Statute: Official Title and Summary (Nov. 6, 2012), *available at* http://vig.cdn.sos.ca.gov/2012/general/pdf/35-title-summ-analysis.pdf.

Conference Report, International Labour Office Conference 93rd Session, Director-General, A Global Alliance against Forced Labour: Global Report under the Follow-Up to the ILO Declaration on Fundamental Principles and Rights at Work (2005), *available at* http://www.ilo.org/wcmsp5/groups/public/---ed_norm/---declaration/documents/publication/wcms_081882.pdf.

COMMIT Sub-Regional Plan of Action (SPA_III 2011–2013) (Jan. 2011), *available at* http://www.no-trafficking.org/reports_docs/commit/commit_resources/commit_spaiii_en.pdf.

Danziger, Richard, Martens, Janathan, and Guajardo, Mariela, *Human Trafficking and Migration Management*, *in* Strategies Against Human Trafficking: The Role of the Security Sector (Cornelius Friesendorf ed., 2009), *available at* http://www.acrath.org.au/multimedia/downld/var/Strategies_Against_Human_Trafficiking-The_Role_of_the_Security_Sector_Vienna&Geneva_Sep2009.pdf.

David, Fiona, et al., Progress Report on Criminal Justice Responses to Trafficking in Persons in ASEAN Region (2011), *available at* http://www.artipproject.org/progress-report/Progress%20Report_Criminal%20Justice%20Responses%20to%20TIP%20in%20the%20ASEAN%20Region_2011.pdf.

Dottridge, Mike, *Introduction* to Collateral Damage 13–14 (Global Alliance Against Trafficking in Women/Amarin 2007), *available at* http://www.gaatw.org/Collateral%20Damage_Final/singlefile_CollateralDamagefinal.pdf.

Dottridge, Mike, *Research Needs Concerning the Monitoring, Evaluation and Impact Assessment of Both Research about Human Trafficking and Projects and Programmes to Address Human Trafficking*, *in* Human Trafficking: New Directions for Research (2008), *available at* http://www.iom.ch/jahia/webdav/shared/shared/mainsite/microsites/IDM/workshops/ensuring_protection_070909/human_trafficking_new_directions_for_research.pdf.

International Council on Human Rights Policy, Irregular Migration, Migrant Smuggling and Human Rights: Towards Coherence (2010), *available at* http://www.ichrp.org/files/reports/56/122_report_en.pdf.

International Labour Office Mekong Sub-Regional Project to Combat Trafficking in Children and Women, The Mekong Challenge—Destination Thailand: A Cross -Border Labour Migration Survey in Banteay Meanchey Province, Cambodia (Jan. 3, 2005), *available at* http://www.ilo.org/asia/whatwedo/publications/WCMS_BK _PB_69_EN/lang--en/index.htm.

International Organization for Migration, Caring for Trafficked Persons: Guidance for Health Providers (Cathy Zimmerman ed., 2009), *available at* http://publications. iom.int/bookstore/index.php?main_page=product_info&products_id=510 (scroll to middle of page and click "You can download the free PDF here").

International Organization for Migration, Trafficking of Fishermen in Thailand (Jan. 14, 2011), *available at* http://publications.iom.int/bookstore/index.php?main_page =product_info&cPath=41_7&products_id=720.

Jampaklay, Aree & Kittisuksathit, Sirinan, Migrant Worker Remittances: Cambodia, Lao PDR and Myanmar (2009), *available at* http://www.ilo.org/wcmsp5/groups/ public/@asia/@ro-bangkok/documents/publication/wcms_111543.pdf.

Macalalad, Rhanch, et al., A Guidebook on Spaces for Children's Participation in ASEAN (2011), http://forum-asia.org/2010/Spaces%20for%20Childrens%20 Participation%20%28May%2012%29%20FINAL.pdf.

Maltoni, Bruno, Analyzing the Impact of Remittances from Cambodian Migrant Workers in Thailand on Local Communities in Cambodia (June 2010), *available at* http://www.iom.int/jahia/webdav/shared/shared/mainsite/published_docs/ studies_and_reports/report_on_remittances.pdf.

Muntarbphorn, Vitit, Development of ASEAN Human Rights Mechanism, EXPO /B/DROI/2012/05 (Sep. 25, 2012), *available at* http://www.europarl.europa.eu/ committees/en/droi/studiesdownload.html?languageDocument=EN&file =76531.

Pearson, Elaine, *Destination Factors in the Trafficking of Children and Young Women in the Mekong Sub-Region, in* The Mekong Challenge- Human Trafficking: Redefining Demand (2005), *available at* http://www.ilo.org/wcmsp5/groups/public/---asia/ ---ro-bangkok/documents/publication/wcms_bk_pb_29_en.pdf.

Roundtable on Using CEDAW to Protect the Rights of Women Migration Workers and Trafficked Women in South and Southeast Asia, Report, May 6–9, 2009, Kuala Lumpur, MalaysiA (2009), *available at* http://www.iwraw-ap.org/publications/doc/ Roundtable_on_Migration_and_Trafficking_report.pdf.

Smith, Gerald, The Criminal Justice Response to Human Trafficking: Recent Developments in the Greater Mekong Sub-RegioN (May 2010), *available at* http:// www.no-trafficking.org/reports_docs/siren/GMS-08_eng.pdf.

South East Asia National Human Rights Institutions Forum (SEANF) Paper on Migrant Workers (2010), *available at* http://www.aseannhriforum.org/attachments/059 _SEANF_Paper_on_Migrant_Workers_-_Final.pdf.

Tangchonlatip, Kanchana & Richter, Kerry, *Gender and Migration, in* Thailand Migration Report 2011: Migration for Development in Thailand: Overview and Tools for Policymakers (Jerrold W. Huguet & Aphichat Chamratrithirong eds., 2011), *available at* http://www.un.or.th/documents/TMR-2011.pdf.

Task Force on ASEAN Migrant Workers, Civil Society Proposal: ASEAN Framework Instrument on the Protection and Promotion of the Rights of Migrant Workers (2009), *available at* http://www.workersconnection.org/resources/Resources_72/book_tf-amw_feb2010.pdf.

United Nations Commission on Human Security, Human Security Now: Protecting and Empowering People (2003), *available at* http://reliefweb.int/sites/reliefweb.int/files/resources/91BAEEDBA50C6907C1256D19006A9353-chs-security-may03.pdf.

Speeches & Addresses

Axworthy, Lloyd, The New Diplomacy: The UN, The International Criminal Court and the Human Security Agenda, Paper presented at Conference on UN Reform, Kennedy School, Harvard University (April 25, 1998), *available at* http://www.radioradicale.it/exagora/icc-havard-university-note-of-the-minister-of-foreign-affair-lloyd.

Co-Chairs Statement, Delivered at the Bali Ministerial Conference on People Smuggling, Trafficking in Persons and Related Transnational Crime (the Bali Process) (Feb. 26-28, 2002), *available at* http://www.baliprocess.net/files/ConferenceDocumentation/BRMC1.pdf.

Pillay Navanethem, United Nations High Commissioner for Human Rights, Keynote Speech at the 4th Regional Civil Society Consultation on ASEAN and Human Rights (Nov. 27, 2011).

Theses & Dissertations

Betz, Diana, Human Trafficking in Southeast Asia: Causes and Policy Implications (June 2009) (unpublished M.A Thesis, Naval Postgraduate School), *available at* http://edocs.nps.edu/npspubs/scholarly/theses/2009/Jun/09Jun_Betz.pdf.

Hwang, Kyu Deug, The Mechanisms of Politico-Security Regionalism in Southeast Asia and Southern Africa: A Comparative Case Research of ASEAN and SADC (Sep. 27, 2006) (unpublished Ph.D. dissertation, University of Pretoria), *available at* http://upetd.up.ac.za/thesis/available/etd-09272006-154344/.

Kidanemariam, Fekadeselassie F., Enforcement of Human Rights under Regional Mechanisms: a Comparative Analysis (Jan. 1, 2006) (unpublished LL.M. thesis, University of Georgia School of Law), *available at* http://digitalcommons.law.uga.edu/cgi/viewcontent.cgi?article=1079&context=stu_llm.

Miller, Rebecca J., What is the Added Value of Coordination?: An institutional Analysis of the United Nations' Response to National and Regional Coordination of Human

Trafficking in the Greater Mekong Subregion (2008) (unpublished Ph.D. thesis, University of Auckland), *available at* https://researchspace.auckland.ac.nz/handle/2292/3396.

Sutthisunsanee Sunsanee, Response of ASEAN to Human Rights Violations in Southeast Asia: Case Studies of Cambodia and East Timor (2006) (unpublished thesis, Mahidol University) (on file with Mahidol University).

Conference Papers

Cheeppensook, Kasira, ASEAN Way on Human Security (Paper presented at the International Development Studies Conference of Mainstreaming Human Security: The Asian Contribution, Oct. 4–5, 2007), *available at* http://humansecurityconf.polsci.chula.ac.th/Documents/Presentations/Kasira.pdf.

GAATW and La Strada International, NGO Priority for EU Anti-Trafficking Day 2009: Focus on Human Rights (Paper presented at the EU Ministerial Conference: Towards Global EU Action against Trafficking in Human Beings, Oct. 18, 2009).

Rahmasari, Aninda, Human Security, Emancipation, and the Challenges towards the Establishment of ASEAN Security Community 2015 (Paper presented at the 4th International Conference on Human Rights & Human Development, Critical Connections: Human Rights, Human Development and Human Security, Chulalongkorn University, Aug. 18–19, 2011), *available at* http://www.humanrights-mu.org/attachments/article/88/Aninda_Paper.pdf.

Thatun Susu, Challenges and Breakthrough in Regional Cooperation: the Case of the COMMIT Process, Paper delivered to Workshop on National and Regional Responses to Trafficking: Lessons for a Global Response, Metropolis Conference, Melbourne, Australia (Oct. 9, 2007).

Paper Series

Anthony, Mely Cabellero, *Regionalization of Peace in Asia: Experiences and Prospects of ASEAN, ARF and UN Partnership* (The Institute of Defence and Strategic Studies, Working Paper No. 42, Jan. 2003), *available at* http://www.rsis.edu.sg/publications/WorkingPapers/WP42.pdf.

Beyond Borders: Exploring Links between Trafficking and Migration (GAATW Working Paper Series, 2010), *available at* http://www.gaatw.org/publications/WP_on_Globalisation.pdf.

Chammartin, G. Moreno-Fontes, *The Feminization of International Migration* (Labour Education Paper, No. 29, Apr. 2002), *available at* http://www.ilo.org/wcmsp5/groups/public/---ed_dialogue/---actrav/documents/publication/wcms_111462.pdf.

D'Amato, Anthony, *Softness in International Law: A Self-Serving Quest for New Legal Materials: A Reply to Jean d'Aspremont* (Faculty Working Paper 89, 2010), *available at* http://scholarlycommons.law.northwestern.edu/facultyworkingpapers/89/.

Feigenblatt, Otto von, *ASEAN and Human Security: Challenges and Opportunities* (Ritsumeikan Center for Asia Pacific Studies Working Paper No. 09-5, July 2009), *available at* http://papers.ssrn.com/sol3/papers.cfm?abstract_id=1442476&download=yes.

Gallagher, Anne T. and Karlebach, Nicole, *Prosecution of Trafficking in Persons Cases: Integrating a Human Rights-Based Approach in the Administration of Criminal Justice* (OHCHR Background Paper, No. 4, July 2011), *available at* http://www.ohchr.org/Documents/Issues/Trafficking/Geneva2011BP_GallagherAndKarlebach.pdf.

Hao, Phan Duy, *The International and ASEAN Legal Framework against Non-Traditional Security Issues* (The China-ASEAN Project Occasional Paper Series, 2006), *available at* http://www.rsis-ntsasia.org/resources/publications/research-papers/Phan%20Duy%20Hao.pdf.

International Council on Social Welfare, Trafficking and Related Labour Exploitation in ASEAN Region (Nov. 2007), *available at* http://www.icsw.org/doc/Trafficking%20Labour%20Exploitation%20in%20ASEAN%2007.pdf.

International Labour Organization, *Ensuring the Right to Social Security for ASEAN Migrant Workers Through Social Security Agreements* (ILO Research Series: Social Security Extension Initiatives in Asia), *available at* http://www.ilo.org/public/english/region/asro/bangkok/events/sis/download/paper20.pdf (last visited Dec. 12, 2012).

Kingsford, Michael, *Can the ASEAN Regional Forum have a Role in Maintaining Regional Security?* (Shedden Papers, 2012), *available at* http://www.defence.gov.au/adc/docs/Publications2012/SheddenPapers12_120306_ARF_Kingsford.pdf.

Nguyen, Thi Hoai Thu et al., *Assessment on Urban Migration Policy* (Parliamentary Committee for Social Affairs Research Paper, 2005).

Roberts, Christopher, *ASEAN Institutionalization: The Function of Political Values and State Capacity* (The S. Rajaratnam School of International Studies, Working Paper, No. 217, Dec. 8, 2010), *available at* http://www.rsis.edu.sg/publications/WorkingPapers/WP217.pdf.

The Academic Association for Contemporary European Studies, The European Union and the Council of Europe: Difference, Duplication or Delegation? (2008), *available at* http://www.uaces.org/pdf/papers/0801/2008_Bond.pdf.

The World Bank, *Human Trafficking: A Brief Overview* (Social Development Notes: Conflict, Crime and Violence, No. 122, Dec. 2009), http:///siteresources.worldbank.org/EXTSOCIALDEVELOPMENT/Resources/244362-1239390842422/6012763-1239905793229/Human_Trafficking.pdf.

Thearith, Leng, ASEAN Security and Its Relevency (Cambodian Institute for Cooperation and Peace E-Book, No. 1, June 2009), *available at* http://www.cicp.org.kh/download/CICP%20E-Book/cicp%20e-book%20no%201.pdf.

Vannarith, Chheang, *Asia Pacific Security Issues: Challenges and Adaptive Mechanism* (Cambodian Institute for Cooperation and Peace Policy Brief, No. 3, July 2010), *available at* http://www.cicp.org.kh/download/CICP%20Policy%20brief/CICP%20 Policy%20brief%20No%203.pdf.

Unpublished Documents

Action against Trafficking in Human Beings, Council of Europe Human Rights and Rule of Law, http://www.coe.int/t/dghl/monitoring/trafficking/Docs/Monitoring/Monitoring_en.asp#TopOfPage (last visited Dec. 12, 2012).

Benedek, Wolfgang et al., The Role of Regional Human Rights Mechanisms, European Parliament, EXPO/B/DROI/2009/25 (Nov. 2010), *available at* http://www.europarl.europa.eu/committees/en/droi/studiesdownload.html?languageDocument=EN&file=33385.

Camroux, David, The European Union and ASEAN: Two to Tango? (2008), *available at* http://www.notre-europe.eu/media/Etude65EU-ASEAN-en.pdf.

Child Exploitation and Online Protection Centre (CEOP), The Trafficking of Women and Children from Vietnam (2011), *available at* http://www.ceop.police.uk/Documents/ceopdocs/NPM_CEOP_FCO_report_-_trafficking_of_Vietnamese_women_and_children.pdf.

Crassard, Suzana, Country Profile: Cambodia, *available at* http://www.iom.int/jahia/webdav/shared/shared/mainsite/activities/countries/docs/country_profile_cambodia.pdf (last visited Dec. 12, 2012).

ECPAT International, Cambodia: Country Progress Card (2010), *available at* http://www.ecpat.net/TBS/PDF/2010_Cambodia_Progress_Card.pdf.

Hames, Caroline et al., Feeling Good about Feeling Bad: A Global Review of Evaluation in Anti-Trafficking Initiatives (2010), *available at* http://www.gaatw.org/publications/GAATW_Global_Review.FeelingGood.AboutFeelingBad.pdf.

Kartusch, Angelika, Reference Guide for Anti-Trafficking Legislative Review with Particular Emphasis on South Eastern Europe (Sept. 2001), *available at* http://www.osce.org/odihr/13986.

Kaye, Mike, The Migration-Trafficking Nexus: Combating Trafficking Through the Protection of Migrants' Human Rights (Nov. 2003), *available at* http://www.antislavery.org/includes/documents/cm_docs/2009/t/the_migration_trafficking_nexus_2003.pdf.

Kranrattanasuit Naparat, Memorandum of Anti-Human Trafficking Law of Vietnam (2011) (unpublished manuscript) (on file with author).

Leiter, Karen, et al., No Status: Migration, Trafficking, and Exploitation of Women in Thailand – Health and HIV/AIDS Risks for Burmese and Hill Tribe Women and Girls (2004), *available at* https://s3.amazonaws.com/PHR_Reports/thailand-women-trafficking-2004.pdf.

Olivie, André, Identifying Cambodian Victims of Human Trafficking Among Deportees from Thailand (Dec. 2008), *available at* http://www.no-trafficking.org/reports_docs/commit/commit_cambodia%20deportees.pdf.

Rule of Law for Human Rights in the ASEAN Region: A Base-line Study (2011), *available at* http://hrrca.org/system/files/Rule_of_Law_for_Human_Rights_in_the_ASEAN_Region.pdf.

Sukma, Rizal, ASEAN and Non-Traditional Security (Dec. 3, 2010), *available at* http://www.waseda-giari.jp/sysimg/imgs/20101203_2c_sukuma_research.pdf.

General Internet Sources

About MTV Exit, MTV Exit: End Exploitation & Trafficking, http://mtvexit.org/about/ (last visited Mar. 5, 2013).

ASEAN – Vietnam Emphasises ASEAN Cooperation to Combat Human Trafficking, Disabled Peoples' International Asia-Pacific Region (Apr. 3, 2010), http://www.dpiap.org/resources/article.php?id=0000472&genreid=15&genre=ASEAN.

Asia, International Justice Resource Center, http://ihrlaw.org/ihr-reading-room/regional/asia/ (last visited Mar. 5, 2013).

Asia Regional Trafficking in Persons Project (ARTIP), http://www.artipproject.org.

Bonded Labour, Anti-Slavery, http://www.antislavery.org/english/slavery_today/bonded_labour.aspx (last visited Mar. 5, 2013).

Corruption Perceptions Index 2011, Transparency International (2011), http://cpi.transparency.org/cpi2011/results/.

Frequently Asked Questions on the ASEAN Charter, MARUAH: Singapore Working Group for an ASEAN Human Rights Mechanism, http://maruah.org/asean-charter/ (last visited Mar. 5, 2013).

Human Trafficking & Modern-day Slavery in the Early Years of the 21st Century—2000 to 2010 [Vietnam], GVNET, http://gvnet.com/humantrafficking/Vietnam.htm (last visited Mar. 5, 2013).

MTV Exist Partners, MTV Exit: End Exploitation & Trafficking, http://mtvexit.org/partners/(last visited Mar. 5, 2013).

Press Release, International Labour Organization, 21 Million People are Now Victim of Forced Labour ILO Says (June 1, 2012), *available at* http://www.ilo.org/washington/WCMS_181961/lang--en/index.htm.

Summary Notes of CS-ACWC Meeting: Work Plan, Human Rights Working Group – Indonesia (Sept 8, 2011), *available at* http://www.hrwg.org/en/asean/acwc/document/item/3278-summary-notes-of-cs-acwc-meeting-sept-8-2011 (scroll down to "download attachment").

Summary of the ILO 2012 Global Estimate of Forced Labour: Executive Summary, International Labour Organization, http://www.ilo.org/wcmsp5/groups/public/---ed_norm/---declaration/documents/publication/wcms_181953.pdf (last visited Mar. 5, 2013).

The 5th SOMTC, 3rd SOMTC+3 (CHINA, JAPAN, ROK), 3rd SOMTC+CHINA, 2nd SOMTC+JAPAN, 2nd SMTC+USA, 2nd SOMTC+AUSTRALIA and 1st SOMTC+INDIA, Siem Reap, Cambodia, June *13–17, 2005*, NCB-Interpol Indonesia (July 19, 2010, 12:09 PM).

Where We Work: Thailand, International Labour Organization, http://www.ilo.org/public/english/region/asro/bangkok/child/trafficking/wherewework-thailand detail.htm (last visited Mar. 5, 2013).

World Vision, GMS Human Trafficking: A Changing Landscape: Mekong Region 2, *available at* http://wvasiapacific.org/downloads/factsheets/regionaltraff.pdf (last visited Mar. 5, 2013).

Presentations

Phavi, H.E. Dr. Ing Kantha Phavi, *Managing Return Migration when Entry or Stay is not Authorized*, *available at* http://www.iom.int/jahia/webdav/shared/shared/mainsite/microsites/IDM/workshops/managing_return_migration_042108/presentations_speeches/idm_pres_apr22.pdf (last visited Dec. 12, 2012).

South East Asia Regional Cooperation in Human Development (SEARCH), *Promoting a Process of Change: The Task Force on ASEAN Migrant Workers*, *available at* http://www.docstoc.com/docs/74046970/Task-Force-on-ASEAN-Migrant-Workers-Civil-Society---Trade-Union-Consultation-Process-Towards-an-ASEAN-FRAMEWORK-INSTRUMENT-FOR-THE-PROTECTION-AND-PROMOTION-OF-THE-RIGHTS-OF-T (last visited Mar, 2013).

Van Dung, Vu, et al., *2011–2015 Action Plan for Anti-Human Trafficking in Vietnam* at the Capacity Building Workshop on Anti-Human Trafficking (Aug. 2011), *available at* http://www.google.com/url?sa=t&rct=j&q=&esrc=s&source=web&cd=1&ved=0CB4QFjAA&url=http%3A%2F%2Fjica-cb-workshop.weebly.com%2Fuploads%2F8%2F0%2F7%2F2%2F8072630%2Fvietnam_action_plan.pptx&ei=_MSTUPOZNcuz0QGp3oHoAw&usg=AFQjCNHtq8qfwOCyQcBLUo4DpNM81n7-bw&sig2=SISoYhGZUnR0ycrrsZp_4g.

Wahyuningrum, Yuyun, *Understanding ASEAN: Its Systems and Structure* (Dec. 2009), *available at* http://www.scribd.com/doc/81600447/ASEAN-Structures-Mechanisms-Yuyun-10-03-04-Copy.

Interviews

Interview with Mr. Matthew Friedman, Regional Project Manager, The United Nations Inter-Agency Project on Human Trafficking (Jan. 6, 2011).

Interview with Ms. Sriprapha Petcharamesree, Professor at Mahidol University, Thailand (June 17, 2011).

Flyer

Office of Anti-Trafficking in Persons Committee, Scope and Elements of Identification of Trafficked Persons (Guideline), *available at* http://www.no-trafficking.org/reports_docs/legal/thailand/se_vicid_pamph_en.pdf (last visited Dec. 12, 2012).

Index

www.ingramcontent.com/pod-product-compliance
Lightning Source LLC
LaVergne TN
LVHW020652300926
849161LV00004B/905
* 9 7 8 9 0 0 4 2 6 5 1 7 2 *